Microsoft® Works Suite 99 For Dummies

Quick Formatting in Your Word Processor

To Do This ...	Press This ...
Add or remove space	Ctrl+0 (zero) before paragraph
Indent	Ctrl+M
Un-indent	Ctrl+Shift+M
Bullet on/off	Click bullets button on toolbar
Format subscript	Ctrl+Equal sign (=)
Format superscript	Ctrl+Shift+Plus sign (+)

Quick Spreadsheet Tricks

To Do This ...	Do This ...
Sum at end of column or row	Press Ctrl+M, or click Σ in the toolbar
Change column width	Drag edge to the right of column letter
Change row height	Drag edge below row number
Insert row above	Choose Insert⇨Row
Insert column to left	Choose Insert⇨Column

Number Formats in Spreadsheets and Databases

To Do This ...	Press This ...
Dollars	Ctrl+4 ($ key)
Percent	Ctrl+5 (% key)
Comma at thousands	Ctrl+, (comma)

Quick Formatting Almost Everywhere

To Do This ...	Press This ...
Undo edits	Ctrl+Z
Bold	Ctrl+B, or click **B** on toolbar
Italic	Ctrl+I, or click / on toolbar
Underline	Ctrl+U, or click U on toolbar
Center	Ctrl+E, or click center align on toolbar
Left-align	Ctrl+L, or click left align on toolbar
Right-align	Ctrl+Shift+R, or click right align on toolbar
Remove font styles	Ctrl+spacebar
Insert page break	Ctrl+Enter
Change page margins	Choose File⇨Page Setup

Microsoft® Works Suite 99 For Dummies®

Navigating in Almost Any Document

To Do This ...	Do This ...
Scroll up/down	Use vertical scroll bar
Scroll sideways	Use horizontal scroll bar
Move right, left, up, down	Press arrow key
End of column/next paragraph	Press Ctrl+down arrow
Start of column, paragraph	Press Ctrl+up arrow
One screen up/down	Press PgUp / PgDn keys
Beginning/end of line or row	Press Home / End keys
Beginning/end of document	Press Ctrl+Home/Ctrl+End keys

Controlling Programs, Windows, and Documents Almost Everywhere

To Do This ...	Do This ...
Start program	Double-click program icon
Start program	Click Start⇨Programs⇨ your program
Exit program	Choose File⇨Exit, or press Alt+F4
Start a new document	Choose File⇨New
Save a document	Press Ctrl+S
Open a document	Press Ctrl+O
Close a document	Press Ctrl+W
Choose an open window	Choose Window then 1 or 2 or 3 ...
Print Preview	Choose File⇨Print Preview
Print	Press Ctrl+P
Get Help	Press F1

Editing Almost Everywhere

To Do This ...	Do This ...
Select something	Click it or drag across it
Select everything	Press Ctrl+A
Select with keys	Press Shift+navigation key
Delete	Press Delete key or Backspace key
Cut selection to Clipboard	Press Ctrl+X
Copy selection to Clipboard	Press Ctrl+C
Paste from Clipboard	Press Ctrl+V
Move	Select, drag to position
Copy	Select, Ctrl+drag to position
Insert file into document	Drag file from My Computer window

...For Dummies: Bestselling Book Series for Beginners

TM

References for the Rest of Us!®

BESTSELLING BOOK SERIES FROM IDG

Are you intimidated and confused by computers? Do you find that traditional manuals are overloaded with technical details you'll never use? Do your friends and family always call you to fix simple problems on their PCs? Then the *...For Dummies®* computer book series from IDG Books Worldwide is for you.

...For Dummies books are written for those frustrated computer users who know they aren't really dumb but find that PC hardware, software, and indeed the unique vocabulary of computing make them feel helpless. *...For Dummies* books use a lighthearted approach, a down-to-earth style, and even cartoons and humorous icons to diffuse computer novices' fears and build their confidence. Lighthearted but not lightweight, these books are a perfect survival guide for anyone forced to use a computer.

> *"I like my copy so much I told friends; now they bought copies."*
>
> — Irene C., Orwell, Ohio

> *"Quick, concise, nontechnical, and humorous."*
>
> — Jay A., Elburn, Illinois

> *"Thanks, I needed this book. Now I can sleep at night."*
>
> — Robin F., British Columbia, Canada

Already, millions of satisfied readers agree. They have made *...For Dummies* books the #1 introductory level computer book series and have written asking for more. So, if you're looking for the most fun and easy way to learn about computers, look to *...For Dummies* books to give you a helping hand.

8/98

MICROSOFT® WORKS SUITE 99 FOR DUMMIES®

by David Kay

IDG Books Worldwide, Inc.
An International Data Group Company

Foster City, CA ♦ Chicago, IL ♦ Indianapolis, IN ♦ New York, NY

Microsoft® Works Suite 99 For Dummies®

Published by
IDG Books Worldwide, Inc.
An International Data Group Company
919 E. Hillsdale Blvd.
Suite 400
Foster City, CA 94404
www.idgbooks.com (IDG Books Worldwide Web site)
www.dummies.com (Dummies Press Web site)

Library of Congress Catalog Card No.: 98-86185

ISBN: 0-7645-0477-0

Printed in the United States of America

10 9 8 7 6 5 4 3 2 1

1B/QZ/RR/ZY/IN

Distributed in the United States by IDG Books Worldwide, Inc.

Distributed by Macmillan Canada for Canada; by Transworld Publishers Limited in the United Kingdom; by IDG Norge Books for Norway; by IDG Sweden Books for Sweden; by Woodslane Pty. Ltd. for Australia; by Woodslane (NZ) Ltd. for New Zealand; by Addison Wesley Longman Singapore Pte Ltd. for Singapore, Malaysia, Thailand, and Indonesia; by Norma Comunicaciones S.A. for Colombia; by Intersoft for South Africa; by International Thomson Publishing for Germany, Austria and Switzerland; by Distribuidora Cuspide for Argentina; by Livraria Cultura for Brazil; by Ediciencia S.A. for Ecuador; by Ediciones ZETA S.C.R. Ltda. for Peru; by WS Computer Publishing Corporation, Inc., for the Philippines; by Contemporanea de Ediciones for Venezuela; by Express Computer Distributors for the Caribbean and West Indies; by Micronesia Media Distributor, Inc. for Micronesia; by Grupo Editorial Norma S.A. for Guatemala; by Chips Computadoras S.A. de C.V. for Mexico; by Editorial Norma de Panama S.A. for Panama; by Wouters Import for Belgium; by American Bookshops for Finland. Authorized Sales Agent: Anthony Rudkin Associates for the Middle East and North Africa.

For general information on IDG Books Worldwide's books in the U.S., please call our Consumer Customer Service department at 800-762-2974. For reseller information, including discounts and premium sales, please call our Reseller Customer Service department at 800-434-3422.

For information on where to purchase IDG Books Worldwide's books outside the U.S., please contact our International Sales department at 317-596-5530 or fax 317-596-5692.

For information on foreign language translations, please contact our Foreign & Subsidiary Rights department at 650-655-3021 or fax 650-655-3281.

For sales inquiries and special prices for bulk quantities, please contact our Sales department at 650-655-3200 or write to the address above.

For information on using IDG Books Worldwide's books in the classroom or for ordering examination copies, please contact our Educational Sales department at 800-434-2086 or fax 317-596-5499.

For press review copies, author interviews, or other publicity information, please contact our Public Relations department at 650-655-3000 or fax 650-655-3299.

For authorization to photocopy items for corporate, personal, or educational use, please contact Copyright Clearance Center, 222 Rosewood Drive, Danvers, MA 01923, or fax 978-750-4470.

is a trademark under exclusive license to IDG Books Worldwide, Inc., from International Data Group, Inc.

About the Author

Dave Kay is a writer, reformed engineer, and aspiring naturalist and artist, combining professions with the same effectiveness as his favorite business establishment, Acton Muffler, Brake, and Ice Cream (now defunct). Dave has written six computer book titles (totally over a dozen editions) by himself or with friends. Dave's books include *Microsoft Works For Dummies, WordPerfect 8 Web Publishing For Dummies, WordPerfect For Windows For Dummies, MORE WordPerfect For Windows For Dummies, VRML and 3D on the Web For Dummies,* and *Graphics File Formats* (all published by IDG Books Worldwide, Inc.)

In his other life, as the Poo-bah of Bright Leaf Communications, Dave creates promotional copy, graphics, and Web site content for high-tech firms. He and his wife, Katy, live in the wilds of Massachusetts where, in his spare time, he studies human and animal tracking and munches edible wild plants. He also has been known to make strange blobs from molten glass, sing Gilbert and Sullivan choruses in public, and hike in whatever mountains he can get to. He longs to return to New Zealand and track kiwis and hedgehogs in Wanaka. He hates writing about himself in the third person like this and will stop now.

ABOUT IDG BOOKS WORLDWIDE

Welcome to the world of IDG Books Worldwide.

IDG Books Worldwide, Inc., is a subsidiary of International Data Group, the world's largest publisher of computer-related information and the leading global provider of information services on information technology. IDG was founded more than 30 years ago by Patrick J. McGovern and now employs more than 9,000 people worldwide. IDG publishes more than 290 computer publications in over 75 countries. More than 90 million people read one or more IDG publications each month.

Launched in 1990, IDG Books Worldwide is today the #1 publisher of best-selling computer books in the United States. We are proud to have received eight awards from the Computer Press Association in recognition of editorial excellence and three from Computer Currents' First Annual Readers' Choice Awards. Our best-selling ...For Dummies® series has more than 50 million copies in print with translations in 31 languages. IDG Books Worldwide, through a joint venture with IDG's Hi-Tech Beijing, became the first U.S. publisher to publish a computer book in the People's Republic of China. In record time, IDG Books Worldwide has become the first choice for millions of readers around the world who want to learn how to better manage their businesses.

Our mission is simple: Every one of our books is designed to bring extra value and skill-building instructions to the reader. Our books are written by experts who understand and care about our readers. The knowledge base of our editorial staff comes from years of experience in publishing, education, and journalism — experience we use to produce books to carry us into the new millennium. In short, we care about books, so we attract the best people. We devote special attention to details such as audience, interior design, use of icons, and illustrations. And because we use an efficient process of authoring, editing, and desktop publishing our books electronically, we can spend more time ensuring superior content and less time on the technicalities of making books.

You can count on our commitment to deliver high-quality books at competitive prices on topics you want to read about. At IDG Books Worldwide, we continue in the IDG tradition of delivering quality for more than 30 years. You'll find no better book on a subject than one from IDG Books Worldwide.

John Kilcullen
Chairman and CEO
IDG Books Worldwide, Inc.

Steven Berkowitz
President and Publisher
IDG Books Worldwide, Inc.

*Eighth Annual
Computer Press
Awards ≥1992*

*Ninth Annual
Computer Press
Awards ≥1993*

*Tenth Annual
Computer Press
Awards ≥1994*

*Eleventh Annual
Computer Press
Awards ≥1995*

Dedication

This book is dedicated to Rusty (the Wonder Dog), the most loving, beautiful, funny, dignified, and well-behaved dog anyone ever had, and to Yankee Golden Retriever Rescue who made Rusty's life with us possible.

Author's Acknowledgments

I would like to acknowledge the support of my wife Katy and of my friends and family, from whose company I am sadly removed while writing these books. Thanks also to Matt Wagner and the rest of the folks at Waterside, and to the congenial editors at IDG Books Worldwide, including:

- ✔ Consistently cheerful project editor Brian Kramer, and the project editors for various editions of this book's precursor, *Microsoft Works For Dummies:* Ryan Rader, Bill Helling, and Kathy Cox. They fainted not, though the hour drew nigh.

- ✔ Copy editors Bill Barton, Ted Cains, Kathleen Dobie, and Billie Williams, for tolerating my tormented sentence structure, and those copy editors upon whose weary (and shrugging) shoulders we stand: Andrea Boucher, Diana R. Conover, and Diane Giangrossi.

- ✔ Technical editor Michael Young, for keeping me as honest as I can stand, and his equally exacting predecessors, Jim McCarter and Michael Partington.

Publisher's Acknowledgments

We're proud of this book; please register your comments through our IDG Books Worldwide Online Registration Form located at: http://my2cents.dummies.com.

Some of the people who helped bring this book to market include the following:

Acquisitions, Editorial, and Media Development

Associate Project Editor: Brian Kramer

Associate Acquisitions Editor: Steven H. Hayes

Copy Editors: William A. Barton, Ted Cains, Kathleen Dobie, Billie A. Williams

Technical Editor: Michael C. Young

Editorial Manager: Leah P. Cameron

Editorial Assistant: Donna Love

Production

Project Coordinator: Regina Snyder

Layout and Graphics: Lou Boudreau, J. Tyler Connor, Angela F. Hunckler, Brent Savage, Michael A. Sullivan

Proofreaders: Christine Berman, Kelli Botta, Nancy Price, Rebecca Senninger, Janet M. Withers

Indexer: Sherry Massey

General and Administrative

IDG Books Worldwide, Inc.: John Kilcullen, CEO; Steven Berkowitz, President and Publisher

IDG Books Technology Publishing: Brenda McLaughlin, Senior Vice President and Group Publisher

Dummies Technology Press and Dummies Editorial: Diane Graves Steele, Vice President and Associate Publisher; Mary Bednarek, Director of Acquisitions and Product Development; Kristin A. Cocks, Editorial Director

Dummies Trade Press: Kathleen A. Welton, Vice President and Publisher; Kevin Thornton, Acquisitions Manager

IDG Books Production for Dummies Press: Michael R. Britton, Vice President of Production and Creative Services; Cindy L. Phipps, Manager of Project Coordination, Production Proofreading, and Indexing; Kathie S. Schutte, Supervisor of Page Layout; Shelley Lea, Supervisor of Graphics and Design; Debbie J. Gates, Production Systems Specialist; Robert Springer, Supervisor of Proofreading; Debbie Stailey, Special Projects Coordinator; Tony Augsburger, Supervisor of Reprints and Bluelines

Dummies Packaging and Book Design: Robin Seaman, Creative Director; Kavish + Kavish, Cover Design

◆

The publisher would like to give special thanks to Patrick J. McGovern, without whom this book would not have been possible.

◆

Contents at a Glance

Cartoons at a Glance

By Rich Tennant

page 241

page 293

page 159

page 333

page 7

page 351

Fax: 978-546-7747 • E-mail: the5wave@tiac.net

Table of Contents

Introduction

- -

*C*ongratulations! You have already proven your superior intelligence. Rather than blowing several hundred bucks on the latest and most muscle-bound software you can find, you're using Microsoft Works Suite 99 — a bunch of software that can do probably everything you need for a lot less trouble and money. Heck, you're so smart that maybe you bought a PC with Works Suite already installed.

So then why, exactly, should you be reading a book for Dummies? Because Dummies are an underground group of people smart enough to say, "Okay, so I'm not a computer wizard. So sue me. Call me a dummy if you will. I still want to use this stuff." The *...For Dummies* books are for people who:

- Want to find out more about their software without being bored silly.
- Feel there should be a manual to explain the software manual.
- Actually want to get some work done. Soon. Like today.
- Don't want to wade through a lot of technical gibberish.
- Don't think like computer software engineers seem to think.

What's in This Book

This book describes how to use the software and tools of Microsoft Suite 99, separately and together (for better or for worse, in sickness and in health, 'til an upgrade do you part). This book also includes an extensive appendix, which reveals all those Windows basics that most other books assume you already know. Specifically, in this book, you can learn about the following topics:

- Windows basics (opening, closing, and painting them shut) for Windows 95 and 98.
- Word processing (like food processing, only messier) in Word and Works.
- Spreadsheets (for soft, comfortable naps on your spreadbed) in Works.
- Databases (for storing all your baseless data) in Works.

✔ Graphics (for charting and general doodling) in Word and Works.

✔ Managing money with Microsoft Money.

✔ Web browsing in Internet Explorer.

✔ E-mail and newsgroup communications in Outlook Express.

✔ Researching in the Encarta computerized encyclopedia.

✔ Creating your own greeting cards, banners, and what-have-you in Microsoft Greetings.

Who Do I Think You Are, Anyway?

Apart from thinking that you are a brilliant and highly literate person (evidenced by the fact that you bought or are considering buying this book), here's what I assume about you, the esteemed reader:

✔ Your PC has Microsoft Works Suite 99 installed on it.

✔ You're more or less a beginner on the PC. You are not necessarily familiar with Works Suite, Windows, PC screens, keyboards, or mice.

✔ Speaking of mice, you don't really give a mouse's eyelash about Windows or PCs except for what you absolutely need to do your work.

✔ Heck, you may even have thought that Works Suite was part of Windows, if it came with your PC. (It's not.)

✔ If you're on a private computer network, you have a computer and network *guru* available — an expert whom you can pay off in cookies or pizza to solve network problems.

Apart from that, you could be darn near anybody. I know of mathematicians, computer scientists, business people, computer book authors, and day care center managers who use the Works Suite programs quite happily.

How to Use This Book

Nobody wants to sit down and read a book before they use their software. So don't. Instead, just look something up in the Index or Table of Contents and "go to it."

The only sane way to use this book is to follow along on your PC, using this book as a tour guide or road map — don't just read. I use pictures sometimes, but I don't throw in a picture of everything because you have the pictures right there on your PC screen, and they're even in color.

This is mainly a reference book, so you don't have to read it from front to back. In fact, if you're new to PCs, start at the back: Read the appendix first. Within each part, the earlier chapters cover the more fundamental stuff. So if you want, you can just read the chapters in order (in each part) to get from the fundamentals to the more advanced tasks.

How This Book Is Organized

This book breaks things down into the following useful parts, including one part for each piece of Works Suite. Each part has something for everyone, whether you've never used a similar tool before or you're an old hand who just needs to figure out how a particular program works.

Part I: Putting Works to Work

Microsoft Works, the namesake of Works Suite, is a single program made up of very different tools. Works gives you a simple word processor, a spreadsheet tool for analyzing numbers, a database tool for organizing lists and inventories, charting and other graphic software. In this part, I discuss how each tool works separately and, in some cases, together — using address databases to send form letters, for instance.

Part II: Putting Words in Word

In Part II, discover how to create documents of all kinds on one of the world's most commonly used word processors, Microsoft Word. (Part II also covers word processing in Works, which is very much the same as it is in Word.) Part II covers word processing starting with really basic basics, such as typing, deleting, moving, and copying, to subtle and elusive facts, such as where paragraph formatting hides. Later chapters introduce editing techniques and important adornments like page numbers, tables, borders, lines, headers, footers, graphics, and footnotes.

Part III: Learning to Love Money

You're probably already fond of money, but Part III will help you feel warmly about Microsoft Money. Learn how to track your income and expenses, create and stick to a budget, print checks, report your taxables and tax-deductibles, and create graphs and reports that make understanding your finances as easy as pie (charts). You can even track your investment values with price data downloaded from the Internet.

Part IV: 'Netting Ventured, 'Netting Gained

There's an information highway out there, all right, but it winds through a vast digital wilderness called the Internet. This part covers how to get connected to the Internet and use Microsoft's Internet Explorer to read information and download free stuff from the World Wide Web. Part IV also tells you how to start sending and receiving e-mail and joining in newsgroup discussions by using Outlook Express.

Part V: Entertaining Enlightenment

All work and no play makes PC users fall asleep on their keyboards. Microsoft, to help software users avoid such embarrassment, includes fun — and even enlightening — "infotainment" in Works Suite. In Part V, discover how Microsoft Encarta encyclopedia lets you explore a topic in half the time it would take in a printed encyclopedia. Part V also shows you how to create, print, and electronically send greeting cards, posters, banners, and other colorful projects with Microsoft Greetings.

Part VI: The Part of Tens

The Part of Tens? Why not the part of twelves? Who knows, but thanks to the perfectly random act of fate that gave humans ten fingers, every *...For Dummies* book has a Part of Tens. Here are Ten Nifty Tricks and Ten Exhortations for Editing, providing recommendations that make your PC a better place to live.

The Appendix: Clues for the Clueless: PC Basics

Some software books leave beginners without a clue about the basics of PCs and Windows. Not this one. If you're new to Windows, files, directories, mice, or disks, , the appendix is the place to turn. Here's how to start programs, make your various windows behave, and get basic keyboard and mouse skills that apply to nearly all programs.

Icons Used in This Book

You'd think we were in Czarist Russia from the popularity of icons in the computer world. Not to be left behind, this book uses icons, too. Here's what they mean:

For an easier or faster way to do something, or to check out something really cool, look for these target-thingies in the margin.

 This icon reminds you that you shouldn't forget to remember something — something that was said earlier but is easily forgotten.

 This icon cheerfully tells you of something that may go wrong, with consequences ranging from mild indigestion to weeping, wailing, and gnashing of teeth.

 You won't see too much of Mr. Science (alias the Dummies guy) in this book. When he does appear, he indicates a little inside information on how things work. But, if you ignore him, you won't be much worse off.

 This icon lets you know that somewhere else in the book is important information related to the topic at hand. Because a lot of Works tools work alike, you see a bunch of these guys.

 Works Suite has two word processors that work very much alike: Microsoft Word, and the word-processor tool of Works. The word processors are so alike, this book refers Works word-processor users to the chapters on Word, where this icon identifies instructions for Works users.

The One Shortcut Used in This Book

This book always uses genuine English words to describe how things work! Well, almost always. (Sorry.) There's one important exception. When you see an instruction that looks something like this,

Choose Blah⇨Fooey from the menu bar . . .

it means: Click Blah in the menu bar, and then click Fooey in the menu that drops down. (If you don't know what *click, menu bar,* or *menu* mean, that's okay — see the appendix.)

This sort of instruction crops up so often that, if I didn't use that shortcut, you'd be bored silly by Chapter 3 — and IDG Books would have to slaughter another forest worth of trees to get the extra paper to print the book!

(You may also notice another very minor typographic habit of this book. This book capitalizes all the first letters of certain features, even though the software itself doesn't. That habit makes sentences like, "Click the check box Center Across Selection" at least slightly readable, whereas, "Click the check box Center across selection" is utter gibberish.)

Where to Go from Here

You've probably already tried to do something with Works Suite, and are perplexed, annoyed, or intrigued by something you've seen. Look it up in the Table of Contents or the Index and see what this book has to say about it.

All authors enjoy hearing from readers, and I'm no different. If you have comments or questions, you can send me e-mail at workssuite@gurus.com. (Attach your file if you're reporting a beginner's-level problem with a document that this book doesn't seem to solve.)

I'm just an author: one guy, working out of his house, with mice. I am not an employee of Microsoft, IDG Books Worldwide, or anyone else, and I have no special connections to anyone. Not even the mice. I can't send you software or book updates. I can't even promise to reply to your message or to solve your problems (although I try). Your e-mail will, however, help make future editions of this book better! (Your e-mail will also automatically generate a confirmation reply from an e-mail robot at gurus.com.)

After you go online to the Internet with Internet Explorer as Part IV describes, you can fill out the online registration form at www.dummies.com/register.html on the World Wide Web!

Part I
Putting Works to Work

The 5th Wave   By Rich Tennant

"I think the cursor's not moving, Mr. Dunt, because you've got your hand on the chalk board eraser and not the mouse."

In this part . . .

"**W**hat the heck is Works?" you may well ask. Well, Works appears to be just one of many products in the Works Suite: Word, Works, Money, Encarta, and so on. But why do they call this particular part of the suite "Works" if it's actually something less than "the entire works?"

The answer: Works originally *was* the whole enchilada. Intended for novice PC users with simple needs and for budget-minded folks, Works combines a set of simple, similarly working tools into a single program. It saves you from needing to buy and figure out a bunch of separate, unrelated, and overpowered programs. The main tools that Microsoft thought Works users wanted — back when Works was first created — were as follows:

- ✔ A word-processor tool for creating things such as letters, books, and reports.

- ✔ A spreadsheet tool for performing calculations, numerical analyses, and charts.

- ✔ A database tool for organizing and analyzing large quantities of information, such as inventories, names and addresses, or purchase orders.

Today, the computer world is a little different, and Works Suite is Microsoft's answer to changing times. Microsoft now offers Word 97, its full-featured word processor, cheap! It's part of Works Suite, too, so you probably aren't going to be very interested in Works' less-powerful word processor tool.

This part of the book explains all the main tools of Works but focuses on the spreadsheet and database tools. These tools are simpler relatives of muscle-bound programs for which you can pay a *lot* more money, such as Microsoft Excel 97 and Access 97 but may be just fine for what you want to do.

Chapter 1

The Works Task Launcher and Other Basics

*U*sing Microsoft Works is kind of like using a food processor: Although it encompasses several different tools, you use them all largely the same way. You start new documents, find old ones, set margins and layout, print documents, and get Help, for example, by using the same commands. This chapter tells you how to perform basic Works tasks, whether you're slicing a spreadsheet or dicing a database. (*Note to self:* Never write on an empty stomach.)

Don't know how to start Works? If you're reading this book, the chances are good that you're new to PCs. If so, first read the appendix, "Clues for the Clueless: PC Basics." You accomplish certain tasks (such as starting programs, using menus, toolbars, dialog boxes, opening windows, and finding files) the same way for nearly all PC programs, so I save a tree by not reprinting the instructions for those tasks elsewhere. I also explain what *menus, toolbars, clicking, disks, files,* and all the other PC basics are in the appendix. If an instruction you read here doesn't seem to tell you enough to follow it, you probably need to read the appendix.

Using, Removing, and Restoring the Task Launcher

I begin my workday by opening my lunch box. Works begins by opening its "launch box," the Works Task Launcher, as shown in Figure 1-1. After the Task Launcher does its job, it disappears. You can perform any of the following steps to get it back:

- ✔ **Choose File⇨New from the menu bar at the top of the Works window.**
- ✔ **Press Ctrl+N on the keyboard.**
- ✔ **Click the Task Launcher button.**

In Figure 1-1, notice that Works' "launch box" contains food for thought: three stacked index cards, each with a tab sticking out on top for you to click. Each card offers one of the following different ways to start working on a document:

- ✔ Going straight to a Works tool.
- ✔ Launching a TaskWizard. (See "Starting new documents by using TaskWizards or templates," later in the chapter.)
- ✔ Opening an existing document.

Works consists of a bunch of mini-programs (which I call *tools*): a word-processor, spreadsheet, database, and communications tool.

The following sections of this chapter describe each of these ways of getting started. The callouts in Figure 1-1 describe how to control the Task Launcher.

Note: The things that you create by using Works are known as either *documents* or (after you save them) *document files*. See the appendix for additional information on what a file is.

Starting by choosing a Works tool

Whenever I lunch, I start by choosing a utensil. Whenever I launch (that is, start a new Works document), I likewise usually start by choosing a tool. Works has four main tools, which I describe in the other chapters of this part. On the Task Launcher, click the Works Tools tab to access the four tool selection buttons and brief descriptions of what these tools do. Click one of the buttons to start that tool. *Bon appétit!*

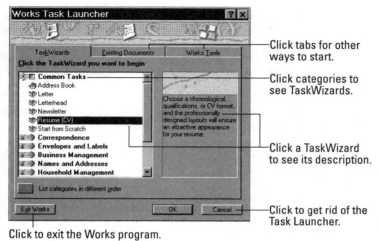

Figure 1-1:
The Works
Task
Launcher,
displaying
its Task-
Wizards —
one of
several
ways to get
started on a
document.

Click tabs for other ways to start.

Click categories to see TaskWizards.

Click a TaskWizard to see its description.

Click to get rid of the Task Launcher.

Click to exit the Works program.

After you choose a tool, a complete menu bar (yum!) and a *toolbar* (a line of buttons) for that tool appears. Works also opens a document window that displays a new, empty document for you to fill up. (The document is temporarily named something such as "Unsaved Spreadsheet 1" until you save it to a disk.)

If you're still working on yesterday's leftovers, you can open a document you created earlier. See the section, "Opening existing documents," a bit later in this chapter, for more information on the latter option.

Starting new documents by using TaskWizards or templates

A *TaskWizard* is like a personal chef that asks you a few questions and then, using one of one of Works' tools, automatically cooks up (or at least begins to cook) the entrée . . . er, document that you need. TaskWizards can save you a lot of work if you don't mind Works making some decisions for you.

Templates are precooked documents with lots of tasty formatting already in place for you, filled with delicious headings and crunchy sample data. You fill in the blanks and replace the sample data with your own.

Legions of TaskWizards and templates, in several categories, are hankering to be your own *Chef d'cuisine.* In the Works Task Launcher, you just choose the TaskWizards card (click its tab) to see the various TaskWizards and descriptions, as the callouts of Figure 1-1 suggest.

Templates are at the bottom. Scroll down to the bottom of the TaskWizards list (or press Ctrl+End) and then click the last category in the list, User Defined Templates.

To start a TaskWizard or open a template, double-click its name in the list. Whenever you first start a TaskWizard, Works displays a silly new dialog box, the Works Task Launcher. So that you're never bothered by this silly dialog box again, click the Always Display This Message check box to clear the check mark. Then click the Yes, Run the TaskWizard button.

For more information on using TaskWizards to perform some of the more common tasks in Works, such as creating mailing lists and newsletters, see Chapter 10.

Opening existing documents

If you've recently created or worked on a document in Works, Works remembers it and displays the document's name in the list shown in Figure 1-2.

To see this list, click the Existing Documents tab in the Task Launcher. To choose a document from this list, double-click the document name.

If you're already working in a Works tool, you don't need the Task Launcher. You can find a short list of recently opened documents by clicking File in the Works menu bar to open the File menu. Click one of the document files listed at the bottom of the File menu to open that file.

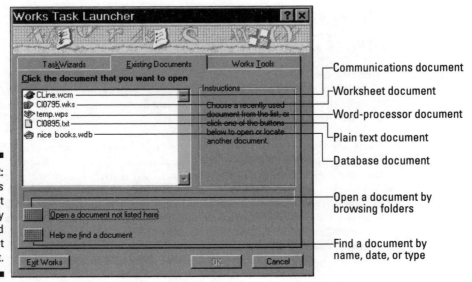

Figure 1-2:
Works lists your most recently used document first.

Communications document

Worksheet document

Word-processor document

Plain text document

Database document

Open a document by browsing folders

Find a document by name, date, or type

Opening existing documents not listed on the Task Launcher

Is your favorite *entrée* not on the menu? If, for some reason, your document doesn't appear on the Existing Documents list, you need to use the usual Windows technique of browsing through folders in a dialog box (similar to browsing through a refrigerator). Works gives you the following two connections to the Open dialog box, as shown in Figure 1-3:

✔ If the Task Launcher is on-screen, click the Open a Document Not Listed Here button (on the Existing Documents card).

✔ If you're currently using a Works tool, choose File⇨Open from the Works menu bar or press Ctrl+O (and that's the *letter* O — not the number zero [0]).

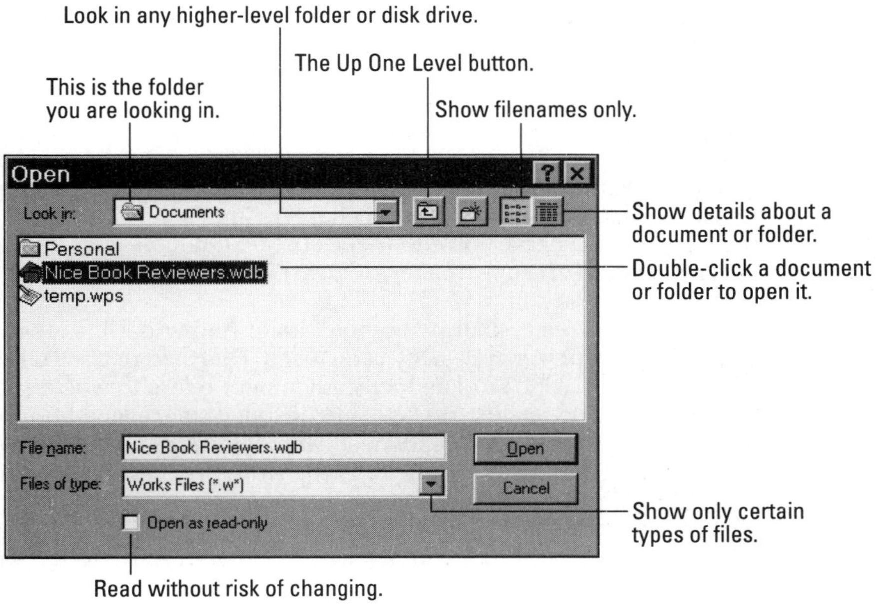

Look in any higher-level folder or disk drive.

The Up One Level button.

This is the folder you are looking in.

Show filenames only.

Figure 1-3:
The Open dialog box initially displays the contents of Works' Documents folder.

Open	? ✕

Look in: Documents

Personal
Nice Book Reviewers.wdb
temp.wps

Show details about a document or folder.

Double-click a document or folder to open it.

File name: Nice Book Reviewers.wdb — Open

Files of type: Works Files (*.w*) — Cancel

☐ Open as read-only

Show only certain types of files.

Read without risk of changing.

The Works document folder is usually set up to be on your C: drive, in the PROGRAM FILES folder, the MSWORKS sub-folder, then the DOCUMENTS sub-sub folder. (Yum! A "sub" sandwich!)

If the file you want appears in the Open dialog box's list, double-click its name. If the file you want isn't in the folder shown here, you need to browse through the other folders of your disk drives, as the callouts of Figure 1-3 describe. (See the appendix if this idea of browsing through folders is new to you.) To open a file that the Works backup system created, click the Files of Type box, as shown in Figure 1-3, and choose `Backup files (*.b*)`. (See my tip in the section "Saving Your Documents," at the end of this chapter, for instructions on creating and using these backup files.)

Choosing Fonts and Other Basic Text Appearances

No matter what Works tool you're using, you can control the appearance of the text you type by using the same techniques. Works gives you several different ways to spice up any text: the toolbar, keyboard shortcuts, and the Font and Style Dialog Box.

You can choose a particular appearance (say, a particular font or boldface type) either before you type or afterward. To choose before you type, use the toolbar, keyboard, mouse menu, or Font and Style dialog box, as I describe in the following text. To choose an appearance after you type, first you must select the text. (See individual tool chapters in this part for details on selecting text, but in general, you either click the text, double-click it, or drag across it.) Then choose an appearance, as I describe in the following text.

You probably already know what bold, italic, and underline mean. A *font* is a name for the type (or typeface) being used. *Font size* refers to the size of that type in *points* (1/72 of an inch). Alignment refers to whether a block of text smooshes up against the left side of something, against the right side, or is nicely centered. In spreadsheets and databases, *alignment* refers to smooshing within the cell or field. In the word processor, alignment refers to smooshing against a page margin.

Clicking toolbar buttons is a quick way to set appearances. A toolbar (see Figure 1-4) appears only after you start working in a particular Works tool. The callouts of Figure 1-4 tell you which buttons to click for various appearance choices.

Finding documents with the Task Launcher

After your pantry (okay, your disk drive) is full of documents and folders, you may need help finding the document that you want. On the Task Launcher, click the Existing Documents tab and then click the Help Me Find a Document button. The Find dialog box springs into view. This dialog box may look familiar to experienced Windows users because it's actually the Windows Find tool! Because this Find tool is actually a Windows feature, not a Works feature, I give you the details of its use in the appendix of this book.

Figure 1-4:
Toolbar buttons for that buttoned-up look. Keyboard alternatives appear in parentheses.

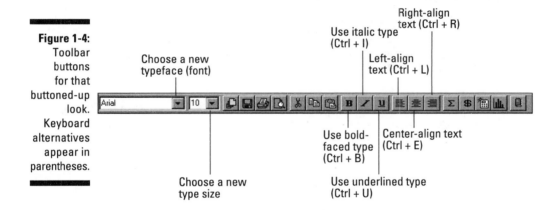

Choose a new typeface (font)

Right-align text (Ctrl + R)

Use italic type (Ctrl + I)

Left-align text (Ctrl + L)

Choose a new type size

Use bold-faced type (Ctrl + B)

Center-align text (Ctrl + E)

Use underlined type (Ctrl + U)

If a button looks depressed at any time, don't fret. It's simply reflecting the state of the text where your *insertion point* (the blinking vertical line) is or of the currently selected (highlighted) text.

If you prefer to use a keyboard, Works offers several keyboard alternatives. The callouts in Figure 1-4 list in parentheses the keyboard alternatives to various toolbar buttons. (See the appendix if these keyboard alternatives make no sense to you.)

For additional font options, you need the Font and Style dialog box, as shown in Figure 1-5. To access this nifty box of stuff, choose Format➪Font and Style from the menu bar of whatever tool you're using.

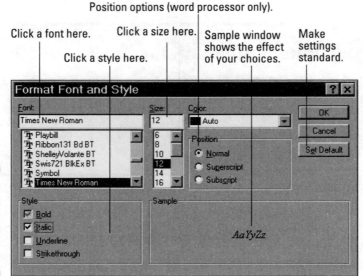

Position options (word processor only).

Click a font here.   Click a size here.   Sample window   Make
                                          shows the effect   settings
            Click a style here.   of your choices.   standard.

Figure 1-5:
The Format
Font and
Style dialog
box does
it all.

If you want Works to use your chosen font and style whenever you begin a
new document, click the Set Default button in the Format Font and Style
dialog box.

Printing

Printing proceeds roughly the same way in each tool of Works. As in all
Windows programs, Microsoft quite unreasonably forces the commands that
have anything to do with printing to live in the File menu: File⇨Page Setup,
File⇨Print Preview, and File⇨Print.

Setting up the page

Ever since humankind moved from scrolls to pages, things have gone
downhill. Now you must worry about top and bottom margins as well as side
margins. Even worse, now you can print the darn pages sideways! Back to
scrolls, I say!

You don't need to set up the page every time you print — just set up the
page once for each document. In fact, if you like Works' normal settings, you
don't need to set up the page at all. If you want to use the same settings for
other documents, create a custom template. See Chapter 9 for details.

Making marginal decisions

Page margins in Works are the spaces between the edge of the page and the regular body text (including any footnotes) of the document. *Headers* and *footers* (text, including page numbers, that appears on the top or bottom of every page) go within these page margins, so header and footer margin settings need to be smaller than page margins.

Choose File⊅Page Setup to open a Page Setup dialog box; then click the Margins tab. The Margins card then graces you with its presence, as shown in Figure 1-6.

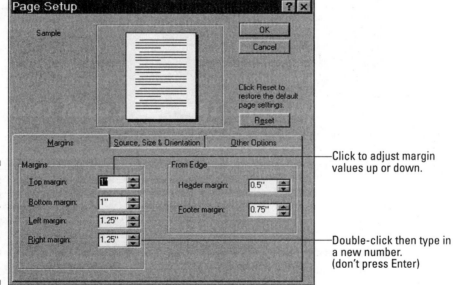

Figure 1-6: A place to do your marginal thinking: the Margins card.

Click to adjust margin values up or down.

Double-click then type in a new number. (don't press Enter)

Setting source, size, and orientation

At least 99 percent of the work you're probably going to print is on standard-sized paper in the normal, or *portrait,* orientation. But for spreadsheets, flyers, and other work, you may want your printer to print sideways, in the *landscape* orientation. (Do *not* put the paper sideways into your printer!)

To set up Works for a different size or orientation of paper, choose File⊅Page Setup to open a Page Setup dialog box; then click the Source, Size & Orientation tab in that dialog box. Figure 1-7 and its callouts show you how to adjust the settings.

See the effects of your settings here.

Page Setup [?] [X]

Sample

OK

Cancel

Click Reset to restore the default page settings.

Reset

| Margins | Source, Size & Orientation | Other Options |

Figure 1-7:
Getting
sourced,
sized, and
oriented all
at once.

Orientation

[A] ⊙ Portrait ○ Landscape

Width: 8.5"

Height: 11"

Click to print page normally (vertically).

Click to print sideways.

Paper

Source: Default Tray

Size: Letter (8 1/2 x 11 in)

Click to select a standard paper size.

If you're using an envelope or special paper and you need to use a special paper-feeding place (or *source*) on your printer, click the Source drop-down list box and choose that source from the list that appears. If that source is a manual-feed slot, Works prompts you at the right time to put the paper in.

Options for printing and displaying

Each type of Works document has certain special quirks, or *options,* for page setup. With spreadsheets and databases, for example, you may or may not want gridlines separating lines and columns of data. See the individual tool chapters in this part for more information on those options.

Previewing coming attractiveness

You've formatted your document, and you think that it's going to look quite attractive on paper. But how do you know? Time for a preview of coming attractiveness! Specifically, time for *Print Preview,* as shown in Figure 1-8. Print Preview shows you how Works thinks your document is going to look in print, without wasting paper.

Most Windows applications provide a Print Preview feature similar to the one you find in Works. Read about Word's Print Preview feature in Chapter 12, for instance.

You can access Print Preview in one of the following three ways:

✔ Click File➪Print Preview in the menu bar.

✔ Click the button in the menu bar that looks like a document with a monocle.

(To determine whether you're on the right button, place your mouse cursor over the button without clicking; if you're on the money, Works shows you a tiny label reading Print Preview.)

✔ Choose File➪Print and then click the Preview button in the Print dialog box that appears.

See the callouts in Figure 1-8 for instructions on using the controls for Print Preview.

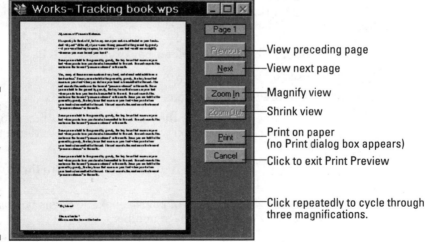

Figure 1-8: Works shows you teeny-tiny print on a minuscule page. Click the page to zoom in.

— View preceding page
— View next page
— Magnify view
— Shrink view
— Print on paper (no Print dialog box appears)
— Click to exit Print Preview
— Click repeatedly to cycle through three magnifications.

To view maximum or minimum magnifications of the document, click the Zoom In or Zoom Out buttons respectively. Or click the document itself. Three clicks takes you through all available magnifications. After magnifying the view, use the vertical and horizontal scroll bars to check out any parts of the document that extend beyond the window. (See the appendix if scroll bars are new to you.)

Printing on actual paper!

What next? Imagine — printing on paper instead of on a computer screen! (Beats printing on an empty stomach!) Printing is a little different for each tool in Works. For the most important printing variations within each tool, see the chapters on that tool. In general, however, printing is pretty simple if things go right. Simply perform the following steps:

1. **Turn on your printer and wait until it comes online**.

   Most printers have an indicator light somewhere to tell you that the printer has had its morning coffee, done its exercises, and is ready to roll. See your printer manual.

2. **To print the entire document without further ado, click the Print button on the Works toolbar (the button with picture of a printer on it).**

   At this point, you're essentially done. Read the following section "Terminating printing," if you change your mind about printing the document.

If you want to print only a part of the document, print multiple copies, change to another printer (or fax modem), or adjust the quality of printing, follow these steps instead:

1. **Choose File➪Print from the menu bar or press Ctrl+P.**

   The Print dialog box comes to your aid.

2. **Make any of the following choices in that dialog box:**

   - For multiple copies, click the Number of Copies box and type the number of copies that you want (but don't press the Enter key yet).

     You can also click the up or down arrows next to that box to change the page count.

   - To print a specific group of pages, click the Pages box and type the starting and ending page numbers.

   - To print faster but with less quality, click the Draft Quality Printing check box.

   - To change to another printer (or "print" to a fax modem to send a fax), click the Name drop-down list box and choose a printer (or fax modem) from the list that appears.

   - To use any of the special options your printer provides, click the Options button.

     A printer-specific dialog box appears. You need to check your printer manual for instructions.

3. Click OK (or press Enter).

If all goes well, you can now just close your eyes and wait for your document to print. If you change your mind about printing — quick, read the following section, "Terminating printing." If you're "printing" to a fax modem, your fax software now takes over.

Terminating printing

Don't just turn off the printer. Your paper may get stuck halfway, and your PC may become confused and send you error messages. Don't just turn off the PC, either, or it may become confused after you restart it.

Depending upon what printer you use, a dialog box for your printer may appear on your screen as soon as you click OK in the Print dialog box (Step 3 of the preceding section). If such a dialog box appears, click the stop button (sometimes marked with a black square). I can't tell you exactly what to click because the dialog box comes from your printer's manufacturer. Check your manual for details.

If no dialog box for your printer appears on your screen, Windows provides a quick "emergency stop" procedure for terminating a printing job. Follow these steps:

1. Click the Windows Start button (on the Windows Taskbar, not in Works) and then choose Settings⇨Printers from the Start menu.

2. In the Printers dialog box that appears, double-click the icon for the printer that you're using.

A dialog box appears with the same name as your printer and displays your file's name.

3. Click your file's name in that dialog box, and then choose Document⇨Cancel Printing from the menu bar of the Printers dialog box and wait for printing to stop.

Printing may continue for a page or so, depending on how many pages already downloaded to your printer's memory.

Hollering for Help

This book, while arguably the finest example of technical documentation since *The Joy of Cooking,* doesn't tell you everything about Works Suite. Sorry. But it does tell you how to access the Works Help feature to fill in the gaps.

Major kinds of Help

Most Windows programs, including Works, offer the following two principal kinds of Help:

- ✔ **Brief explanations of dialog box thingies:** Dialog boxes are like a box of chocolates sometimes. If a dialog box filled with mysterious thingies confronts you, just right-click any thingy; then click the What's This? box that appears. A brief explanation of what it is and does appears on-screen. Click anywhere else or press the Esc key to make the explanation go away.

- ✔ **Detailed documentation:** This form of Help appears in various dialog boxes and in a panel in the right-hand side of the Works window. I describe this type of Help in the rest of this section.

Works also offers First-Time Help. First-Time Help comes in dialog boxes, one example of which is shown in Figure 1-9. These boxes appear the first time you start some task that Works considers complex, such as creating a database. The choices that these dialog boxes offer are fairly obvious, as the callouts in Figure 1-9 indicate. I suggest that you take the tour once.

Each time you start Works anew, First-Time Help forgets that you benefitted from its services the last time around, so it annoyingly reappears if you undertake the same task again. The next time that the same First-Time Help dialog box appears, click the Don't Display This Message in the Future check box and then click OK.

Works also offers several other flavors of Help, including additional tours or tutorials (worth taking once) and online Help. (Online Help requires a Web browser such as Internet Explorer and a connection to the Internet.)

Figure 1-9:
First-Time Help is nice, but after it becomes annoying, you can make it go away.

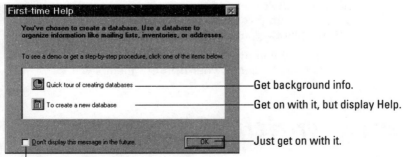

Get background info.

Get on with it, but display Help.

Just get on with it.

Never see this box again.

Getting — and getting rid of — Help

Okay — you need help. Call the various members of Works' Help squadron into action by performing the following actions:

✔ Press the F1 key at any time to get help related to whatever you're currently doing.

✔ Choose Help➪Contents to browse topics from a table of contents.

✔ Choose Help➪Index to use an alphabetical index to locate topics.

✔ Choose Help➪Introduction to Works to get a quick tour of Works.

✔ Choose Help➪How to use Help to get help on Help. (Help!)

✔ Choose Help➪Microsoft on the Web and then any subsequent menu selections you want. If your PC is set up to go online, this choice launches your Web browser and displays information from the Microsoft Web site.

To clear Help off your screen, choose Help➪Hide Help. (You can banish Help in other ways, too, but this one is the fastest.)

Using Help's index and contents

After you choose Help➪Index or Help➪Contents from the menu bar, you see two new goodies on-screen that work together. As shown in Figure 1-10, they're the Help Topics dialog box (on the left) and the Works' Help panel (on the right). As you choose topics in the Help Topics dialog box, instructions appear in the Help panel.

To look in a table of contents of Help, click the Contents tab. If you prefer an alphabetical index, click the Index tab. If you use the Index tab, you may click the text box that the callout in Figure 1-10 indicates and type a word or phrase describing what you want help on. As you type, Works looks at what you've typed so far and scrolls the list of topics to match, if it can.

When you see the subject you want appear in the Help Topics dialog box, click the name of that subject. (If the subject has a folder icon, click the folder to reveal subtopics.) Help on that subject then usually appears in the Works Help panel. A What If or How dialog box may appear instead. If so, click its Done button after you read it.

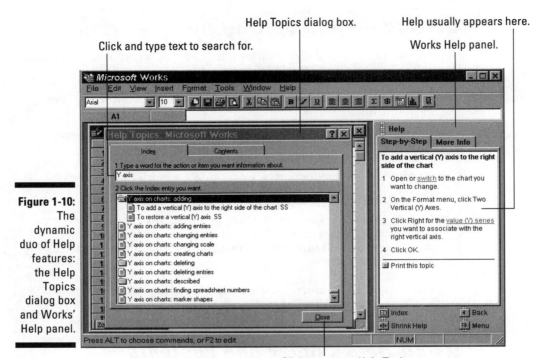

Help Topics dialog box.

Click and type text to search for.

Help usually appears here.

Works Help panel.

Click to remove Help Topics.

Figure 1-10:
The dynamic duo of Help features: the Help Topics dialog box and Works' Help panel.

In the Works Help panel, you can get more information in several ways, as the following list describes:

- For an explanation of any green, underlined text, click that text.
- Click the More Info tab (if visible) to read background stuff.
- Click anything that a bullet or tiny square button precedes. (Click the Menu button at the bottom of the panel to see some of these items.)
- Click the Back button to return to panels you viewed previously.

After you finish with Help, choose Help⇨Hide Help to clear your screen. To restore Help, choose Help⇨Show Help.

Saving Your Documents

Computer documents disintegrate faster than cake at a picnic after you exit from the program or lose power to your PC. To preserve documents, you must save them as files on a disk, whether that disk is your permanent *hard disk* or a removable *diskette* (or *floppy disk*). See the discussion of files, disks, folders, and directories in the appendix for more information on files and their residences.

Works gives you three ways to save your document as a file. Choose your favorite from among the following:

- ✔ Choose File⇨Save from the menu bar.
- ✔ Press Ctrl+S.
- ✔ Click the button displaying the disk icon (on the toolbar).

As you save a document for the first time, Works opens the Save As dialog box, as shown in Figure 1-11. This dialog box enables you to give the file a name and a location. Whenever you subsequently save a document by using one of the preceding methods, Works doesn't open any dialog box but, instead, simply updates the file on your hard or floppy disk.

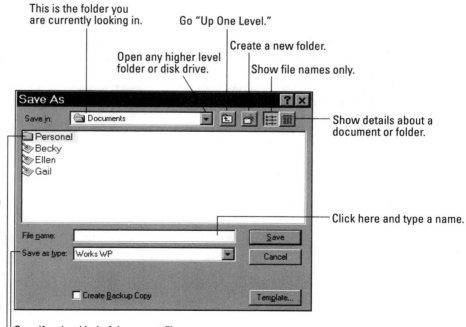

Figure 1-11: Giving your documents a name and a place to live.

This is the folder you are currently looking in.

Go "Up One Level."

Open any higher level folder or disk drive.

Create a new folder.

Show file names only.

Show details about a document or folder.

Click here and type a name.

Specify what kind of document file.

Double-click a folder to open it.

The only action that you absolutely must take to save your file is to click the File Name text box and type a descriptive name, as Figure 1-11 shows, and then click the Save button or press the Enter key. That name can be up to 256 characters long and may include spaces or any punctuation except the characters / \ : ? * " < > or | . If you use the name of a file that already appears in the Save As dialog box (which you can do by clicking that name), the document you're saving replaces the existing one.

Works automatically specifies the location (folder) and file type of your document in the Save As dialog box by *default*. (What a program does unless you tell it otherwise is its default action.) Works' default location for your document file is the Document folder within the MS Works folder, which is within the Program Files folder on your hard disk. As you can with any Windows program, you can save your document in any folder or disk drive on your PC. See the appendix and the callouts of Figure 1-11 for help in understanding and using this Windows folder and file system.

At some later date, you may want to make copies of your file under different names or in different locations. If so, open the original file, use the File⇨ Save As command to open the Save As dialog box, and type a new name or choose a new folder or disk drive. This procedure is helpful if you need slightly different versions of the same file. (If you're sending the same letter to three different people, for example, and need to change the address each time, you may save it as TOM.WPS, DICK.WPS, and HARRY.WPS.)

Works automatically keeps a *backup* copy of your document if you click to enable the Create Backup Copy check box in the Save As dialog box. Then, if you accidentally ruin or delete your document file, you can open the backup file as I describe in the section, "Opening existing documents not listed on the Task Launcher," earlier in this chapter. Then choose the File⇨Save As command to open the Save As dialog box and enter a new file name in the File Name text box. Your document returns to its preruined state.

Chapter 2
Spreading Your First Sheets

. . . .

In This Chapter

▶ Understanding spreadsheets

▶ Creating a new, blank spreadsheet

▶ Examining the spreadsheet window and toolbar

▶ Using cells and ranges

▶ Typing text and numbers

▶ Changing column widths and row heights

▶ Inserting and deleting rows and columns

▶ Entering sequential headings and data automatically

. . . .

So you're ready to set sail into the uncharted seas of calculation? With the Works spreadsheet hoisted squarely to the wind, you can sail to exotic lands where budgets, business plans, alphabetized lists, expense analyses, profit-and-loss statements, surveys, scientific experiments, and sales forecasts live.

If you've never used spreadsheets before, however, you need to know a few basics first, which is where this chapter comes in. In here, you find out what you can do with a spreadsheet, what's what in the spreadsheet window, how to navigate around in spreadsheets, and how to enter text and numbers. To perform calculations and tackle the more exciting stuff, see Chapter 3.

Understanding and Appreciating Spreadsheets

Truth to tell, you can't fully appreciate a spreadsheet until you use one (sort of like with an electric toothbrush but even more fun — if you can imagine that). But to understand a spreadsheet, try to think of it as a table of numbers and calculations where the results of the calculations change to reflect any changes you make in the numbers. A simple form of spreadsheet, for example, is one that automatically sums up rows and columns of numbers and adjusts the sums whenever you change a number.

Some of the main reasons spreadsheets are so popular follow:

✔ Because spreadsheets automatically recalculate every time you change a value, they enable you to carry out "what-if" analyses — for example, what if inflation goes from 4 to 8 percent? When can I retire?

✔ Spreadsheets provide formulas to perform the complex calculations you need for such analyses as mortgages, retirement plans, and statistics.

✔ You can also use spreadsheets for simple lists and collections of data — for example, the names of students in your class and their grades. Spreadsheets overlap with databases in this role. Spreadsheets are more useful for small lists that perhaps require a calculation for every item, while databases are more useful for ever-expanding collections of data (such as mailing lists) or those requiring summary reports (such as inventories).

✔ After you have data in a spreadsheet, you can turn that data into a chart in minutes. I look at this process in more detail in Chapter 5.

Starting Out

To review how to start Works and the different ways of starting a spreadsheet document, check out Chapter 1. If you're starting a new spreadsheet, you can use a wizard or a template to do a lot of the work for you. Or, to start by creating a blank document, choose the Works Tools tab on the Task Launcher and then click the Spreadsheet button. You're now gazing at a window like the one in Figure 2-1.

What's what in the spreadsheet window

Figure 2-1 shows you what's what in your spreadsheet window. (*Spreadsheet window* is my name for how the Microsoft Works window looks if you're using the spreadsheet tool.) Works has given the spreadsheet document shown in the spreadsheet window the forlorn name of Unsaved Spreadsheet 1 — one of the nerdy sort of start-up names Works gives new documents that you haven't yet saved as a file. Near the top of the Works window is the usual Works menu bar with all the commands and underneath that menu bar is the spreadsheet toolbar with all its buttons and icons.

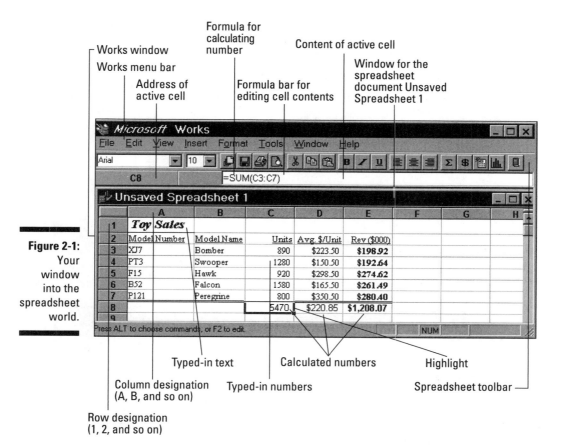

Figure 2-1:
Your
window
into the
spreadsheet
world.

The spreadsheet toolbar

A popular way to give commands to Works (other than traditional shouting methods) is by using the toolbar — the thing with all the pictures (see Figure 2-2). The toolbar is just a faster way than the menu bar to do some of the same things. You click a button and stuff happens.

As you discover in the other chapters of this part, much of the spreadsheet toolbar is similar to the toolbars in other Works tools. All buttons but four (the AutoSum, Currency, Easy Calc, and New Chart buttons) are the same as the ones in, for example, the word processor tool, which I discuss in Chapter 8.

I don't go into detail about any of the toolbar buttons here, but I discuss them as I go along. Here's where to go to read about the buttons that are particularly interesting for working with spreadsheets:

✔ **Left-, Center-, and Right-Align in a cell:** See the section in Chapter 4 on changing alignment in a cell.

   ✔ **Currency (format a number as dollars and cents):** See the section in Chapter 4 on formatting numbers.

   ✔ **AutoSum:** See the section in Chapter 3 on shortcuts for creating formulas.

   ✔ **Create a chart:** See Chapter 5.

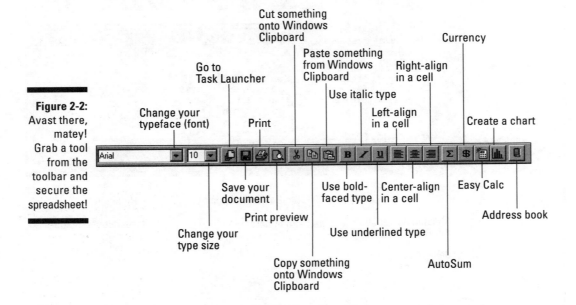

Figure 2-2:
Avast there,
matey!
Grab a tool
from the
toolbar and
secure the
spreadsheet!

The spreadsheet document

The spreadsheet document looks like a big table, which is gratifying, because that's what a spreadsheet is. Here are two important points to note:

   ✔ Each horizontal row in this table has a number (at the far left) and each vertical column has a letter (at the top) in tasteful battleship gray.

   ✔ A spreadsheet has no pages (until you print it); it's one vast table. To see spreadsheet stuff beyond your screen limits, scroll the document up or down, left or right, using the gray scroll bars along the right and bottom sides. (See the appendix if scroll bars are new to you.)

Cells

A *cell* is one of those little rectangles on the spreadsheet shown in Figure 2-1; it's the intersection of a row and a column. Everything that you type into a spreadsheet goes in cells.

Each cell has an address so that you can talk to Works about it in your calculations, graphs, and other activities. A cell address is made up of the column letter and row number, smushed together as, for example, B12, which is the cell at column B and row 12.

Entering and Editing Data in Cells

As you can in most Windows programs, if you make a mistake, you can press Ctrl+Z or choose Edit⇨Undo *Something* to undo your most recent action (which is the *Something* that appears after the word Undo on the Edit menu).

Moving from cell to cell

The cell you're about to type in, edit, format, or otherwise muck around with Microsoft calls the *active cell*. It's surrounded by a rectangular halo that Microsoft calls the *highlight*. (In computer heaven, the halos are rectangular.) The address of the active cell (cell C8 in Figure 2-1) appears near the upper left of the Works window, under the font window of the toolbar.

The easiest way to choose a new active cell is to move your mouse so that the mouse cursor — a big, fat plus sign (+) — hovers over the new cell and then click.

Of course, you can't click what you can't see. To view various areas of your spreadsheet, use the scroll bars on the right side and bottom of the document window.

You can also move the highlight by using the navigation keys on your keyboard. See the section "Navigating in Almost Any Document," on the Cheat Sheet inside the front cover of this book, for information on using these keys.

If you know the address of the cell that you want but it's nowhere nearby, press the F5 key. An itsy-bitsy Go To dialog box appears. Type the cell address — **Q200** for example — and click the OK button to access that cell.

People often type headings on top of columns or to the left of rows to identify what data the row or column contains. After you create column and/ or row headings, you can *freeze* those headings in place on-screen for convenience while you move around in the rest of the spreadsheet. Click the cell just under the column-headings row (or row 1 if you have no column headings) and to the right of the row-headings column (or column A if you have no row headings). Then choose Format⇨Freeze Titles. Repeat to unfreeze.

Typing stuff in cells

Typing something into a cell involves the following simple procedure:

1. **Click a cell.**

   You can also move your highlight to it by using an arrow key or other navigation keys.

2. **Type what you want in the cell.**

   Use the Backspace key to delete any mistakes. If you decide not to save what you type, press the Esc key.

3. **After the text, number, or formula is the way you want it, press the Enter key or move to another cell by using a mouse-click, the Tab key, or a navigation key.**

Typing more stuff than can fit into a cell's width is okay. You can always increase the cell width later. Don't worry if the stuff appears to overlap the empty cell to the right.

If you type more text than you can display in a cell, or if you type a number that turns into a bunch of ##### characters, your column is too skinny. See the following section, "Changing column widths and row heights."

Changing column widths and row heights

Following are several ways to set the column widths and row heights.

To quickly set a column's width, double-click the column letter at the top of the column. Works sizes the column to fit the largest entry in that column. (What about row height? Works sizes row height automatically to the largest font size you use.)

An intuitive way to change the width of a column (or height of a row) is to "drag" its edge by using your mouse. In the gray area where the column letters (or row numbers) are, position your cursor over the right edge of the column (or bottom edge of the row) until the cursor reads "Adjust." Click and drag to adjust.

A more precise way to change the width of a column or row is to first click anywhere in that column or row. To adjust several adjacent columns (or rows) drag across them (highlight them) with your mouse at any row (or column). Then choose Format⇨Column Width (or Row Height).

The Format Column Width (or Format Row Height) dialog box springs into action. Type a new width number into the Column Width (or Row Height) text box and then click OK. If you're setting column width, the width number specifies approximately how many characters wide the column is, using 10-point type. For row height, the number is in *points* (as in a 12-point font). (A point is roughly $1/72$ of an inch.)

To put multiple lines of text in a single cell, you need to both increase row height and enable the line-wrapping feature. To enable line wrapping, choose Format⇨Alignment. On the Alignment card of the Format Cells dialog box that appears, click the Wrap Text check box to put a check mark in it. Text now wraps automatically to a second line if the length exceeds the column width.

Entering different kinds of cell contents

Spreadsheets can contain three different kinds of contents and treats each of them differently. A cell can contain only one kind of content. The three kinds of cell content are as follows:

- ✔ **Text** (In Figure 2-3, the model names are text.)

- ✔ **A typed number** (In Figure 2-3, the revenues are typed numbers.)

- ✔ **A calculation, which displays its result** (In Figure 2-3, the totals in the last row and column are the results of calculations.)

Text   Typed-in numbers

Figure 2-3:
Contents
of a few
example
cells in the
Toy Sales
spreadsheet.

	A	B	C	D	E
1	*Toy Sales*				
2	Model Number	Model Name	Units	Avg. $/Unit	Rev ($000)
3	XJ7	Bomber	890	$223.50	**$198.92**
4	PT3	Swooper	1280	$150.50	**$192.64**
5	F15	Hawk	920	$298.50	**$274.62**
6	B52	Falcon	1580	$165.50	**$261.49**
7	P121	Peregrine	800	$350.50	**$280.40**
8			5470	$220.85	**$1,208.07**

Calculations

The following sections explain how to enter the first two kinds of cell contents: text and typed numbers. I explain calculations in Chapter 3.

Unless you tell Works otherwise, it aligns text entries against the left side of their cells and numeric entries against the right side. I tell you how to "tell Works otherwise" in the section on cell alignment in Chapter 4.

Typing text

To simply enter some text, such as a column heading or title — something that you don't use in a calculation — just click the cell and type the text. Press the Enter key after you finish typing. Works recognizes any entry containing letters as being a text entry.

After you type your text and press Enter, you may notice that, up in the formula bar, Works sticks a quote character in front of what you typed. The quote mark doesn't appear in the cell, just in the bar. This character is Works' subtle way of saying that it interprets the contents of this cell as text, not as a number or calculation.

Sometimes you must enter that quotation mark yourself: before Zip codes (or any all-numeral code or identifier beginning with zero); before any text beginning with =, +, or –; or before any text that already begins with a quotation mark (in other words, you must enter two quotation marks to start).

Note: Text entries require only a single, opening quotation mark for reasons lost in the dim mists of spreadsheet history. You don't need one at the end of the entry.

Typing numbers

Entering numbers into a cell is as simple as entering text into a cell. Just click a cell and type the numbers. Here are a few of the most popular options you have for entering numbers, some of which Figure 2-4 illustrates:

- ✔ You can precede a number with a minus sign (–) if it's negative, or you can use a dollar sign ($) if it's money. Use –$ or parentheses for negative money amounts. Use as many decimal places as you need, but Works rounds off the numbers to two decimal places if you use the dollar sign or parentheses.

- ✔ For percentages, add a percent sign (%) immediately after the number. Just as mathematics dictates, if you type **100%** Works understands it to mean 1.00.

- ✔ If you're a scientific type, you can use scientific notation: You can type 1,253,000,000 as 1.253e9, for example, or as 1.253E+09. In fact, if you type a big number, Works automatically displays it in this format.

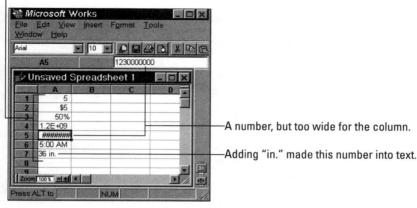

Figure 2-4:
A few
popular
formats in
which you
can write
numbers
(and one in
which you
can't).
Chapter 4
gives you
more
number
formats.

—These are all valid numbers.

—A number, but too wide for the column.

—Adding "in." made this number into text.

What actually happens after you type a number a certain way is that Works automatically chooses a *number format* for that cell. If you begin with a $ symbol, for example, Works chooses *currency* format. For more information on number formats, see Chapter 4.

If a number has units, such as *fathoms,* enter the units as text in the next cell to the right. Don't type *36 fathoms* all in a single cell, or Works thinks that the entry is text, not a number, and can't perform calculations with the entry at all.

Editing the contents of a cell

You may notice something a bit odd as you type things into cells. Works is normally set up so that, as you type things into cells, you're actually typing in two places at once! Works (as it comes out of the box) is set up to enable you to edit cell contents in either of the following places:

 ✔ In the formula bar.
 ✔ In the cell itself.

Here's how to edit the contents of a cell, either in the formula bar or in a cell:

1. **Click the cell you want to edit.**

 The cell shows its little rectangular halo and displays the contents of the cell in the formula bar.

2. **Click the formula bar to edit in the formula bar or double-click the cell to edit in the cell.**

   You can also press F2 and have Works decide where you edit.

3. **Edit the contents of the cell just as you edit text in a Windows dialog box.**

   Type new text, use the Backspace key for errors, and so on. See the appendix for details on editing in dialog boxes.

4. **To enter your changes into the cell, press the Enter key or click the check mark button on the formula bar.**

   If you decide that you don't want to change the cell contents after all, press the Esc key on your keyboard or click the X button on the formula bar.

If the data you're editing is too long to fit entirely in the editing area of the formula bar, the navigation keys (left/right arrow keys, Home, and End) are an easier way to move the insertion point than the mouse.

Trying Out a Sample Spreadsheet

One of the fastest ways to understand spreadsheets is to create one yourself. Figure 2-5 shows an example of a spreadsheet with the first week of a diet plan for an anonymous, but very earnest, calorie-counting person.

$!@($?)&$!!! What's all this ##########?

If you're typing a number that's too wide for the column, you often get a distressing result. You get a bunch of pound (or "score") symbols, #####, in the cell, which is a message from Works saying, "I can't print this number here; make the column wider, will ya?" (Refer to Figure 2-4.) Sometimes this situation occurs because the cell in question has the wrong number format — some formats are wider than others. If you use Works' default format for numbers, the *General* format, Works simply switches to nice, compact scientific notation if a number gets too large. You may or may not approve of this switch. For details on number formats, see the section on formatting numbers in Chapter 4.

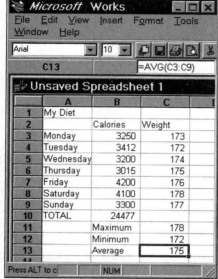

Here's how to duplicate this spreadsheet (18 quick steps to weight control!):

1. **To start out with a fresh spreadsheet, press Ctrl+N and, after the Task Launcher screen appears, click the Works Tools tab and then click the Spreadsheet button.**

   A fresh, new spreadsheet appears on-screen. The current active cell (where the highlight is) is A1.

2. **Type** MyDiet **in the active cell and press the Enter key.**

3. **Click cell B2 (column B, row 2), type** Calories, **and press the Enter key.**

4. **Press the right-arrow key to highlight cell C2, type** Weight, **and press the Enter key.**

5. **Click cell A3 and type** Monday.

6. **Press the down-arrow key and type** Tuesday; **keep pressing the down-arrow key and entering days of the week through** Sunday.

   On the seventh day, rest.

   To avoid manually typing the days of the week, you can try out Autofill here, instead. See the section, "Entering Sequential Headings and Data Automatically by Using Autofill," later in this chapter.

7. **Click cell B3 and type** 3250.

8. **Press the down-arrow and type** 3412; **refer to Figure 2-5 for the other calories and keep on like this through** Sunday.

9. **Click cell C3 and type** 173; **refer to Figure 2-5 for the other weights and keep on like this through** Sunday.

10. **Click cell A10 and type** TOTAL.

    This text is simply a label.

11. **Press the right-arrow key to highlight cell B10, type** =SUM(B3:B9), **and press Enter.**

    Wow! Magic! The total calories for the week.

12. **Press the down-arrow key to highlight cell B11 and type** Maximum.

13. **Press the down-arrow key to highlight cell B12 and type** Minimum.

14. **Press the down-arrow key to highlight cell B13 and type** Average.

15. **Click cell C11 and type** =MAX(C3:C9).

16. **Press the down-arrow key to highlight cell C12 and type** =MIN(C3:C9).

17. **Press the down-arrow key to highlight cell C13, type** =AVG(C3:C9), **and press Enter.**

    If you followed these directions, you're looking at an exact duplicate of Figure 2-5.

Notice that you save some effort by not pressing Enter every time you type something (although you may press Enter if you want). All you need to do to enter what you just typed is to move the highlight to a new cell.

Try changing some of the calorie or weight values to see what happens to the calculated values at the bottom.

Working with Ranges: Groups of Cells

One essential feature of spreadsheets is the ability to perform calculations and other operations on groups of cells. You can move a group of cells, for example, copy it, format it, sum a column of numbers, or average all the data in a group.

Any rectangular block of cells is a *range*. A range can be a large, small, skinny, or wide rectangle of cells anywhere in your spreadsheet. A range can consist of just two adjacent cells, a column, a row — even the entire spreadsheet. The following sections tell you how to work with ranges.

Selecting a range of cells

The easiest way to point out a range of cells to Works, either because you're about to format them all in some way or because you're referring to them in a calculation, is to select them. (The other way is to refer to them by their range address, as I describe in the following section.)

To select any group of cells (any row, column, or rectangular area), click at one end or corner of the group and drag the mouse cursor across the cells you want to select. Release the mouse button when you're done.

To select an entire row or column, click the column letter or row number (in the gray area of the spreadsheet). To select the entire spreadsheet, click the unmarked button where the row-number and column-letter areas intersect (at the upper-left corner).

To select a columnal group of filled cells (as opposed to selecting the entire column, from row 1 to row 16384), click the top cell of the group and then press Ctrl+Shift+↓. To select a row of filled cells, click the left-most cell and then press Ctrl+Shift+→. The selection stops at the first blank cell in the column or row.

Referring to a range by its address

The way Works describes a range in its formulas (calculations) and in various dialog boxes is by using the range's *address*. You need to understand range addresses to use these formulas and dialog boxes. A range's address combines the addresses of the two cells in opposite corners of the range, with a colon (:) in between. Which cell address comes first doesn't matter. To refer to two separate ranges at once, use a comma between them.

Here are the addresses of a few of the ranges in Figure 2-3, which appears earlier in this chapter:

Contents of spreadsheet in Figure 2-3	Range of content
All the model names	B3:B7 or B7:B3
Everything concerning the XJ7	A3:E3 or E3:A3
Revenues for all models	F3:F7 or F7:F3
Unit sales for every model but Hawk	C3:C4, C6:C7

Copying, Moving, and Deleting

Works provides a variety of features that enable you to copy, move, and delete chunks of your spreadsheet. These features work pretty much the same way in every tool in Works. Here's how these things work in your spreadsheet:

- To delete a cell or range, select it and then press the Delete or Backspace key.

- To move a cell or range, select it and then slowly move your mouse cursor across the thickish frame that appears around the selected area until the cursor changes to an arrow labeled *drag*. At that point, click the mouse and drag the copy of the frame that appears to the new location. Release the mouse button, and the cells are moved.

- To copy, carry out the same actions as you do for moving cells but hold down the Ctrl key while you drag.

- Another way to copy is to use the Windows Clipboard. Select the cell or range that you want to copy and then press Ctrl+C. Click the cell where you want the copy to appear and press Ctrl+V to paste. If you're pasting a range of cells, click where you want the upper-left-corner cell of that range to go and then press Ctrl+V

- To cut the contents of a cell or range out and paste them it elsewhere in the spreadsheet, select the cell or range to be cut and then press Ctrl+X; then click the cell where you want to paste and press Ctrl+V. (If you're pasting a range, click where you want the upper-left corner of the range to go.)

- To make multiple copies of a single cell, click the cell to copy and press Ctrl+C. Then highlight a range and press Ctrl+V. All the cells in the range are filled with a copy of the original cell's contents.

- To *fill* a row or column of cells with copies of an adjacent cell, click the cell, position the mouse cursor over the cell's lower right-hand corner so that the cursor reads "Fill," and then drag across adjacent cells.

You have three alternatives to using the Ctrl key combinations for copy, cut, and paste. You can use the Copy, Paste, and Cut buttons on the toolbar, as shown in Figure 2-2; you can right-click a selection with your mouse and then choose Copy, Cut, or Paste from the menu that appears; or you can choose Edit⇨Copy, Cut, or Paste from the Works menu bar.

Following are a few things to remember while moving and copying things:

- If you move or copy something to already-occupied cells, you wipe out the earlier contents of those cells.

✔ If you move a cell (say, you're moving what's in A1 to B5) that contains data that you use in a formula anywhere in the spreadsheet (say, =A1/3), the formula changes to follow its data. (In this example, it changes to =B5/3.) See Chapter 3 if you're not familiar with formulas.

   ✔ If you copy a formula, the addresses in it change. See the section on the mysteries of copying formulas in Chapter 3.

Inserting and Deleting Rows and Columns

Imagine that you're a high-priced lifestyle consultant, typing up your monthly invoice for September. You've got a row for each day that you worked. You've made it to September 30, and suddenly you remember that you taught your client swing dancing on Saturday the 18th. Swell — what do you do now?

Well, you can select everything after the 18th and move it down a row, but how tedious and pedestrian! No, no, — a with-it, turn-of-the-millennium kind of person such as you should be inserting rows. Or columns — whatever. To do so, follow these steps:

1. **To insert a new row *above* an existing row, click anywhere in the existing row.**

   To insert a row *above* row 5, for example, click row 5.

2. **To insert a new column *to the left of* an existing column, click anywhere in the existing column.**

   To insert a column *to the left of* column D, for example, click column D.

3. **Choose Insert⇨Insert Row or Insert Column.**

   You can also right-click the existing column or row with your mouse and choose Insert Row or Insert Column from the menu that appears.

Deleting a row or column (as opposed to just deleting its contents and leaving the row or column blank) is a similar procedure: Click anywhere in the row or column you want to delete; choose Insert⇨Delete Row *or* Delete Column. Selecting Insert to delete may seem odd, but that's the way it is.

If you insert a row or a column (say, a new row 5) into the middle of a range that you use in a formula (say, =SUM(A1:A10)), the formula now includes the new row or column. If, however, you insert a new row or column *on the edge* of a range of numbers (say, a new row 1 or row 11), the formula does *not* include the new row or column. So if you have an alphabetic list and add an Aaron or Zykowski, you may want to check to make sure that your totals are still correct. If they are not, you must edit your formulas, as Chapter 3 describes.

Entering Sequential Headings and Data Automatically by Using Autofill

Sometimes the entries in a row or column — especially row and column headings — follow some predictable sequence. That sequence may be 1, 2, 3; or Monday, Tuesday, Wednesday (refer to Figure 2-5) where an equal interval lies between each entry. Unfortunately, typing in these predictable sequences can become really boring. After a while, you find yourself thinking, "This sequence is so predictable. This thing I'm typing on is a computer. Couldn't the computer, like, *predict* or something?" The answer is yes: by using Autofill. Follow these steps:

1. **Type the first two items from the sequence in adjacent cells.**

   In Figure 2-5, for example, you'd type **Monday** in A3 and **Tuesday** in A4.

2. **Select the two cells in which you just typed. (Drag across them.)**

3. **Move your mouse cursor to the lower-right corner of the two-cell block that you just selected, until the word *FILL* appears under your cursor.**

4. **Click and drag over all the cells that you want Works to fill automatically.**

   In the example in Figure 2-5, you drag until the highlighted area includes the two cells that you typed, plus the next five in the same column.

5. **Release the mouse button.**

Presto! Works extends the sequence to fill the selected cells. Was figuring all this stuff out worth the effort just to avoid typing the names of five days? Maybe . . . maybe not. But if you ever need to type all the days of a *year* into a row or column, you may come to think very fondly of the Autofill feature.

Chapter 3

Making Calculations

. . . .

In This Chapter

▶ Using Easy Calc

▶ Creating and understanding formulas

▶ Using and understanding mathematical operators

▶ Understanding functions

▶ Using shortcuts to create formulas

▶ Copying formulas

. . . .

*I*f doing calculations is not your idea of how to have fun with spread-sheets, you need to try Works spreadsheets. (And avoid marrying a mathematically inclined sailor.) Works gives you the following two nifty ways to perform the amazing variety of calculations that a spreadsheet can do:

✔ **Works Easy Calc:** An automated take-you-by-the-hand approach to creating calculations.

✔ **The traditional write-it-yourself approach:** Also the approach you can use for editing calculations.

This chapter explores both techniques. It also gives you labor-saving tricks, tips, and insights into the way spreadsheets work.

Never try to write while you're thinking about sheets.

Basic Ideas behind Spreadsheet Calculations

You need to understand a few basic concepts to do calculations in spreadsheets. Here are the biggies:

- ✔ You do calculations by putting *formulas* in cells. Those formulas compute their results by using data from various other cells in the spreadsheet.

- ✔ You put the formula *in the cell where you want the answer.* The formula displays the *result,* not the formula itself.

- ✔ If you change any of the numbers on which the formula works, the formula immediately recalculates a new result.

- ✔ You can use a formula cell as data for another formula. You can sum a row of sums, for example.

- ✔ You can often save time by copying a formula from one row or column to another.

Microsoft has checked the version of Works you have in Works Suite for Year 2000 (Y2K) calculation bugs and deloused it. No millennipedes in your sheets!

Using Easy Calc in Works

Works' designers created a special tool called Easy Calc that builds a formula for you. Of course, you need to know what sort of data the calculation you're doing requires. If you're computing Net Present Value, for example, Works expects you to give it a value for the Rate of Return.

I designed the spreadsheet in Figure 3-1 to compute the average cost per night for lodging during our vacation in Canada (where the sheets are always nice and clean). I've entered the data, including an exchange rate for how many Canadian dollars I get for my American dollars. I'm now ready to enter my calculations.

I will add my first formula here.

	A	B	C	D	E	F
1	Our Canadian Vacation Lodging Expenses					
2		No. of	$$ Paid	$$/night	U.S.	
3	Hotel	Nights	(Canadian dollars)		dollars	
4	Calgary Value Hotel	2	$167.90			
5	Banff Discount Lodging	1	$126.75			
6	Rancho Cheapo Cabins	1	$110.65			
7	Castle Mtn. Campground	2	$24.00			
8	Lake Louise Campground	2	$30.00			
9	Wabasso Campground	5	$75.00			
10	Riverside Cabins	1	$144.85			
11	Kootenay Hootnanny Lodge	1	$155.95			
12	Marble Canyon Campground	3	$36.00			
13	Jasper Honeysuckle Lodge	1	$189.55			
14	Totals:					
15	Exchange Rate: CN$/1 US$	1.56				
16	Average Cost Per Night:					
17						

Figure 3-1:
A spreadsheet, ready to add formulas.

Here's how to use Easy Calc to perform basic calculations on data you enter in your spreadsheet:

1. **Choose Tools⇨Easy Calc from the Works menu bar or click the Easy Calc button (the calculator with a gleam) near the right end of the toolbar.**

   The Easy Calc dialog box appears, as shown in Figure 3-2.

2. **Click the button for the kind of calculation you want to do.**

   If you don't see the calculation you want among the buttons shown in the dialog box, click the Other button. (See the sidebar "Doing 'other' calculations in Easy Calc," later in this chapter.)

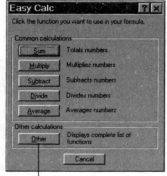

Figure 3-2:
Choose your calculation in Easy Calc.

Calculations other than those listed

In the example shown in Figure 3-1, I first want to compute the dollars per night for each lodging place, which means that I click the Divide button to divide the total dollars in column C by the number of nights in column B.

A different Easy Calc dialog box now appears, as shown in Figure 3-3.

3. Enter the values (numbers used in the calculation), or cell addresses containing those values, that the Easy Calc dialog box prompts you to enter.

You can either type the actual values into the text boxes; or if the value appears in a cell of your spreadsheet, you can type its cell address (such as B12 for column B, row 12) or click that cell. (To click a cell, you may need to drag the Easy Calc dialog box to one side, or use the vertical or horizontal scroll boxes on the right or bottom side of your spreadsheet window to see the portion of the spreadsheet that you need.)

If Easy Calc prompts you for a range (as it does for Sum and Average), you can either type the range (such as **B1:D20**) or click and drag your cursor across the range to highlight it.

See Chapter 2 if you don't understand cell addresses or ranges.

If you make a mistake, click the text box containing the mistake and try again. If you made a mistake in a previous step, click the Back button.

At the bottom of the Easy Calc dialog box, as the callout for Figure 3-3 shows, Works displays the formula it constructs for you. This display is a good example of how to write formulas. You can also click this display and edit the formula if you need to.

Figure 3-3:
Telling Easy
Calc how to
divide one
cell's
contents by
another's.

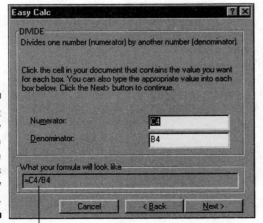

Click the formula to edit.

4. **Click the Next button and enter additional numbers, text, ranges, or cell addresses, as the Easy Calc dialog box prompts you.**

   Depending on the sort of calculation you ask for, Easy Calc may need additional information. You may need to go through one or two more dialog boxes, clicking Next each time to proceed.

   The final piece of information for which Easy Calc asks is the cell address where you want the result to appear.

5. **In the Result At text box you may either type the cell address or click that cell; then click the Finish button.**

   In the example shown in Figure 3-1, I'd choose cell D4 for my result and then click the Finish button.

Here are some of the other calculations I can do for the spreadsheet in Figure 3-1:

- *Compute American dollars from Canadian.* This calculation involves dividing the Canadian dollars in column D (beginning with D4) by the currency exchange rate in cell B15 and putting the results in column E (beginning with E4).

- *Compute the total number of nights,* just as a check to make sure that I didn't miss any. This calculation would involve summing the range B4:B13 and putting the result in cell B14.

- *Compute the total cost* by summing C4:C13, with the result in cell C14 (for Canadian dollars), and then doing the same for the American dollars in column D.

- *Compute the average cost per night for lodging* **in American dollars.** I can perform this calculation by averaging the range E4:E13 and putting the result in cell B16. Or I can do it by dividing the total cost in cell D14 by the total number of nights in cell B14.

Some of this calculation work is easier if you copy formulas. I can copy from cell C14 the formula that summed Canadian dollars, for example, and I can paste it in cell E14, where it sums American dollars.

The same trick doesn't, however, work well for copying the formula for computing American dollars in cell E4 to the other cells in column E. The copied formulas fail to refer to the exchange rate in cell B15. If I copy the formula for each of the nine rows, the copies refer instead to cells B16, B17, and so on, through B24. To understand why this error occurs and how to prevent it, see the section "The Joys and Mysteries of Copying Formulas," later in this chapter.

Doing "other" calculations in Easy Calc

If basic arithmetic and averaging can't do the job that you have in mind, Works can carry out lots of other calculations, known as *functions*, which you can access by clicking the Other button in the initial Easy Calc dialog box. (See the section "You're Invited to a Function," later in this chapter, for more details about these mathematical marvels.)

If you choose Tools➪Easy Calc and click the Other button, the Insert Function dialog box swings into action. For instructions on using this dialog box, see Figure 3-5 and the numbered steps in the section "Shortcuts for Creating Formulas," later in this chapter.

After you click the Insert button in the Insert Function dialog box, Easy Calc resumes its helpful dialog, as I note in Step 3 of the preceding instructions.

Writing Formulas: Beyond Easy Calc

Writing your own formulas (as opposed to using Easy Calc to write them for you) enables you to make more powerful calculations in a single cell. To do a calculation, you type a formula into a cell. You can design a formula to do a lot of work all at once, as does the following example:

```
=(SUM(B1:B8))/(SUM(C9:C17))*A17-3.7
```

Believe it or not, this formula is not a random collection of symbols. It means something — or at least it does to Works. This section helps you write formulas like that one (or simpler ones).

Works doesn't care whether you write formulas, cell addresses, or ranges in uppercase or lowercase letters. Works may convert some of the lowercase letters to uppercase letters, but that's its business.

Entering a formula

To enter a formula into a cell (whether you type directly into the cell or into the formula bar), follow these steps:

1. **Click the cell where you want the formula to go.**

   Or use the navigation keys to move the highlight to that cell. Use a blank cell; don't try to put the formula in the same cell that holds the numbers that you're using in the calculation.

2. **Type an equal sign (=) and then a mathematical expression.**

   Spreadsheet formulas are mathematical expressions, which look something like the following example:

   ```
   =5.24+3.93
   ```

   Starting Works formulas with an = sign tells Works that you're doing a calculation and not entering text or a number.

3. **Press Enter.**

   Or click the check mark on the formula bar . . . or move the highlight by clicking another cell . . . or press a navigation key.

   These actions enter the formula into the cell, which then displays the result. The formula remains in the cell, but only the result appears.

If you type **=5.24+3.93** into a cell and press the Enter key, the cell shows the answer: 9.17. Isn't that exciting! This is why people spend thousands of dollars on computers and software. Well, maybe not; you may have been able to do that more easily on a five-dollar calculator. What you can't do on a five-dollar calculator, however, is type something like the following example:

```
=5.24+B1
```

Hmmm. Shades of algebra. What this formula really means is "Show me the sum of 5.24 and whatever is in cell B1." If B1 has the number 3.93 in it, you get 9.17. If B1 has the number 6 in it, you get 11.24. You can keep plugging new numbers into cell B1 and watch the answer change in the cell that contains this formula.

Okay, this stuff is amusing — but wait! There's more! What if you want a formula to add up a bunch of cells? You can type the following:

```
=B1+B2+B3+B4+B5+B6+B7+B8
```

Pretty boring. You can see where this type of thing may drive you back to your calculator. So to avoid losing your business, the software folks came up a way to tell Works to "Sum up the range B1 through B8." You do so by entering the following:

```
=SUM(B1:B8)
```

You don't even need to type **B1:B8** while you're entering the formula! You can stop typing for a moment, select that range with your mouse, and then type the final parenthesis. See the section "Shortcuts for Creating Formulas," later in this chapter, for more information on this technique. See Chapter 2 for more information on ranges and range addresses such as B1:B8.

SUM and other built-in calculations are known as *functions*. And, if you use them correctly, they do — function, that is. Works includes a whole passel of other functions for doing all kinds of things. (More information about those functions is in the section "You're Invited to a Function," later in this chapter.)

All calculations, no matter how complex, are performed this way in the spreadsheet: by mixing numbers, mathematical operations (such as addition and subtraction), and functions together to make formulas.

Seeing and editing formulas

The spreadsheet displays only the result of a formula, although the formula actually remains in the cell. "So," you may well ask, "how can I see my formula?"

You can see an individual formula at any time by clicking its cell (or using the navigation keys to place your highlight on the cell) and looking in the formula bar.

You edit a formula the same way that you edit any other contents of a cell: To edit by using the formula bar, click the cell, and then click the formula bar. To edit directly in the cell, double-click the cell. (See the section on editing inside a cell in Chapter 2.)

To see all the formulas in your spreadsheet, choose View➪Formulas from the menu bar. This command turns on a Formula view that's pretty ugly but does show all your formulas. You can work using this view, if you want. To turn off the Formula view, do the same thing you did to turn it on.

Hello, operator?: Mathematical operations

In the earlier section, "Entering a formula," I employ the + symbol to represent addition in a formula. Among the common operators (math actions) that you can use to create your mathematical formulas are + (add), – (subtract), / (divide), * (multiply), and ^ (raise to the power of . . .).

In a formula that uses several operators, put the expressions you want to compute first in parentheses to make sure that Works computes things in the order you want. Works evaluates the expression (2+3)*4, for example, as 5*4, giving 20 as the result. Without the parentheses, the expression is 2+3*4. Works does multiplication first, creating 2+12; then it does addition, giving 14 as the result, not 20! Without parentheses, Works evaluates expressions according to the operator that you use, in the following order of priority: ^, *, or /; then + or –. To break any ties (if the formula uses, say, both * and / operators), Works evaluates the formula from left to right.

You're Invited to a Function

Works has quite a few convenient built-in functions, such as SUM, which are very inviting. Functions produce some sort of value as, which you can, in turn, use within a formula, as in SUM(A2:A22)/B4. The following lists some functions, in addition to SUM, that you often use.

AVG(*cells*)   The average of the values in the cells

MAX(*cells*)   The maximum value among the cells

MIN(*cells*)   The minimum value among the cells

ROUND(*cell, # of digits*)   The value in the cell rounded off to some number of digits

The word *cell* in italics in the preceding minitable means that you type in a single, specific cell address, such as **B1**, not the word *cell*. And the word *cells* means that you type in a range, such as **B1:B8** or a set of ranges, such as **B1:B8, D5:D13, F256**. (Microsoft uses the term *range reference* instead of *cells*.) You may also use actual numbers in formulas instead of addresses containing numbers.

The phrase *# of digits* in the minitable means to use a specific number, such as 2 or 3. Alternatively, *# of digits* may be the address of a cell that contains the number of digits, but that's getting complicated.

If a function uses its own result, you're in trouble. The formula =SUM(A1:A10), for example, had better not appear in any of the cells A1 through A10. If you're lucky, Works tells you that you've got a *circular reference*. If you're not lucky, Works just merrily calculates something bizarre and doesn't tell you why.

So many functions are available that even a short list is more than this book can handle. Two places describe these functions: the spreadsheet tool itself and the Works Help feature. I discuss the spreadsheet tool's listing in the section "Shortcuts for Creating Formulas," later in this chapter. To read about functions by using the Help feature, follow these steps:

   1. **Choose Help⇨Index to display the Index card of the Help Topics window.**

   2. **Type** functions: **(including the colon) in text box number 1.**

3. **Click the folder covering the type of function that you seek.**

   If you want a function that calculates averages, for example, click the Functions: Statistical folder, which gives you a list of documents describing all the functions of this type.

4. **Click the document (which all begin "To use . . .") describing any function.**

   Help appears in a window on the right side of the screen.

5. **In the Help window, click the More Info tab and then click the Overview button to find out about the function.**

6. **Click the Close button in the Help Topics window to return to your document.**

Shortcuts for Creating Formulas

As you create formulas, Works provides several typing shortcuts, as the following list describes:

- ✔ **Don't type the range address.** As you're typing and you reach the point where you need a range address (say, for example, that you just typed =SUM( ), take your mouse in hand and drag across the range you want or click the cell you want in the function. Then type the closing parenthesis and any subsequent parts of the formula you need.

- ✔ **When summing a row or column, don't bother to type** SUM **function.** Whenever you have a column (or row) of numbers that you want to add up, just select the empty cell at the bottom of the column (or at the end of the row) and click the Autosum button — the button on the toolbar with the Greek letter sigma on it (Σ). The sum formula then appears in the empty cell with the column or row range address automatically entered.

- ✔ **Don't type the function you want to use.** Instead, Works provides you with a feature for inserting the function itself, as the remainder of this section describes.

To insert a function without typing it in a formula, follow these steps:

1. **Click a cell and start typing your formula.**

   At the point where you need a function, type an = sign or click the formula bar.

2. **Choose Insert⇨Function.**

See specific categories of functions.

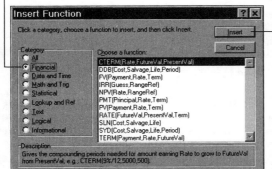

Put this function in your formula.

Figure 3-4:
Getting
functional
with the
Insert
Function
dialog box.

The Insert Function dialog box swings into action, as Figure 3-4 shows. At this point, the big Choose a Function list box shows all the functions that Works offers. Scroll down the list to find the function that you want.

3. **If you don't see what you want on the main list, click the radio button for a specific category in the Category area to reduce the display of functions to a specific type.**

   To see only mathematical and trigonometric functions in the Choose a Function box, for example, click Math and Trig. (Oddly, the SUM function is in the Statistical collection.)

4. **Click a function in the Choose a Function list box.**

   You can see a brief description of what the selected function does at the bottom of the Insert Function dialog box.

5. **Click the Insert button.**

   The dialog box goes away, leaving you with your chosen function in the formula bar. Works doesn't yet know what cell or cells you want the function to apply to, however, so it leaves text (such as RangeRef) as a placeholder in the places where cell addresses go.

   For a detailed explanation of the function from Works Help files, turn on Help by choosing Help⇨Show Help. See Chapter 1 for other Help controls.

6. **Edit the formula to add cell addresses.**

   You have two ways to do so: You can type the cell addresses you need and delete any extraneous text, or you can drag across the placeholder text to highlight it and then use your mouse to click a cell or drag across a range in your spreadsheet. As you do so, their addresses replace any highlighted placeholder text.

7. Press Enter after you finish entering the entire formula.

The Joys and Mysteries of Copying Formulas

Spreadsheets usually contain tables, which are rows and columns of numbers. In these tables, you often use essentially the same formula over and over again. If you're summing columns, for example, the only difference from column to column is the range you're summing.

If you're doing calculations on columns or rows of a table, you can often save yourself work by copying the formula instead of retyping it — especially if the formula is complex. Works automatically takes care of changing the range in the formula from, say, A1:A10 to B1:B10.

In fact, in a table, you can successfully copy *any* formula (not just a sum) that doesn't use data from outside its own column (or row) to another column (or row). The column (or row) of data must be the same size as the original.

Copy a formula just as you'd copy a number or text or anything else — for example, copy by using Ctrl+C and paste by using Ctrl+V. Remember that by selecting (highlighting) several cells before pasting, you can make several copies at once (one copy in each selected cell). See Chapter 2 for various ways of copying stuff.

For formula copying to work without special tricks, one condition must be true: The location of a formula relative to its data must be the same for all copies as for the original. If the original formula uses a cell that's three columns over and one row down from its address, you must provide each copy with data three columns over and one row down from *its* address.

What happens if you copy formulas

The best way to explain what happens if you copy a formula is by presenting an example: Figure 3-5 shows part of a spreadsheet just after I finished copying a bunch of formulas in column D. The task before me was to calculate the D column (average price per unit sold) from the C (unit sales) and E (total

	A	B	C	D	E
1	*Toy Sales*				
2	Model Number	Model Name	Units	Avg. $/Unit	Rev ($000)
3	XJ7	Bomber	890	$223.51	$198.92
4	PT3	Swooper	1280	$150.50	$192.64
5	F15	Hawk	920	$298.50	$274.62
6	B52	Falcon	1580	$165.50	$261.49
7	P121	Peregrine	800	$350.50	$280.40
8			5470	$220.85	$1,208.07

sales revenues) columns. Instead of entering a formula for each cell of the D column, I typed the formula only once, for the total in cell D8, and then I copied it to the other five cells, D3 through D7 (shown highlighted in Figure 3-5).

As I began, column D had no formulas in it. My procedure for adding the formulas went as the following steps describe:

1. **Enter the formula** =1000*E8/C8 **into cell D8 and press Enter.**

   (The 1000 is there because I express the revenues in column E in terms of thousands of dollars.) Wouldn't this formula be a pain to type five more times just to put it in rows 3 through 7?

2. **Click the Copy button on the toolbar to copy the formula in D8.**

3. **Select the range D3:D7.**

4. **Click the Paste button on the toolbar to paste copies of the formula into cells D3 through D7.**

Notice that each copy of the formula uses only cells in its own row. You can see the formula in the formula bar after you click those cells. The formula in cell D5, for example, is =1000*E5/C5; in cell D6, it's =1000*E6/C6; and so on. Pretty neat, huh?

Here's what happens to cell addresses if you copy formulas:

✔ **After you copy a formula to a new column, the letter (column) portion of the cell address changes.**

   If you copy something one column to the right and you have an address of A1 in your formula, it changes to B1; Q17 changes to R17 and so on.

✔ **After you copy a formula to a new row, the number (row) portion of the cell address changes.**

   If you copy something one row down and you have an address of A1 in your formula, A1 changes to A2; Q17 changes to Q18 and so on.

(If you copy a formula to a new row *and* column, *both* the row and column change in any cell addresses in that formula.)

Note: If you *move* a formula (by dragging it) or cut and paste the formula, the addresses in the formula don't change. Addresses change only if you *copy* something — either by dragging or by using the Copy and Paste commands (Ctrl+C and Ctrl+V).

Fixing formulas that don't copy correctly

You can often still copy formulas that don't copy correctly if you tweak them a bit beforehand. Following is a simple example that you can generalize to fix many of your formula copying problems.

A typical formula copying problem is that the formula you want to copy refers to a single cell containing a key value or fudge factor. Back in Figure 3-1, for example, the formula in cell E4 (American dollars) depends on the exchange rate in cell B15. If you copy that formula in cell E4 to the other rows (E5, E6, and so on), the reference to B15 changes rows — to B16, B17, and so on — and is wrong.

The solution is to keep the reference to that one cell from changing as you copy. To keep a reference from changing, put a dollar sign in front of the column letter and/or row number in the formula. In cell E4 of Figure 3-1, for example, you'd type **=D4/B15** instead of **=D4/B15**. After you copy that formula to the next row, the E4 changes to E5, but B15 remains the same. This trick is called *absolute addressing*.

If, instead of typing your cell addresses into a formula, you prefer to point to them with the mouse, press the F4 key after you point to create an absolute address such as B15. Press F4 again to get B$15 and again to get $B15. This trick also works if you enter cell addresses in Easy Calc.

The dollar sign here has *absolutely nothing* to do with dollars (U.S. or Canadian) *or* currency formatting; use of the dollar sign is just an ancient convention in spreadsheets, probably started by Dan Bricklin when he did VisiCalc or by one of the other spreadsheet pioneers.

Chapter 4

Formatting and Printing Your Spreadsheets

● ●

In This Chapter

▶ Formatting the entire spreadsheet using AutoFormat

▶ Formatting characters and numbers

▶ Aligning within a cell

▶ Entering and formatting dates and times

▶ Doing basic arithmetic on dates and times

▶ Using borders and gridlines

▶ Making and sorting lists

▶ Printing your spreadsheet

● ●

*M*aking a spreadsheet is one thing. Getting the spreadsheet ready for prime time — formatting its numbers and dates correctly, giving it a face lift, and, finally, printing it out — is another.

Dates are a particular challenge (as many unmarried people understand), as are times. This chapter helps you deal with dates, times, and basic date-and-time arithmetic. (You can read this chapter while you're waiting for your date to arrive, which should impress him or her with your intellectual capacity.)

Feeling out of sorts (possibly because your date is late)? This chapter shows you how to sort lists and data into alphabetical or numerical order.

Finally, this chapter delves into the unique opportunities that spreadsheets present for really messing things up as you print. Why, this chapter even provides some solutions!

Formatting in One Swell Foop!

Back when disco ruled and quiche was the trendy food of the day, spreadsheets were dull, boring grids. No more! Today's spreadsheet sports designer colors, shadings, lines, borders, and fancy fonts in different sizes and styles.

You can apply all of these fancy formats individually if you want. But Works also combines a bunch of formatting into various stylish ensembles, which Works refers to as *automatic formatting*. Automatic formatting, or *autoformatting,* is truly a great idea (unless you don't want all those particular changes).

If you copy a cell, you also *copy all its formatting*. Formatting includes number formatting, alignment, borders, and shading.

Figure 4-1 shows what happens to the toy sales spreadsheet from Chapter 3 after you deck it out in an automatic format called *3-D Effects 2*. All kinds of stuff has changed here — even the formats of some of the numbers. Zowie! All these changes result from a few mouse clicks.

Figure 4-1:
Auto-
formatting:
Just a few
clicks can
get you a
whole new
look.

	A	B	C	D	E
1	*Toy Sales*				
2	Model Number	Model Name	Units	Avg. $/Unit	Rev ($000)
3	XJ7	Bomber	890	223.505618	198.92
4	PT3	Swooper	1280	150.5	192.64
5	F15	Hawk	920	298.5	274.62
6	B52	Falcon	1580	165.5	261.49
7	P121	Peregrine	800	350.5	280.4
8			5470	220.8537477	1208.07

The AutoFormat feature presumes that you have a fairly classic table structure: rows, columns, and maybe (although not necessarily) totals. If you meet these standards, AutoFormat away by following these steps:

1. **Make sure that you have column and row headings.**

   Or, if you don't have 'em, at least have a blank row above and a blank column to the left of your table. (Use these "empties" for your title row and column in Step 2.)

2. **Select all the rows and columns, including title row and column and total row and/or column.**

   If you have a title for the entire spreadsheet, you can include or exclude it, as you want. I excluded the "Toy Sales" line in Figure 4-1.

3. **Choose F̲ormat⇨AutoFor̲mat from the menu bar.**

   The AutoFormat dialog box leaps into action, as shown in Figure 4-2.

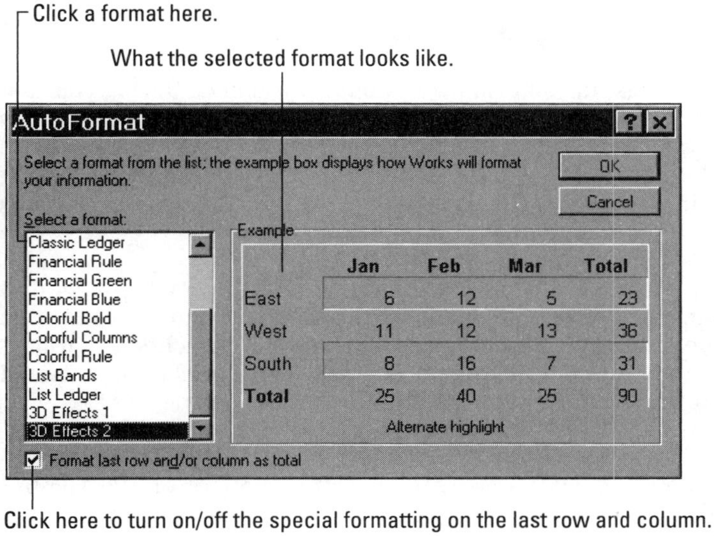

Click a format here.

What the selected format looks like.

AutoFormat `? X`

Select a format from the list; the example box displays how Works will format your information.

`OK`

`Cancel`

Select a format:

| Classic Ledger |
| Financial Rule |
| Financial Green |
| Financial Blue |
| Colorful Bold |
| Colorful Columns |
| Colorful Rule |
| List Bands |
| List Ledger |
| 3D Effects 1 |
| 3D Effects 2 |

Example

	Jan	Feb	Mar	Total
East	6	12	5	23
West	11	12	13	36
South	8	16	7	31
Total	25	40	25	90

Alternate highlight

☑ Format last row and/or column as total

Figure 4-2:
The AutoFormat dialog box. If only reformatting my auto was this easy.

Click here to turn on/off the special formatting on the last row and column.

4. **Click any interesting-sounding format in the Select a Format list box.**

   The Example area shows you how the format looks. If you don't like this format, click another format. If you don't like any of 'em, press the Esc key.

5. **Examine the Format Last Row and/or Column as Total check box.**

   If you're not using a total row or column or if you have your total somewhere other than at the end of the range, make sure that this check box is blank. If you do have a total row or column, click the check box to add a check mark but look at the example to see whether this particular format puts the total in the same place that you did.

   In the toy sales example, I chose to leave the box blank because cell D8 is an average, not a total.

6. **Click the OK button.**

   Foop! A brief flurry of activity takes place, and suddenly, your spreadsheet looks like the inside pages of a quarterly report. If you don't like the results, press Ctrl+Z immediately to undo the formatting — before you make any other changes to the spreadsheet — and try again.

7. **Throw in some finishing touches if you want.**

   In Figure 4-1, for example, I'd probably do something to get rid of all those digits after the decimal point in D3 and D8, either by using the ROUND function or by selecting column D and changing to currency format. (See the section "Formatting Numbers," later in this chapter.)

Formatting Cells Yourself

If AutoFormat doesn't ring your chimes, you need to ring your own chimes. The basics of font, font size, colors, and text alignment all work the same way for all the tools of Works. Press Ctrl+R to right-align, for example, or Ctrl+E to center-align text. See Chapter 1 for instructions on using the Works toolbar, the keyboard, and the Font and Style dialog box to change characters and their alignment.

For a greater variety of cell formatting, select the cells that you want to format; then either right-click with your mouse and choose Format off the pop-up menu that appears or, from the menu bar, choose Format⇨Font, Alignment, Number, Border, or Shading. The Works Format Cells dialog box appears, where you can click a card for each of those types of cell formatting.

This chapter deals mainly with formatting options on the Number and Border cards. The Shading feature is pretty self-explanatory.

The Alignment card offers a few other choices besides the toolbar's standard left, right, and center options. To use one, select the cells you want to align and then choose Format⇨Alignment.

For *vertical alignment,* click Top, Center, or Bottom to position your cell contents at the top, center, or bottom of a cell. Row height must exceed text height to see any effect! To have *multiple lines of text* in your cell, click to put a check mark in the Wrap Text check box.

Additional interesting *horizontal alignment* tricks exist. To *fill* a cell that contains a single character with copies of that character, click Fill. To *center a title across several cells,* choose Center Across Selection as your horizontal alignment. To restore Works' usual text and number alignments, click General.

Formatting Numbers

Formatting numbers is not quite the same as formatting text. If you format numbers, the actual characters and punctuation change to different characters and punctuation, adding dollar signs or parentheses, for example. The number itself doesn't change, but it puts on a radically different face. Sometimes it doesn't even look like a number any more.

If, for example, you put the number 3284.2515 in a cell and use your formatting options (which Table 4-1 lists), you can make that number look like any of the stuff in the How It Looks column of Table 4-1.

Table 4-1		Different Formatting for the Number 3284.2515
How It Looks	*Format Name*	*About That Format and Options You Can Specify*
3284.25	General	As precise as possible for the column width; this style is how Works formats numbers unless you tell it otherwise.
3284.251	Fixed	Specifies decimal places (in this example, *three*).
$3,284.25	Currency	Dollar sign, comma, specifies decimal places; negative numbers appear in parentheses. *Optional:* Negative numbers also in red.
3,284.25	Comma	Similar to Currency but no dollar sign.
328425.15 %	Percent	Displays number multiplied by 100, adds percent symbol; specify your decimal places.
3.28 E+03	Exponential	Single digit number with power of ten; specify your decimal places (in this example, *two*).
03284	Leading Zeros	No fraction; displays as many digits as you specify (in this example, *five*); adds zeros or trims leading digits to do so. Good for Zip codes.
3248 3/10	Fraction	Expresses fractional part as fraction: Choose halves, thirds, quarters, eighths, tenths, and so on (in this example, *tenths*).
TRUE	True/False	If zero, displays FALSE; if not zero, displays TRUE.
November 21, 1908	Date	Interprets number as number of days since midnight, December 31, 1899; Works uses this format if you enter a date.
6:02 AM	Time	Interprets fractional part of number as fraction of one day; displays fraction as hour of that day. Works uses this format if you enter a time.
3284.2515	Text	If you apply format *before* entering a number, turns number into text. Useful for serial numbers or other numeric codes.

Date and time formats are among the weirder ones in this list because they make numbers look like text. For more information on how Works handles the passage of time, see the section "Working with Dates and Times," later in this chapter.

Currency format is the easiest to apply: Select the cell or cells to format and click the toolbar button with the $ icon on it.

Note: You don't actually format numbers in the spreadsheet tool; you format *cells.* The cell can be empty as you format it, and after you type a number in that cell, the number takes on formatting the cell. If you type text in that cell, the formatting doesn't affect the text. If you delete an entry from a cell, the number format remains.

Works starts with every cell in the General format. To change the format of specific cells, follow these steps:

1. Select a cell or bunch of cells.

Click the cell or highlight the bunch of cells.

2. Choose F__o__rmat➪__N__umber.

The Number card of the Format Cells dialog box presents itself for duty, as shown in Figure 4-3.

Choose a format first.   Choose options second.

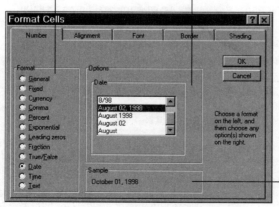

Figure 4-3:
You can make numbers look like darned near anything.

A sample appears here.

3. Click any format in the Format area of the dialog box.

As Figure 4-3 shows, Works displays a sample in the Sample area. If a number is already in the cell, Works uses that number in the sample. If you don't like what you see, click another format. See Table 4-1 for notes about these formats.

Some formats enable you to specify precision: How many digits are to the right (or left, in the case of Leading Zeros format) of the decimal point? Normally, Works uses two digits here. To change the precision, type a number in the Decimal Places text box (which only appears for formats that use decimal places).

The Currency and Comma formats enable you to optionally put negative numbers in red; just click the Negative Numbers in Red check box (which appears if you choose these formats).

The Fractions format normally rounds numbers to a fraction you specify, and reduces them to the lowest possible denominator. *Reduction* means, for instance, that if you choose $1/32$ for Round To (which appears for fractions format), and your number ends in .125, that fraction displays as $1/8$. If you really want that fraction to appear as $4/32$ or whatever fraction you've chosen, click the Do Not Reduce check box.

4. Click OK.

Changing formatting doesn't change what's really in the cell — it changes only the appearance of what's there.

Working with Dates and Times

The secret of using dates and times successfully in a spreadsheet is to realize that, to a spreadsheet, dates and times are numbers! Works just formats the number to *look like* a date or time. You don't usually need to understand the details of how Works represents time, but if you want to understand it, see the accompanying sidebar, "The clockwork behind Works' dates and times."

The clockwork behind Works dates and times

Here's what's behind the scenes: Works keeps track of time by giving every day a number; Works starts the sequence at 12 AM, January 1, 1900, which is represented as 1.00. Days are whole numbers. Hours and minutes in that day are represented by a fractional portion. So 8:00 AM on January 1, 1900 is 1.333333333. Just plain 8:00 AM is 0.33333.

If you type in a date or a time, Works shows it to you as a date or a time, which is nice. But Works secretly changes the entry to a number. If you type **8 AM**, for example, Works enters 0.33333 and chooses a *time format* for the number. If you type in a date, Works enters the number for midnight on that date and applies a *date format* that duplicates the format in which you typed the number.

Ever heard of a "year 2079 bug?" Works (Release 4.5a, anyway) can't handle dates later than June 3, 2079, so don't make any hundred-year plans.

Typing dates and times

If you want to do calculations based on your dates and times, you must type them in valid Works date and time formats. Table 4-2 shows valid formats for entering dates and times.

If you enter a date or time in a format that Works doesn't recognize, your entry may end up as simply text, not a number, and you can't use it for calculations.

Table 4-2	Valid Formats for Entering Dates and Times
Dates	**Times**
August 28, 1945	2:30PM
8/28/45	14:30
8/28/1945	2:00
August	2 AM
August 2	2:00 AM
8/2	

You can enter times without using AM or PM, but Works interprets them all as a.m. unless they're in 24-hour time format (for example, 14:00). Works interprets dates (such as August 28, 1945) as 12 a.m. on that date. You can enter dates without adding a year designation (as 8/28, for example), but Works actually takes them to be in the current year. Likewise, you can enter months alone (August, for example), and Works translates them as 12 a.m. (midnight) on the first of that month, the current year.

To enter today's date, press Ctrl+; (that's Ctrl and the semicolon key). To enter the current time, press Ctrl+Shift+; (that's Ctrl+Shift+semicolon).

To enter a date that's current all the time, such as on a day/date watch, type in the function =NOW( ) and format the cell by using a date format. The date updates every time you change a cell or press the F9 (recalculate) key. To display a time that's always current, format the same cell with a *time format*.

Formatting dates and times

Working with dates and times in a spreadsheet often produces weird numbers, such as 16679 or 0.33333, that don't resemble a date or time. No problem. Really. What you get is the number that Works secretly uses for handling dates or times: the number (and any fractional portion) of days between the date in question and January 1, 1900. For more info, see the sidebar, "The clockwork behind Works dates and times," a bit earlier in this chapter.

If your date or time appears in such an un-date-and-time-like format, you need to format this number as a date or time yourself. (Unless, of course, you don't care how the date looks.) Choose Format⇨Number and, on the Number page of the Format Numbers dialog box that appears, click Date or Time. For details, see the section, "Formatting Numbers," earlier in this chapter.

Doing basic date and time arithmetic

The Works spreadsheet tool enables you to do calculations based on time, but you need to be a little careful. Works secretly uses numbers to represent dates and makes them look "date-ish" by using a date *format.* If you do calculations, the results may come out as funny numbers instead of the date, number of days, or number of hours that you were hoping for. The following instructions can generally keep things working well.

Subtracting dates and adding days to dates

If you have two dates, you can easily calculate the time between them by subtracting exactly how much time elapses between them.

Calculating intervals between dates can be depressing if you're single and your social life is less than satisfactory.

You subtract dates just as you subtract regular numbers. To type a date directly into a formula, however, you must enclose it in apostrophes and use the slash-date format, as in **=B4 – '4/14/95'**. The result is the number of days between the dates, so use a regular number format, not a date format, for the cell containing this formula.

Adding dates is silly. (December 25 plus July 4 equals . . . what?) But adding *days* to dates is quite reasonable in a Works formula. For example, **='9/15'** **+ 35** adds 35 days to September 15. You format this formula by using a date format, because the result is a date.

Subtracting and adding times

You subtract and add time in much the same way that you subtract and add dates. For example, enter **=B4-'0:15'** to subtract 15 minutes from the time in cell B4. As in that example, if you type a time value directly into a formula, you must enclose it in apostrophes.

If you add or subtract times, the result may need some mathematical correction and time formatting. If, for example, you're paid by the hour and keep time records, whenever you subtract, say, 10:17 a.m. from 10:32 a.m. the result is 0.0104167! You have two problems: 0.0104167 doesn't look like 15 minutes; and (even if you format it correctly) if you multiply that number by your hourly rate (say, $100), you end up billing for only $1.04!

Works keeps track of hours as fractions of a day. One hour is $1/24$ of a day, so to fix the problem in this example, multiply by 24 in your billing formula. (If the time is in cell B4, type **=B4*100*24** where the asterisks are times symbols.) To convert the result of time subtraction to hours, multiply by 24; to convert the result of time subtraction to minutes, multiply by 24*60.

To fix the appearance problem, use a time format. (See the section "Formatting Numbers," earlier in this chapter.)

Adding Borders, Viewing Gridlines

Works takes much of the pain and strain out of prettying up spreadsheets with its AutoFormat feature. (See the section "Formatting in One Swell Foop!" earlier in this chapter.) Alas, sometimes you still need a few lines to dress things up further.

Borders are lines that you add along the top, bottom, or sides of a cell. Some borders are so thin that the *gridlines* that normally cover a spreadsheet mask them. To turn off the gridlines, choose View➪Gridlines. The same action turns the gridlines back on. The highlight that appears around selected cells can also mask your borders. Click elsewhere to move the highlight.

Select (highlight) the cell or block of cells to which you want to apply borders and, then choose Format➪Border. The Border card of the Format Cells dialog box materializes, as shown in Figure 4-4.

To create a border, choose one first (Outline, Top, Bottom, Left, or Right). Then click any of the Line Style examples shown in the dialog box. Choose a color, if you want. Click OK when you're done.

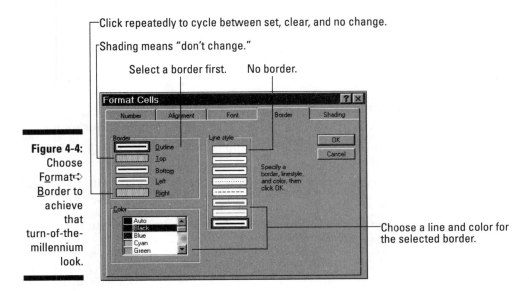

Click repeatedly to cycle between set, clear, and no change.

Shading means "don't change."

Select a border first.   No border.

Figure 4-4:
Choose
Format⇨
Border to
achieve
that
turn-of-the-
millennium
look.

Choose a line and color for
the selected border.

Following are a few tips for using the Border controls of this dialog box:

✔ To create a single horizontal or vertical line in your spreadsheet, simply apply a top, bottom, left, or right border to a row or column.

✔ In applying borders to a range (block) of cells, the Outline option in the Border area refers to the entire range; Top, Bottom, Left, and Right refer to the borders of each and every cell in that range.

✔ To change or clear (remove) a border, repeatedly click its selection box in the Border area. Clicking cycles the border through three states: set to the currently selected line style; clear; or (if a border already exists) remain unchanged. "No change" is signified by shading in the box.

✔ To remove an outline border, you must clear all individual borders.

Sorting Your Data

One of the nice things that Works can do for you is sort your data. If, for example, you're keeping a spreadsheet that lists students and computes their grades, you may want to alphabetize the list by name or sort by class rank. Works can sort alphabetically or numerically. It can also sort by "primary," "secondary," and "tertiary" considerations, such as last name, first name, and middle initial. Such sorting groups all the Smiths together, sorting them by first names, and then sorts the John Smiths by middle initial. The procedure for sorting follows:

1. **Save your spreadsheet as a file (by pressing Ctrl+S), in case anything goes wrong.**

   If anything *does* go terribly wrong and Ctrl+Z doesn't undo the error, close the spreadsheet without saving it and then reopen the original file.

2. **Select (highlight) only the rows and columns that contain the data you want to sort.**

   You may include or not include a row of column heads if you have one.

3. **Choose Tools⇨Sort from the menu bar.**

   The Sort dialog box appears. Go along with its suggestion: to sort only the columns selected.

4. **Click OK.**

   This action opens the second Sort dialog box, as shown in Figure 4-5, which asks which column to sort on and whether to sort in ascending or descending order.

Figure 4-5:
Sorting on one column. Clicking Advanced gets you a triple-decker version.

5. **Choose from the Sort By list box the column by which you want to sort.**

6. **Choose either the Ascending or Descending radio button.**

   Ascending means that, reading from top to bottom, numbers or letters go from low to high. *Descending* means, well, the opposite.

7. **Choose either the Header Row or No Header Row radio button.**

   If the cells you highlighted in Step 2 include a header row, click Header Row. Otherwise, click No Header Row.

8. **If you want secondary or tertiary sorting (say, sorting multiple Smiths by their first name and middle initial), click the Advanced button.**

   A sort of triple-decker version of the Sort dialog box appears. The top deck contains the column and sort order you just specified. The second and third decks are available for you to specify additional columns for Works to sort on in the event of identical entries in the primary sort column.

9. **Click the Sort button.**

   Works sorts your list (that is, it shuffles your rows around in the order that you specified). To return to the original order, you can press Ctrl+Z as long as you haven't made any other changes.

If you're clever and created a column in which you give each record (row) a serial number, you can always sort by using that column for Sort By and restore the original order.

You can dress up your list by using the AutoFormat feature, just as you can any other spreadsheet. A couple of formats are even made especially for lists: List Bands and List Ledger. See the section "Formatting in One Swell Foop!" earlier in this chapter.

Calculating in sorted areas

By sorting, you can unintentionally change the data to which your formulas refer! Here's how to avoid problems: You can use a formula that refers to a range of the sorted area safely only if that range covers an *entire column* of data (as a sum or average does). If a formula refers to *specific cells in the sorted area*, it should refer only to *cells in the same row* as that formula. You must include the column containing the formula in the sort. Otherwise, after

you sort the rows, the range address that the formula specifies remains unchanged, but it now refers to different data.

If you add rows to the list, do so by inserting a new row, not by moving other rows. Check your formulas after inserting new rows to make sure that the formulas include the new data rows.

Dealing with Printing Peculiarities

Printing spreadsheets is pretty much like printing anything else in Works, so for the general picture, see Chapter 1. Following, however, are a few peculiarities about printing spreadsheets:

✔ To print only a range of the spreadsheet, not the entire spreadsheet, select a range and use the Set Print Area command: Choose Format➪Set Print Area. To go back to printing the entire spreadsheet, select the entire spreadsheet (Ctrl+A) and repeat the Set Print Area command.

✔ Works splits up your spreadsheet to get it to fit on a printed page. If the spreadsheet is bigger than the page, you literally must cut and paste paper pages together to re-create the original layout. Use the Print Preview feature (by choosing File➪Print Preview) to see how your spreadsheet is going to print.

To control page breaks yourself, you can split up the document horizontally and/or vertically and create page-sized pieces. Follow these steps:

1. **For a horizontal break, click the row below where you want the break; for a vertical break, click the column to the right of the break.**

2. **Choose Insert➪Page Break from the menu bar.**

   A tiny Insert Page Break dialog box appears.

3. **In the Insert Page Break dialog box, click Column for a vertical break or Row for a horizontal one and then click OK.**

If you repeat the process, keeping your highlight at the same cell you use in Step 1, Works automatically assumes that you want the new break to run in the opposite orientation (vertical if the existing one is horizontal, for example). It doesn't open an Insert Page Break box to ask you.

To get rid of a page break, put your cursor to the right of the page break (for vertical) or under the page break (for horizontal); then choose Insert➪ Delete Page Break.

Chapter 5

Creating Charts from Spreadsheets

• •

In This Chapter

▶ Strolling the gallery of charts

▶ Getting from spreadsheet to chart

▶ Using the chart window, menu, and toolbar

▶ Naming, saving, and managing multiple charts

▶ Customizing axes and other lines

▶ Customizing charts by adding and formatting text and numbers

▶ Printing charts

• •

*F*or a multitool package with plenty of other things on its mind, Works offers a rather nice selection of chart types and variations and makes the job of charting a breeze. Or is it a snap? Whatever. A snapping breeze perhaps. Very easy, in any event.

You produce charts from data in your spreadsheets. You can print the charts or copy them to other documents that you create in Works, Word, and many other Windows programs. This chapter tells you how to make the jump from dry rows and columns of numbers to graphical "eye scream" that delights the soul and satisfies the intellect.

A Gallery of Chart Types and Variations

Works has more kinds of charts than *Ben & Jerry's* has kinds of ice cream. Works displays the array of possibilities whenever you create a chart in Works, as shown in Figure 5-1. The following list describes how each chart relates to the cells of your spreadsheet:

✔ **Bar:** If you make a bar chart, each cell inspires a separate bar on the chart; the cell's value determines the height of its bar. For multiple rows or columns of data, bars appear differently colored (like popsicles) and can sit side by side or stacked to show the sum.

✔ **Pie:** If you make a pie chart, each cell determines the size of a slice of a pie. By using Works *variations,* you can display your pie charts whole, with one slice partially removed, or exploded into separate slices (a microwaved pie). *A la mode* is not an option.

✔ **Line:** In a line chart, each cell determines the height of a dot, and the dots run horizontally, connected by lines. Variations include lines alone, dots alone, or high/low/close (for tracking your *Ben & Jerry's* stock values).

✔ **Stacked line:** Stacked-line charts are for multiple sets *(series)* of data that you want to display together but in a way that reveals what portion of the total comes from each set. A stacked-line chart can show how ice-cream sales from your Eastern, Western, Northern, and Southern sales divisions contribute to your total sales. The divisional sales "stack" on top of each other to show the total.

✔ **Area:** An area chart is like a stacked-line chart but filled in with color underneath the lines.

✔ **Scatter:** A scatter plot enables you to compare two sets of data. If your data is in two columns, each row gives the X,Y coordinates of a point. To the extent that the dots appear to form a straight line, the two sets correlate (as do, for example, daily ice-cream consumption and cholesterol level).

✔ **Radar:** A radar chart is kind of like a line chart that's going around in a circle: Instead of the line's height varying, its radius from a center point varies. Radar plots are useful for showing variations in cyclical events — for example, consumption of ice cream by month. See Figure 5-1; radar charts are kind of hard to describe.

✔ **Combination:** Enables you to mix lines and bars in a single chart. A Neapolitan ice cream kind of chart!

I'm not going to get into all of these chart types here. After you know about the basic types, you can pick up the others pretty easily.

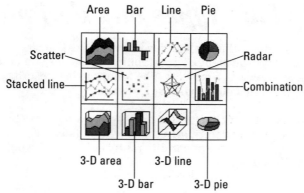

Figure 5-1:
The Works gallery of charts.

You can get the basic types of charts in several *variations* and with various features. (Not including chocolate sprinkles.) See the section "Changing Chart Types and Variations," later in this chapter.

You can also size the charts to any size you need; put a border around them; and change the fonts, colors, shading, gridlines, and even the shapes of the data points. I don't discuss all these variations here, but you should be aware of what's possible.

Creating Any Chart, Step by Step

To create a new chart, start with a spreadsheet — preferably, one that's laid out with row and column headings, although you can chart any spreadsheet that you want. Just follow these steps:

1. **Select a range containing the data that you want to chart.**

   Select only the data that you want to plot; if you don't want to plot a column or row, leave it out. If headings are immediately adjacent to the row or column you want to plot, include them in your selection; otherwise leave them out. See Figure 5-2.

   For a pie chart, select just the one column (or row) containing the numbers you want to chart; if headings are in an adjacent column, include them.

2. **Choose Tools⇨Create New Chart or click the New Chart button (which looks like a tiny bar chart) on the toolbar.**

   The New Chart dialog box swings into action, as shown in Figure 5-3. It shows you a sample of a bar chart based on the data you selected. It also tries to figure out whether you included line and column headings; if so, it uses them as labels in the chart.

Figure 5-2: Include both headings and data in your selection, if possible.

	A	B	C	D	E	F
1	Seedling density	6/89	6/90	6/91	6/92	6/93
2	Red oak	453	437	470	497	452
3	Hickory	27	32	36	43	52
4	Birch	240	260	277	297	319
5	White pine	181	164	149	135	128
6	Hemlock	140	145	148	151	145
7	Sassafras	32	30	27	24	22
8	Sycamore	88	75	67	63	58
9	White birch	23	21	20	17	16
10	White oak	54	49	42	40	37
11						

seedlings.wks
Zoom 100%

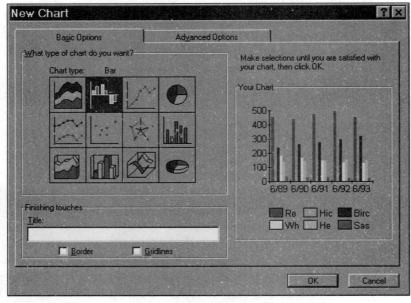

Figure 5-3:
The New
Chart dialog
box initially
suggests a
bar chart.

3. **Choose a chart type from the graphical picture gallery.**

   The sample area on the right shows you what your chart looks like. Works always starts out by showing you a bar chart. To review your other choices, see the section "A Gallery of Chart Types and Variations," earlier in this chapter.

4. **If the chart in the sample area looks incorrect, click the Advanced Options tab to see a card with various options you can change.**

   Works makes some guesses based on what it finds. Works may have misinterpreted your spreadsheet data and is, for example, reading your data series across instead of down or vice versa.

   • If necessary, change selection 1, Which Way Do Your Series Go?

   Remember that a series is a column or row of data that you want to chart in a single color. If your data is in columns, choose Down. I often find thinking about this too confusing. If the chart looks wrong, I just choose the alternative: either Across or Down. For more help, see the sidebar, "What the heck are series and categories?"

   • If necessary, change the settings for First Column Contains and First Row Contains.

   If you have numbers in the first row or column that you actually intend as *labels* for your data, not as the data to chart, click Legend text.

What the heck are series and categories?

Works keeps yammering about series and categories. What the heck are these things anyway?

A *series* is the group of numbers that you're plotting — a single row or column of data. A series always appears in a single color.

A *category* is a name for each of the numbers in the series. January, February, and March, for example, are each a separate category in a series of 12 monthly sales figures. If your series are in columns, your categories are the rows.

A *series label* is a description of what the numbers represent, such as Sales or Rainfall. Usually Works copies labels from the headings on your columns or rows of data. If you include that heading in your initial selection of cells, the label appears automatically in the legend. The legend identifies what series a particular color represents.

If you have dates or times in the first row or column and you actually intend them to be data and not labels, click A value (Y) series.

- All better now? Click the Basic Options tab to return to the other card in this dialog box.

5. **Enter a title for the chart in the Title text box at the bottom of the Basic Options card.**

   Click the Title text box and type something descriptive, such as **Sales by Quarter**. The sample chart in the dialog box reflects your choice.

6. **If you want a border around the whole chart, click Border; if you want gridlines, click Gridlines.**

7. **Click OK.**

A chart window appears with your lovely work of numeric art in spunky primary colors. To enhance or change your chart, see the section "Changing Chart Types and Variations," later in this chapter.

Using the Chart Window, Menu, and Toolbar

After you finish creating a new chart, Works creates a chart window as shown in Figure 5-4. Even though the chart appears in a separate window, it's part of your spreadsheet and is saved with the spreadsheet file.

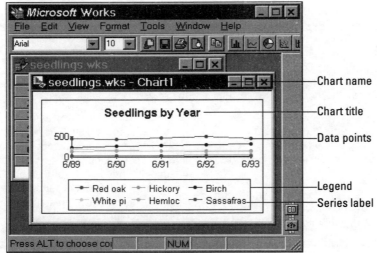

Figure 5-4:
The chart
window
with a line
chart.

Notice that the menu bar has changed a little, and the toolbar has changed a lot. That's because, as long as the chart window is active, you're in the *chart tool* — the thing this chapter has been talking about. If you switch to the spreadsheet (by, say, clicking its title bar), you're in the *spreadsheet tool,* where you make spreadsheets.

Another way to switch between your chart and its spreadsheet is to press F3 and then choose View⇨Chart or View⇨Spreadsheet. Because you can switch to several different charts, a View Chart dialog box appears displaying the list of available charts. Double-click the one you want to use.

If the chart looks rather squished and crowded and the words appear chopped off, don't panic. That's just how Works deals with a too-small chart window. Click and drag a side or corner of the chart window to make it bigger.

The chart menu bar

The chart menu bar looks and works like menu bars everywhere, but it contains some commands that don't appear in any other Works tool, as the following list describes:

- ✔ The *Edit* selection on the chart menu bar gives you not only the usual cut-and-paste stuff, but also everything that you need for changing the range of data in the spreadsheet which you're charting or editing the text in the chart.

- ✔ The View command on the chart menu bar enables you to switch between the spreadsheet and any of the charts that you may attach to it.

- Choosing Format➪Chart Type enables you to change the type and variation of the chart. See the section "Changing Chart Types and Variations," later in this chapter. The toolbar buttons also enable you to do the same thing.

- Clicking Format also gives you commands that control the chart's appearances: its fonts, patterns, colors, axes, borders, legends, and 3-D-osity.

- Clicking Tools gives you commands to create, name, and delete charts that attach to the spreadsheet.

I cover the most important menu choices in more detail in the remainder of this chapter.

The chart toolbar

The toolbar, as always, is just another vehicle for giving commands to Works (instead of the traditional semaphore flags). About half the buttons (the ones on the left side) are identical to the buttons on the spreadsheet toolbar, covering options such as font, size, saving, printing, and copying.

You can always discover the purpose of a toolbar button by placing your mouse cursor over it (but don't click!). A tiny tag appears with actual English words on it, telling you what the button is or does.

The buttons on the right half of the toolbar are, for the most part, WYSIWYG (*What You See Is What You Get*) — that is, they have pictures of charts on 'em. (Really! Just get out your magnifying glass.) Click 'em, and your chart can look something like what you see on the icon, only bigger and prettier. See the following section, "Changing Chart Types and Variations," for more information.

The second-to-last button (displaying the white arrow and the number 1) is a secret passage to the spreadsheet — specifically, to the first data series in the spreadsheet. If you have a big spreadsheet and are charting just a portion of it, clicking this button is a quick way to get to the right place.

Changing Chart Types and Variations

To change the chart's *type* or *variation,* either choose Format➪Chart Type from the chart menu bar or click a toolbar button. Either way, you get a lovely graphical display of various ways to display your data.

If, for example, you click the button that looks like downtown Chicago (the 3-D Bar Chart button), you open the Chart Type dialog box, as shown in Figure 5-5.

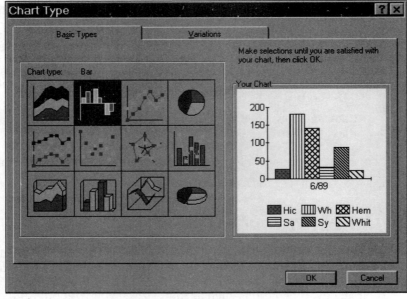

Figure 5-5:
A graphical
selection of
basic chart
types; for
variations
on that
type,
click the
Variations
tab.

The top card in the Chart Type dialog box shows you the basic types of charts available, such as bar, line, or 3-D bar. (If you click a toolbar button to get here, your chosen chart type is already selected.) Choose a different type of chart by clicking one of the pictures.

Click the Variations tab, the second card in this dialog box, to explore different versions of the basic chart type that you choose. Browse through the variations by clicking them and carefully watching the changes in the example chart shown on this card.

If you change your chart type or variation, do so before you apply finishing touches, such as data labels (which I discuss later in this chapter). Changing the chart type or variation may remove these niceties if the new type of chart doesn't use them. Even if you change back to the old type, your finishing touches are still gone.

Click OK to close the dialog box and choose the variation at which you're looking. The following list describes some of the variations from which you may choose:

- **3-D bar, line, and pie charts:** Works doesn't really mean 3-D; it means that the chart appears to have thickness and shading, as if it were made of chunks of plastic. Very trendy.

- **Titles:** You can have two lines in a title that identifies the chart.

✔ **Labels:** You can add *data labels,* which label the top of each bar or each point along a line with text or numbers (the cell values). You can also add *category labels* (such as text that identifies each bar in a bar chart).

✔ **Legends:** A *legend* is a box that identifies what sets of data the various colors or shades represent. Sales figures, for example, may appear in blue and costs in green.

✔ **Axes:** You can have two Y axes if you plot two different kinds of data, such as temperature and weight, on the same chart.

Naming, Saving and Managing Multiple Charts

Creative artist that you are, you're probably not content with a single chart of your spreadsheet. No, you want two charts — maybe a line chart to compare annual sales by region and then a bar chart to show total sales by product.

Works enables you to create multiple new charts and keeps them as part of the spreadsheet file. You don't save charts as separate files. If you save your spreadsheet (by choosing File⇨Save), you save all the charts associated with it. If a chart is utterly wrong and you don't want to bother trying to rehabilitate, delete it by choosing Tools⇨Delete Chart, as I describe in the following list.

To create, name, delete, or duplicate a chart, choose Tools and then one of the following selections from the Tools menu:

✔ **Create New Chart:** This command performs the customary routine with the New Chart dialog box, as I describe in Chapter 18.

✔ **Rename Chart:** To keep your charts straight and to buttress their self-esteem, give your charts names. Choosing this command opens the Rename Chart dialog box. Click the chart you want to rename in the Select a Chart list. Click the Type a Name Below text box at the bottom of the dialog box and then type a name for the current chart. Click the Rename button. The chart name now appears in the chart title bar. Click OK.

✔ **Delete Chart:** This command opens the Delete Chart dialog box (surprise). Click the chart you want to delete in the list of charts and then click the Delete button. Click OK.

✔ **Duplicate Chart:** This command is handy for creating a slightly different version of an existing chart. In the Duplicate Chart dialog box that appears, click the chart that you want to duplicate and then click the Name text box. Type a new name, click the Duplicate button, and then click OK.

To switch among charts, just choose View⇨Chart from the menu bar. A humble View Chart dialog box appears, displaying a list of charts by name. Double-click a name to open that chart window.

Customizing Axes and Other Lines

All those spiffy types and styles of charts, such as 3-D area charts, are artistic as all heck — but without lines going across them, the charts may occasionally leave your viewers wondering exactly what values they're looking at: "Is that bar 10, 12, or 15 units high?"

Unless you've already done a lot of customizing of your chart, the simplest way to get horizontal or vertical lines across your chart is to choose a style that gives the lines to you. (Choose the Format⇨Chart Type command or click the buttons on the toolbar that depict various chart types.) The other way to add lines is by formatting the axes of your chart, as I describe in the following two sections.

Figure 5-6 shows some options for a 3-D bar chart. Lines that run across the chart horizontally (at intervals along the vertical, or *Y*, axis) are perhaps most in demand. To get these lines, see the following section, "Customizing the Y axis." For lines that run up the chart vertically (at intervals along the horizontal, or *X*, axis) see the section "Customizing the X axis," later in this chapter.

Figure 5-6:
Horizontal
lines at
intervals of
25 along the
Y axis
improve this
chart.

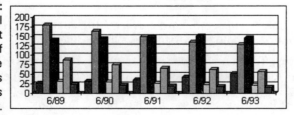

Customizing the Y axis

The Y axis is the axis that goes up toward the heavens. An axis with such lofty ambitions deserves a bit of dressing up. To extend horizontal lines out from the Y axis or to otherwise fool around with the Y axis, choose Format⇨Vertical (Y) Axis. The Format Vertical Axis dialog box appears, looking like the example shown in Figure 5-7.

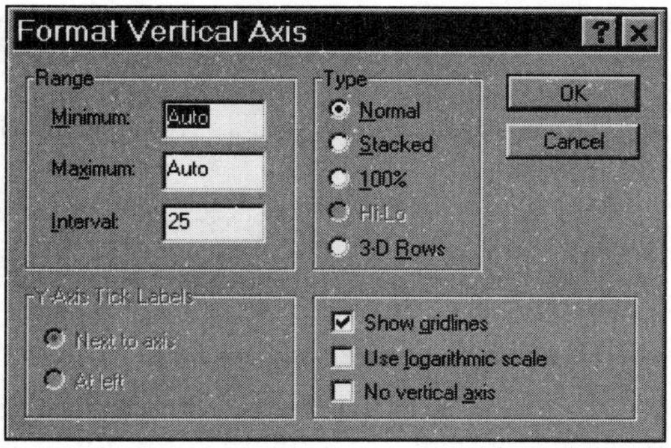

Figure 5-7:
The place
to go for
a more
refined axis.

Following is a rundown of what you can accomplish in the Format Vertical Axis dialog box:

- For gridlines at each interval along the axis, click Show Gridlines.

- For more or fewer intervals along the axis, click Interval and type a new value. For a numbered tick-mark along the axis every $50 (or 50 ducks or 50 inches of rain or whatever), for example, enter **50**.

- To start or end the axis at a different value, edit the values in the Minimum or Maximum text boxes, respectively. This option is good if you have a couple extreme values you're embarrassed about and don't care to present.

- If you have values over a very wide range (for example, over several powers of 10 — say, from 1 to 1,000), click Use Logarithmic Scale. (This option isn't available in area charts.)

- To eliminate the vertical axis altogether (economists and PR folks, take note), click No Vertical Axis. Hey, if you let folks see actual numbers, you just get a lot of picky debate.

- You can fool around with what I call the chart's variation by clicking one of the (nongrayed out) entries in the Type area. Sometimes you find variations here that aren't available if you use the Format⇨Chart Type command or the toolbar buttons (such as line charts expressing themselves as percent fractions).

Customizing the X axis

The X axis is the one that goes across the bottom of the chart. To extend vertical lines up from the X axis or otherwise fool around with the X axis, choose Format⇨Horizontal (X) Axis. The Horizontal Axis dialog box appears.

Following are some of the things you can accomplish in the Horizontal Axis dialog box:

- ✔ Click Show Gridlines to, well, show gridlines — the vertical-line thingies at every interval.

- ✔ In an area-type chart, where gridlines disappear behind the curve, you can also click Show Droplines: Works superimposes these lines on the area curve.

- ✔ To eliminate the horizontal axis altogether, click No Horizontal Axis.

- ✔ To trim out some of the category labels along a crowded X axis, type a larger value in the Label Frequency text box. Type **3**, for example, to show every third label.

Customizing Charts: Text and Numbers

Works enables you to put text — including titles, series labels, and data labels (the very numbers that you're charting) — in several places in your chart.

Font and style

Charts use a single font and style for all text. You can change the chart font and style in the charting tool just as you do in any other Works tool: by using the toolbar, keyboard shortcuts (such as Ctrl+B for bold) or the Format⇨Font and Style menu command. See Chapter 1 for details.

You can also change the font and style by double-clicking any tick-mark along an axis or a data label. Or right-click any text and choose Font and Style from the pop-up menu that appears. The Font and Style dialog box then appears.

Don't be too quick to reduce font size. If the text seems too large, you may simply be looking at the chart in a rather small window. Check your chart by using the Print Preview command before you assume that the type is too large (by choosing File⇨Print Preview).

Number formats

If your numbers need dollar signs, a different number of decimal places, or any of the other number formatting with which you're familiar from spreadsheets, this problem is not your chart's! No, it's your spreadsheet's problem.

Return to your spreadsheet window (by pressing F3, for example) and change the number formatting of your data. See Chapter 4 for details of number formatting.

Chart and axis titles

Titles are important. I once had a cartooning teacher who said that if you can't draw a rabbit, make sure the title says rabbit somewhere. So if you create an incomprehensible chart, at least give it a good title.

Remember the following points about titles:

- ✔ *Chart titles* are the one or two lines at the top of the chart.
- ✔ *Axis titles* go along an axis and tell you what the axis represents: months, furlongs, doughnuts, and so on.

To create chart or axis titles, choose Edit⇨Titles. The Titles dialog box moves regally into view. (Regally because — after all — you're conferring a title!) Just click the appropriate text box and type your title, as the following list describes:

- ✔ You can enter two lines of title for the chart in two separate text boxes: Chart title and Subtitle.
- ✔ To type an identifier that prints alongside the X or Y axis, click Horizontal (X) Axis or Vertical (Y) Axis and type the identifier.
- ✔ Enter an identifier for Right Vertical Axis is for a second Y axis if you have one.

Click OK after you finish titling your chart.

If your titles don't look very good in the chart window, remember that they don't really look like that after you print them. To see how the chart really looks, use the Print Preview feature (by choosing File⇨Print Preview).

Data labels

Data labels display actual data values (such as the number 181) in the chart. (The values may appear along the line, atop the bars, or alongside the pie slices — depending on what kind of chart you choose.) Take a look at the example shown in Figure 5-8, which includes data labels.

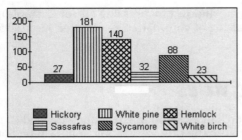

Figure 5-8:
Data labels
leave no
doubt about
what the
numbers
are.

Data labels for all points

To simply print the numbers corresponding to all the points on the chart for every data series, follow these steps:

1. **Choose Edit⇨Data Labels.**

   The Data Labels dialog box puts in an appearance.

2. **Click the Use Series Data check box.**

3. **Click OK.**

Data labels are great but can become confusing if you have several data series on the chart at once. The example in Figure 5-8 displays only one data series, so it's pretty easy to read. The trouble with the procedure I just gave you is that it puts numbers on every point of the chart; if you have many points or several data series, the numbers may overlap or crowd each other. If that problem arises, see the following section, "Data labels for a select few points."

Text may look crowded in the Works chart window, but it may appear okay on the printout. Use the Print Preview feature (by choosing File⇨Print Preview) to see how your chart is going to look after you print it. If your text still looks crowded after you print the chart, another alternative is simply to choose a smaller font size from the toolbar.

Data labels for a select few points

To put data labels on a particular data series (one line of a line chart, or one set of bars in a bar chart, for example), I suggest you use the following copy-and-paste approach:

1. **Choose Window⇨Tile so that you can see both spreadsheet and chart.**

2. **In the spreadsheet window, select (highlight) the range of cells that you want to use as data labels and then press Ctrl+C to copy the range of cells to the Windows Clipboard.**

(You usually want to choose the same range that you use for the series, but you can choose a completely different range, too, as long as it contains the same number of cells.)

3. **Click anywhere in the chart window and then choose Edit⇨ Data Labels.**

   The Data Labels dialog box appears.

4. **If a check mark appears in the Use Series Data check box, click the check box to clear the mark.**

5. **Click the text box for the series that you want to label (Series 1 or Series 2, and so on) and click the Paste button to paste the range address.**

   Don't press Ctrl+V, the usual way to paste.

6. **Click OK.**

7. **Repeat Steps 2 through 6 for each series that you want to label.**

   Leave a series box blank if you want no data labels on that series.

Printing a Chart

A great piece of industrial art such as your chart deserves to appear proudly on canvas. Because your printer probably doesn't do canvas very well, however, you must settle for printing your chart on paper (and proudly displaying it on the refrigerator door perhaps?).

First make sure that the chart window is open and active (by choosing View⇨Chart). Then choose whichever of Works printing commands or buttons you normally prefer to set up, preview, and print documents.

Following are a few tips for printing charts, all concerning the Page Setup dialog box:

✔ Many, if not most, charts fit better if you print them sideways (in *landscape* mode). Choose File⇨Page Setup; click the Source, Size and Orientation tab; and choose Landscape. Click OK.

✔ To proportion the chart just as it appears in the chart window, open the Page Setup dialog box (by choosing File⇨Page Setup), click the Other Options tab, and choose Screen size. Click OK. The graphics keep the same proportion; the text is whatever point size you select.

✔ Other options (not surprisingly) also appear on the Other Options card of the Page Setup dialog box. The Full Page, Keep Proportions option keeps the same proportions as the chart window but fills the paper page either to the side margins or to the top and bottom margins. Full Page expands height and width to the margins and doesn't worry about proportions.

✔ To set the dimensions more precisely by using the Page Setup dialog box, choose either of the two Full Page options on the Other Options page and then set the page margins on the Margins tab.

To see how a chart is going to look on your printer, choose the command View⇨Display as Printed from the menu bar.

To put your chart in another document (say, a Works or Word word-processing document), see Chapter 14.

Chapter 6

Organizing Your Data with a Database

● ●

In This Chapter

▶ Understanding and getting started with databases

▶ Designing databases

▶ Working in different views

▶ Entering fields and data

▶ Creating an example database

▶ Using printing options

▶ Saving your work

▶ Editing in the formula bar

▶ Inserting and removing fields

▶ Adding, inserting, and deleting records

▶ Copying and moving data

▶ Fooling around with formats

● ●

*T*he time has come to give your data a little discipline. Have your scraggly lists of names and addresses, inventory lists, and sales or inventory records report for duty at the database and give them the Works. Anything that you currently do using paper forms, or about which you've thought, "I'd like to computerize that," is a possible candidate for becoming a Works database. In this chapter, you find out how to create a database and enlist your data in electronic form.

Using a Database

If you've ever used a library-card index, a Rolodex file, a dictionary, or a phone book, you've used a database. A *database* is just a collection of information that has some organization to it. (Every card in a Rolodex, for example, has the same structure: a line for a name, usually last name first; a couple lines for an address; a line for the phone number; and so on.)

If you put a database on a computer, a *database manager* or *database tool* is the software that you use to read the database and to put information into the database. Because database tools always accompany databases, people get lazy and lump the terms together, calling the whole ball of wax a "database."

What does the Works database do for you?

The most basic benefit of computerizing your data in a database is tidy record keeping and the capability of neatly printing your forms, receipts, invoices, or reports. The bigger deal with computer databases, however, is that they help you find, group, and sort things quickly and also help you analyze and summarize your records. Following are the three main functions that the Works database tool can perform for you:

- ✔ **Sorting** enables you to organize *records* alphabetically (by last name, for example) or numerically. (See the following section for an explanation of records.) Sorting your database records also groups similar records together. If you sort based on Zip code, for example, the database groups all the records sharing a common Zip code together.

- ✔ **Filtering** reveals certain records in your database. You can, for example, create a filter that, by using the Age and Town *fields* of your student database, screens out say, every child except the 12-year-olds from Mudville. (See the following section for an explanation of fields.) You can then create mailings specifically for that group or any other group.

- ✔ **Reporting** filters, sorts, and organizes records into a report or summary form for printing and provides mathematical summaries of certain fields. You can, for example, create a report of your customers in the state of California that you group by Zip code, with total sales by month.

A Works database can also serve as an address book from which you, too, can do your very own junk mailing! Yes — you, too, *Mr. Smith* of *345 Smithtown Road,* may already be a wiener. See Chapter 9 for the exciting details!

Fields and records: How Works stores information

Works talks a lot about fields and records, so you need to understand what they are. The Rolodex file metaphor is great for understanding fields and records, which are part of every database program.

Each card in your Rolodex file is like a *record* in a database. (If you don't have a Rolodex file, think of a recipe card file; each recipe card is a record.)

Each card has the same blank areas to fill out: name, telephone number, and address, at the very least. These blank areas are known as *fields* in computer databases. Each field has a name, similar to the *Address* field in a Rolodex file (or *Cooking Time* if you're thinking of recipe cards). Each record has different entries in those fields, which typically describe a person (as in the Rolodex), a transaction (such as a sale or a phone call), an object, or a location.

The Database Window

Figure 6-1 shows what I call the *database window*, which is simply how the Microsoft Works window looks while you're using the database tool. Your window looks like this example after you create or open a database.

Make a mental note that Figure 6-1 shows you only one of two main *views* of a database. The view shown here is known as *Form* view, and the other view, which looks like a spreadsheet, is known as *List* view. (A third view, *Form Design* view, looks like Form view but is actually an editing feature to enable you to change how Form view looks.)

The basic file and edit menu commands work as they do in all Works tools. Be aware, however, that in this database tool certain menu commands and toolbar buttons change between Form view, List view, and Form Design view. See Figure 6-2 for the database toolbar.

Don't try to memorize all the stuff in these figures. Stick a pencil here or an unused stick of gum or turn back the corner of the page and come back whenever you need to refresh your memory.

The buttons nearer the right-hand end of the toolbar are specific to databases. Here's where to go for a discussion of what each of these buttons refers to:

- ✔ **List, Form, and Form Design view:** See the section "Viewing Your Database," later in this chapter.

- ✔ **Insert a record:** See the section "Adding, Inserting, and Deleting Records," later in this chapter.

- ✔ **Insert a field:** See the section "Adding and Deleting Fields," later in this chapter.

- ✔ **Create or apply a filter:** See Chapter 7.

- ✔ **Create a report:** See Chapter 7.

- ✔ **Use the Address book:** See Chapter 9.

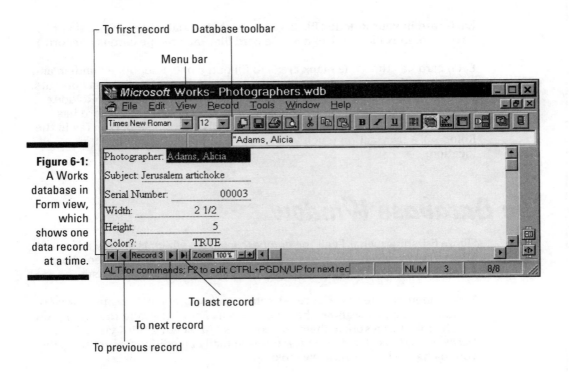

To first record — Database toolbar

Menu bar

Figure 6-1:
A Works
database in
Form view,
which
shows one
data record
at a time.

To last record

To next record

To previous record

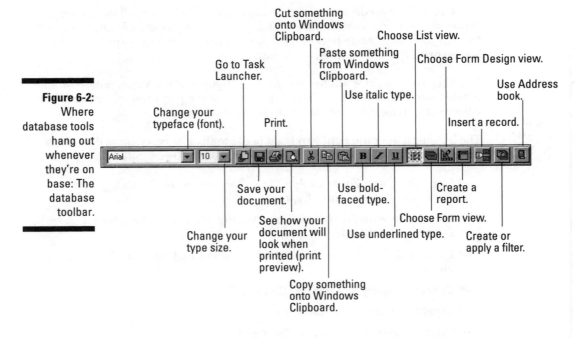

Cut something
onto Windows
Clipboard.

Choose List view.

Paste something
from Windows
Clipboard.

Choose Form Design view.

Go to Task
Launcher.

Use italic type.

Use Address
book.

Figure 6-2:
Where
database tools
hang out
whenever
they're on
base: The
database
toolbar.

Change your
typeface (font).

Print.

Insert a record.

Save your
document.

Use bold-
faced type.

Create a
report.

See how your
document will
look when
printed (print
preview).

Use underlined type.

Choose Form view.

Create or
apply a filter.

Change your
type size.

Copy something
onto Windows
Clipboard.

To quickly see what a button on the toolbar does, place your mouse cursor over the button (don't click) and wait half a second. A tiny sign appears and gives you a tiny description.

Starting the Database Tool

You can start a new document in the database tool as you do in any other Works tool. From the Works Tools card of the Task Launcher, for example, choose the Database tool. (See Chapter 1 if you're unfamiliar with the Task Launcher.)

Alternatively, you can use a TaskWizard to create one of many predesigned databases Microsoft has conjured up. To review the various ways of starting a new document or opening an existing document in Works, check out Chapter 1. Chapter 9 further discusses TaskWizards and templates. If you're a new PC user and commands, menus, and dialog boxes are still new to you, see the appendix.

Creating a New Database

If you launch the database tool by clicking the Database button on the Tools card of Works Task Launcher, rather than using a template or TaskWizard as mentioned in the preceding section, Works begins creating a fresh, clean database document. Here are the first steps you take:

If the Task Launcher isn't currently on-screen, choose File⇨New from the menu bar or press Ctrl+N.

From the Task Launcher, choose the Works Tools card and then click the Database button.

The first time you start a database document you may see a First-time Help dialog box, as shown in Figure 6-3. If so, please refer to Chapter 1, where I discuss First-time Help.

Works now displays the Create Database dialog box.

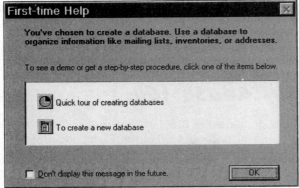

Creating New Database Fields

Whenever you create a new database without using a TaskWizard, your principal job is entering fields. Here, in New England, we wear our rubber boots and watch where we step whenever we enter fields. No such precautions are necessary for entering fields into your database. Following, however, are some guidelines for creating fields:

- ✔ Create a field for anything you may want to search for, report on, or print on a form, envelope, or label: a date, a manufacturer, color, price, vendor, nickname, neck size, Zip code, and so on. If in doubt, create a field.

- ✔ Use a separate field for anything that's separable. For example, the names of many people in your database may begin with Mr., Ms., Mrs., or Dr.; keep this information in a separate field.

- ✔ Always create a serial-number field, which contains a unique number for each record of the database. Doing so ensures that each record has something unique by which to identify it, in case the descriptions are otherwise identical. A serial-number field also ensures that you can later reconstruct the original order in which you entered the data.

Following is the procedure for creating new fields by using the Create Database dialog box (see Figure 6-4). Repeat the following procedure for each field that you think you need.

1. In the Field Name text box, enter a name for a field.

The field's name must be shorter than 15 characters. In Figure 6-4, for example, I'm starting to create a database of photographs that I use in my business. The first field I want is one for the photographer's name. (Don't append the colon you see in Figure 6-4 at the end of the field name; Works adds one for you in Form view.)

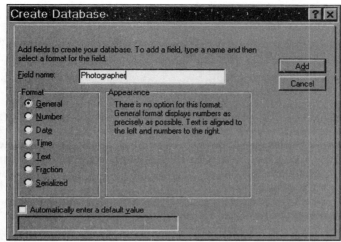

Figure 6-4:
Enter fields
one at a
time in the
Create
Database
dialog box.

2. **In the Format area of the dialog box, choose a format for the field by clicking the appropriate radio button.**

The following formats are very much like the number formats for spreadsheets. Refer to the section on formatting numbers in Chapter 4 of this book. You can change formats later, so don't worry too much about your choice now. (See the section "Applying and Changing Formats," later in this chapter, for more information.)

- **General:** You can use the General format for most fields, but you run across a few special circumstances — such as fields containing dates, dollars, or fractions — where you may want to choose something other than General.

- **Number:** Choose this format if you want dollar signs, commas, percentages, or scientific notation to appear without your needing to type them. Number formats also include TRUE/FALSE for fields such as the Color? field that appears in Figures 6-1, 6-5, and 6-6, where you can enter a **1** for TRUE or a **0** for FALSE.

- **Date** and **Time:** Use these formats for date or time fields. These formats give you flexibility to change the way dates or times appear in your database, and enable you to summarize your data in reports, such as in calculating total labor time.

- **Text:** Use this format to enter certain data, such as Zip codes that begin with zero. Otherwise, the Zip code 01776 turns into 1776.

- **Fraction:** Use this format and Works automatically rounds off data that you enter in decimal form, such as 2.125, into mixed-number fractional form, such as $2^1/_8$. Choose what fraction you want the number to round off to from the list that appears. This format is useful for listing things in nonmetric dimensions, such as inches. Works "reduces" a fraction such as $^4/_8$ to $^1/_2$ unless you click the Do Not Reduce check box.

- **Serialized:** Most databases benefit from having a unique number for each record, which a serial-number field provides. Choose the Serialized format to create such a field, and you don't even need to enter the numbers yourself: Works does it for you automatically each time you enter a new record. In the Next Value text box, enter the number with which you want the next record to start. If you want the number to increase by increments of something other than 1, enter that increment in the Increment text box.

3. **Specify a default value for the field if this field is often going to contain the same value.**

   At the bottom of the Create Database dialog box, click the Automatically Enter a Default Value check box and then type the value in the box at the very bottom. A *default value* is data that appears automatically whenever you create a new record, and it saves you time. If, for example, most of the photographs in my photography database are by the same person — say, Johnson — I can make *Johnson* my default value. Then, whenever I record a new photograph in my database, Johnson automatically appears in the Photographer field. (I can replace the default with another name if the photographer is someone other than Johnson.)

   Fields that use default values behave oddly as you enter data into a record: *The default value doesn't appear until you enter data in at least one other field.*

4. **Click the Add button.**

   This action adds the field you just specified to the database, and it enables you to move on to the next field. If you're done creating fields, go to Step 5. Otherwise, return to Step 1 and keep adding fields until you have all that you need — and then go to Step 5.

5. **Click the Done button to exit the Create Database dialog box.**

After you finish, your database is ready for you to add some data. But wait! How come it looks just like a spreadsheet? Well, the odd thing about databases is that they can look like darned near anything. The following section gives you the details on viewing your database.

Viewing Your Database

One reason people sometimes get a bit confused using a database tool is that the tool can show your data in different ways, known as *views*. Figures 6-5 and 6-6, for example, show the same database in two different views.

Figure 6-5:
My database for cataloging photographs in Form view, showing record 6.

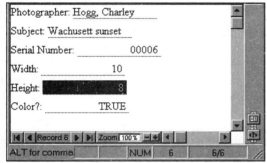

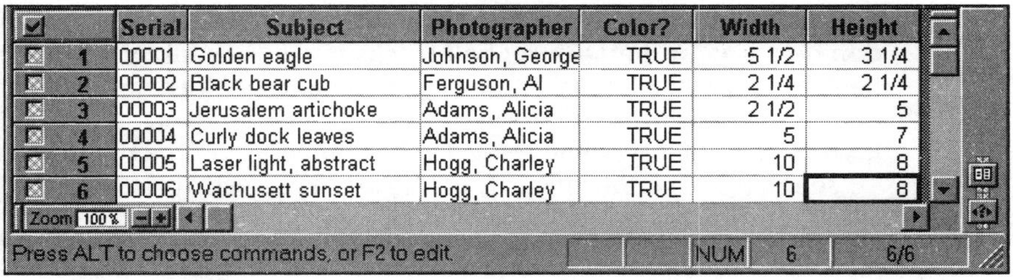

Figure 6-6:
The same database as shown in Figure 6-5, but now in List view, showing records 1-6.

☑		Serial	Subject	Photographer	Color?	Width	Height
☒	1	00001	Golden eagle	Johnson, George	TRUE	5 1/2	3 1/4
☒	2	00002	Black bear cub	Ferguson, Al	TRUE	2 1/4	2 1/4
☒	3	00003	Jerusalem artichoke	Adams, Alicia	TRUE	2 1/2	5
☒	4	00004	Curly dock leaves	Adams, Alicia	TRUE	5	7
☒	5	00005	Laser light, abstract	Hogg, Charley	TRUE	10	8
☒	6	00006	Wachusett sunset	Hogg, Charley	TRUE	10	8

Zoom 100%   Press ALT to choose commands, or F2 to edit.   NUM   6   6/6

Here are the different views of Works, and what they do for you:

- **Form view** enables you to enter, look at, and print data as if you entered it on a paper form. Figure 6-5 shows a database in Form view. A blank line, where you enter data follows the field names (Photographer, Subject, Serial Number, Width, Height, and Color? in Figure 6-5).

- **List view** looks like a pad of lined paper on which you copied all the information from your Rolodex, using columns for the fields of, say, Name, Address, and Phone Number. You can see several records at once. Figure 6-6 shows the same database as Figure 6-5 does but in List view. In this view, your database is a big spreadsheet-like table of rows and columns. The rows, which Works numbers along the left side, are individual records. (Blank rows are records in which you haven't yet entered data.) The columns are your fields.

✔ **Form Design view** enables you to design the form you see in Form view. In this view, you can move, resize, reformat, or otherwise change how the fields are going to look in Form view. You can also use Form Design view to add text, such as headings or explanations, or even add illustrations to your forms (say, a logo, if you're printing invoices).

✔ **Report view** is complicated. In principal, it enables you to create printed summary reports. In fact, it's too complicated for most Works users. Fortunately, you can create useful reports without using it.

To switch between views, take any of the following actions:

✔ Choose View⇨List, Form or Form Design from the menu bar.

✔ Click the List view, Form view, or Form Design button on the toolbar (see Figure 6-2).

✔ Press the F9 key to go to Form view, Shift+F9 to go to List view, or Ctrl+F9 to go to Form Design view.

Navigating in Different Views

An important part of your basic training at the database is navigation. You don't want your metaphoric half-tracks wandering all over your metaphoric field. Here's how to get around with minimal casualties and good gas mileage.

If you apply a filter, some records are hidden as you navigate your database. To see them all, choose Record⇨Show⇨1 All Records from the menu bar. See Chapter 7 for more information on using filters.

The spreadsheet connection

In List view, the Works database tool has a great deal in common with the Works spreadsheet tool, except that the database tool performs calculations differently. You cannot sum columns in List view, nor can you put a formula in any old cell as you can in a spreadsheet. Nonetheless, the List view of a Works database looks very much like a spreadsheet and you can control it very much like you do a spreadsheet. You can easily cut and paste data between the List view of a database and a spreadsheet without too much confusion. You may want to find out more about spreadsheets at some point to pick up some tricks for working with databases in the List view. Take a look at Chapters 2 through 4 for more information on spreadsheets.

Navigating in Form view or Form Design view

In Form or Form Design view, you're looking at a representation of a page that's 8¹/₂ x 11 inches, unless you fooled with the Page Setup commands. You can look at any part of the page or (in Form Design view) type anywhere on the page. The dashed lines indicate page boundaries.

To scroll around vertically or horizontally, use the scroll bars on the right side and bottom of the document window. (See the appendix if you don't know how to use scroll bars.) To move around vertically on the page, you can also use your keyboard's arrows and other navigation keys.

To advance from one field to the next, press the Tab key. Press Shift+Tab to move in the opposite direction.

To move between records, use one of the following methods:

- ✔ To advance one record, press Ctrl+Page Down. To back up, press Ctrl+Page Up. Pressing the Tab key after making the last entry on the page (record) also advances you to the next record.

- ✔ Another way to advance or go back one record is to click the inner left- or right-arrow in the following gadget, which you find in the bottom-left border of your document window:

  | ◄◄ | ◄ | Record 3 | ► | ►► |

- ✔ To go to the first or last record in your database, click the outer left- or right-arrow in that gadget.

- ✔ Or, to go to the first record, press Ctrl+Home; to go to the last record, press Ctrl+End.

Navigating in List view

Navigating a database in List view is almost exactly like navigating a spreadsheet, which I describe in Chapter 2. Following is a short review.

To select a cell (the intersection of a row and column) to type in or to format, simply click that cell. Click and drag to select several cells at once. Click the field name (in gray) at the top of a column or the record number (in gray) of a row to select the entire column or row. An alternative way to move the rectangular highlight around a cell is by using the navigation keys on your keyboard. To look around your database in List view, use the scroll bars on the right side and bottom of the document window.

Entering Data

To enter data into your database, you generally fill out one record at a time, starting with the first record. Form view is usually the best choice for conventional, one-record-at-a-time data entry. In a nutshell, the procedure is just to click a field in Form view (or click a cell in List view) and then type.

Use any of the techniques mentioned in the preceding section ("Navigating in Different Views") to move from one field or record to the next. A popular method is to use the Tab key to advance from one field to the next (use Shift+Tab to go backward) and to advance to the next record after one is complete.

Following are a few tips for entering data:

- ✔ To put a new record into your database, just add it at the end: Press Ctrl+End in Form view; in List view, press Ctrl+End and then press Tab.

- ✔ For fields that you format as TRUE/FALSE fields, you can enter the number **1** for TRUE or **0** for FALSE, or you can type the words **TRUE** or **FALSE**.

- ✔ If the symbol ###### appears after you enter some data, the field isn't wide enough to display the data. A quick fix, if you're in List view, is to double-click the field name in the top cell of the column. See the section "Moving and Resizing Fields," later in this chapter, for other techniques.

Creating a Sample Database

Show time! Here's an example of how to create a database. (The example is a very simple, five-field database for cataloging photographs.)

The Rule of This Design, as dictated by its omnipotent creator (me), is that you shall have five fields: Photographer, Subject, Width, Height, and Color?.

I like having *standards* for data, as illustrated by the following Rules: The Photographer field shall contain the last name first, a comma, and then the first name; the Subject field shall contain a short description of what's in the photo; the Width and Height fields shall give the dimension in inches and $1/8$ fractions of an inch; and the Color? field shall be a TRUE/FALSE field indicating whether the photo is in color (TRUE) or black and white (FALSE). If I want to be on the safe side, I use a separate field for the first and last name of the photographer, but I'm feeling reckless.

To go ahead and create this example of a database, just follow these steps:

1. **To start a new database document, press Alt+F and then N.**

2. **After the Task Launcher appears, choose the Works Tools card and then click the Database button.**

   A First-time Help dialog box may appear. If so, click the To Create a New Database button. The Create Database dialog box appears.

3. **Type** Photographer **into the Field Name box and click the Add button or press the Enter key.**

   Every time that you click Add from now on, a new, blank field form appears in the Create Database dialog box.

4. **Type** Subject **in the Field Name text box and click Add.**

5. **Type** Serial **into the Field Name text box; then, in the Format area, choose the Serialized radio button and click Add.**

6. **Type** Width **in the Field Name text box; then, in the Format area, choose the Fraction radio button; from the Appearance list box, choose** $^1/_8$**; and click Add.**

7. **Type** Height **in the Field name box; then, in the Format area, choose the Fraction radio button; from the Appearance list box, choose** $^1/_8$**; and click Add.**

8. **Type** Color? **in the Field name box; then, in the Format area, choose the Number radio button; in the Appearance list box, scroll to the bottom and choose True/False; click the Add button and then click the Done button.**

You created a database! Well, the structure of it, at least. But your database still needs some data.

Now start entering data. You can do so in either List view (which is what you're looking at) or Form view. Simply click a cell (in List view) or a field (in Form view) and start typing. Use the Tab key to advance to the next field.

Moving and Resizing Fields

If you don't like the position or size of your fields, changes are a simple matter. You can make the changes in either Form Design view or List view.

Moving fields in Form Design view

To move the position of a field as it appears in Form and Form Design view, perform the following steps:

1. **Switch to Form Design view, if you're not there already.**

   To switch to Form Design view, click the Form Design button on the toolbar, choose View➪Form Design from the menu bar, or press Ctrl+F9.

2. **Click and then drag the field where you want it.**

   To move a bunch of fields at once, hold down the Ctrl button and click each field that you want to move. Release the Ctrl key and then click and drag the entire group of fields.

Moving fields in List view

To move a field (column) in List view, follow these steps:

1. **Click the top cell of the column — the one containing the field name.**

   This action selects the field/column.

2. **Click the top cell of the column again and then drag the column to the left or the right.**

   The dark vertical line that appears between columns indicates where the column appears after you release the mouse button.

Resizing fields in Form Design view

If a field is too small to display your data in Form or Form Design view, you can resize the field. (You may need to move adjoining fields to allow for the change in size.) Follow these steps:

1. **Switch to Form Design view, if you're not there already.**

   To switch to Form Design view, click the Form Design button on the toolbar, choose View➪Form Design from the menu bar, or press Ctrl+F9.

2. **Click the underlined area to the right of the field name.**

   This action highlights the field, and three tiny, gray squares, known as *handles,* appear in the highlight. Figure 6-7 shows a blown-up view of the highlighted area.

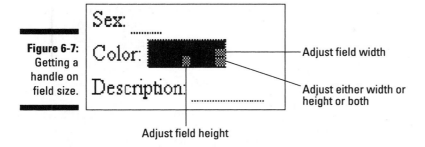

Figure 6-7:
Getting a
handle on
field size.

Adjust field width

Adjust either width or
height or both

Adjust field height

3. **Adjust the field size by dragging the handles.**

   To make a field wider, drag the handle at the center of the right edge to
   the right. To make the field higher (to add lines), drag the handle at the
   center of the bottom edge down. The handle at the corner enables you
   to drag both width and height at the same time.

   To adjust field size more precisely, click the underlined area next to the
   field name; then choose Format⇨Field Size to open the Field Size dialog
   box. Enter a width (how many characters) in the Width text box, and a
   height (how many rows) in the Height text box for the data entry.

Resizing fields in List view

To resize a field (change column width) in List view, you can either drag a
column edge or use the Field Width dialog box, as the following paragraphs
describe:

✔ **To change the width of the column by dragging,** move your cursor to
   the gray row at the top of the columns, where the field names appear. In
   this row, slowly move your mouse pointer across the right-hand edge of
   the column that you want to change. After the pointer changes to a
   double-headed-arrow-sort-of-deal with the attached word *Adjust,* click
   and drag the column edge left or right.

✔ **To set the width of a column more precisely,** use the Field Width
   dialog box. First click any cell in that column to choose the column.
   Then choose Format⇨Field Width from the menu bar. After the Field
   Width dialog box appears, type a number slightly larger than the
   maximum number of characters you expect for data in this field and
   then press Enter.

To make your field size just large enough to hold the longest entry in your database, double-click the field name (in the top cell of the column).

Editing Data and Field Names

If you need to change some data or a field name in your database, the tool you can rely on in all views is the *formula bar*. The formula bar works just the same as the formula bar in the Works spreadsheet tool, which I describe in Chapter 2. You can see the formula bar located just under the toolbar in Figure 6-8.

Click a field name or data and then make your changes in the editing area of the formula bar (refer to Figure 6-8). Click the check mark button or press Enter on your keyboard to make the change permanent. Click the button displaying the X or press the Esc key to abandon your edits and leave whatever you were editing in its original state.

If the data you're editing is too long to fit entirely in the editing area of the formula bar, the navigation keys (left/right arrow keys, Home, and End) offer an easier way to move the insertion point than does the mouse.

In List view, just as in spreadsheets, you can edit data right in its cell: Just double-click the cell, and the insertion point you need for editing appears in the cell.

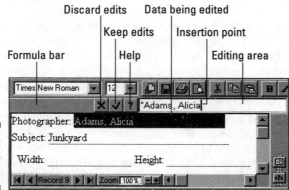

Figure 6-8:
Using the
formula bar.

Surviving (Or Using) the Protection Racket

If you find that Works complains whenever you try to edit data, the complaint probably arises because Works is protecting the field in which you're working against data changes. This situation arises if you use certain TaskWizards. Here's what to do to defeat this protection scheme:

1. **Switch to either List view or Form Design view.**

2. **Click the protected field.**

3. **Choose Format⇨Protection from the menu bar to open a Format Protection dialog box.**

4. **If you find a check mark in the Protect Field check box, click that check box to clear it and then click OK.**

On the other hand, you may want to use this protection racket yourself. By protecting a field, you can help avoid accidental changes to important data. This protection is especially valuable if you're working with another person who may not realize how important some data's value is. To protect a field, follow the same four steps in the preceding list, but turn the check mark *on* by clicking the Protect Field check box.

Adding and Deleting Fields

As any general knows, sometimes you advance on a field and sometimes you retreat from a field. Similarly, in database work, you add fields at certain times and remove them at other times. The following sections describe how to add or remove a field.

Adding new fields

You can add new fields in either the List view or the Form Design view. The advantage of using List view is that the process is very simple. The advantage of using Form Design view is that, after you add a field, you're then conveniently in the correct view for positioning or sizing the field. The choice is yours!

Adding new fields in List view

In List view, the fields are columns. New fields are columns that go to the right or left of existing columns. Follow these steps to create new fields in List view:

1. **Click the column next to which you want to add a new column.**

2. **Choose Record⇨Insert Field from the menu bar; then choose 1 Before (to put a new field to the left of your chosen column) or choose 2 After (to put a new field to the right of your chosen column).**

   An Insert Field dialog box appears to grace your screen, bearing a familiar face: It looks and works just like the Create Database dialog box you use to create your database. See the section "Creating New Database Fields," earlier in this chapter if you need instructions on how to use the Insert Field dialog box.

3. **Type in a name for the field (and a special format if you need it) and then click the Add button.**

4. **For additional fields, repeat Step 3.**

5. **After you finish adding fields, click the Done button, which now appears in the Insert Field dialog box.**

Adding new fields in Form Design view

Here's how to add fields in Form Design view:

1. **Click the place on the page where you want the field to appear.**

   Don't click to the right or below any dashed line you see at edges of the window. That dashed line is the page margin area, which is visible if your Works window is sufficiently large.

   A set of coordinates tells you where you are on the page, if you care. Look in the upper-left corner of the Works window, just under the font box in the text bar. The number after X gives the horizontal position from the left edge of the page; the number after Y gives the vertical position from the bottom edge.

2. **Type a field name of fewer than 15 characters, followed by a colon — as in Last Name: — and press Enter.**

   A dialog box appears, asking for a field name and format, just as a similar dialog box appears when you first create your database. Click OK after you're done creating all the fields that you need.

If you enter a field name in Form Design view, don't forget to end the field name with a colon. If you don't, Works assumes that you're just putting an annotation on the form, not adding a new field.

Deleting (removing) fields

If you remove a field, you also remove all the data that's in it — data that represents a lot of work on somebody's part. If you think that you may want to access the field and its data again sometime, do the following: Before you delete the field, save your unmodified database under a new name by using the File⇨Save As command.

Removing a field in List view is a little safer than is removing a field in Form Design view because you can undo the removal in List view using Ctrl+Z.

Here's how to remove a field in both views:

✔ **In Form Design view:** Just click the field name and press the Delete key. A warning box appears to ask whether you want to Delete this field and all of its contents? and warns that you can't undo this delete. If you really do want to delete the field, click OK.

✔ **In List view:** First, click anywhere in that field's column; then choose Record⇨Delete Field from the menu bar. A warning box appears, asking whether you in fact want to Permanently delete this information?. If you really do want to delete the field, click OK.

Zap! It's dead, Jim.

Adding, Inserting, and Deleting Records

Many unprincipled people have wished, over the years, that they could add or delete certain records in their files. If only they knew how easily you can add or delete records in a Works database.

Adding a record

After you acquire yet another antique popsicle stick for your collection, you undoubtedly want to add another record to your popsicle stick database. Remember that a record is an entire page or row of related data, not just one piece of data. The easiest way to add a record is to add it to the end of your database. To get to the end, take one of the following actions:

✔ In Form view, press Ctrl+End.

✔ In List view, press Ctrl+↓ and then press the down arrow (without the Ctrl key).

Either way, a blank, new record appears. (If you're of the pre-compact disc, or *vinyl,* generation, think of these records as albums, not singles.)

Inserting or deleting a record

To add a record at a particular point in your database, you *insert* it. First, indicate to Works where you want to insert the new record. In Form view, just navigate to that record. In List view, click that row. Then take one of the following actions, as appropriate:

- ✔ **To insert a record:** Choose Record⇨Insert Record from the menu bar or click the Insert Record button. (Refer to Figure 6-2, the toolbar illustration at the beginning of this chapter, or slowly move your mouse pointer across the buttons and read the pop-up labels that appear.) A blank record appears for you to fill in.

- ✔ **To delete a record:** Choose Record⇨Delete Record from the menu bar. Works then deletes the record, and you're left gazing on the next higher record in the database.

You can alternatively delete just the contents of a record rather than the record itself. This trick is useful if you're replacing an item in your database (say, a deceased computer in your inventory). In List view, click the row number (in the gray area on the left) to highlight the entire row — or highlight just as much as you want to delete — and then press the Delete key. The record is now blank (except for serialized fields), and you can enter new data into it.

Applying and Changing Formats

Just as your mother said, appearances are important. You can take a number of actions to change the way your field names and data appear in a Works database. The following list describes the formats you can change.

- ✔ **Field:** How Works interprets and displays your data: as a number, time, or text.

- ✔ **Alignment:** Whether data or a field name is left- or right-justified or centered, for example.

- ✔ **Font:** What typeface and style the data or field name appears in.

- ✔ **Border:** For borders around data or field names.

- ✔ **Shading:** To apply a background color or shade to data or field names.

Fonts, borders, and shading that you apply in one view don't apply to the other view. Field and alignment formats do apply to all views.

To format the data of a particular field, first click that field. Then choose Format⇨Field, Alignment, Font, Border, or Shading. The Format dialog box appears, as shown in Figure 6-9.

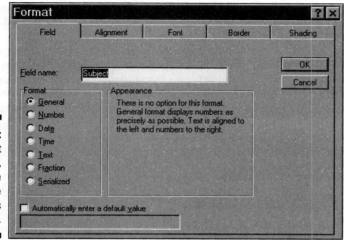

Following is the executive summary of what you can accomplish in each card of the Format dialog box:

✔ **The Field card** enables you to specify the same formatting that you specified when you first created the field, telling Works to display the value as, for example, a date, a fraction, or a dollar amount. (For a discussion of field formats, see the section, "Creating New Database Fields," earlier in this chapter.) Changes to Field formats affect all views.

If you change a field from General or Text to a Date or Time format, you may need to reenter the data in that field.

✔ **The Alignment card** enables you to click Left, Right, or Center respectively to left-justify, right-justify, or center text in its field. Choosing General aligns text to the left and numbers to the right. If you're using List view, you can choose to make text wrap within a cell in List view by clicking the Wrap Text check box. If, in List view, your rows are higher than a single character height, you can also align text vertically. To do so, click Top, Center, or Bottom.

✔ **The Font card** works just as it does elsewhere in Works. See Chapter 1 for more information.

✔ **The Border card** enables you to put an outline around a field or data for emphasis. Click a line style from the list of style boxes on the card. Click the top line-style box (containing no line) to turn off a border.

✔ **The Shading card** enables you to apply a background color or pattern. Choose a pattern from the Pattern selection box; patterns are made up of two colors, taken from your selection of foreground and background colors. Unless you have a color printer or don't intend to print at all, sticking to Auto for both colors is best.

If you print from Form view, as you may for address labels, you probably don't want a big gap between the city and the state. As you design the form, however, you must use a City field wide enough for, say, "Lake Memphremagog," which pushes your State field way over to the right. If the name of a city in a given record is short, such as Big Sky, Montana, a lot of open space appears before Montana as you print. (As it does in real life, come to think of it.) Works provides a trick to get rid of this excess space during printing. Using Form Design view, click either the field name or data area of the field on the right (the State field, for example). Choose Format➪Alignment. Choose the Alignment card and then click the Slide to Left check box. Use print preview to check the result.

Printing Your Database

How and what you print depends what you need. To print address labels, you may want to print out your entire address database in Form view or only certain addresses that you select by *filtering*. To print a sales invoice, you probably want to print only the record that's currently on-screen, in Form view. To print an inventory report, you generally print from Report view. The basic procedure for printing databases is pretty much the same as the procedure for printing anything else in Works, so for procedural details, see Chapter 1. Following, however, are a few peculiarities about printing databases:

✔ To print only certain groups of records, you first need to hide the other records. Works hides records that you filter out or that you specifically select for hiding. See Chapter 7 for details on hiding and filtering. To print only the record you're currently viewing in Form view, choose File➪Print; then, in the Print dialog box, click Current Record Only.

✔ If you print in Form view, you normally print one record on a page. To print multiple records on a page, as you may do for mailing labels, choose File➪Page Setup, choose the Other Options card in the Page Setup dialog box, and then click to clear the Page Breaks Between Records check box. Adjust the spacing between records by clicking the up- or down-arrows in the Space Between Records box.

✔ Printing from List view normally prints data only — no headings and no gridlines. To change this situation, choose File➪Page Setup to open a Page Setup dialog box. Choose the Other Options card in this box. Click the appropriate check box: Print Gridlines and/or Print Record and Field Labels.

✔ To force a page break prior to a particular row or column in the List view, click the column or row header (the cell that's gray) and then choose Format➪Insert Page Break.

Chapter 7

Getting Answers from Your Database

● ●

In This Chapter

▶ Finding data

▶ Hiding and showing records

▶ Creating, applying, and deleting a filter

▶ Using multiple criteria

▶ Using math in filtering

▶ Sorting data

▶ Creating standard reports

▶ Viewing your report

▶ Improving the appearance of your report

▶ Reporting on selected records

▶ Doing calculations on your database

● ●

*A*s Chapter 6 notes, the real value in a database is not that it enables you to amass an army of data on your computer or print out rank upon rank of uniformly typed and regimented data. The real value is that a database helps you interrogate your data: to find, display, print, and compute meaningful answers from legions of data.

Finding, filtering, sorting, and *reporting* are the biggest features for getting results in Works. You can also perform *calculations* based on the contents of records. In this chapter, you discover how to put these features to work.

Finding Specific Records

To locate records that contain a specific word, phrase, or number, the simplest thing you can do is to use the *Find* command. You can tell Works to find either the *first* example of that word, phrase, or number, or to show you *all* examples. Here's how to do it:

1. **Press Ctrl+Home.**

   This action takes you to the top of the document so that Works begins its search with the first record of the database.

2. **Choose Edit⇨Find from the menu bar (or press Ctrl+F).**

   A small but helpful Find dialog box appears.

3. **Type the word, number, or phrase for which you're searching in the Find What text box.**

   You must specify lowercase or uppercase letters. Searching for *Copy Paper* doesn't find records containing *copy paper.*

   Type only as much as you remember or need. To find copy paper, printer paper, or any kind of paper, type **paper**. The symbol **?** can substitute for a single character and help you find a broad range of records. If searching for Zip codes, for example, typing **0792?** finds all the Zip codes beginning with 0792. The symbol * can substitute for one or more characters as long as you precede the * by at least one other character. Typing **M*.**, for example, finds *Mr.*, *Mrs.*, and *Ms.* (but not Miss — because this particular search specifies that a period must come at the end).

4. **To find only the next matching record, choose Next Record in the Match area of the Find dialog box. To find all matching records (and hide the other records) choose All Records.**

5. **Click OK.**

   In Form view, Works displays the next record it can find that matches what you're searching for. In List view, Works moves the rectangular "active cell" highlight to the next matching record and field.

   Note: If you choose to find All Records in Step 4, Works hides the records that don't match your search text! (See the following section for details on showing and hiding records.) To unhide (or show) those records again, choose Record⇨Show⇨1 All Records.

Using Selected Records: Marking, Showing, and Hiding

Often you ask Works to display or make use of only certain records: to print mailing labels for one Zip code only, for example, or show all the employees you hired this month. To accomplish your command, Works *shows* certain data and *hides* the other data. Works "automagically" hides data if you ask it to "find all records" that match certain criteria, or to *filter* your data (which I describe in a minute). In addition, you can manually specify which records Works hides and which ones it shows.

The following list describes the operations involved in showing and hiding data, whether Works does the job automatically or you do it manually:

- ✔ **Hiding** is a way to make records invisible in List or Form view or to omit them from printouts or reports.
- ✔ **Showing** is the opposite of hiding. Works initially shows all records.
- ✔ **Marking** is a convenient way to identify a group of records for manual hiding or showing.

To hide an individual record, either click the record in List view or display it in Form view; then choose Record⇨Hide Record from the menu bar.

To show or hide a specific group of records, mark them first: In List view, click the check box in the leftmost column (the *marking column*) of each row that you want to hide. To mark a group that's all together, click and drag down the marking column. (In Form view, choose Record⇨Mark Record for each record.)

Then, to show the marked records (and hide the rest), choose Record⇨Show⇨2 Marked Records. To hide the marked records instead, choose Record⇨Show⇨3 Unmarked Records from the menu bar.

To reverse the logic and make the currently hidden records the shown ones, choose Record⇨Show⇨4 Hidden Records.

To undo all this hiding stuff and show all records, choose Record⇨Show⇨1 All Records from the menu bar.

To clear all your marks, go to List view and click the check mark at the very top of the marking column.

Filtering Your Data

Sometimes the Find command isn't enough. You may need Works to look for a certain range of values or for combinations of data in multiple fields. To print address labels for a letter targeting potential big donors to your organization, for example, you may want to select people in your donor database who either contributed $100 or more in the past *or* who live in a wealthy community. The Find command can find only records containing one specific hunk o' text or a specific number.

To find records based on more complex criteria, you need to *filter* your data. When Works filters your data, it goes through your database, record by record, comparing what's in those records to certain criteria that you give it and hiding those records that don't meet the criteria.

The gadget that you use for applying a filter is the Filter dialog box, as shown in Figure 7-1. To access one of these little gems, perform either of the following actions:

> ✔ Choose Tools⇨Filters from the menu bar.

> ✔ Click the Filters button on the toolbar.

The first time you create a filter, Works displays a First-time Help dialog box. See Chapter 1 for notes on such help boxes. Click OK to proceed.

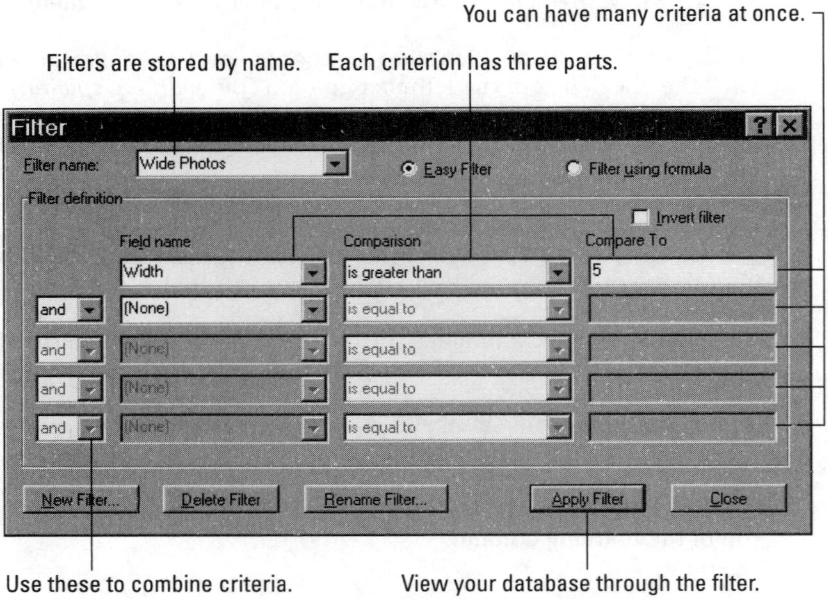

You can have many criteria at once.

Filters are stored by name.   Each criterion has three parts.

Figure 7-1:
Use this
dialog box
to tell
Works your
criteria for
picking out
certain
records.

Use these to combine criteria.   View your database through the filter.

If your database currently has no filters, a Filter Name dialog box appears; enter a descriptive name no longer than 15 characters, such as **Big Contributor**. If your database currently has filters, you can choose a filter to edit by clicking Filter Name in the Filter dialog box. To create a new, additional filter, click the New Filter button.

To construct the description of what records you want, you must enter three pieces of information into the following text boxes of the Filter dialog box:

> ✔ **Field Name:** Click to choose the name of the field where you want Works to look. Choose the *No. of Children* field, for example, if you have such a field and want to find families based on the number of children they have.

✔ **Comparison:** Click to choose the way you want Works to test the data in the field. You may, for example, test that the data in the No. of Children field is greater than some value. For purposes of comparison, later dates and times are "greater than" earlier ones. Letters that fall later in the alphabet are "greater than" earlier ones.

✔ **Compare To:** Type whatever value (text or a number) that you want Works to compare the data to — such as **2** for two kids. In filters (unlike in finds), Works doesn't take note of capitalization. The words *Potato* and *potato* are identical to Works. You can use the **?** and ***** characters just as you do in a Find command, if you want. See the section "Finding Specific Records," earlier in this chapter, for more information on using these characters.

The following list offers some examples of the records for which you may filter in different databases. (The terms you'd choose in the Filter dialog box are in italics.)

✔ In a Families database, you may want those records in which the *No. of Children* field *is equal to 2.*

✔ In a Members database, you may want those records in which a *Town* field *is not Mudville.*

✔ In a mailing list, you may want those records in which an *Age* field *is greater than or equal to 21.*

Press the Enter key or click the Apply Filter button to execute the filtering. For the clearest view of your results, use List view (press Shift+F9).

You're done! In List view, Works shows you only those records that meet your criterion. The other records are hidden. After you finish looking over your success, choose Record⇨Show⇨1 All Records to make the other records reappear.

Applying, changing, and deleting filters

Creating a filter takes a bit of work; so, for your future convenience, Works saves your filter, under the name that you give it, as part of your database file.

Because Works saves filters, you can fool around with them until they're correct, and you can easily switch from one to the other, applying them to your database whenever you need them. The idea is that you're likely to want a few standard filters that you apply to your database regularly. One Works quirk, however, is that you can't have more than eight saved filters.

To apply the filter you used most recently, just press F3. To apply any other filter to your database, choose Record⇨Apply Filter and then choose a filter from the Filter drop-down list. List view (press Shift+F9) now shows you all the records that match your filter criteria. To restore all the hidden records, choose Record⇨Show⇨1 All Records.

To change or delete a filter, choose Tools⇨Filters (or click the Filters button on the toolbar). After the Filter dialog box appears, click the Filter Name box, and choose the filter on which you want to work. Then you can perform any of the following actions:

✔ To edit an existing filter, choose new criteria. (See the preceding section, "Filtering Your Data," for information.)

✔ To change the name of the filter, click the Rename Filter button. Enter a new name in the Filter Name dialog box that appears and click OK.

✔ To delete a filter, click the Delete Filter button. Click the Yes button in the warning dialog box that appears to make sure that you want to delete this filter. (If the Filter Name dialog box appears now, click its Cancel button.)

Click the Close button of the Filter dialog box after you finish changing or deleting a filter.

Using more than one criterion

You can have Works use up to five criteria at one time in a filter, which is why the Filter dialog box contains five rows. This five-criteria feature enables you to narrow down or expand your search.

If, for example, you want only the families in your database that have more than two kids and that also live out of town, you create one row for the kids criterion and a second row for the Town field. You specify that the town Works selects should not equal your town of Mudville. Figure 7-2 shows such a two-part filter, using a different example.

To use more than one criterion, just select and fill in the first one as usual. Choose either and or or from the drop-down list box that begins the next line; then select and fill in the second criterion in a similar fashion. Do the same for any other criteria that you need.

For the example shown in Figure 7-2, you need to tell Works that it must meet both of the following criteria on each record that it finds:

The photograph Width is greater than or equal to 7 inches.
AND
The photograph Height is less than or equal to 5 inches.

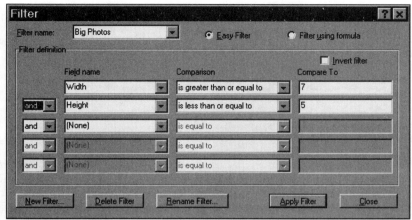

Figure 7-2:
Using two
criteria for
a query.

So you click the and selection from the drop-down list on the second line.

You use the or selection to specify that a record can meet either criterion. If you change and to or in Figure 7-2, the search results include photographs that are less than or equal to five inches high (but can be any width) as well as photographs that are at least seven inches wide (but any height).

You can also have multiple criteria lines using the same field, one on each line — for example, width is greater than or equal to 7 on the first line and width is less than or equal to 14 on the second line. This search finds all photos with a width between 7 and 14 inches.

If you set your logic up incorrectly and end up filtering *out* things that you want to filter *in,* click the Invert Filter check box in the Filter dialog box. This method is also a good way to look at the filtered-out crowd and make sure that the filter is working correctly.

Trickier filtering using formulas

Sometimes you need to filter on something that just isn't in your database. My Photographs database, for example, has a *width* and a *height,* and I can create a filter for a certain range of those dimensions. But if I want a photograph that fits a certain ratio of height to width, I can't make a filter using straightforward criteria. No field for *ratio* is available.

One solution to this sort of problem is to use formulas that use field names, mathematical expressions, and Works functions to describe the filter that you want. If I want to filter for all photographs where the height is 80 percent or less of the width, for example, I enter the criterion shown in Figure 7-3.

Figure 7-3:
By using a
field name
and some
math, I can
filter for
height-to-
width ratio.

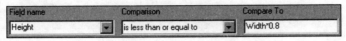

Note: Works functions for databases are the same as for spreadsheets. For a complete listing of functions by type, choose Help⇨Index from the menu bar, and type **functions:** (note the colon). Click any folder that begins with *Functions:*.

Sorting

Sorting is useful for grouping similar records together for your viewing or printing convenience. Are you printing mailing labels from an address database? You may want to sort by Zip code to make bulk mailing easier. Do you want to sort your inventory records alphabetically by location or numerically by dollar value? Either way; the choice is yours.

The database sorting process is very similar to the spreadsheet sorting process. For background information on sorting, see Chapter 4.

Works enables you to sort by up to three fields. This capability, in turn, enables you to sort your records into categories (say, by the Zip code field), subcategories (say, by street name within each Zip code), and sub-subcategories (say, the last names of people living on the street).

List view gives you the clearest picture of your results, so if you're currently in Form view, I suggest that you switch to List view (by pressing Shift+F9). Now, here's how to sort:

1. **Choose Record⇨Sort Records from the menu bar.**

   The Sort Records dialog box jumps gaily into your lap (so to speak), as shown in Figure 7-4. (The first time you sort, Works displays a First-time Help dialog box, as I describe in Chapter 1. Click OK to continue.)

2. **Click the Sort By drop-down box to choose the principal field to sort by.**

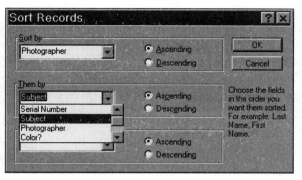

Figure 7-4:
Choosing
what fields
to sort by in
the Sort
Records
dialog box.

3. **Choose a sorting direction for that field by clicking the appropriate radio button.**

   Ascending is the order A, B, C or 1, 2, 3. *Descending* is the opposite.

4. **Optionally, perform the same actions for a second field (your subcategory) and a third field (sub-subcategory).**

   If your principal field is, say, Zip code, the Then By field enables you to sort the identically Zip-coded records in, perhaps, alphabetical order by street name. If you don't fill out this information, the records don't sort in any particular order within each Zip code. Similarly, the final Then By field provides sorting among any duplicate entries in the second field (for example, several people on the same street).

5. **Click OK.**

If you're in List view, you now see your database with its records shuffled around in the order you specified. Records don't keep their original record numbers (the number at the far left of each row in List view) after you sort them, which is one reason that having a serial-number field is important (as I mention in Chapter 6). The serial number field enables you to reconstruct the original order by sorting by that field.

Figure 7-5 shows the result of sorting a database by photographer's name and then subject.

Reporting

The Works report feature provides nifty summaries of the data in your database. I need to make sure that you know what I'm talking about when I say *report,* however, because it's a vague term.

Figure 7-5:
Sorting
groups of
records
with
identical
data.

☑		Serial	Subject	Photographer	Color?	Width	Height
▣	1	00004	Curly dock leaves	Adams, Alicia	TRUE	5	7
▣	2	00003	Jerusalem artichoke	Adams, Alicia	TRUE	2 1/2	5
▣	3	00007	Red sails in the sunset	Adams, Alicia	TRUE	10	8
▣	4	00008	Earthworms	Allworthy, Fred	FALSE	7	5
▣	5	00002	Black bear cub	Ferguson, Al	TRUE	2 1/4	2 1/4
▣	6	00005	Laser light, abstract	Hogg, Charley	TRUE	10	8
▣	7	00006	Wachusett sunset	Hogg, Charley	TRUE	10	8
▣	8	00001	Golden eagle	Johnson, George	TRUE	5 1/2	3 1/4

Works sorted on this field . . .

. . . then on this field

A Works report is something for you to print, not view on your PC screen (although you can see it in Print Preview). A Works report shows the following two kinds of information:

✔ A list of records very much like that of the List view, typically sorted into categories.

✔ A summary based on your records.

A mail room, for example, may have a database consisting of the packages that it's shipped, the date of shipping, the destination Zip codes, the package weights, the shipper, and the cost of shipping.

From this shipping database, management may want reports on how cost-effective various shippers are; how much product is being shipped by weight every month; how much is shipping to each Zip code; the average weight shipped; and other typical, nosy management requests. All these reports require either a summary of some sort, or a list, or both.

What's a standard report?

To make creating a report easier for you, Microsoft's *ReportCreator* steps you through the creation process. The result of using ReportCreator is what I call a *standard report*. You could make a custom report by using Report view, but the process is too complicated for many users.

A standard report from the shipping department's database may show all the packages sent, together with a summary of total weight and total cost. Such a standard report may look something like the example shown in Figure 7-6.

The report in Figure 7-6 contains lists of shipments grouped by shipper, with total weight and average weight shipped for each group and total and average weight at the bottom. Not bad for a little database program!

```
                                    shipping.wdb - Wt. by Shipper

     Shipper   Weight

     CityZIP     0.73
     CityZIP     0.94
     CityZIP     0.21
     CityZIP     0.67
     CityZIP     0.75
     CityZIP     0.95
     CityZIP     0.18
     CityZIP     0.82
     GROUP TOTAL Weight:              5.26
     AVERAGE Weight:                  0.66

     DinEx       0.80
     DinEx       0.44
     DinEx       0.63
     GROUP TOTAL Weight:              1.86
     AVERAGE Weight:                  0.62

     Hercules    0.05
     Hercules    0.03
     Hercules    0.37

      ---- ( I cut out some stuff here )----

     PSU         0.04
     PSU         0.76
     PSU         0.60
     GROUP TOTAL Weight:              1.40
     AVERAGE Weight:                  0.47

     Rural Xpres 0.87
     Rural Xpres 0.58
     Rural Xpres 0.08
     GROUP TOTAL Weight:              1.53
     AVERAGE Weight:                  0.51

     Zowiefast   0.98
     Zowiefast   0.80
     Zowiefast   0.96
     Zowiefast   0.76
     Zowiefast   0.86
     GROUP TOTAL Weight:              4.36
     AVERAGE Weight:                  0.87

     TOTAL Weight:           14.98
     AVERAGE Weight:          0.58
```

Figure 7-6:
One of the
standard
reports that
Works can
make. (I
chopped
out the
middle so
that the
report fits
on this
page.)

Creating a standard report

Works makes creating a standard report fairly simple, but you must play
your cards right! The ReportCreator dialog box deals you six different cards
that you need to fill out.

You may not need to create a report at all if you make your database by using a Works TaskWizard. Such databases include very nice, formatted reports for special purposes such as business inventory or accounts payable. If you create your database by using a TaskWizard, you need only to choose the report you want by choosing View⇨Report from the menu bar.

To begin your quest for a standard report, awaken the mighty ReportCreator from its slumber by choosing Tools⇨ReportCreator from the menu bar.

A tiny Report Name dialog box requests that you name your report. Use 15 characters or fewer. This name doesn't appear on your report; it just identifies your report so that you can use it again.

Then the ReportCreator dialog box swings into action and displays six cards, as shown in Figure 7-7.

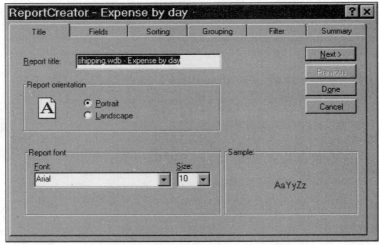

Figure 7-7:
The Report Creator Title card. Fill out all six cards, and you win a report!

You don't need to take the six cards in strict left-to-right order, but Works presents them to you in that order if you use the Next button in the ReportCreator dialog box. To work on a different card at any time, just click that card's tab.

First card: Title, orientation, and font

The top card the ReportCreator shows you is the Title card. The title is what appears on the top of your report. Works suggests a title for you that it makes up from the database filename and the name that you give the report, but you can probably come up with a better one. Works also suggests that you create the report in portrait orientation (taller than it is wide) and the 10-point Arial font; but Works also enables you to change these selections. To fill out this card, follow these steps:

1. **Click the Report Title text box and enter a title (such as** Shipping Costs**) if you don't like the suggestion Works gives you.**

2. **Choose Landscape orientation, if you're making a w – i – d – e report — that is, a report with a lot of fields in it; choose Portrait orientation if your report is tall.**

   The number of fields in your report depends on how wide your fields are.

3. **Choose a Font and Size from the drop-down lists in the Report font area.**

After you finish, click the Next button or the tab for the Fields card.

Second card: Choose your fields

The second card the ReportCreator deals you is the Fields card, as shown in Figure 7-8. Here you choose which of the fields in your database you want to appear in your report and in what order. (In the report, fields appear in columns, going left-to-right in the order that you specify here.) You can also specify whether you want field names as headings for those field columns.

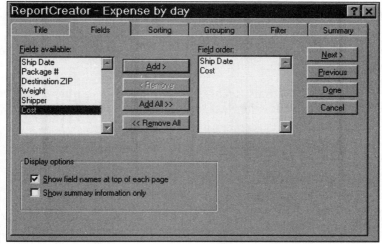

Figure 7-8:
Copy field names from the left box to the right box.

Follow these steps to choose the fields that you want to appear in your report, along with their order:

1. **Click a field name in the Fields Available list box.**

   The list in the Fields Available box is a list of the fields in your database. The basic procedure in this dialog box is to copy field names from the left-hand box to the right-hand box.

2. **Click Add to copy that field to the Field Order list box.**

   The right-hand box is where you accumulate a list of the fields that you want to appear in the report.

   (Every time you add a field, the highlight in the left-hand box moves down, for your pleasure and convenience. So to copy a consecutive series of field names, you can just keep clicking the Add button.)

3. **Repeat Steps 1 and 2 for each field that you want in the report.**

   If you want them all, click the Add All button.

   If you change your mind about a field, click that field's name in the Field Order list box and then click the Remove button that is now available. To remove all the fields from the right-hand box and start again, click the Remove All button.

4. **If you don't want the field names to appear at the top of your page, click the Show Summary Information Only check box.**

   Normally, you want them. Figure 7-6, for example, has 'em.

After you finish, click the Next button or the tab for the Sorting card.

Third card: All sorts of stuff!

This card may look familiar to you if you've already done sorting in the Works database or spreadsheet tool. *Sorting* is the ordering of records alphabetically, numerically, or by date or time.

For sorting instructions, see the section "Sorting," earlier in this chapter. After you finish, click the Next button or the tab for the Grouping card.

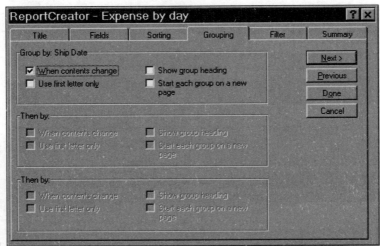

Figure 7-9:
Choosing
to group
by one
field only.

Fourth card: Groupings

Whenever you sort any kind of data, similar items inherently wind up grouped together. All the Zimmers in the telephone book, for example, end up grouped together because the phone book sorts entries by last name. Similarly, sorted databases inherently group records. So why the heck does Works now ask about grouping?

Grouping in Works simply puts *breaks* (space) between the natural groupings that occur during sorting. Works needs breaks if you want headings above each group ("Zimmer" above the Zimmer group, for example), if you want a separate page for each group, or if you want to create a statistical summary of some kind for the group (say, total package weight for each Zip code).

The following list gives you the scoop on grouping:

- ✔ You don't need to group at all. If you want one long list of sorted records with a summary at the end, just click the Next button.

- ✔ To create a group, click to place a check mark in the When Contents Change check box. The other check boxes then come alive.

- ✔ You can group by only those fields that you select to appear on this report (on the Fields card) and choose for sorting (on the Sorting card). If I want to group on, say, the Cost field, I must go back to the Sorting card and add that field. Each field you select for sorting appears on the Grouping card.

- ✔ You can have groups, subgroups, and sub-subgroups — that's why three identical areas appear on this card. If, on the Sort card for example, I sort shipments by date and "Then By" shipper and "Then By" Zip code, the group is all the shipments on that date. Within that date group are the weight totals for each shipper that I used on that date. Within each shipper group are that shipper's shipments, grouped by Zip code.

- ✔ You can create groupings based strictly on the first character of a data entry. If you have a list of last names, for example, you probably don't want to group by each name (because many groups would end up only one name long) but by initial letter: all the As together, the Bs together, and so on. To accomplish this type of grouping, click the Use First Letter Only check box.

- ✔ You can use a heading to identify each group. If you're grouping by Zip code, for example, you can head each group with its Zip code. Heading each group with its Zip code is somewhat redundant, however, because the Zip code appears in every line of that group anyway, making what group it is rather obvious. Nonetheless, if you like this sort of thing, click the Show Group Heading check box.

Works' ReportCreator doesn't handle dates as group headings correctly. The ReportCreator doesn't format them correctly, so the dates appear as numbers (the number of days since January 1, 1900)!

> ✔ For some reports, you may want to print each group on a separate
> page. In a national sales database, for example, you may need to send a
> separate page to each region's sales office. To accomplish this task,
> click the Start Each Group on a New Page check box.

After you finish, click the Next button or the tab for the Filter card.

Fifth card: Filters

Filters enable you to separate the sheep from the goats, so to speak (or the
wheat from the chaff, if you're a vegetarian). The filters that you can use
here are exactly the same as the ones I discuss in the section "Filtering Your
Data," earlier in this chapter.

The executive summary on filters is that filters enable you to selectively
hide certain records from your report. Packages that you ship by the U.S.
postal service, for example, may not belong in this report, so you can create
a filter that says (in filter-ese) *Shipper is not equal to U.S. Postal Service.*

To create a filter, click the Create New Filter button and see the section
"Filtering Your Data," earlier in this chapter for further instruction. After you
create a filter, the filter appears in the Select a Filter text box. You can
modify that filter by using the Modify Filter button, if you need to.

If you haven't created any filters, the ReportCreator gives you two filtering
options in the Select a Filter text box anyway. Choose one of the following:

> ✔ **Current Records** means that you want to include in your report only
> the records that are currently *shown* (not *hidden*) in your database. (To
> include or exclude certain records, see the section "Using Selected
> Records: Marking, Showing and Hiding," earlier in this chapter.)
>
> ✔ **All Records** means just that: Include all the records in the database.

Be brave; you're almost done. Click the Next button or click the Summary
tab of the ReportCreator to wrap up your report with a few summaries.

Sixth card: Statistical summaries

At this point, you're gazing (glassy-eyed) at the Summary dialog box of
Figure 7-10.

Statistical summaries are useful things. Statistical summaries give you the
answers to such questions as, "What are the total sales for January in the
Eastern region?" or "What is the batting average for each team?" or "Why are
my eyes glazing over?"

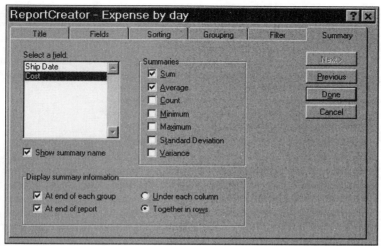

Figure 7-10:
Time to
sum up,
counselor!

Summaries are optional. If you don't specify any summaries and you just click the Done button in the ReportCreator, you get a report that simply lists all the records currently shown (not hidden) in your database, displaying the fields that you chose on the Fields card — sorted and grouped, if you chose those features.

If you want statistics (including sums) on a certain field or fields, here's what to do:

1. **Click the field name in the Select a Field list box.**

2. **Choose the kind of statistical summary (or summaries) that you want for that field by clicking the appropriate check box(es).**

   Click any check box in the Summaries area to select a particular kind of summary. Heck, click a batch of 'em if you want several different kinds of summaries. *Average* computes the average of all the numbers in the field, *Minimum* shows you the smallest (or most negative) value, and so on.

3. **Repeat Steps 1 and 2 for each field that you want to summarize.**

   Each field can have its own set of summaries.

   You must work very carefully in this card, because you can't easily change summaries after you click the Done button. Be careful that you don't sum if you want to count. Sum adds up the numerical value of all the records in the selected field. Count just counts the records in a field. And don't accidentally sum up the wrong field (such as the date field)!

4. **Click the Show Summary Name check box.**

   This option makes Works label the summary as a sum, as an average, or as whatever you choose.

5. Choose where you want your summaries to appear in the report by clicking the appropriate check box(s) in the Display Summary Information area.

If you create groups on the Grouping card, you can have a summary appear under each group by clicking the At End of Each Group check box.

Click Under Each Column to put your field summaries at the bottom of their respective columns.

Click Together in Rows to put each of your field summaries in a separate row at the bottom of the report (or at the bottom of each group, if you chose that option).

6. Click the Done button.

Things whiz around on your screen, ultimately delivering . . .

. . . a big, confusing mess and then one of those little boxes with the exclamation point in it! What the heck?!? This result isn't what you had in mind! Where's that nice report??

Hang in there. Read the little dialog box, which is assuring you that The report definition has been created and asking whether you want to preview the report or modify it. I suggest that you choose Preview. Choosing Modify doesn't gain you much — it just leaves you gazing at the big confusing mess (called the Report view).

Click the Preview button, and Works shows you your report in Print Preview mode. Remember that the main purpose of a report is to make a nice report to print out — not to view on-screen. The following sections helps you to figure out exactly what's going on here.

Laying your cards on the table: Viewing your report

If you've filled out the various cards of the ReportCreator, as I describe in the preceding sections, you're probably now viewing your report in Print Preview. For details on how Print Preview works, see Chapter 1. Click the Cancel button after you finish viewing your report.

After you leave Print Preview, what's on-screen at this point isn't your actual report. Instead, what's on-screen is the Report view — a view most people find nearly incomprehensible and that's not necessary for most work. This view displays the rather intimidating report definition that tells Works how to construct your report. Don't be too upset — if not for that nice ReportCreator dialog box, you'd need to enter all that intimidating stuff by hand.

You probably want to get out of Report view and go back to a List or Form view. To do so, just choose View⇨List or View⇨Form from the menu bar.

After you finish defining a report in the ReportCreator, your named report exists as part of your Works database document. As you can with filters, you can access this report at any time, and the report takes into account any new or changed data in your database. Also, as with filters, you can have only eight reports; any more, and you must delete one by choosing Tools➪Delete Report and double-clicking the report name in the dialog box that appears.

You can reuse a report over and over as you add data. Just choose View➪Report. Double-click the report name in the dialog box that appears.

Modifying your report

Works makes modifying your report easy — within limits. You can easily modify the sorting, grouping, and filtering, although certain options that were available at the time you created the report are no longer available. You can't very easily change what fields or summaries your report displays. The following list gives you the scoop on how to modify report settings:

- ✓ **Sorting:** Choose Tools➪Report Sorting.
- ✓ **Grouping:** Choose Tools➪Report Grouping.
- ✓ **Filtering:** Choose Tools➪Report Filter.

All these menu choices open a Report Settings dialog box, where the cards look exactly like the cards in the ReportCreator, except that only these three functions (instead of six) are available. Refer back to the discussions of sorting, grouping, and filtering in the preceding sections for instructions. Options that are no longer available appear grayed out in the dialog box. If you need an option that's grayed out, sometimes the easiest solution is to construct a completely new report using the ReportCreator.

Modifying your report by using Report view

To change your report any way other than by using the Tools menu, you need to use the Report view. Report view, frankly, is messy to deal with — too messy to cover in this book. The modifications and enhancements that you can make in Report view (including adding fields to the report; performing more sophisticated calculations; and formatting report text, borders, and other features) are invaluable to a some users, but most Works users can live without them. If you need a fancier report, consider creating your database by using one of the TaskWizards instead, such as Accounts or Business Inventory in the Business TaskWizard folder. (See Chapter 1 for information about TaskWizards.)

If you need to enhance your Works report, you can find instructions for basic report enhancements in *Microsoft Works 4.5 For Dummies* by yours truly, David Kay, (IDG Books Worldwide, Inc.). The book is available at fine bookstores near you and through www.dummies.com on the Web!

Chapter 8

Word Processing in Works

● ●

In This Chapter

▶ Things that work the same in Word as in Works

▶ Using Easy Formats

▶ Creating Easy Formats

▶ Using headers, footers, and page numbers

▶ Creating and printing envelopes

● ●

*M*icrosoft Works is for people who want a little bit of everything. Microsoft Works *Suite* is for people who would like a little bit more. One of the first things that people want more of is word-processing power, so the Suite user ends up with two — count 'em, two — word processors: the one in Works plus Microsoft Word 97. Which one should you use? Or should you use both?

Works' word processor has certain advantages over Word: It comes with nice, automatic TaskWizards; it's simpler; it's similar to other Works tools (and, therefore, more easy for a Works user to pick up); and it plays well with the other Works tools if a task calls for cooperation, such as creating form letters from an address database or inserting spreadsheets or charts into a word-processor document.

Most people still prefer Word, however. Word offers more features; comes with nice, automatic templates; plays reasonably well with Works' other applications; and isn't all *that* much harder to pick up than Works' word processor. Moreover, Microsoft has made Word into one of the business world's most widely used word processors. For the ultimate in compatibility with that world, you want to use Word.

Given that preference, I'm going to short-change Works' word processor in this book. Fortunately, the two word processors use nearly identical commands and techniques for basic word processing. So, if you prefer to use

Works' word processor, you find the basic word processing instructions in Part II, "Putting Words in Word." Instructions that apply to users of Works' word processor I mark there with a special "Works for Me!" icon. Works does have certain unique word-processing features, however, which I cover in this chapter.

What Works the Same In Word?

What Works instructions can you get from the Word chapters of this book? Check out the features that I describe in the following list:

- ✔ Typing and deleting
- ✔ Paragraph marks and other invisible characters
- ✔ Fonts and other basic text formatting
- ✔ Tabs, bullets, indents, and other paragraph formatting
- ✔ Finding text
- ✔ Margins and other basic page setup

Turn to Chapters 11 through 14 for instructions on these subjects. For features that are unique to Works, read the following sections of this chapter.

The Word-Processing Window and Toolbar

See Chapter 1 for different ways to start using the word-processor tool in Works. Figure 8-1 shows you what's what in your word-processing window.

You're looking at one of two possible views of your document in Figure 8-1; this view is called *Normal view,* and the other view is called *Page Layout view.* Page Layout view shows you page margins and gives a somewhat more accurate picture of what your document really looks like.

Figure 8-2 shows you what the various buttons do on the toolbar of Works' word processor tool. Many of them will be familiar to you from the other tools of Works, such as the spreadsheet tool.

Menu bar

Word-processing toolbar

Document window title bar

Ruler bar

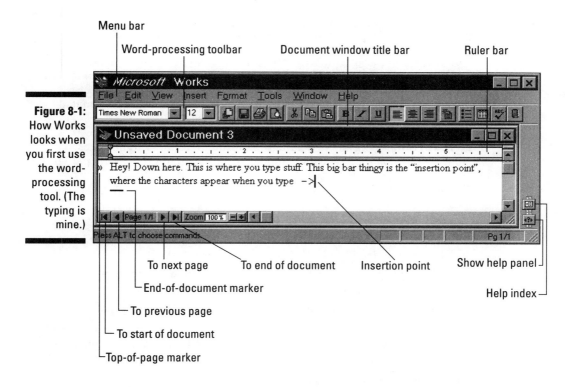

Figure 8-1:
How Works
looks when
you first use
the word-
processing
tool. (The
typing is
mine.)

To next page   To end of document   Insertion point   Show help panel

End-of-document marker   Help index

To previous page

To start of document

Top-of-page marker

Figure 8-2:
Where tools
hang out
whenever
they're off
duty: the
toolbar.
(Its motto:
"Where
nobody
knows your
name.")

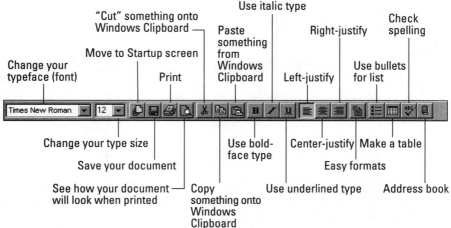

"Cut" something onto
Windows Clipboard

Move to Startup screen

Print

Change your
typeface (font)

Use italic type

Paste
something
from
Windows
Clipboard

Right-justify

Left-justify

Check
spelling

Use bullets
for list

Change your type size

Save your document

See how your document
will look when printed

Copy
something onto
Windows
Clipboard

Use bold-
face type

Use underlined type

Center-justify Make a table

Easy formats

Address book

Having It Their Way: Easy Formats

If your taste in paragraph formatting is at all like the taste of most other humans on the planet, you're in luck. (Actually, you're in luck even if your taste is pretty weird, as long as it matches the taste of somebody at Microsoft.) Works has a couple dozen real pretty, off-the-shelf formats, called *Easy Formats,* from which you can choose.

An Easy Format consists of a paragraph format — and, in some cases, a character format as well, which applies to all the characters in the paragraph.

To use an Easy Format, follow these steps:

1. **Select (highlight) the paragraphs that you want to format.**

   If you don't select anything, Works assumes that you want to format the paragraph in which the insertion point is sitting.

2. **Choose Format⇨Easy Formats from the menu bar to open the Easy Formats dialog box, as shown in Figure 8-3.**

3. **Click any format name in the list at the left side of the box.**

   Check out the Sample box to see whether your selection makes the text look how you want. If your selection doesn't suit you, click another format name.

4. **Click the Apply button.**

   The Easy Formats dialog box goes away, and your reformatted paragraphs await you.

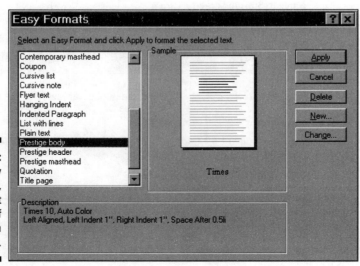

Figure 8-3:
Easy
Formats,
the fast
food of
paragraph
formatting.

Having It Your Way: Creating Your Own Easy Formats

If you find yourself using the same combination of character and paragraph formatting again and again (and the combination isn't already an Easy Format), you can put it on the Easy Format list. All you need to do is follow these steps:

1. **Select a paragraph that's already formatted the way that you want.**
2. **Click the Easy Formats button on the toolbar.**

   A drop-down menu appears.
3. **Choose Create From Selection from the drop-down menu to open the New Easy Format dialog box.**
4. **Name your format by typing in the box with the blinking cursor.**
5. **Click the Done button.**

Now your newly named format can appear on the Easy Formats menu. (See the preceding section, "Having It Their Way: Easy Formats.")

Headers, Footers, and Page Numbers

Headers and *footers* are chunks of text that appear on every page of a document within the top page margin (for headers) or the bottom page margin (for footers). You typically use headers and footers for chapter or section titles, but in Works you also use them for page numbers. They may also include an always-current date and time or the document's name. To put a header or footer into your document, follow these steps:

1. **Choose View⇨Header (or Footer) from the menu bar.**

   Your document goes into Page Layout view, and the insertion point moves to the header (or footer) box on the current page. (If a First-Time Help dialog box appears first, click its OK button.)
2. **Type in the box the text that you want to appear on each page.**

   Anything that you can put in ordinary text, you can put in a header or footer: bold, italic, giant fonts, alignments, Easy Formats — anything goes.
3. **If you want page numbers, the date or time, or the document name to appear in your header or footer, choose Insert on the menu bar, and make the appropriate selection from the menu that appears.**

4. **If you want to prevent header or footer text from appearing on the first page or to specify the starting page number, choose File⇨Page Setup.**

   The Page Setup dialog box appears. Choose the Other Options card; on that card, you may choose any of three check boxes: No Header on First Page, No Footer on First Page, and Print Footnotes at End. Click the one(s) that you want. To choose what number you want to appear on your first page (as you may if the document were a single chapter of a book), type that number into the Starting Page Number text box. Click OK.

To change your header or footer margin, choose File⇨Page Setup to open the Page Setup dialog box. Click the Margins tab and type a new margin value for your header or footer in the Header margin or Footer margin box. Make sure that the header or footer margin is less than the page margin.

Creating and Printing Envelopes

Works includes a unique envelope tool for either printing a single envelope or, as Chapter 9 discusses, printing a series of envelopes from an address database. (Word can do either task, too, but operates differently.)

If you're addressing an envelope for a letter created in Works, open that letter document and highlight the address text in that letter. Otherwise, start a new word processor document for the envelope.

Choose Tools⇨Envelopes to access Works' envelope tool. The tool has several cards for you to fill out. After you fill out a card, click the Next button to advance to the next card. For a single envelope, choose No Database on the Database card. After you finish, Works attaches the envelope to the top of your current document. You can print it separately from the main document by clicking Envelope in the What To Print area of the Print dialog box.

Chapter 9

Works Wizardry for Popular Tasks

● ●

In This Chapter

▶ Using and creating templates

▶ Starting an address book

▶ Sending your own junk mail

▶ Working with wizard and template documents

● ●

*T*hrough the magic of TaskWizards and templates, Works can create some amazing documents for you very quickly. Without the help of a template or TaskWizard, you'd need to thoroughly study Works to create such delightful documents.

What are TaskWizards and templates? *TaskWizards* are automated programs that first ask you a series of questions by means of dialog boxes. Then, using one of Works' tools — such as the word processor — the TaskWizards create and format a custom document for you (letterhead stationery, for example) by using the name and address information that you supply. You finish that document by inserting or editing text and by adjusting the formatting. *Templates* are prebuilt, general-purpose Works documents (for example, a game schedule for sports teams) from which you can create documents that you customize to your specific needs. Works comes with a bunch of prebuilt templates, or you can create your own.

TaskWizards and templates are available from the Works Task Launcher that appears whenever you start Works or begin a new document (by choosing File⇨New, for example). Chapter 1 explains how to choose TaskWizards and Templates on the TaskWizard card of the Task Launcher.

Because Task Wizards and templates use advanced features and subtle tricks, sometimes they can be a little overwhelming. This chapter provides some instructions and hints to help make things come out right. Works has too many TaskWizards and templates to cover thoroughly in this book, so this chapter provides details on the most popular TaskWizards as well as general hints and tips for other TaskWizards and templates.

Tempting Templates

Templates are a fabulous feature for intelligent people who'd just as soon not do the same thing twice. They're essentially just the bare bones of a certain type of document that you use over and over again.

If you're a consultant, for example, almost all your invoices look the same, except for the details of dates and charges and who you're doing the work for. An invoice template supplies everything but those details, which you fill in. You can then save that invoice document as a file, and the original template remains untouched. (Some computer users simply modify their last invoice to create a new one, using Save As to save it with a new name. But using a template is better because you don't run the risk of accidentally modifying the original.)

Works supplies more than 100 pre-designed templates, complete with nice formatting, for a variety of uses. You can also create your own templates.

Using a pre-designed template

Using a pre-designed template is simply a way to start a new document with most of the work already done. In the Task Launcher (which you access by choosing File⇨New), click the TaskWizards tab. Way down at the bottom of the list of TaskWizard categories, you find the User Defined Templates selection. Click this selection and then double-click the template of your choice; a new document appears.

Your new document is just like any other document, except that it's already partly complete! Make edits and fill in the blanks. (Click at the beginning of a blank to fill it in. Blanks are actually underlined Tab characters, by the way.) After you finish with your changes, you save your new document as you do any other document (by pressing Ctrl+S, for example).

Creating a template

To create a template, begin by creating a document that contains all the text and graphics that don't change (such as your address and logo). Format the document and set up the page layout. If you want the text that that you're going to add later to have a particular format, put in *dummy,* or *placeholder,* text and format that. To later replace the dummy text, select it, type new text, and the new text takes on the same format.

To save the document as a template, follow these steps:

1. **Choose File⇨Save As to open the Save As dialog box.**

2. **Click the Template button at the lower right of the dialog box.**

   A Save As Template dialog box then appears and requests a name for your new template.

3. **Enter a name for the template.**

   If the only type of word-processing, database, spreadsheet, or commu-nications document that you ever use is the one for which you created a template, click the Use This Template For New *whatever* Documents check box (with *whatever* being Word Processing, Database, and so on). This action turns your template into the *default* template. Now, when-ever you start a new document of that type — a word-processing document, for example — your document automatically takes the form of that template. To turn off this feature, open the template by choosing File⇨Open, return to the Save As dialog box by using Steps 1 through 3, and click the check box again.

Works stores your template in the Template folder within the MSWorks folder. If you need to modify the template in any way, choose File⇨Open and open that folder to find the template.

Creating an Address Book

Obviously, Microsoft thinks that you really need an address book. After all, Microsoft put an Address Book button on the toolbar. Because no one wants to disappoint Microsoft, you should probably create an address book. Here are some other good reasons for creating an address book:

✔ You call lots of people often — usually while you're sitting next to your computer.

✔ You have lots of friends and want to keep track of their birthdays and anniversaries.

✔ You're in charge of sending out letters or information to a lot of people on a regular basis.

✔ You want to create your own junk mail: "Dear Mr. ___, I know you and others of the _____ family would love to send us your money."

> ✔ You're a salesperson and need to keep a record of all your prospects and clients. If Ms. Steinway calls, you want to be able to say, "Oh, hi, Barbara. I was just thinking of you. How are, um . . ." (brief pause while you look up her entry in the address book) "George and the kids? Isn't little . . . Sustenuto 12 now?"

Computerized address books make the preceding tasks easier because you can quickly search for people by name, by birthday, by company, or by other criteria. You can also reorganize your address book easily — for example, grouping together all the people who work for the same company.

You may want several address books — one for friends, another for clients, and another for members of the professional organization that you run. You can print out these address books as well as use them on the computer.

Address books are really database documents. Each entry (last name, first name, phone number, and so on) is a *field* in database lingo. For more information on creating, modifying, and using databases, see Chapters 6 and 7 of this book.

Here's how to create an address book by using one of the cool TaskWizards that Works supplies:

1. **Choose File⇨New and then click the TaskWizards tab in the Task Launcher.**

   See Chapter 1 if you need an introduction to the TaskWizards card of the Task Launcher.

2. **In the Common Tasks category of the TaskWizards list, double-click Address Book.**

3. **If a Works Task Launcher dialog box appears, click the button marked Yes to run the TaskWizard.**

   The address book TaskWizard fires up and asks you to choose what type of address book you want.

4. **Click a type of address book that sounds good.**

   If the one you pick now isn't perfect for your needs, you can go back and choose another one later or modify this one.

5. **Click the Next button to see what sort of information goes in this address book.**

   To go back and try another type of address book, click the Back button. To add other types of information to the address book that you choose, hang on until you get to the next screen.

6. **Click the Next button to add fields or to specify *reports* (printout versions of your address book).**

For each type of address book, Works has some standard additional fields that it thinks you may like, such as extended phone numbers and an area for notes. (*Extended phone numbers* include fax, home/business phone, pager, cellular phone, and electronic mail addresses.) To add these fields, choose Additional Fields, and the Additional Fields dialog box appears. Click check boxes in the Additional Fields dialog box to add the fields you want. Click OK after you're done.

To add your own fields, such as a Dues Paid field, choose Your Own Fields. In the dialog box that appears, you can add up to four fields of your own choosing; click a field check box and enter a name for the field in the adjacent text box. Click OK when you're done.

To create printed reports, click Reports. In the Report dialog box that appears, click the Alphabetized Directory check box to create a report that shows an alphabetized listing of people in your address book. Click the Categorized Directory check box to create a report that's broken up into groups based on a field called "category" in your address book. Click OK after you're done.

7. **Click the Create It! button to check over your choices before creating the book.**

   To make this address book the one that pops up after you click the Address Book button on your toolbar (or after you choose Tools➪ Address Book), click the Yes, I Want This To Be My Default Address Book option.

8. **Click the Create Document button.**

   The address book TaskWizard, the world's fastest typist, tosses together a database document: your new address book.

9. **Save your address book by pressing Ctrl+S.**

   Give your file a name and folder to live in.

Of course, now you must fill out your address book. Ugh. For more details on navigating around your address book database and entering information, see Chapter 6. But for now, here's the executive summary:

✔ You're looking at one page, or *record*, of your address book.

✔ To advance from one field to the next as you enter data, click the field you want or press the Tab key.

✔ Type to enter data, pressing the Enter or Tab key after you're done.

✔ To advance or go back one record, press Ctrl+Page Down or Ctrl+Page Up, respectively.

✔ If you request a *category* report, decide how you want to group people (for example, members/nonmembers/prospects) and, for each person, enter the group in the Category field.

- To edit an entry, click the entry, press the F2 key, and edit in the formula bar just under the toolbar. Press Enter after you finish.

- To find someone by name or other information, the easiest way is to choose Edit⇨Find from the menu bar. In the Find dialog box that appears, type the word or phrase you want in the Find What box, choose All Records, and then click OK. Choosing All Records hides records not containing your search word; press Ctrl+Page Down to step through the visible ones. After you're done, choose Record⇨Show⇨ 1 All Records to make everything visible again.

To open your address book, you can use any of the following methods:

- If you made this address book your default address book, just click the Address Book button (the last button on the right end).

- To open an address book other than your default book, open it as you do any other (database) document by choosing File⇨Open or using the Task Launcher.

To change your default address book, choose Tools⇨Options, click the Address Book tab, and double-click an address book in the list shown.

Creating Your Own Junk Mail

For that personal touch without actually being personal, you just can't top junk mail. (Miss Manners, please call your office.) Yes, now you, too — *<your name here>*, of *<your address here>* — can send junk mail just like the pros!

This popular feature, also known as *mail-merge* or *form letters,* enables you to write a single letter in the word processor, leave blanks in the text, and have Works automatically fill in the blanks *(merge)* from a database (such as an address book). Works prints out one letter for each lucky person in your database.

Of course, in addition to sending falsely personal letters, you can use this feature for more valid personalization, such as in the following examples:

- Sending a letter to members of your organization, telling them how much they've paid and have left to pay of their annual dues or pledge.

- Welcoming each attendee to some event and telling the attendees what room they're staying in.

In these examples, a piece of information that your database contains about that person appears in the letter.

Of course, you must have a database document with this information in it for the information to appear in a letter! You can use any database TaskWizard to create the database document, such as the address book TaskWizard that I describe in the preceding section, "Creating an Address Book." In the Task Launcher, look through the various TaskWizard categories (such as Names and Addresses) for wizards with a database icon (a tiny picture of Rolodex-style cards). Or create a database from scratch — see Chapters 6 and 7.

After you have a database, you need to create the letter. You have the following two alternatives:

✔ Write the letter from scratch, modifying it for mail-merge.

✔ Have Works write the letter with a TaskWizard, although this action typically doesn't do any more than begin the letter with the recipient's name and address.

If you're new to this mail-merge stuff or if you just need some assistance in writing and correctly formatting a letter, I suggest the second option: Use a TaskWizard to start the letter and then modify the letter to add any personal information that you want in the body of the letter. By seeing how the TaskWizard handles the task, you can find out how to create your own form letters. See the section "Form letters by using a letter TaskWizard," coming up in this chapter.

Otherwise, you can create your own form letters from scratch fairly simply, as the following section describes.

Form letters from scratch

Works has a tool for creating form letters, but it seems unnecessarily complicated to me for most purposes; you need to pop in and out of the tool to write the letter. Here's what I think is the simplest approach: Write your letter using the word processor. Click wherever you need to fill in some personal data for the addressee, perform the following steps.

1. **Choose Insert⇨Database Field.**

   If a First-Time Help dialog box appears, click To Write A Form Letter.

   An Insert Field dialog box appears. Click Use A Different Database and, in the Use Database dialog box that appears, double-click the name of your chosen database.

2. **Click the field that contains the personal data you need and then click the Insert button.**

   You may, for example, have a Child Name field, which you use to write an acceptance letter for summer camp, drawing from a database of applicants. You can enter several fields from this dialog box.

3. **Click Close after you finish choosing fields.**

After you finish composing your letter, you can best see the results of your work by using Print Preview. Choose File⇨Print Preview from the menu bar, click OK in the dialog box that mutters about "all records," and enjoy the view.

In Print Preview, you can see each of the many letters you're going to print! Just click the Next button to see the next letter. Continue editing the form letter if necessary and print it for real after you get the form letter ready. If the data is wrong, you need to edit the database, as Chapter 6 describes.

Form letters by using a letter TaskWizard

You can choose from several TaskWizards; just about any "letter" TaskWizard does the trick, but a good, basic one to use is the form letter TaskWizard in the Correspondence folder. Follow these steps:

1. **Choose File⇨New and then click the TaskWizards tab in the Task Launcher.**

2. **Click Correspondence in the TaskWizards list and double-click Form Letter.**

3. **If a Works Task Launcher dialog box appears, click the Yes, Run The TaskWizard button.**

   The Letter TaskWizard fires up and asks you to choose the letter layout that you want.

4. **Click the picture of the layout that looks good to you (such as Professional) and click the Next button.**

   In the next Works TaskWizard dialog box that appears, you get to specify the details: Letterhead, Address, Content, Text Style, and Extras.

5. **Click Letterhead.**

   Two choices appear in a Letterhead dialog box: I Want To Design My Own and I Want To Use My Pre-Printed Letterhead Stationery. Click the first choice to go to a letterhead design specialist; click the second choice to arrange body text around preprinted items if your letterhead is already preprinted on your paper.

Whichever choice you make, the TaskWizard presents a series of dialog boxes, one at a time. Just follow the steps that the TaskWizard provides, adding your own particular information in the blanks in these dialog boxes.

6. **Click Address, and in the Address dialog box that appears, click I Want To Use Addresses From A Works Database; click Next.**

7. **Select the database containing your names and addresses from the address dialog box that appears.**

   If the database you want doesn't appear in the list, click The File I Want Isn't In The List. Works tells you how you can continue to make the form letter and then go back and merge the database later.

8. **Build an address for the addressee area of the letter by using the Address dialog box, as shown in Figure 9-1.**

   The task in this step is to choose which fields print, the order in which they appear, and on which line they appear. The procedure goes as follows:

   a) Click the name of a field at the left side of the Address dialog box; then click the Add button to copy it to the right side.

   b) If you make a mistake, click the Remove button to remove the last field you added.

   c) To begin a new line of the address, click the New Line button.

   d) Click the Comma button to type a comma — for example, to separate city from state.

   Don't use all the fields in your database! Use only the ones that you want to print at the top of the letter. After you finish selecting the fields, click the Next button.

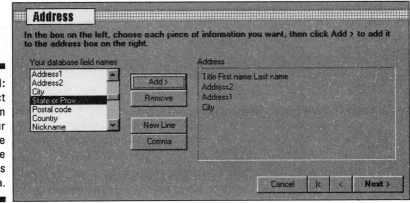

Figure 9-1:
Select
fields from
your
database
for the
Address
area.

9. **Create a greeting or salutation line (Dear ____) in the Address dialog box by using the same method as in Step 8 and then click Next after you finish creating the greeting.**

   For a formal letter, you can use **Dear <Title> <Last name>** for Dear Ms. ____ or Dear Mr. _____.

10. **Click OK in the next dialog box.**

    You're not done yet! Back to deciding the other features of your letter.

11. **Choose Content, click any type of letter listed in the Content dialog box, then click OK.**

    Wow! Works even provides prewritten letters! Use one if you want (although many of these aren't particularly suited for bulk mailing — for example, the Acceptance Of Job Offer letter — unless you live a very interesting life!). I am occupationally predisposed toward writing, so I choose Blank Letter.

12. **All right, you get the idea. Finish up your form letter by choosing ClickText Style and clicking various style check boxes in the Text Style dialog box that appears. Click Extras and do likewise.**

13. **Click the Create It! button.**

    At last!!! How exciting!!!! Check over the specifications for your form letter in the Checklist dialog box that appears, and if the letter needs changes, just click Return To Wizard. Otherwise, click the Create Document button.

After all the dust settles, you're left gazing at an ordinary Works word-processing document. Well, not entirely ordinary: As you can see in Figure 9-2, some odd entries appear in it.

The items in << >> symbols are placeholders. Works replaces these with actual data from your database. The thing within the << >> symbols is the name of the field from which the data comes. (Paragraph and space symbols that don't actually print also appear, so don't fret about them.)

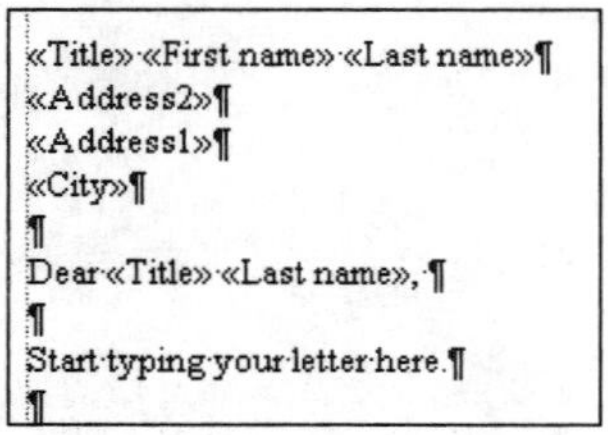

Figure 9-2:
What you
end up with:
a letter with
odd text
in it.

```
«Title» «First name» «Last name»¶
«Address2»¶
«Address1»¶
«City»¶
¶
Dear «Title» «Last name», ¶
¶
Start typing your letter here.¶
¶
```

Finish your letter. Whenever you come to a place where you need to fill in some personal data for the addressee, follow these steps:

1. **Choose Insert⇨Database Field.**

   If a First-time Help dialog box appears, click To Write A Form Letter.

   An Insert Field dialog box appears.

2. **Click the name of the field that contains the personal data you need and then click the Insert button.**

   You can enter several fields from this dialog box.

3. **Click Close after you finish selecting fields.**

After you finish composing your letter, you can best see the results of your work by using Print Preview. Choose File⇨Print Preview from the menu bar, click OK in the dialog box that mutters about "all records," and enjoy the view.

In Print Preview, you can see each of the many letters you're going to print! Just click the Next button to see the next one. Continue editing the form letter if necessary and print for real after you ready the letter. If the data is wrong, you need to edit the database.

You may not want to send mail to everyone in your database, so you need to *filter, hide,* or *mark* certain records. For information about filtering, hiding, and marking, see Chapter 7.

Tips for Using Wizard and Template Documents

Works pulls out all the stops for wizard and template documents. Works uses lots of advanced features in such clever ways that you may not recognize exactly what feature it's using. The following sections provide some tips for working with these clever wizard and template documents.

Working with word-processing documents

Wizard and template word-processing documents are full of graphical and layout tricks. Here are a few of the most common tricks:

✔ In Newsletter documents, Works shows multiple columns, WordArt, charts, and graphics. To change any of these features, double-click what you want to change; whatever tool is responsible appears.

- ✓ In Letterhead and other wizard documents, Works uses paragraph formatting and borders extensively. Click some text and choose Format⇨Paragraph and Format⇨Borders And Shading to see what's going on.

- ✓ Works wizard documents use tabs in creative ways. To see where tab characters appear, choose View⇨All Characters. Tiny arrows represent tab characters on-screen. You often create fill-in blanks by using underlined tab characters.

Working with spreadsheet documents

Wizard and template spreadsheet documents use lots of tricks with borders, column widths, and gridlines. Here are tips for working around a few of those tricks:

- ✓ If a spreadsheet appears to have headings with text indented under them, you are actually looking at a very narrow column for the heading text, with the indented text in the next column.

- ✓ If you can't edit the text in a spreadsheet, select the area and choose Format⇨Protection. In the Protection dialog box that appears, click the Protect Data check box to clear the check mark. Click OK.

- ✓ If a spreadsheet uses colored text that doesn't work well for you, remember that colors are an option in the Font card of the Format Cells dialog box.

Working with database documents

Wizard and template database documents come with built-in reports and some tricky formulas, as well as fancy formatting. Here are a few tips for making sense of what you see:

- ✓ In label templates, you enter your name and address only once, in the upper left-hand corner. You don't need to enter it for every label. (Formulas automatically make copies.)

- ✓ Check out what reports are available by choosing View⇨Report; click a report in the View Report dialog box that appears, then click Preview.

- ✓ To change the formatting, layout, or content of a database document, Form Design view generally works best; see Chapter 6.

- ✓ If you need to change a field, but Works prevents you from doing so, choose Format⇨Protection to open the Protection dialog box and then click the Protect Field check box to remove the check mark.

Chapter 10

Dating Yourself with Works' Calendar

● ●

In This Chapter

▶ Understanding what's what in the calendar window

▶ Viewing by month, week, or day

▶ Looking ahead or back in time

▶ Creating appointments or events

▶ Entering birthdays and other recurring events

▶ Editing and moving appointments and events

▶ Using categories

▶ Setting up reminders

▶ Printing calendars

● ●

*P*ersonally, I have trouble remembering the old rhyme, "Thirty days hath whatever, April, March, and whenever, and all the rest have something different." On the other hand, Works Calendar (or just Calendar to its friends) has the entire next century figured out.

All Calendar needs to help you take over the world is for you to put your business, personal, and other appointments or day-long events into its calculating little brain. Do so, and you not only can see all your upcoming happenings displayed by day, week, or month, but you can also get automatic reminders of appointments, review your notes before meetings, and print out calendars for business associates.

So what are you waiting for? To start Works calendar, go to the Windows Taskbar and choose Start⇨Programs⇨Microsoft Works Calendar (assuming you installed the program in the usual location).

After you start it up, Works Calendar repeatedly asks you whether you want to give it the honor of being your default calendar. If you're not currently using another calendar, click Yes. If you're using another calendar but want to check out Works Calendar before deciding which to use, click No. To get it to stop asking the question, click Always Perform This Check When Starting Works Calendar.

What's What in the Calendar Window

The calendar window displays the kind of menu bar and toolbar that you find in any Windows program, plus one of the several views of your calendar among which you can choose (see Figure 10-1). Initially, you see an entire month, but you can choose to view a single day or week instead. (See the following section, "Viewing by Month, Week, or Day," for details.) You can also view your appointments by different categories — displaying, for example, just personal or just business appointments. (See the section, "Using categories," later in this chapter, for details.)

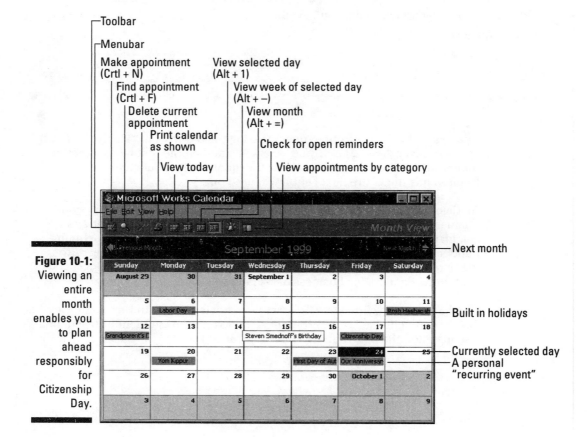

Figure 10-1:
Viewing an entire month enables you to plan ahead responsibly for Citizenship Day.

As do most Windows programs, Calendar offers you several alternative ways to perform any given task: toolbar buttons, keyboard shortcuts (see Figure 10-1 for buttons and shortcuts), a pop-up menu that appears after you right-click a date, or the menu bar. The method you use is up to you. I find that using the toolbar buttons and the right-mouse menu are the most convenient methods, but you may prefer to use a different method.

Viewing By Month, Week, or Day

Calendar enables you to choose your view: month, week, or day. (I prefer an ocean view, but they refuse to give me a room with a window.) Click the appropriate button on the toolbar, as shown in Figure 10-1, or choose View⇨Day, Week, or Month from the menu bar.

Here are a few tips for choosing views; I find Day and Month views to be the more useful ones:

- ✔ Choose Day view for easiest scheduling of appointments at particular hours. Day view displays all-day events in light gray above the list of time slots.

- ✔ Choose Month view for easiest scheduling and viewing of all-day events. If an appointment title isn't fully visible in Month view, position your mouse cursor over it and wait a second. The title appears in full (as shown in Figure 10-1 for Steven Smednoff's birthday).

Looking Ahead or Behind

If you're like me (and I don't say that you are), you're always nervously looking ahead and behind to see what's coming or what you forgot to do. In Calendar, each view provides the following two ways to move your view forward or back in time:

- ✔ Click the Previous *whatever* or Next *whatever* arrows at the left and right sides of the calendar, respectively, just under the toolbar. (By *whatever*, I mean *Day* in Day view, *Week* in Week view, or *Month* in Month view.)

- ✔ Click the month or date text that appears in large type just under the toolbar. Choose a new date from the list of selections that drops down.

If the window isn't large enough to show the time that you want to see, you can scroll the calendar. Use the scroll bar along the right side of the window, or press the up- or down-arrow key on the keyboard.

Setting Up Appointments or Events

Works' Calendar program distinguishes *appointments* such as meetings or lunch dates from *all-day events* (or *events* for short). (The program is superior to some business people I've known in that regard.) Appointments are happenings that begin and end at particular hours. All-day events are happenings such as holidays, birthdays, or casual day at work. I use the term *happenings* in this chapter if the text applies to both events and appointments.

The key Calendar feature you use to set up happenings of either kind is the New Appointment dialog box (or its nearly identical twin, the Edit Appointment dialog box). Calendar also offers a few shortcuts for creating and editing happenings. I show you how to use all these features in the following sections.

Making happenings happen

Works Calendar gives you multitudes of ways to enter various happenings. Some ways are obvious because they appear right on-screen and say Click here to add... If you click where Calendar indicates, a blank line and cursor appear so that you can type a title for the happening.

Following, however, are my two favorite, universal alternatives for entering a happening of any kind — universal because they work in any view:

 ✔ Click the New Appointment button (or press Ctrl+N or choose File⇨New Appointment). You may want to select the date or time first (by directly clicking the date or the time slot) so that Works enters that date or time for you in the New Appointment dialog box.

 ✔ Right-click directly on the date (in Month or Week view) or time slot (in Day view) and then choose the *top selection* in the list that drops down. (The selection reads either New Appointment or New All Day Event. Don't worry about the difference right now; you can choose the type of happening you want in the New Appointment dialog box that appears.)

A shortcut for entering an appointment (not an event) — as long as it happens on the half-hour — is to switch to Day view and then simply click any of the half-hour time slots there and type the appointment title.

Whichever of those two ways you choose, you end up gazing at the New Appointment dialog box, as shown in Figure 10-2.

If you edit an appointment, you use a nearly identical dialog box known as the Edit Appointment dialog box.

Tricky clicking

You must click carefully in Works Calendar, or you may find yourself doing something other than you intend. To select a date in Month view, click the day number and *not the appointment or event in the gray bar.* Similarly, to enter an appointment or event by right-clicking, right-click the day number and not the appointment or event. And make sure that you don't left-click before you right-click. Clicking or right-clicking the appointment or event is only for editing it. Press the Esc key if you find yourself accidentally editing a title or viewing a menu with Edit commands.

The following steps are the only essential ones for entering an appointment or event in the New Appointment dialog box:

1. **Click the Title box (shown in Figure 10-2) and type a descriptive title for the appointment or event.**

   This title is what appears in the calendar.

2. **Enable or disable the check mark in the All-Day Event check box, if necessary.**

   If you're entering an all-day event (like a birthday or holiday), make sure that the All-Day Event check box contains a check. (Click the check box if it doesn't contain a check mark.)

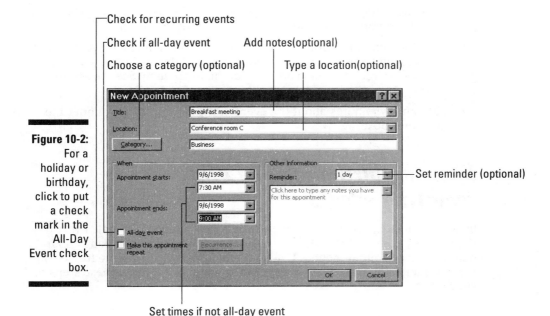

Check for recurring events
Check if all-day event
Choose a category (optional)
Add notes(optional)
Type a location(optional)
Set reminder (optional)
Set times if <u>not</u> all-day event

Figure 10-2: For a holiday or birthday, click to put a check mark in the All-Day Event check box.

If you're entering an appointment (which needs starting and ending times), make sure that the All-Day Event check box does *not* contain a check mark. (Click the check box to remove the mark if it does.)

3. Adjust the dates and/or times for this happening, if necessary.

To change the date or make a *multiday event,* you may edit the dates in the Appointment Starts and Appointment Ends drop-down list boxes. If you prefer to pick dates from a calendar, click the down arrows adjoining those boxes.

For appointments, type a starting and ending time for the appointment, as Figure 10-2 shows. If you prefer to pick half-hour intervals from a list, click the down arrows adjoining those boxes. You may also enter a new date above the time boxes. (If you make an appointment span more than one day, it appears in its time slot on each of those days.)

4. Click the OK button when you're done.

Some of the options you can choose in the New Appointment dialog box are as follows:

- ✔ Click the Make This Appointment Repeat check box to make your happening *repeat* every day, week, month, or year. See the following section, "Entering birthdays and other recurring events," for details.

- ✔ Click the Location box and type a *location* for the event. Calendar keeps a list of locations you've used in the past. To choose from that list, click the down arrow at the far-right end of the Location text box.

- ✔ Click the Category button to *categorize* your happening. See the section "Using categories," later in this chapter, for instructions.

- ✔ Click the Reminder drop-down list box and type a time interval (or click the adjoining down arrow and choose a time interval from the list) to have Works remind you in advance of the happening. See the section "Setting up reminders," later in this chapter, for details.

- ✔ Click and type notes about the event in the large white box under the Reminder box.

Entering birthdays and other recurring events

If your event or appointment occurs once a year, a month, a week, every day of the week, or every work day, you're in luck (unless you're talking about dental surgery appointments). Calendar enables you to enter the happening just once and make it repeat on any of those intervals. Follow these steps to success:

1. **To enter a new, repeating event or appointment, either click the New Appointment button (or press Ctrl+N or choose File⇨New Appointment), or, in Month or Week view, right-click the date you want.**

   To *change an existing event or appointment* to a repeating one, begin by right-clicking it. Then choose Open from the pop-up menu that appears. You get an Edit Event dialog box, which is identical to the New Event dialog box.

2. **Click the Make This Appointment Repeat check box in the New Appointment (or Edit Appointment) dialog box.**

3. **Click the Recurrence button; the Recurrence Options dialog box appears, as shown in Figure 10-3.**

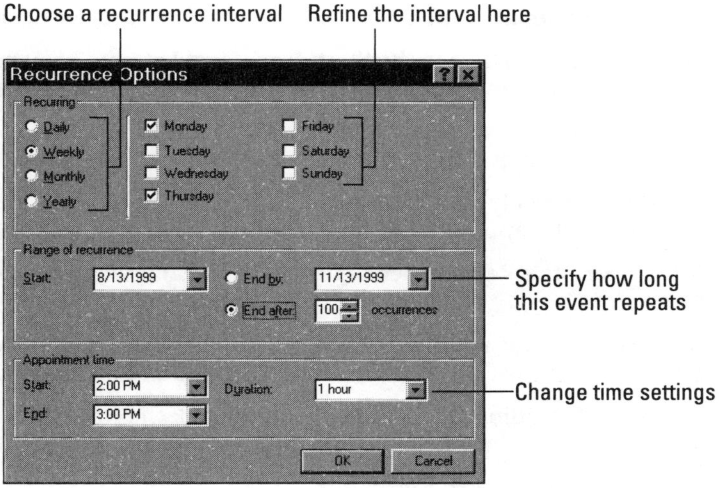

Figure 10-3:
A hypothetical appointment occurs weekly on Mondays and Thursdays. The Recurrence Options dialog box enables you to add all these appointments to your calendar easily.

Choose a recurrence interval   Refine the interval here

Specify how long this event repeats

Change time settings

Specify how often your happening occurs and for how long it continues to recur, by following these steps in the Recurrence Options dialog box:

1. **Click the radio button for your choice of interval: Daily, Weekly, Monthly, or Yearly.**

2. **Choose from among the options that each different interval offers, by clicking check boxes:**

   • **Daily options:** Every day (seven days a week) or Every weekday (Monday through Friday).

   • **Weekly options:** Choose a day of the week.

   For happenings that occur several times a week, you can choose multiple days. If you're a computer book author, for example, this choice is perfect for your electroshock appointments.

   • **Monthly options:** Choose by *day number* (On the 6th day, for example) or by the *day and week* (such as Every second Thursday).

   • **Yearly options:** Choose by *date* (August 13th, for example) or by *day*, *week*, and *month* (such as Every second Thursday in August).

3. **Specify how long this happening continues to repeat by giving a beginning date and either an end date or a number of occurrences.**

   Enter a beginning date in the Start drop-down list box. (You may use the "slash" format shown in the figure or type the date as in **August 15, 1999**.)

   Enter an ending date in the End By box, or click End After and enter a number of occurences.

   By editing the values in the Start, End, and/or Duration boxes, you can also adjust the appointment times if necessary.

4. **Click OK in the Recurrence Options dialog box when you are done there.**

5. **Review — and, if you like, change — the information in the New Appointment (or Edit Appointment) dialog box to which you return.**

   If you need to adjust appointment times, click the Recurrence button again.

6. **Click OK when you're done.**

Editing and moving appointments and events

If you're like me, your appointments change and move even faster than those giant man-eating chameleons. (You know — the ones crawling up your walls?) Well, maybe you're not like me — you may have fewer mental health appointments — but I bet your appointments change.

To edit the title of an appointment in any view, simply click the appointment. A blinking cursor appears, and you can type, backspace, select text, and delete text just as you do in the text box of a dialog box. (See the appendix if these activities are unfamiliar to you.)

To edit any aspect of an appointment, including its dates, times, notes, or title, right-click the appointment and choose Open from the pop-up menu that appears. The Edit Appointment dialog box appears, which works identically to the New Appointment dialog box (refer to Figure 10-2) and enables you to change any aspect of the appointment. If the appointment is a repeating one and you need to change its date or time, click the Recurrence button and make the changes in the Recurrence Options dialog box.

In Calendar, dragging is the easiest way to move any happening (appointment or event) to another date or time. Click that happening and, holding down the mouse button (don't let up!), drag the happening to another date on the Calendar.

Copying an appointment or event is similar, except that you press and hold the Ctrl key on your keyboard while you drag the appointment.

To move an appointment or event to a date farther in the future than you care to drag it, edit the appointment or event (as I describe in the second paragraph of this section) and change its date.

Using categories

If you get really serious about using Calendar to manage your life, consider using the Calendar *categories*. (Or consider getting a simpler life!) If you have lots of happenings in Calendar — meetings, trips, lunches, therapies, kids' activities, holidays, classes, or the Ludlow, Vermont Zucchini Festival — your calendar gets pretty cluttered.

By using Calendar's categories, you can assign any happening to one or more categories: business, education, medical, personal, and so on. Then you can restrict (or *filter*) the display to show only certain categories of happenings at a time. Calendar comes with a set of standard categories among which you can choose, and you can create, rename, or delete categories as well.

The place to go to assign categories is the Choose Category dialog box. You can access this dialog box in any of the following several ways — whichever is most convenient for you:

✔ To assign a category while you're creating a *new* happening by using the New Appointment dialog box (refer to Figure 10-2), click the Category button (or the text box to the button's right).

✔ To assign a category to an *existing* happening, right-click that appointment or event and choose Categories from the pop-up menu that appears. Or, if you're editing the happening anyway by using the Edit Appointments dialog box, click the Category button in that box.

The Choose Categories dialog box consists simply of a list of check boxes, one for each category. Check one or more categories for your happening and then click OK.

To add a category of your own design or to delete or rename a category, you need to access the Edit Category dialog box. Choose Edit⇨Categories from the menu bar or click the Edit Categories button in the Choose Categories dialog box.

In the Edit Categories dialog box, click a category to delete or rename and then click the Delete or Rename button. To create a new category, click the blank text box at the bottom of the dialog box, type a new name, and then click the Add button.

To make your calendar display only certain categories of appointments or events (say, medical appointments), you *filter* out the other happenings by using the filter control panel. Click the Category Filter button (the right-most button in the toolbar, shown in Figure 10-1) to display or hide that panel.

A list of check boxes appears to the left of your calendar; check marks indicate which categories Calendar is displaying. Click to clear the check marks for categories that you don't want to see, and your calendar changes accordingly.

To restore all happenings to your calendar, click the words Category Filter at the top of the filter panel, and choose Show Appointments in All Categories from the menu that appears. To hide the filter panel, click the Category Filter button again.

Hiding the filter panel doesn't remove filtering. Only by choosing Show Appointments in All Categories do you remove filtering.

Setting up reminders

Calendar can remind you of upcoming happenings (events or appointments) by popping up a reminder window and, optionally, making a sound. All you need to do is tell Calendar how far in advance to remind you.

To create a new event or appointment that includes a reminder, either click the New Appointment button (or press Ctrl+N or choose File⇨New Appointment), or, in Month or Week view, right-click the date of the happening.

To add a reminder to an existing event or appointment, begin by right-clicking it. Then choose Open from the pop-up menu that appears.

In the New Appointment (or Edit Appointment) dialog box that appears (refer to Figure 10-2), you enter an interval into the Reminder drop-down list box that reflects how far in advance of the happening you want Works to remind you about it. Either type an interval (in minutes, hours, days, weeks, months, or years) or click the down arrow adjoining the Reminder text box and choose a standard interval from the drop-down list that appears.

Calendar doesn't need to be running for the reminder to work. You can now exit Calendar by choosing File➪Exit.

At your specified interval before the appointment or event begins, a View Reminders dialog box appears. You may leave the View Reminders dialog box on-screen to help you remember the appointment. The dialog box displays all current (*active*) reminders in its Reminders text box. To view your notes on a given happening, click the happening in the Reminders text box, and then click the Open button.

After you're sure you're going to remember an upcoming happening (or after it passes), you may clear (*dismiss*) its reminder in the View Reminders dialog box. Click that happening and then click the Dismiss Item button. To dismiss all current reminders, click Dismiss All; they don't appear again. Dismissing a reminder is the same as deleting or canceling it.

Click the Close button to remove the View Reminders dialog box from your screen. You can check your reminders at any time by choosing View➪ Reminders from the Calendar menu bar or by clicking the Reminders button on the toolbar, which sports a bell icon.

To cause a sound to play whenever the View Reminder dialog box appears, follow these steps:

1. **From the Windows taskbar (not the Calendar menu), choose Start➪Settings➪ Control Panel.**

 2. **In the Control Panel, double-click the Sounds icon.**

3. **In the Events box of the Sounds Properties dialog box that appears, scroll down to Microsoft Works Calendar and click Reminder.**

   At this point, you can choose what sound file plays by clicking the Browse button, or you can just go with Calendar's current choice.

4. **Click OK in the Sounds Properties dialog box.**

Printing Calendars

Computers — phooey! Nothing beats a paper calendar or appointment book for keeping you current with events and appointments and for sharing a schedule with others. Works Calendar gives you more ways to print your schedule than you probably can ever use.

Choose File⇨Print (or click the Print button on the toolbar or press Ctrl+P). The Print dialog box appears.

Begin by selecting a calendar style. To print out a day's appointments, choose one of the following Day styles from the Style box.

- ✔ **Day by appointments:** Similar to Day view; shows a space covering each appointment's duration.

- ✔ **Day by hours:** Similar to Day view but lists every half-hour time slot and shows what appointment begins in that half-hour.

- ✔ **Day list:** Lists each appointment in order and its start and end times; shows no time slots.

- ✔ **Day list by sections:** Groups appointments into Morning, Afternoon, and Evening, showing start and end times for each appointment.

Calendar also offers Week and Month calendar styles in the Style box. Choose Month-Portrait for a calendar that prints vertically on a page or Month-Landscape for the horizontal orientation that you more usually use for calendars.

Enter a Start and End date and time in the Range area of the Print dialog box. (Or use the default dates and times that Calendar suggests.)

Make sure that Calendar applies any filtering the way you actually want it to appear. In the Include area of the Print dialog box, Calendar assumes by default that any filtering you're currently applying (displaying Personal appointments only, for example) also applies to this printed calendar. If you want to print all appointments and events instead, click All Appointments.

Part II
Putting Words in Word

In this part . . .

Microsoft Word 97 is the big bargain of Works Suite 99. Thanks to the power of Microsoft, Word is probably the most commonly used word processor in the business world today. Know Word, and your skills are useful in nearly any job in business. (Academic, legal, and government organizations tend to prefer Corel WordPerfect.) Word, as are other top-end word processors, is also packed to overflowing with features. Many features are useful to everyone, some are useful to only a select few people, and nearly all are as confusing as heck to new users!

If you've never processed a word electronically in your life, this part gets you past the confusion and into creating and formatting basic documents. It gives you key fundamentals behind the power of word processing, such as using paragraph formatting and styles. It then tells you how to add common and essential features, such as tables, headers and footers, columns, charts, and illustrations.

Chapter 11

Creating and Editing a Document

● ●

In This Chapter

▶ Starting and exiting Word

▶ Starting and saving documents

▶ Navigating the Word window and toolbar

▶ Typing and deleting

▶ Dealing with Word paragraphs

▶ Using document views

▶ Getting around in your document

▶ Selecting text for editing or formatting

▶ Moving and copying

▶ Finding and replacing

▶ Using the thesaurus

▶ Checking spelling and grammar

● ●

*I*n the beginning, there was Word. Yes, Microsoft Word has been around for many years, and in that time has acquired a lot of fancy features. In this book, however, I'm focusing on the basics. (Well, okay, maybe a few fancy features.) If you want to get seriously into Word, I suggest you pick up a copy of Dan Gookin's *Word 97 For Windows For Dummies* (IDG Books Worldwide, Inc.).

This chapter gives you the really basic basics: getting the words right. I include information on starting a document and getting the words typed, plus finding, editing, and checking those words. Anything having to do with appearances and other frilly stuff is in the next chapter.

Attention: Works word-processor users!

The word-processing basics of Word 97 and the Works word-processing tool are so similar that they often use the same commands. In this part of the book, the *Works for Me!* icon guides Works users to instructions that work for them. If the icon isn't present, the instructions are for Word users.

If the Works for Me! icon appears at the first paragraph of a section, the whole section also applies to the Works word processor. Likewise, if the icon appears before a numbered list, the whole numbered list applies to Works. I call any exceptions in the section or list to your attention.

Starting and Exiting Word

Just as you do for any other Windows program, you can start Word from the Windows Start button or with a program icon. Do one of the following:

- On the Windows Taskbar, choose Start⇨Programs⇨Microsoft Word.
- If you have a Microsoft Word icon on your screen, double-click that icon.

To exit the Word program, choose File⇨Exit. If you haven't already saved your work (your "changes" in Word-speak), a pop-up box asks you if you want to do so. Choose Yes to save your work, No to discard your work, or Cancel to return to Word.

To read more about starting Windows programs, see the appendix. Likewise, turn to the appendix if you're a little shaky on using the mouse or keyboard, windows, menus, or dialog boxes.

The paper clip guy

Word may occasionally display a very cute animated paper clip, called *Office Assistant*, who tries to help out. He gives you pretty explicit directions, so you don't need me to repeat them. You type a question, and he lists subjects that he thinks are related.

Unfortunately, he's not very smart. But then, he's a paper clip. Click one of the listed subjects to read about it. To make him go away, click the tiny X in the upper-right corner of his box. To wake him up, click his "?" button on the toolbar. (See Figure 11-1.)

Starting Documents

When you start Word (unless you start Word by double-clicking a Word document), it gives you a brand-new, daisy-fresh document right from the start: that big area of sparkling white you're looking at in the Word window. Just start typing! See "Typing and Deleting," later in this chapter, if you're new to word processing.

To start a new document while Word is already running, do as you would in Works or most other Windows programs. Do any of the following:

- Choose File➪New
- Press Ctrl+N
- In Word, (not Works) click the New button on the standard toolbar (shown in Figure 11-1)

If you choose File➪New or press Ctrl+N, you get a choice of what kind of new document you want. The New dialog box appears, with an icon labeled Blank Document highlighted. To start a normal, blank document, simply click the OK button on the New dialog box. If you would rather create a fancier document, Word's New dialog box provides a variety of templates and wizards on what appears to be several tabbed cards. If you click the New button in the Word toolbar, you get a blank document.

To open an existing document, do as you would for most other Windows program documents: Chew open the wrapper. No, just kidding. Do one of the following:

- Choose File➪Open or press Ctrl+O (the letter, not the numeral zero).
- Click the Open button on the standard toolbar.
- Choose File, then at the very bottom of the File menu, choose a recently-worked upon document by its name.

In the first two instances, you then choose the file from the Open dialog box that appears. Double-click the file in the Open dialog box to open it. If the file you want is not displayed, use the standard Windows file-finding techniques that I describe in the appendix.

Saving Documents

As with any program, you must save your document as a file on your hard drive or on a diskette before exiting Word (assuming you want to keep the document). Saving Word documents is very much like saving a document in any Windows program, so please see the appendix for basic instructions on saving and managing files. Following are some tips for saving in Word:

✔ Click the Save button in the standard toolbar (shown in Figure 11-1), choose File➪Save, or press Ctrl+S to save your document.

✔ The first time you save a new document, a Save As dialog box asks you for a name and a location in which to save your document. Word suggests a name taken from the first word of your document. Type a new name if you like, then press the Enter key (or click the Save button).

✔ You don't have to type the .doc part of the file name, Word does that for you.

✔ Unless you give a different location in the Save As dialog box, Word saves your documents in its default directory, typically the folder "My Documents" on your C: drive.

The Word Window and Toolbar

Figure 11-1 shows the names of parts of the Word window. In the window is a document with one of the dweeby sort of startup titles that Word gives new documents, "Document 2," for instance, appearing in the title bar.

Figure 11-1 shows one of several possible *views* of your document. This view, which Word uses unless you choose otherwise, is called *Normal view*. Another common view is *Page Layout* view. See "Document Views," later in this chapter for more information.

To find out the name of a button in Word, position your mouse cursor over the button and pause for a second. Word displays the button's name. You can then move your cursor over the other buttons to see their names. Word offers so many buttons and so many of them are rarely used that I don't waste space discussing them all here. In the appendix I identify basic buttons shared by nearly all Windows programs.

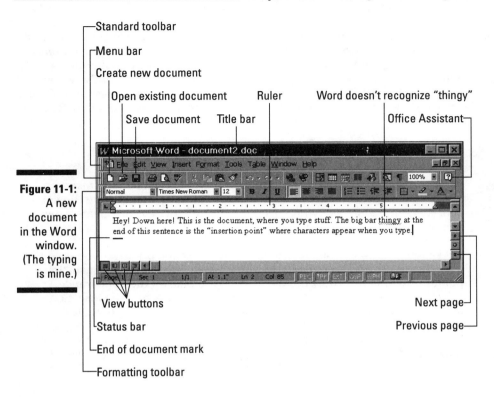

Standard toolbar
Menu bar
Create new document
Open existing document
Save document
Title bar
Ruler
Word doesn't recognize "thingy"
Office Assistant

Figure 11-1: A new document in the Word window. (The typing is mine.)

Hey! Down here! This is the document, where you type stuff. The big bar thingy at the end of this sentence is the "insertion point" where characters appear when you type.

View buttons
Status bar
End of document mark
Formatting toolbar

Next page
Previous page

Typing and Deleting

Typing and deleting are the big existential issues of word processing: existence and nonexistence; calling into creation and returning to the void. All else is illusion (or maybe illustration).

Typing

If you're looking at a Word window, away you go. Just start typing. All the regular keys on the keyboard — the letters, numbers, and punctuation — put characters on the screen when you press them. The space bar, Tab key, and Enter key put invisible (white space) characters in your document.

If you are new to word processing, remember: Do NOT press the Enter (or Return) key when you get to the end of a line. Just keep typing. The text you type automatically starts on the next line, a phenomenon called *line wrap*. When you get to the bottom of the document window, the document scrolls up, like paper in your typewriter. Press the Enter key when you get to the end of a paragraph — *not before!!!*

To get space between your paragraphs, you can press the Enter key twice at the end of the paragraph, but there's a better way, called *paragraph formatting,* which I get into in the next chapter. For now, try this technique: To put a line's worth of space above the paragraph that you're currently typing (and a line's worth of space above subsequent paragraphs), press Ctrl+0 (that's zero, not the letter O). If you want that space to go away, press Ctrl+0 again.

The insertion point

As you type, you start pushing around that big vertical bar, the *insertion point.* The insertion point's main function in life is to mark where the next character appears when you type or where a character disappears when you delete.

Click anywhere in existing text to place the insertion point. As you type new text, the existing text moves to the right. When you place your insertion point in existing text, the characters you type take on the appearance *(character formatting)* of the character immediately *before* the insertion point — even if that character is a space or other invisible character!

You can nudge the insertion point up, down, or sideways by pressing the arrows and other navigation keys on your keyboard. Or you can just click the mouse pointer at the place in your document where you want to start typing.

Notice what happens to your mouse pointer when you move it into the white area where you type. The bulky, arrow-shaped mouse pointer changes into an *I-beam* shaped cursor which is a little easier to fit in between characters than the pointer is.

Beware the insidious Insert key

Word provides two ways for you to type with your keyboard: *insert mode* and *overtype mode.* (A third mode, *a la mode,* is when your ice cream cone drops onto the keyboard.) Normally, you're in insert mode, which means that if you move the insertion point into the middle of text and type, the existing text scoots to the right to make room. If, however, you accidentally press the Insert key (which lives over by your navigation keys, just waiting to be pressed accidentally), you find yourself transported to the parallel dimension of overtype mode. (A little OVR shows up near the bottom-right corner of your Word window.) Now, if you move the insertion point into the middle of text and type, the existing text vanishes as you type over it. If you find yourself typing over existing text, you probably pressed Insert. Press the Insert key again to return to your home dimension.

Undoing your doings

Word (and many other programs) lets you *undo* whatever you just did. For instance, to undelete (that's *un-delete*, not *undulate* — don't get excited) something that you deleted by accident, press Ctrl+Z or choose Edit⇨Undo. To untype something you just typed, you can also use Ctrl+Z. Word lets you undo many actions into the past; just keep pressing Ctrl+Z.

Deleting

You can delete stuff with either the Backspace key or the Delete key. To delete a character you just typed, press the Backspace key (usually on the upper-right corner of the typewriter keys). Technically speaking (geek-speak), the keys work as follows:

- ✔ The Backspace key deletes the character *before* the insertion point.
- ✔ The Delete key deletes the character *after* the insertion point.
- ✔ Either key deletes a block of text that is selected. (You typically select text by clicking and dragging your mouse cursor across it.) The selected area can span as many words, lines, paragraphs, or even pages as you want. For more on selecting text, see the appendix.

Typing spaces, tabs, and other invisible characters

You probably already suspect that your document is haunted by powerful invisible beings. What you probably didn't know is that you pressed the keys that brought them into existence.

Some of these characters are common-sensical and fairly innocuous. Other characters, such as the following, are somewhat more mysterious:

- ✔ The space bar puts a space mark (character) in your text that is (unlike the space on a typewriter) much thinner than most other characters that you type.
- ✔ When you press the Tab key, you insert a tab mark. The tab mark creates space in your text between the preceding character and the next *tab stop* location. See Chapter 12 for more on tabs.

✔ The elite of these invisible beings, the paragraph mark that you get when you press the Enter key, is so powerful that it gets its own section in this chapter, "Understanding paragraphs and paragraph marks," coming up soon.

"What tab mark? What paragraph mark?" you ask. Well, these marks are *invisible,* of course, which is why they don't stand out in a crowd. They're easy to overlook when you format or delete. But they do affect the way your document looks, and they can cause weird, spooky, inexplicable things to happen, such as a big gap appearing in your text (due to a tab mark or a line of spaces you didn't know was there), or one paragraph merging with another (when a paragraph mark gets deleted), or finding a font you didn't expect (when the insertion point gets plunked down next to an invisible character that has a different font attached to it).

For all these reasons, you need to be able to see these invisible characters, at least occasionally. Read on.

Seeing invisible characters

To see the creepy invisible characters inhabiting your document, click the Show/Hide paragraph button (the backwards-P thingy) on the standard toolbar. (If you're using a Microsoft Works word processor, you don't have that button. Choose View⇨All Characters instead.)

AAAaaggghh! Your document is filled with nasty dots and funny marks! In fact, it looks almost as bad as the document shown in Figure 11-2! Those dots between your words are spaces. The little backwards-P-looking thing is a paragraph mark, and it hangs out with the text that precedes it. If you have any tab marks, they look like arrows with deodorant-failure problems (lots of space around them). Manually inserted page breaks are dotted lines.

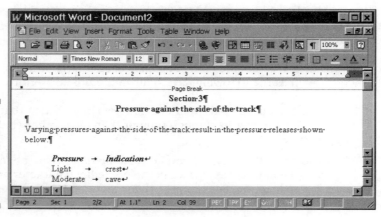

Figure 11-2:
Invisible characters are lurking in your document.

Now, if any of these invisible dudes are giving you trouble, just revoke their existence (delete them). The visible text moves around to fill the gap.

To make these characters invisible again, click the Hide/View paragraph button again. (Choose View⇨All Characters if you're a Works user.) Frankly, however, until you get used to having these characters lurking around, your life may be easier if you leave the characters visible.

Understanding paragraphs and paragraph marks

You remember what your English teacher told you a paragraph is, right? Topic sentence? Two or more related sentences? Well, Word has its own ideas about paragraphs. A Word paragraph is created when you press the Enter key and create one of those secret, invisible paragraph marks that I talk about in "Typing spaces, tabs, and other invisible characters" earlier in this chapter.

That paragraph mark is very powerful, as invisible beings tend to be. Here are three extremely important and utterly critical things to know about the paragraph mark:

- ✔ **A paragraph mark tells Word, "Do not line wrap beyond this point; start a new line."** A paragraph mark is what that keeps paragraphs apart.

- ✔ **The paragraph mark controls paragraph formatting for its paragraph.** In other words, the mark affects all the text preceding it (up to the preceding paragraph mark).

  Paragraph formatting is indentation, spacing between paragraphs, tab stops, alignment, justification, and other stuff that I talk about in the next chapter. When you format a paragraph, all this formatting information is *owned* by the paragraph mark and applies to the text preceding it. So if you copy a paragraph mark and paste it somewhere else, *it brings its paragraph formatting with it!* (The paragraph mark does *not,* however, specify type: meaning the typeface [font] or any aspect of type, such as style or size.)

- ✔ **Every time you press the Enter key (creating a new paragraph mark), the new paragraph inherits all the formatting of the paragraph you were just in.** The indentation, the spacing, the tab stops, and all the other paragraph stuff is just the same. In other words, just type, and new paragraphs look just like the first one. To change appearances of new paragraphs, adjust the final paragraph's formatting. Any new paragraphs you create from it inherit its appearance.

What these points mean for you is:

- Don't press the Enter key at the end of every line; press it only at the end of your paragraphs. Otherwise, Word thinks your paragraph is actually a bunch of paragraphs. And then, if you want to do something stylish with your paragraphs — like indenting every line except the first one — the format won't work properly because (as far as Word is concerned) every line *is* the first line!

- Do press the Enter key at the end of short lines in a list, like this one.

- To split one paragraph into two, put the insertion point where you want the split and press the Enter key. The two new paragraphs share identical paragraph formatting.

- To create a new paragraph in front of the one that you're currently in, move your insertion point to the beginning of the current paragraph and press Enter.

- To create a new paragraph to follow the one that you're currently in, move your insertion point to the end of the current paragraph (click the last line and press the End key to be sure) and press Enter.

- If you delete text that includes a paragraph mark (for example, if you select and delete text crossing two paragraphs), the two paragraphs merge. The remaining single paragraph takes on the paragraph formatting of the bottom of the original pair. Try pressing Ctrl+Z to undo whatever you did, if you need to.

Unfriendly mergers and takeovers of paragraphs

The Backspace and Delete keys delete invisible characters the same way they delete visible characters. If your insertion point is at the beginning of a paragraph and you press the Backspace key, you delete the preceding character: the invisible paragraph mark at the end of the preceding paragraph! Likewise, if you press the Delete key at the end of a paragraph, you delete the paragraph mark. Without a paragraph mark to hold it back, the first paragraph spills into the following one and forms one humongous paragraph. What's worse, if the two paragraphs were formatted differently — say that the first paragraph was centered and the second paragraph wasn't — both of them are now formatted like the second paragraph.

You can get out of this mess by pressing Ctrl+Z (or choosing Edit⇨Undo) immediately. Another option is to reinsert the paragraph mark by clicking where you want the paragraph break and pressing the Enter key, but you still may need to reformat the first paragraph.

Moving around

To work on another area in your document, move the insertion point. To move your insertion point by using the mouse, just click somewhere in your document. To move to another page, click the double-arrow buttons (shown back in Figure 11-1) in the vertical scroll bar.

To move your insertion point by using the keyboard, press the arrow or other navigation keys, like Page Up and Page Down. Table 11-1 shows you how.

Table 11-1	Navigating with Keys
Navigation Key	*Where It Moves the Insertion Point*
Left-arrow/right-arrow	One character's worth left or right
Up-arrow/down-arrow	One line's worth up or down
Page Up/Page Down	One window's worth up or down
Home	Beginning of the line
End	End of the line
Ctrl+Home	Beginning of the document
Ctrl+End	End of the document

Document Views

One of the weird things about word processors is that they're all a little reluctant to show you *exactly* what your document looks like. Word offers you several ways of looking at your document (apart from printing it), with varying amounts of fidelity to how the document looks on the printed page.

Choose View⇨Normal or Page Layout to select one of the two main views:

✔ **Normal view** is best for actually writing text. It doesn't show page margins or page breaks. It treats your document like a long, continuous scroll.

✔ **Page Layout** view is a bit more exact. You can see your page breaks and margins realistically. If you use page numbers, headers, or footers, Page Layout view shows them. Normal view doesn't.

Print Preview is not exactly a view, but lets you see something that's as close to the paper printout as your word processor can manage. For more on this feature, see Chapter 12.

As you add and delete text in your document, the page breaks move fairly often. In the Normal view, the top of each page is marked by an unobtrusive little >> symbol. In the Page Layout view, your pages actually break. A gap and a dividing line appear between one page and the next. This gap makes working in the vicinity of the page break — doing things like selecting text across the break — rather awkward. You probably want to use Normal view for most of your composing and then switch to Page Layout for final editing.

Selecting Text for Editing or Formatting

To format or otherwise change a whole chunk of text at one time, you *select* or *highlight* that text. Because selecting works pretty much the same in all Windows programs, I put the details in the appendix.

In a nutshell, however, to select text, you can either hold down your mouse button and drag the cursor across text, or hold down the Shift key and press the arrow or other navigation keys on the keyboard. (The navigation key method is sometimes easier to control.)

Your word processor has some funky selection quirks not found in other tools:

- ✔ When selecting with your mouse, the highlight envelops one character at a time within the first word, but in subsequent text it switches to enveloping one word at a time. Sometimes that behavior selects more text than you want. In Word, however (not Works), if you back up the cursor, you then release individual characters from the selection.

- ✔ To select a line, click in the white area to the left of that line; to select several lines, hold down the mouse button and drag the mouse.

- ✔ To select a paragraph, double-click anywhere in the white area to the left of the paragraph. To select several paragraphs, hold down the mouse button when you make the second click, then drag up or down.

- ✔ To select the whole document, choose Edit➪Select All (or press Ctrl+A).

Moving and Copying

When your document has to change, Word provides a variety of features that let you change it by moving and copying it.

Basic cutting and pasting are pretty much the same in every Windows program, so I give details of those activities in the appendix. Following are two special tricks for word processing:

✔ **To move text:** Select it, and then click that selection and drag it with the mouse. The vertical bar that follows you as you drag shows you where the selection will go when you release the mouse button.

✔ **To copy text:** Do the same thing as for moving text, but hold the Ctrl key down while you drag.

Finding Elusive Fauna (Or, Where's That Word?)

In the jungle of words that is the typical document, losing track of important words and phrases is easy. Finding a word or phrase is no problem for your efficient and jungle-wise guide, the Find dialog box.

Before you give the Find dialog box its marching orders, click to put the insertion point wherever you want Find to start looking. (Press Ctrl+Home to put it at the beginning of the document.) Or, if you know that what you seek is in a certain area, highlight (select) that area. The Find feature then restricts its search to the selected area.

1. **Choose Edit⇨Find or press Ctrl+F.**

   The Find and Replace dialog box springs into action and presents itself for duty.

2. **Type the word or phrase that you want to look for in the Find What box.**

   In Works (not Word), if the word or phrase you want to find includes a question mark, type the symbol ^ (Shift+6 on your keyboard), and then the question mark. The ? symbol alone, when used in the Works Find dialog box is a wild card — a symbol that you can use to stand for any character.

3. **Click Find Next or press the Enter key.**

   Word scurries forward into the underbrush, and highlights (selects) the first *wildebeest* (or whatever you are searching for) it finds. Highlighting makes doing stuff to the word (deleting, formatting, copying, or just observing) easy. Click in the document window to make any changes.

Repeat Step 3 until you finish searching. Word displays a dialog box to tell you when it has searched your entire document. Click the OK button. Repeat Step 2 to change your search word. Press the Esc key or click the Cancel button in the Find box when you're done.

Finding words by using fragments

Is it *wildebeest* or *wildebeast?* Your Find feature lets you type just the portion of the word or phrase that you are sure of (*wilde,* in this instance), or that identifies the stuff you're looking for (all *Microsoft* products, for instance). This method also works if you want both singular and plural *wildebeest(s).* Just leave off the *s.* (The Find Whole Words Only check box, described in the next section, must *not* have a check mark in it if this technique is to work.)

A useful alternative is to use a *wild card* in place of text you're not sure of — especially if that text is in the middle of a word or phrase. A wild card is a symbol that takes the place of one or more characters.

In the Word Find dialog box, you must first click the More button to reveal advanced features, and then click to enable the Use Wildcards check box. Now you can type wild card symbols to represent parts of a word. The two most popular wildcards are the following: * for any set of characters (as in wildeb*t; not useable in Works); and ? to represent any single character (as in wildebe?st). Word's Find dialog box offers additional symbols when you click its Special button, but they are too tricky to describe here. You can safely explore the special world of the Special button on your own, however!

Searching for Oscar Wilde and finding wildebeests

If you send the Find feature off to locate the word *Wilde* (a *Wilde* goose chase) the Find feature may return from the hunt with a *wildebeest* instead of Oscar Wilde. Very embarrassing for everyone. A more annoying example is when you are searching for text like *man,* which also appears in *man*y other words like *man*ufacture and hu*man*.

To tell the Find dialog box to search for whole words only (a bunch of characters set off by spaces or punctuation), first click the More button in the Find dialog box. Then enable the Find Whole Words Only check box. (In Works, there is no More button; that check box is always visible.)

To find only capitalized words like Wilde, another alternative in the Find dialog box is to check off the Match Case check box (revealed in Word by clicking the More button in the Find dialog box). Then use a capital W in Wilde.

Replacing Wildebeests with Whelks

If you're typing along about wildebeests and suddenly realize that you meant *whelks,* not wildebeests, you have some personal problems that go beyond software, and I can not attempt to deal with them here. I can, however, tell you how to replace *wildebeest* with *whelk.* Here's how:

1. **Narrow the area for your search and replace, if you can, by highlighting (selecting) that area.**

2. **Choose Edit⇨Replace or press Ctrl+H.**

   The Find and Replace dialog box springs into action. (In Works, the Replace dialog box appears.)

3. **Type the word or phrase (say,** wildebeest**) that you want to find in the Find What box.**

4. **Type the replacement word or phrase (say,** whelk**) in the Replace With text box.**

5. **Click the Find Next button or press Enter.**

   Replace scurries forward into the underbrush, and when it discovers your search word *(wildebeest),* it highlights (selects) the word so that you can see whether this particular *wildebeest* is one that you want to replace.

6. **To replace the highlighted text, click the Replace button. To leave it alone, click the Find Next button.**

   Click Replace and — Poof! Your wildebeest is a whelk and happy as a clam. If the wildebeest was capitalized, Word likewise capitalizes your whelk (which is pretty businesslike for an ungulate).

   To replace *all* instances of the search text without pausing for your permission in each case, click the Replace All button. If, however, you selected a region of text back in Step 1, only that region is affected.

   Replace pops up a message box when it finishes searching the whole document (or whatever text you selected). Click OK.

When you're done with your replacing, press the Esc key or click Cancel to clear the dialog box.

Here are two tips for replacing:

✔ To replace a noun throughout your document, use the singular form (say, *wildebeest* or *whelk*) so that where you once had either wildebeast or wildebeests, you now have *whelk* or *whelks*.

✔ The Replace All button can be dangerous. If you want to change *days* to *weeks,* for instance, make sure that you're not changing Sun*days* to Sun*weeks.* Enabling the Find Whole Words Only check box (described in the preceding section) can help in these special instances.

Meeting the Mighty Thesaurus

Among the various critters roaming around in your word processor is a thesaurus. Its basic job is to help you find alternative words. This thesaurus is convenient, although it's kind of a baby thesaurus that can't really hold a candle to a printed thesaurus (which is good, because they're generally flammable).

The following steps give you a click-by-click description of how to use the thesaurus:

1. **Select (highlight) the word or phrase that you want to look up.**

2. **Choose Tools⇨Language⇨Thesaurus (or press Shift+F7).**

   The Thesaurus dialog box shown in Figure 11-3 lumbers out of the wilderness. (Works users: the Works Thesaurus dialog box is practically identical.)

Figure 11-3:
The baby
thesaurus
in Word is
not purple,
but it still
wants to be
your friend.

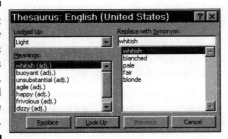

3. **Click any replacement word or phrase you like, either in the Meanings box or in the list of synonyms just below the Replace With Synonym box.**

   Your substitute word can come from either list. If you click a *meaning,* you get a new list of synonyms to play with.

4. **To look for synonyms to your chosen synonym, click the Look Up button.**

   You can go from synonym to synonym all day. If at any point you want to return to an earlier synonym, click the down-arrow adjoining the Looked Up window, and the whole list of what you've looked up so far drops down.

5. **When, in either list, you find a good substitute word or phrase, click it and then click the Replace button.**

   Your original word or phrase in the document is replaced.

Your new word or phrase may not be any better than your old one, but what a good time you had getting it there. Beats working!

Checking Your Spelling and Grammar

One of the classic advantages of using a word processor is that it supposedly can check your spelling. Actually, what the spell checker does is make sure that your document contains 100 percent genuine words — or words it thinks are genuine, anyway, because the words appear in a list of words called a *dictionary*. Word also checks your grammar at the same time that it checks your spelling, so I just call this feature a checker.

The checker does not make sure that you use words write. For example, the word *write* in the preceding sentence is indisputably a word; it just happens to be in the wrong place at the wrong time. The checker doesn't turn up anything wrong with that that sentence. The checker does, however, catch the repeated word *that* in the previous sentence. The spell checker also catches capitalization and hyphenation errors.

Word checks your text as you type, and anything that it doesn't like is underlined with a wavy line: red for spelling problems, green for grammar. If the problem isn't obvious to you, do the following:

1. **Press F7, or on the toolbar click the checker's button (the check mark with ABC on it).**

   You get the Spelling and Grammar dialog box shown in Figure 11-4, which gives you some interesting suggestions for replacing the word or phrase it doesn't recognize. (The Works spelling checker is very similar to the Word checker in Figure 11-4.)

Possible misspelling

Suggestions

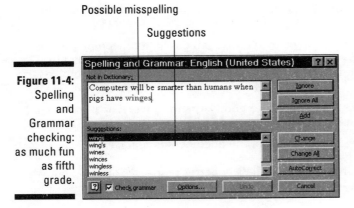

Figure 11-4:
Spelling
and
Grammar
checking:
as much fun
as fifth
grade.

Fortunately, the Spelling and Grammar dialog box often includes a good suggestion among the amusing ones (such as pigs having *wines,* the third suggestion in Figure 11-4), and all you have to do is choose that good one.

2. **To replace your original word with a word in the Suggestions list, click the word, then click the Change button.**

3. **If the word is actually okay, either click Ignore, or click Add to add the word to the dictionary.**

   Click Ignore if the word is okay here, but may be incorrect later in this document or in another document.

   Click Ignore All if the word is okay in this document (as *athwartships* may be in a document about sailboats) but may be a typo or misspelling in some other document.

   Click Add if the word is a real word (such as *atlatl*) that you may use again and again. The word is then added to the spell checker's Custom Dictionary and is thereafter and forever ignored in *any* document that you check. Be certain that the word is spelled correctly before you do this!

   After you choose one of the above actions, the checker moves on to scan the remainder of the document.

4. **You may also edit the original text directly in the checker's dialog box.**

   If you know a correction is necessary, click the text in the upper text box (the Not In Dictionary text box in Word; the Change To Text box in Works), and edit. Click the Change button to transfer the edit to your document and move along to the next apparent blunder in your text.

   Eventually, the spell checker reaches the end of your document and puts up a little box letting you know that the checking process is done. Click OK.

Chapter 12

Controlling Appearances and Printing

*O*ne must keep up appearances. There is no excuse for frumpy fonts, untidy indentation, improper alignment, unkempt tab stops, and mismanaged margins. Indeed, those who format fastidiously can even print sideways and control where their pages start and end.

In this chapter, I show you how to attain all those niceties of civilization — first-line indentation, line spacing, paragraph spacing, and more — automatically, without typing a bunch of tabs and blank lines. I work from the small to the large — from characters to paragraphs to documents — and explore how Word can help give your document a civilized and smart look.

Attention: Works word-processor users!

The word-processing tool of Works is so similar to Word for word-processing basics that you can often use the same instructions. If you are using Works, you'll find instructions that work for you wherever the *Works for Me!* icon appears. If the *Works for Me!* icon isn't present, the instructions are for Microsoft Word users.

If the Works for Me! icon appears at the first paragraph of a section, the whole section applies to the Works word processor. If the icon appears before a numbered list, the whole numbered list applies to Works. I'll call any exceptions in the section or list to your attention.

Charming Characters

When your characters are losing their charm, it's time to look for a prettier face — typeface, that is (or *font,* as it is misnamed in the geeky world of computers). Word can put your type in any font or any size. But wait! There's more! You can also easily change your font's *style,* making it **bold-face,** *italic,* underlined, superscript, subscript, or ~~strikethrough~~!

All told, you have three different kinds of formatting to play with: font, size, and style. These different aspects of type are called *character formatting.*

Word offers three alternatives for formatting your characters, as follows:

✔ Using the formatting toolbar's Font box and Font Size box, shown below.

Times New Roman | 12

To use either box, click the box and choose from the list that drops down. For bold, italic, or (single) underline style, click the **B,** *I,* or U buttons, respectively, just right of the center of the toolbar.

✔ Using the Font dialog box (shown in Figure 12-1) to choose from the complete range of fonts, sizes, and styles. Choose Format⇨Font to get this box. (If you're using the Works word processor, you choose Format⇨Font And Style, and the dialog box is called the Font And Style dialog box. See "Choosing Fonts and Other Basic Text Appearances" in Chapter 1.)

✔ Pressing Ctrl+B for bold, Ctrl+I for italic, and Ctrl+U for underline, to change the style.

Additional effects   Sample display

Underline styles   Color!

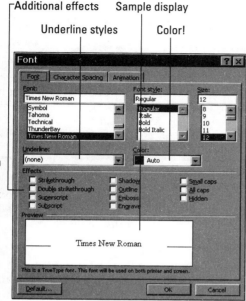

Figure 12-1:
The Font
dialog box
offers more
formatting
options
than the
toolbar.

To change the format of the text you are currently typing, use one of the preceding alternatives with no text selected. The formatting toolbar's boxes and buttons reflect the character formatting in effect at the point you are typing. To change the format of text after you type it, first select (highlight) that text and then choose one of the alternatives.

Pretty Paragraphs

There's no accounting for taste. (In fact, there's no Personnel, Purchasing, or any other department for taste.) Some folks like the first line of their paragraphs indented. Others, perhaps plumbing professionals, like them flush right. Some folks like their text double-spaced, and maybe they like bigger-than-average spaces between paragraphs, too. All this stuff is called *paragraph formatting,* which boils down to a few things you can fool with:

✔ **Indentation:** How far the paragraph's margins are indented from the page's margins.

✔ **Alignment:** How all the lines of the paragraph line up: against the left and/or right page margins, centered between them, or evenly spaced between them.

Spooky formatting changes

If you find yourself typing in a format you didn't intend, you probably placed your insertion point just before a formatted character. The character may even be invisible (like a space, tab, or paragraph mark). Text entered at the insertion point always takes on the format of the character that precedes it. Press the Backspace key to remove the invisible character. (Check out Chapter 11 for details on seeing, typing, and deleting these invisible characters.)

✔ **Breaks:** Whether to split up a paragraph when it crosses over onto the next page or to keep the paragraph as one solid lump; also, whether two paragraphs stay with each other on the same page.

One big deal about using paragraph formatting is that often you need to format only the first paragraph you type. As you type, you spawn new paragraphs from the original whenever you press the Enter key, and the same paragraph formatting applies to those descendants.

Alignments: Making your lines line up

Alignments are the simplest kind of paragraph formatting, so I get them out of the way first. You can choose from four kinds of alignment.

Left, left.

Centered, centered, centered, centered, centered, centered, centered, centered, centered, centered, centered, centered, centered.

Right, right.

Justified, justified.

Check out these two really easy ways to change alignment. First, select the paragraphs you want to realign (or, for a single paragraph, simply click to place your insertion point anywhere within it), and then either:

✔ **Click one of the four formatting toolbar buttons below:**

The buttons are, in order, Align Left, Align Center, Align Right, and Justify. (The Works word processor doesn't provide a Justify button.)

✔ **Use the Format Paragraph dialog box, and click one of the four alignment buttons there.**

I explain the Format Paragraph dialog box later in this chapter. Check out Chapter 7 for a picture of it.

✔ In Works (but not in Word), you can also **press the following keys on the keyboard:**

- Ctrl+L for align left
- Ctrl+Shift+R for align right
- Ctrl+E for align centered
- Ctrl+J for justified

Spaced-out paragraphs

Space is the final frontier of paragraph formatting. If you need a little air in your text, you can always ventilate your paragraph by double-spacing or adding space between paragraphs. But you don't add spaces the way your grandparents did on their old Dumbrowski-Stanowitz steam-powered typing machine:

✔ Don't press the Enter key twice at the end of every line to double-space. (Don't even press it once at the end of every line.)

✔ Don't press the Enter key twice at the end of every paragraph to put space between your paragraphs.

The quick way to get space between paragraphs is by pressing Ctrl+0. (That's zero, not the letter O.) This puts one line of space before the current paragraph if that space isn't there already. If a line of space is already there, this action takes it away. You can also use keyboard commands to set the line spacing within a paragraph:

✔ Ctrl+1 single-spaces the current paragraph (where your insertion point is).

✔ Ctrl+2 double-spaces the current paragraph.

✔ Ctrl+5 imposes one-and-a-half-line spacing on the paragraph.

You can also do this stuff (and lots more) with the Format Paragraph dialog box. See "Having it your way: The Paragraph dialog box," later in this chapter.

Quick indenting and outdenting

Indentation is one kind of paragraph format. A quick way to add left-side indentation to your paragraph is to select the paragraphs you want to indent (or, to indent a single paragraph, click anywhere in it), and then use Ctrl key combinations as follows:

> ✔ **To indent the left side:** Press Ctrl+M; the paragraph indents to the next tab stop (which, unless you add a tab stop, is the first so-called *default* tab stop, normally at $1/2$ inch). Press Ctrl+M again, and your paragraph indents to the next tab stop, and so on. (The *default* is the setting that Word uses until you tell it otherwise.)
>
> ✔ **To left-indent every line but the first line of the paragraph (called a *hanging indent*):** Press Ctrl+Shift+H.
>
> ✔ **To undo any left-side indentation:** Press Ctrl+Shift+M; this action *outdents* (reverses indentation) by one tab (moves the left edge of the paragraph left one tab stop).

In Word (but not Works), you also have toolbar buttons that do indenting and outdenting. The *out*denting button is on the left, as shown below; the *in*denting button is on the right:

What's wrong with simply using the Tab key to indent everything, as you would on a typewriter? In Word (and in Works), the Tab key does peculiar things. See "The tab stops here," later in this chapter. If you want to use the tab key for indentation, I suggest you use it only for left-side indentation of the first line or of the whole paragraph, and use it only after typing the paragraph. That is, click at the beginning of an existing line, and then press the Tab key.

Pressing the Tab key normally inserts a tab character in Word, and always does so in Works. (For more about tab characters, see the next section, "The tab stops here.") However, in Word, when you click at the beginning of an existing line and press the Tab key, Word actually decides, "Whoa! This dude wants to add indentation to the paragraph formatting." It does not insert tab characters at the beginning of the line.

The indentation described here is limited to the default intervals (initially ¹/₂ inch). For more control over the indentation of a paragraph, you can either use the Format Paragraph dialog box or the ruler bar. Check out "Having it your way: The Paragraph dialog box" and "Indenting with the ruler," later in this chapter.

The tab stops here

You know all about tab stops, right? Those things that you used to set on your Smith-Corona where, when you pressed the Tab key, you moved to the next stop? Nice and simple. Well, tabs are a tad (or a tab) more complex than they were on the old Smith-Corona, but they also do a few new tricks.

Using the Tab key

The Tab key worked fine on typewriters, but it is kind of a problem for word processors, for complex reasons. (The reasons have to do with the fact that text flows freely from line to line as you edit on a PC, whereas on a typewriter, text stays put.)

As a result of this problem, the Tab key is actually rather obsolete for most uses. Indenting lines and creating tables are the most common reasons people use the Tab key. But indentation is best done by paragraph formatting; see the earlier section "Quick indenting and outdenting" for indentation instructions. And you are usually better off using an official Word table for tables.

For more information on indentation, see "Having it your way: The Paragraph dialog box," later in this chapter.

Most of the time, the Tab key work much like it does on a typewriter: When you press the Tab key, the insertion point jumps to the next tab stop. (In Word and Works, unless you change the Tab stops yourself, stops are at every ¹/₂-inch from the left margin.)

The big difference between tabs in your word processor and tabs on a typewriter is that in Word (or Works), when you press the Tab key in the middle of a line, you insert a special tab character (normally invisible), whose job could be described as "creating a space between the preceding character and the next tab stop." (If you want to see the Tab character in Word, click the Show/Hide paragraph button on the toolbar. In Works, choose View⇨All Characters.) "Fine," you say, "Who cares?" You care — if you edit the line after the tab! If, for instance, you delete enough text preceding a tab character that currently skips to the 1 inch tab setting, the tab skips to the ¹/₂-inch tab setting instead! Because all subsequent text in the paragraph moves left to fill the space, subsequent tabs in the same line or paragraph may also be seriously wrong!

Newfangled tab stops

Your old Smith-Corona typewriter had only one kind of tab stop. Word and Works (like most word processors) have four kinds of tab stops:

- ✔ **Left tab stop:** The conventional tabs that you're accustomed to are called left tabs in a word processor because, after you press the Tab key, what you type begins after the stop; therefore, the text has its left edge at the tab. Your word processor uses left tab stops unless you tell it otherwise (the default tab setting), preset to appear every $1/2$-inch.

- ✔ **Decimal tab stop:** To better align numbers that appear in a column, you may want to use the decimal tab stop, which aligns every number at the decimal point. You set the tab stop in the position where you want the decimal point to be (or at the end of a number without a decimal point). After setting up the tab stop, press Tab to advance to this stop, then type a number. Your word processor types — oddly enough — to the left of this stop. It continues to type to the left of the stop until you type a decimal point; then it types to the right of the stop.

- ✔ **Right tab stop:** Unsurprisingly, the right tab stop is the opposite of the traditional or left tab stop. Instead of the left edge of text aligning with this stop, the right edge does. When you type (having first set up the tab and then pressed the Tab key to move to this stop), your word processor shifts text over to the left, keeping the right edge of the text aligned with the tab stop.

- ✔ **Center tab stop:** After you set up one of these guys, press the Tab key to move to it and then start to type. Your word processor shuffles your characters left and right as you go, in order to keep your text centered on the tab position. Whatever you type ends up centered at the tab stop.

To see the four kinds of tab stops in action, skip ahead in this chapter and check out Figure 12-3.

How do you set tab stops? You can set all four types of stops with the help of the Tabs dialog box (Format Tabs dialog box in Works), which I address in the next section. Unless you need to set tabs very precisely, however, your word processor's *ruler* is often an easier tool to use for setting tabs. See the section "The ruler: A benevolent monarch," later in this chapter.

Setting, clearing, and changing tab stops in a dialog box

If you want something other than the conventional, every $1/2$-inch tab stop, try using Word's Tabs dialog box (called Format Tabs in Works), shown in Figure 12-2. You, too, can get one of these lovely dialog boxes by choosing Format⇨Tabs. (The Works Format Tabs dialog box is arranged a bit differently but has nearly identical controls.)

Modify an existing tab

Add a tab to your paragraph

Enter a tab   Choose your tab type

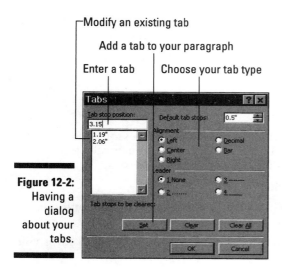

Figure 12-2:
Having a
dialog
about your
tabs.

The tab-setting dialog box works like this: You create one tab stop at a time, specifying its position, its alignment, and its (optional) leader (the character, if any, that fills the space that the tab creates), and then click the Set button. As you create each new stop, your word processor adds it to the list of stops.

The blow-by-blow instructions for using the Tabs dialog box to add, remove, or modify a tab stop are as follows:

1. **Select the paragraphs whose tab stops you want to set or change.**

   If you don't select anything, your word processor assumes that you want to set tabs in the paragraph where the insertion point is. Select multiple paragraphs to give them all the same tab stops.

2. **Choose Format⇨Tabs.**

   Any tab positions already set in the selected paragraph are listed in the largest white box at the left side of the dialog box. The interval at which default tab stops appear (0.5 inch initially) is listed in the box labeled Default Tab Stops.

3. **To add a new tab stop, enter its position in the box labeled Tab Stop Position.**

   Click the box immediately under the Tab Stop Position label and type in the position you want the tab stop to take (in tenths of an inch as measured from the left margin). Whatever you do in the dialog box — changing alignment and so on — now applies only to that Tab stop.

To modify or delete (or clear) an existing tab stop, click it in the list box (the largest white area) at the left of the Tabs dialog box.

4. Click an alignment for this tab stop in the Alignment area.

See the preceding section, for a discussion of the different types of alignment.

5. Click Set to add this tab stop to your paragraph.

When you add your own tab stops, your word processor removes any default tab stops between the left margin and your new tab stop. To review the tab alignments, just click them in the list box.

6. To remove this tab stop, click Clear.

7. To clear out all the tab stops in this paragraph (except default tabs), click Clear All.

8. Repeat with additional tab stops until you have just the tab stops you want in the Tab Stop Position list box.

To review the tabs' alignments, just click them in the list box.

9. Click the OK button.

The Tabs dialog box also says something about a leader. No, the tabs haven't formed a political system. A *leader* is what your word processor puts in the area occupied by the tab character. For example, in a *table of contents,* you use a right-tab between the topic and the page numbers, and may want a line of dots or something in that space (as in the table of contents of this book). To have a leader associated with a tab stop, click one of the styles shown in the Leader area; otherwise, click None.

Finally, if you really don't want to set a bunch of individual tab stops but want to change the intervals between the tab stops that your word processor provides (the default tab stops), just type a new interval in the Default Tab Stops text box. These tab stops are important because your word processor uses them for indenting paragraphs.

The ruler: A benevolent monarch

Nothing keeps order like a good ruler, so your word processor comes equipped with a royal one. Sometimes your word processor is a *royal* something else, but this ruler is a benevolent monarch.

If your ruler is missing, choose View⇨Ruler. Don't be shy; if a cat can look at a king, you can View your ruler. (The same command also lets you hide the ruler if it takes up too much real estate.)

The ruler reigns over indentations, alignments, and tab stops. A modest kingdom, perhaps, but an important one. See how it rules the indentations, alignments, and tab stops in the nonsensical paragraph of Figure 12-3.

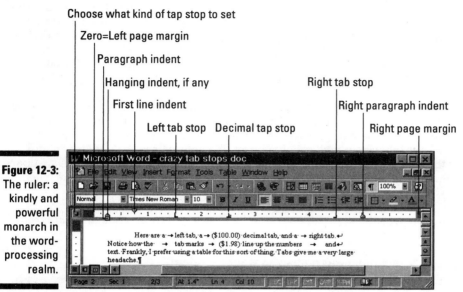

Choose what kind of tap stop to set

Zero=Left page margin

Paragraph indent

Hanging indent, if any

First line indent

Left tab stop   Decimal tap stop

Right tab stop

Right paragraph indent

Right page margin

Figure 12-3:
The ruler: a kindly and powerful monarch in the word-processing realm.

The Works word-processor ruler is very similar to the one Word uses. It displays all tabs, but it lets you set only left tabs.

Notice how the left side of the paragraph in Figure 12-3 aligns with the paragraph indent mark. Also, the first line aligns with the first line indent mark. (Pretty reasonable, huh?) Notice how text aligns in the paragraph with the left, decimal, and right tab stops, and with the right indent mark.

The ruler shows you what's going on in the paragraph your insertion point is in. Or, if you select a paragraph, the ruler tells about the paragraph you selected. The ruler can apply itself to only one paragraph at a time. If you select a bunch of paragraphs, it shows you what applies to the first one.

The totally, utterly cool thing about the ruler is that it not only *shows* you the paragraph stuff, it also lets you *control* the paragraph stuff. Exciting, right? (If you find it exciting, I fear for your well-being, but read on, regardless.)

Indenting with the ruler

The exciting thing about using the ruler for indents is that the ruler lets you adjust them graphically. Just click the left or right indentation mark (check out Figure 12-3 to see where they are) and drag it. As you drag, you move the edges of the paragraph that your insertion point is currently on! To set the edges of a bunch of paragraphs, select the paragraphs before you drag the marks. (To set the edges of all paragraphs in your document, press Ctrl+A to select everything!) These edges are technically called the left and right *paragraph indentations,* not paragraph margins. (Not to think of them as margins is hard, but that would be marginal thinking.)

The tricky thing about the pair of indentation marks on the left side is that they are related, like twins. The top half of this split pair controls only the first line of the paragraph. The bottom half of the pair controls the entire paragraph. One peculiar behavior of this split pair is that when you move the bottom half, the top half always moves along with it! The idea is, apparently, that you probably want to keep the first line indent the same when you change the paragraph indent.

So having said all that, I give you the blow-by-blow on changing paragraph indentations with the ruler:

1. **Select the paragraphs you want to indent.**

   If you don't select anything, Word assumes that you want to format the paragraph where the insertion point is.

2. **To indent the first line, drag the top of the pair of indentation marks on the left of the ruler bar.**

3. **To indent the whole paragraph, drag the bottom of the pair.**

4. **To indent the right side of the paragraph, drag the triangle on the right side of the ruler bar.**

You can also change indentations by using a dialog-box approach. The dialog box is not as cool and graphical as the ruler, but the dialog box is more precise and is easier to use for those of us with poor eye-hand coordination. See "Having it your way: The Paragraph dialog box," later in this chapter.

Tab stops on the ruler

Your word processor already provides a nice set of built-in (default) tab stops, spaced every ¹/₂ inch. If you want other tab stops, follow this complicated instruction:

Click in the ruler where you want your tab.

In Word's ruler (but not Works'), you can choose what kind of tab stop to set: left, right, center, or decimal. As you click the button that shows a tab symbol at the far left the symbol cycles through the different varieties of tab stops you can set. When the symbol for the variety of tab you want appears, click in the ruler where you want that variety of tab.

What if you don't like your tabs once you've got them? Try the following:

- ✔ To move your tab marks around, drag 'em. The built-in default tabs that fall before or between your marks are removed.

- ✔ To remove one of your tab marks, drag it off the ruler and into the document, where it evaporates in the rarefied atmosphere of your prose.

- ✔ In Works, you can double-click the ruler bar to access the Format Tab dialog box. See the section "The tab stops here," earlier in this chapter for instructions on using that dialog box.

Having it your way: The Paragraph dialog box

For one-stop shopping in the world of paragraph formatting, use the Paragraph dialog box shown in Figures 12-4 and 12-5. This two-card dialog box supplies nearly all your paragraph formatting needs. Indentations, alignments, breaks, mufflers — you name it; everything for the well-formatted paragraph except tab stops.

Works users: Your dialog box is called Format Paragraph. As in Word, you can access it with Format⇨Paragraph, and as in Word, its features are distributed on two cards. The indentation, alignment, and paragraph-spacing controls are nearly identical to the ones Word uses, just located on different cards: the Indents and Alignment card and the Spacing card. Your Indents and Alignment card also provides a Bulleted check box for applying bullets to your paragraphs.

Begin formatting a paragraph by placing your insertion point in a paragraph to be formatted or selecting several paragraphs. Then get a Format Paragraph dialog box in either of two ways:

- ✔ Choose Format⇨Paragraph.
- ✔ Double-click the left or right indent marks on the ruler bar.

The dialog box looks like two index cards — Indents And Spacing and Line And Page Breaks. You can switch between them by clicking the top tab of the hidden card. Both cards have preview boxes that show you what the reformatted paragraph looks like on a page.

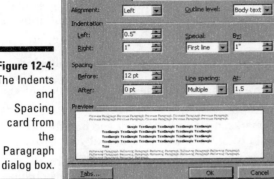

You use the Format Paragraph box by making whatever changes you want on the two cards and then clicking the OK button. Nothing changes in your document until you click OK. If you click the Cancel button at any time, you return to your paragraph without making any changes.

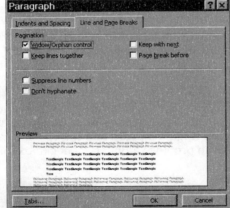

Indents and spacing

The Indents and Spacing card (refer to Figure 12-4) controls not only indentations, but also text alignment, the spacing between lines of the paragraph, and spacing between paragraphs. (In Works, these controls are distributed between the two cards.) The options are as follows:

✔ **Alignment:** Click to choose Left, Right, Center, or Justified.

✔ **Outline Level:** A Word (not Works) format that applies only in the Outline view, which I don't discuss in this book.

- ✔ **Left Indentation:** Sets the distance between the left paragraph margin and the left page margin.

- ✔ **Right Indentation:** Sets the distance between the right paragraph margin and the right page margin.

- ✔ **Special:** Specifies a first line indentation or a hanging indent. Click Special to choose an indentation style, then click By to enter the indentation distance. (In Works, click First Line and type a positive value for an indented first line, and a negative value for a hanging indent.)

- ✔ **Before Spacing:** The spacing you want preceding the selected paragraph(s).

- ✔ **After Spacing:** The spacing you want following the selected paragraph(s).

- ✔ **Line Spacing:** Specifies the spacing within the paragraph: Single, Double, or 1.5 lines. Or, choose Multiple and enter the spacing in lines (enter **3** if you want triple-spaced text) in the At box. Choose Exactly if you prefer to specify spacing in points (typesetting measurements) in the At box; in-line characters or graphics that are too tall to fit in that space will be chopped off. Choose At Least to specify points, but to allow your word processor to adjust for tall characters or graphics on a line.

Line and page breaks

The Line and Page Breaks card of the Format Paragraph dialog box (refer to Figure 12-5) tells Word how each paragraph relates to its neighboring paragraphs and where to place page breaks with respect to paragraphs. Following are the various options on this card and what they do:

- ✔ **Widow/Orphan Control:** Prevents Word from leaving a single line of a paragraph on one page, if the page happens to break mid-paragraph.

- ✔ **Keep Lines Together:** Keeps the entire paragraph on one page. (In Works, use the Don't Break Paragraph check box).

- ✔ **Keep with Next:** (Keep Paragraph With Next, in Works.) Keeps the paragraph on the same page as the following paragraph. (Of course, if the combined paragraphs are more than a page long, there's no way to keep them on the same page.)

- ✔ **Page Break Before:** Forces a page break before the paragraph. (This choice can be useful for the first paragraph of a chapter or section.)

- ✔ **Suppress Line Numbers:** If you're using line numbers (which this book does not discuss), this choice hides the number of the paragraph.

- ✔ **Don't Hyphenate:** Turns off Word's automatic hyphenation feature for the paragraph.

(Clicking the Tabs button, naturally enough, takes you to the Tabs dialog box.)

Having it their way: Styles

Often, you want to use a particular kind of formatting over and over again for consistency. All headings of a particular level in a document, for instance, should be similarly formatted, and most body text should appear the same. Word lets you format text with named *styles,* which can be character formatting, paragraph formatting, or a combination of both. If you change the definition of the style (say, increasing the font size), everything in that style that has not been individually formatted changes accordingly.

Works users can read about Easy Formats, which are similar to styles, in Chapter 8.

In fact, Word has several built-in styles, including the default style, Normal, which is what it uses unless you choose a different style. Word also offers three levels of heading styles and several body text styles. You can use Word's styles as they are, change them to your own preferences, or create your own from scratch.

The quickest way to apply one of Word's standard styles is to click or select the paragraph(s) you want to format and then choose a style from the formatting toolbar. Click the down-arrow on the Style selection box, at the far left end of Word's formatting toolbar. (Unless you've fooled around with styles, the Style selection box probably has the word Normal in it.) Each style has a name and shows a format; click one to apply it.

The list you get from the toolbar doesn't display the details of the formatting very clearly, however. If you need to review the details before applying a style, choose Format⇨Style to use the Style dialog box. Click any style listed in the Styles box and read the description provided. Click the Apply button to apply that style to the paragraph where your insertion point currently resides (or to currently selected paragraphs).

Having it your way: Creating your own styles

If you find yourself using the same combination of character and paragraph formatting again and again, you can add it to Word's list of styles. All you have to do is:

1. **Click or select a paragraph that is already formatted the way that you want.**

2. **Choose Format⇨Style and click the New button in the Style dialog box that appears.**

3. **In the New Style dialog box that appears, type a name for your style in the Name box.**

4. **If you want this style to be available to you in future new documents (those created using the current *template* — usually the Normal template), click the Add to Template check box.**

5. **Click the OK button in the New Style dialog box and then click the Close button in the Styles dialog box.**

   Now your newly named style appears on the list of styles on the toolbar, where you can easily choose it to format any future paragraph.

Perfecting Your Page Layout

Most of this chapter talks about the small stuff: character and paragraph formatting. But what about the big picture? How big is a page, which way does it print, and what are the margins? Good questions. I'm glad you asked.

Word begins by assuming a bunch of stuff about the page — the *page defaults:*

🖊 You're using 8¹/₂-x-11-inch paper, oriented the normal way for a letter.

🖊 Top and bottom margins are 1 inch. Left and right margins are 1.25 inches. If you're using headers and footers, they are .5 inch from the top and bottom of the paper.

Word automatically places page breaks based on these settings and based on how you format your characters and paragraphs. You can also add page breaks manually.

Most of the formatting-of-the-overall-document stuff is tucked away inside the Page Setup dialog box.

Page setup

To set up your document's overall appearance (which is not to imply that it looks like a pair of old overalls), do the following:

Choose File⇨Page Setup.

This action wins you a Page Setup dialog box. When you first use this Page Setup command, the top card is the Margins card shown in Figure 12-6. These cards all deal with different aspects of page setup and printing. Click a card's tab, sticking out at the top, to choose it.

Figure 12-6:
Page Setup
has cards
like Mom's
recipe card
file, but
without the
blueberry
pie stains.
One of
these is the
Margins
card.

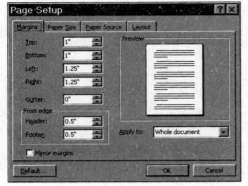

Works users: The Page Setup dialog box in Works is very similar. Chapter 1 has the details.

Each card in the dialog box also shows you a preview to give you a rough idea of what your document looks like using the changes you make. One quirk to be aware of is that if you type something into one of the boxes on these cards (say, Top Margin), the preview doesn't show your changes until you click a different box on that card (say, Bottom Margin) or press the Tab key.

Margins

Using the Page Setup dialog box in Figure 12-6 (choose File➪Page Setup if the Page Setup dialog box is not already up), click the tab marked Margins. Enter new values in the various margin boxes. Following are a few tips for setting margins:

✔ Headers and footers are supposed to fit within the top and bottom page margins, respectively. If you make the header or footer margin larger than the page margin, Word increases the page margin.

✔ The default unit is inches, so if you want inches, just type the number of inches you want. If you want to use another unit, type the number and then one of the following abbreviations for the unit: **cm** for centimeters, **mm** for millimeters, **pi** for picas, and **pt** for points. (Whatever you type, it will be converted to inches when you return to this dialog box later!)

✔ Remember that the Preview doesn't show your changes until you click in a different margin box from the one you just edited, or you press the Tab key.

> ✔ To change margins, place your insertion point where you want the margins to change before choosing File⇨Page Setup, then click the Apply To box and choose This Point Forward from the selections that appear.
>
> ✔ If you're printing an *edge-bound document* printed on two sides (a book, for example), increase the left margin to allow for binding space, then click the Mirror Margins check box. The left margin becomes the inside margin (for the bound edge) and the right margin becomes the outside margin.

Click OK when you're all done setting up the page.

Sideways documents

Most printers these days let you print sideways (known to printers as landscape). You just have to let Word know that sideways printing is what you have in mind. Use the Page Setup dialog box (choose File⇨Page Setup if the box is not already up).

In the Page Setup dialog box, click the tab marked Paper Size. Then click Landscape in the lower-left corner to print sideways. (Portrait is the other, more customary printing orientation, like the portrait of *Mona Lisa*.) The page icon, with the letter A, illustrates how type is to be printed on the page. The preview also changes to show you how the lines of text run.

To change printing orientation within a document (perhaps where large tables begin), first place your insertion point where you want the change to begin. Choose File⇨Page Setup to get the Page Setup dialog box; then click the Paper Size card, choose your orientation, click the Apply To box and choose This Point Forward. To resume your earlier printing orientation on a later page, move your insertion point to that page and repeat the process.

Click OK unless you need to set up something else, such as the paper size.

Different-sized documents

If you're using anything other than 8½-x-11-inch paper (or if you're using an envelope), you need to tell Word about it. (Word has special features for envelopes; see Chapter 13.) Use the Page Setup dialog box (choose File⇨Page Setup if the box is not already up).

1. **In the Page Setup dialog box, click the tab marked Paper Size.**

2. **On the Paper Size card, click the Paper Size selection box.**

3. **Click one of the standard paper or envelope sizes in the box that drops down.**

   If you're using a paper size that's not shown, click the box marked Width and enter a new value; then do the same for Height. (Width always refers to the direction that a line of text runs.) After your last change, click in a different box from the one that you're in and check the preview to see if things look roughly correct.

4. **Click OK when you're all done setting up the page.**

Page breaks

When you fill one page, Word begins another page automatically as you're typing. If you want the page to break at an earlier location, you can put in a page break yourself. If you want the page to break later, forget it. Word can't squeeze any more on a page unless you change some formatting.

Most of the time, the automatic page breaks are just fine because Word counts lines and measures spaces much better than you can (it being a computer program and all). But occasionally you know something that Word doesn't, such as the fact that this particular line is the start of a new chapter and really needs to come at the top of a page. Then you want to be able to put in a page break yourself.

You can tell Word not to put a page break within a paragraph or between two consecutive paragraphs. Look at "Having it your way: The Paragraph dialog box," earlier in this chapter.

You can also put in a pair of page breaks to make a blank page or insert a page break to force a page to appear on the right side in a bound document (such as this book). Don't try this last trick until you finish all the editing. (Otherwise, you may have to repaginate the entire book.)

How to put in your own page break in two easy steps:

1. **Click exactly where you want the page break to occur.**

   Click the first line of a paragraph, then press the Home key to ensure you are at the very start of a paragraph, to avoid any problems with tabs or other invisible characters.

2. **Press Ctrl+Enter or choose Insert⇨Break, then choose Page Break.**

   (In Works, choose Insert⇨Page Break.)

   A dotted line appears; this is your page break symbol. You can delete, cut, paste, or drag the page break symbol just like any other symbol on the page. To select the page break by itself, click the left margin next to the symbol.

After your page break, Word continues to do its own normal, automatic page-breaking thing. Let it. Don't do any more manual page-breaking than you absolutely must.

Printing

You may think that with all this computer wizardry, humans would advance beyond flattening a bunch of trees into thin sheets, smearing ink on them, and then tossing them away when we finish reading them. But no, computer use has actually increased paper consumption. In this section, I tell you how to get good printing results without wasting any more paper than absolutely necessary.

Works users: Your printing features are similar to Word's (minus a few features). See Chapter 1 for details.

Previewing: Printing without paper

If you really want to save a tree, try Print Preview, shown in Figure 12-7. Print Preview shows you how your document will look in print, without wasting paper.

Most Windows applications provide a Print Preview feature similar to the one in Word.

You can get into Print Preview in one of two ways:

> ✔ Choose File⇨Print Preview in the menu bar.
> ✔ Click the Print Preview button in the standard toolbar, shown here:
>
>

Figure 12-7 identifies the various options in Print Preview.

To switch between maximum and minimum magnifications of the document, click the document itself. To magnify at intermediate levels, click the Zoom control and choose a magnification level.

When magnifying, use the vertical and horizontal scroll bars to view parts of the document that extend beyond the window. (See the appendix if scroll bars are new to you.)

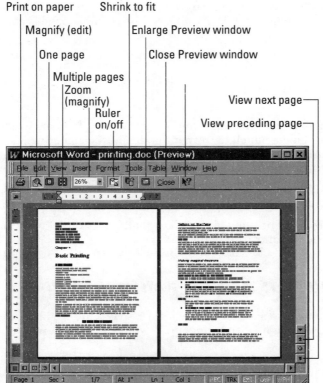

Print on paper
Magnify (edit)
One page
Multiple pages
Zoom (magnify)
Ruler on/off
Shrink to fit
Enlarge Preview window
Close Preview window
View next page
View preceding page

Figure 12-7:
Print Preview
shows you
microscopic
print on a
minuscule
page. Click
the page to
zoom in.

Following are some additional tips for the Preview window:

- ✓ The Print button starts printing immediately, without displaying a Print dialog box.
- ✓ The Magnify button is normally enabled (depressed), which means that clicking the document zooms you in or out. Click the Magnify button to disable it and then click the document to edit.
- ✓ Click the Multiple Pages button and move your cursor diagonally across the array that appears to display a similar multipage array.
- ✓ The Shrink to Fit button adjusts font size to avoid having a fractional last page. Press Ctrl+2 to undo.
- ✓ The Full Screen button fills your monitor with a preview.
- ✓ Click Close to return to your regular editing view.

Printing on actual paper!

The time has come to smear ink on dead trees. Printing is pretty simple when things go right. Do the following:

1. **Turn on your printer and wait until it comes online.**

   Most printers have an indicator light somewhere to tell you when the printer is paying attention to your PC. Consult your printer manual if you have questions.

2. **To print the whole document right now** (that is, you "don't need no stinking Print dialog box"), **click the Print button on the standard toolbar (the button with picture of a printer on it).**

   At this point, the rest is up to Windows and your printer. Read "Terminating printing" later in this chapter if you change your mind about printing the document.

3. **To print the document in any other way, choose File⇨Print or press Ctrl+P.**

   The Print dialog box shown in Figure 12-8 comes to your aid. Click OK when you are ready to print.

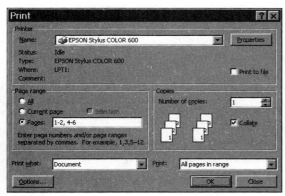

Figure 12-8:
Printing what you want, how you want it.

Use these features to make good use of the key printing options Word provides in the Print dialog box:

> ✔ For *multiple copies,* click the Number of Copies box and enter the number of copies you want (but don't press the Enter key). If you want to print all the page 1 copies, then all page 2 copies, and so on, click to uncheck the Collate check box.

✔ To print just the *current page* (where your insertion point is), choose Current Page.

✔ To print *selected (highlighted) text in the document,* choose Selection.

✔ To print a specific *group of pages,* click Pages and enter page numbers as the instructions under the Pages box describe.

✔ To *print on both sides of the paper* (as for a bound document), unless you have a two-sided printer, first check your printer manual to make sure that you can manually reinsert paper. If all systems are go, print the odd-numbered pages first by choosing Odd Pages in the Print selection box. When the odd pages finish printing, reinsert the pages blank-side-up in the printer (with the top edge pointing the same direction as before) then go back to the Print selection box and choose Even Pages. Before printing the Even pages, check the stack of pages to be sure Page 1 will be taken first (so that page 2 goes on the flip side of page 1). If the order is reversed, click the Options button to enable the Reverse Print Order check box.

✔ To *change to another printer* (or "print" to a fax modem [another way to say *send a fax*]), click the Name box and choose a printer (or fax modem) from the list that drops down.

✔ To use any of the *special options of your printer,* click the Properties button. A printer-specific dialog box appears. Check your printer manual for instructions.

Terminating printing

If you just sent your resume to the printer and you discover your boss is standing next to the printer, you need to take action, fast! Here's what to do.

Don't just turn off the printer. Your paper may get stuck halfway, and your PC may get confused and send you error messages. Don't just turn off the PC, either, or it may be confused when you restart it.

Depending upon what printer you use, a dialog box for your printer may appear on your screen as soon as you click OK in the Print dialog box (Step 3 of the preceding section). If such a dialog box appears, click the stop button (sometimes marked with a black square). I can't tell you exactly what to click because the dialog box comes from your printer's manufacturer. Check your manual for details.

If no dialog box for your printer appears on your screen, Windows provides a quick emergency stop procedure.

1. **Click the Windows Start button (on the Windows Taskbar, not in Word), then choose Settings⇨Printers.**

2. **In the Printers dialog box that appears, double-click the printer you're using.**

   A dialog box appears with the same name as your printer, and displaying your file's name.

3. **Click your file's name in that dialog box, then choose Document⇨ Cancel Printing from the Printers dialog box's menu, and wait for printing to stop.**

   Printing may continue for a page or so, depending on how many pages are already downloaded to your printer's memory.

Chapter 13

Dressing Up Your Document and Sending It Out

*Y*ou've seen your document through the basics: writing, editing, formatting, and printing. Now your document is grown up enough for you to dress it up, introduce it to society, and generally have a little fun. (*Fun* in the highly abstract, metaphoric sense of the word, that is. If you really find yourself eagerly looking forward to word processing, you may want to consider enlisting the aid of a competent lifestyle advisor.)

Dress your document in top hat and tails: add some headers and footers! Teach its pages to do a few numbers; show it how to dance some footnotes, sit down correctly at a table, go to a few shady places across the border, and still get written up nicely in columns. Then send it out "enveloped" with pride!

One way to make a fancier document is to add graphics of various kinds, such as charts, photographs, or other pictures. This chapter discusses charts; See Chapter 14 for tips on dealing with every photo issue *except* the paparazzi.

Attention: Works word-processor users!

The word-processing basics of Word 97 and the Works word-processing tool are so similar that they often use the same commands. In this part of the book, the *Works for Me!* icon guides Works users to instructions that work for them. If the icon isn't present, the instructions are for Word users.

If the Works For Me! icon appears at the first paragraph of a section, the whole section applies to Works' word processor. If the icon appears before a numbered list, the whole numbered list applies to Works. I call any exceptions in the section or list to your attention.

Bulleted Lists: Shooting from the Toolbar

It's a jungle out there, and a few bullets may come in handy — bulleted lists, that is. Bulleted lists are made up of indented paragraphs, each with a little dot next to its first line.

If you want simple, big-black-dot-style bullets, you can get them easily from the Bullets button on the toolbar. (The icon on the Bullets button looks like a bulleted list.) All you have to do is type your paragraphs in the usual way, select (highlight) the ones you want bulleted, and click the Bullets button.

The Bullets button indents your paragraph text from the bullet by $1/4$ inch. (In Word, you can adjust this indentation in the Bullets and Numbering dialog box, discussed in the next section.) For some bulleted lists, you may also want to indent the whole bulleted paragraph: Press Ctrl+M to increase indentation by one tab stop. Press Ctrl+Shift+M to reduce the indentation by one tab stop.

You can remove bullets without an anesthetic. Just select the proper paragraphs and click the Bullets button again.

Bullets behave like paragraph formats do: When you press Enter within any bullet-formatted paragraph, you get a new, pre-bulleted paragraph. This feature lets you type with bulleting *on* and spawn new bulleted paragraphs as you go. To stop using bullets, click the Bullet button.

In Word, a bullet is a special character, separated from the text by a tab character. Word uses a hanging indent of $1/4$ inch and places a left tab stop at the $1/4$-inch point to make the text line up. In Works, bullets are actually a paragraph format; so you can enable or disable them in the Format Paragraph dialog box (choose Format⇨Paragraph) but you can't actually delete a bullet character. In both word processors, a hanging indent is used so that the bullet stands out from the paragraph text.

Heavy Ammo: The Format Bullets Dialog Box

Bullets of any make and caliber are available from the Bullets and Numbering dialog box. To use this dialog box for your ammo, click in the paragraph you want to be bulleted (or select several paragraphs by dragging across them); then choose Format⇨Bullets and Numbering.

If you select one or more paragraphs, you can also get the Bullets and Numbering dialog box by right-clicking the selection and choosing Bullets and Numbering from the menu that drops down.

In the Bullets and Numbering dialog box, simply click a bulleting style — or disarm your selected paragraphs (remove their bullets) by clicking the None selection. Then click the OK button.

Works users, your instructions are slightly different: Choose Format⇨Bullets, and you get the Format Bullets dialog box. Click the bullet of your choice in the Bullet Style box. Adjust the bullet's caliber in the Bullet Size box by either typing a number into the box or clicking the up- and down-arrows next to the box. Click the Hanging Indent check box to set or clear the check mark there, and watch the effect in the Sample window. Click the Remove button to remove bullets altogether.

Need a custom style or caliber of bullet? Need more space between your text and its bullet? Visit the custom bullet shop by clicking the Bullets and Numbering dialog box's Customize button. The Customize Bulleted List dialog box opens its doors to you.

Any character in any font on your PC can become a bullet; just click the Bullet button to choose your symbol. Click the Font button to adjust the bullet size or choose a different font, using the familiar old Font dialog box that I introduce in Chapter 12.

Page Numbers, Headers, and Footers

Headers and *footers* are chunks of text that appear in a special location, either at the top (headers) or at the bottom (footers) on every page of a document. You typically use headers and footers for chapter or section titles or to remind everyone who the author is.

A *page number* is an automatically computed number that appears in a footer or a header. It appears either by itself or with other text, such as after the word Page. You can insert page numbers while creating headers or footers, or use the separate Page Number dialog box, described in the following section.

To use headers, footers, or page numbers in Works, please see Chapter 8.

Inserting automatic page numbers

If all you want is plain old page numbers without having to think about this footer and header stuff, choose Insert⇨Page Numbers. The Page Number dialog box gives you several options:

- ✔ **Position:** Choose Top of Page (Header) or Bottom of Page (Footer)

- ✔ **Alignment:** Choose Left, Right, or Center; or for documents like bound books, Inside (the edge the binding is on) or Outside (used in the very book you're holding).

- ✔ **Show Number on First Page:** Most documents don't bother numbering the first page. Click this check box if you prefer to number page 1.

- ✔ **Format:** This button leads you to a dialog box where you can choose fancy ways to number pages. Several options involve complicated schemes for automatically numbering sections or chapters — topics I don't explore in this book. The others are:

  - • **Number format:** Click to choose Roman numerals or letters.

  - • **Page Numbering:** In the Start At box, click to start at some number other than 1 (or *i* if you are an ancient Roman). Enter that number here.

Word automatically keeps page numbers up-to-date as you add or delete pages.

Creating headers and footers

A header or footer is text that is reproduced on every page of a document. Usually the text of a header or footer is exactly the same on every page, but there are a few special cases, all of which the headings of this very book illustrate. One special case is page numbers, which change automatically for every page. (For every page to have the same number would be kind of useless.) Another special case is the first page of a document (like the first page of each chapter in this book). The third special case is header or footer text that differs between odd-numbered and even-numbered pages.

To put a header or footer into your document, just follow these instructions:

1. **Choose View⇨Header and Footer. (Or if you are in Page Layout view, where the headers and footers appear in light gray, double-click the header or footer.)**

   This step does several things. First, it plops a floating Header and Footer toolbar (a toolbar you can drag around) on your screen, as shown in Figure 13-1. Second, it puts your document into Page Layout view. Third, it moves the insertion point to the header area on the current page. Header and footer areas are enclosed by a dashed line marked with a Header or Footer label.

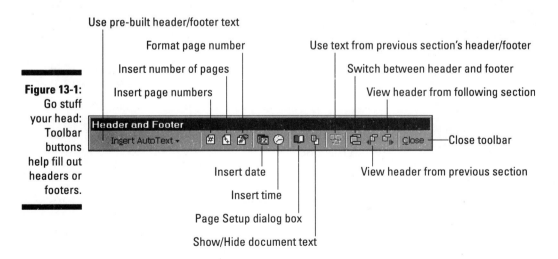

Use pre-built header/footer text

Format page number

Insert number of pages

Insert page numbers

Use text from previous section's header/footer

Switch between header and footer

View header from following section

Figure 13-1:
Go stuff
your head:
Toolbar
buttons
help fill out
headers or
footers.

Header and Footer

Insert AutoText ▾

Close — Close toolbar

Insert date

Insert time

Page Setup dialog box

Show/Hide document text

View header from previous section

2. **Choose whether to work on a header or footer.**

   If you start out working in a header, you can switch to a footer by either scrolling down in your document window to the footer and clicking there, or by clicking the Switch between Header and Footer button shown in Figure 13-1.

3. **Click Insert AutoText (refer to Figure 13-1) to choose from pre-designed header or footer text that includes various page numbering styles, and options for inserting the date, time, your name, or the document name — or any combination of these.**

   The AutoText selections may well be everything you need. If they're not quite perfect, you can edit them or type in your own stuff.

4. **Edit or type your own header or footer text.**

   Anything that you can do in ordinary text, you can do in a header or footer. Use italics, giant fonts, different alignments, Word styles — anything goes.

   In addition to typing, you can insert special text from the toolbar: the page number, the total number of pages in the document (for text like "Page 3 of 15"), or a date or time that is updated every time you open or print the file. Figure 13-1 shows you which buttons to click.

   Page numbers are numbered automatically as the header or footer is reproduced on each page. Although you only see the current page's number at the moment, each page always displays its proper page number. Don't think you need to make a new header or footer for each page!

5. **For a special header on the first page, or for different headers on odd and even pages, click the Page Setup button (refer to Figure 13-1).**

   The Page Setup dialog box appears, laying out its Layout card. Click either or both check boxes: Different Odd and Even, and Different First Page. Click OK in that dialog box to return to your document. Scroll your document to the appropriate page (the first page, or an odd or even numbered page), and click in its header or footer area to create your header.

6. **For special page numbering, like Roman numerals, click the Format Page Number button.**

   See the discussion of the Format button in the preceding section, "Inserting automatic page numbers."

   When you're done with the Page Setup dialog box, click OK.

Adjusting header and footer margins

Anyone who has ever slept in a short bed is sensitive to having suitable margins for their headers and footers. To change your header or footer margin, choose File⇨Page Setup to get the Page Setup dialog box. Click the tab marked Margins and type in a new margin value for your header or footer.

Headers and footers are supposed to appear within (be less than) the top and bottom page margins, respectively. If you make header or footer margins larger than the page margins, Word adjusts the page margins.

Footnote Fundamentals

When I get old (which should be by next Friday, at the very latest), I won't bore younger people with tales of how I trudged miles to school in the deep snow. Oh, no — I plan to bore younger people by telling them how we used to do footnotes before there were word processors. But if you want to be bored, you don't need me; you can just read the Word manual. (Besides, how can I tell whether you're younger than I am?)

Here's how to do automatically numbered footnotes:

1. **Put the insertion point just after the text you want to footnote.**

2. **Choose Insert⇨Footnote.**

   The footnote footman (in the form of a Footnote and Endnote dialog box) comes to your aid.

   If you're using Works, not Word, your dialog box is different. For a standard numbered footnote, click the Insert button in the Insert Footnote dialog box that appears. If you prefer symbols over numbers, click Special Mark, type the mark that you want (usually * or **) in the Mark box, then click the Insert button. Skip to Step 4.

3. **Choose either Footnote (to put your note at the bottom of the page) or Endnote (to put your note at the end of the document), and click OK if you want a normal, numbered footnote.**

   If you prefer asterisks or some other symbol, click the Custom Mark box. Then type the mark that you want (usually * or **) in the Mark box and click OK.

4. **The insertion point moves to the footnote area at the bottom of your current page, right after an automatic footnote number. Type in your footnote text, beginning with a space (for appearance's sake).**

5. **To return to your place in the text, double-click the footnote number (or other symbol).**

   Step 5 doesn't work in Works. Instead, press the Page Up key or scroll up to get back to where you were typing.

To delete a footnote, just delete its reference mark in the text. The mark *and* the footnote go away, and the remaining footnotes are renumbered.

 Serious scholars may need to adjust the location of footnotes, choose a different number format, or adjust the starting numbers. Word provides controls for such changes, which you can find by clicking the Options button. Their use is straightforward, and so is "left as an exercise for the student."

Tables

Word lets you create nearly any kind of table you can imagine, but its table-handling features can be a bit overwhelming. The following sections should help reduce the confusion.

Creating a table

Tables work best if you first make a new paragraph and then start your table — although you may certainly insert a table in the middle of an existing paragraph if you like.

Each cell (square) of your table has the same formatting as the paragraph in which you insert the table. For a nice, cleanly formatted table, choose Normal from the style box on Word's formatting toolbar and check the toolbar to make sure bullets and numbering are turned off.

Word gives you several ways to make tables. Here's the most straightforward way:

1. **Choose Table⇨Insert Table.**

   The Insert Table dialog box appears on the scene.

2. **Size your table.**

   Enter the number of rows and columns that you need into the Number of Columns and Number of Rows boxes. Don't forget to add a row for your column heads and a column for your row heads.

3. **Click AutoFormat to format your table.**

   The Table AutoFormat dialog box shown in Figure 13-2 makes an appearance. On the left side of the dialog box is a list of possible formats. Each time you click a name, the Preview box on the right changes to show you how that format looks.

   To further customize a format, you can disable its borders, colors, chosen font styles, or the heading row or column. Click to clear or enable various check boxes in the bottom of the Table Autoformat box,

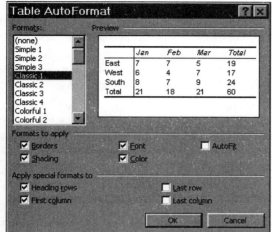

	Jan	Feb	Mar	Total
East	7	7	5	19
West	6	4	7	17
South	8	7	9	24
Total	21	18	21	60

Figure 13-2:
Use
AutoFormat
to set your
table.

as Figure 13-2 shows, and watch the result in the Preview window. If your table has a row or column of totals, click to enable the Last Row or Last Column check box. To automatically size the table to fit its contents, click to enable the AutoFit check box.

4. **OK! OK! Click OK in the Table AutoFormat dialog box, and then OK in the Insert Table dialog box.**

Pouf! Your table is ready, *monsieur* or *madame*. Simply click any cell and type to fill it in. You can put or format nearly anything in a table, including tab stops (decimal tabs are useful for columns of numbers), illustrations, and bulleted paragraphs — but you can't insert a table in a table!

Modifying your table

Tables in Word are immensely flexible. Following are some tips for modifying your table. Most tips involve commands on the Table menu of the menu bar; you can often give the same commands by right-clicking the table and choosing off the menu that drops down.

✔ To select multiple cells, drag across them.

✔ To select (highlight) an entire row, column, or the entire table so you can format its contents, delete it or its contents, or do something else to it, click the row, column, or table and choose Table⇨Select Row, Select Column, or Select Table.

✔ To insert a new row above the row where your insertion point lies, choose Table⇨Insert Rows.

✔ To insert a new column, choose Table⏵ Select Column, then Table⏵Insert Columns. To insert multiple new columns, drag across the many existing columns before issuing the commands.

✔ To insert new cells, select one or more existing cells, then choose Table⏵Insert Cells. The Insert Cells dialog box that appears lets you choose which direction to shift existing rows or columns.

✔ To adjust column width or row height, slowly move your cursor over the dividing line between rows or columns until the cursor changes to a double-line-with-arrows. Then click and drag the line.

Borders and Shade

Nothing like a few good lines and a little shade to liven up a party! Word's got 'em, in the form of *borders* and *shade* around paragraphs or pages. Borders are boxes around text; shade (well, *shading*, actually) is a colored background behind the text.

Here are a few shady, borderline tips:

✔ To create a horizontal line, apply a bottom or top border to a paragraph.

✔ To create a vertical line, apply a left or right border to your paragraph(s).

✔ You can apply borders or shade to nearly anything — one paragraph, a group of paragraphs, or every page in your document — using different styles, line types, and colors.

✔ Because borders and shade are actually a sort of paragraph formatting, if you spawn a new paragraph by pressing the Enter key in a bordered or shaded paragraph, the new paragraph is bordered or shaded, too.

✔ Consecutive, identical paragraphs, identically bordered or shaded, merge into one bordered or shaded block.

Selecting what to border or shade

You can apply borders or shade to darn near anything. Just select the "anything" first:

✔ **To border or shade a single paragraph, click anywhere within the paragraph.**

✔ **To border or shade a group of paragraphs, select the group (double-click in the left margin and drag).**

For this effect to work well, the selected paragraphs should all have the same left and right indents. With the group selected, drag the left and right indent marks on the ruler to set common indentations.

🖛 **To border or shade any old chunk of text, select the text.**

🖛 **To border an illustration, click it. (Shading is not available for illustrations.)**

Marking your borders

Here's how you, too, can create borderline documents, just like the pros. With your target selected, do the following:

1. **Choose Format⇨Borders and Shading.**

   The border patrol arrives on the scene in its three-card, four-wheel-drive dialog box. Have your passport ready.

2. **Click the tab of the Borders card to put borders on paragraphs. Choose the Page Borders tab to border entire pages.**

   Figure 13-3 shows the Borders card. The Page Borders card is nearly identical.

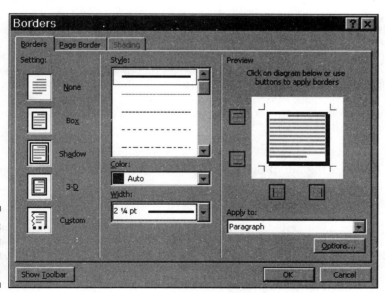

Figure 13-3:
Selecting
fine
bordeaux.

3. **Choose a border Setting (appearance), line Style, Color, and line Width.**

   Click stuff and see what happens in the Preview box. You need not make your selections in any particular order.

4. **If you don't want a complete outline border, click individual borders (left, right, top, bottom) in the Preview box to turn them off. (Click again to restore a border.)**

5. **To use different line styles, colors, and widths for different borders, adjust those attributes in the Style, Color, and/or line Width boxes, and then click a border in the Preview box.**

6. **Examine the Apply Style To box and make sure your border is being applied as you intended (to one or more paragraphs, some selected text, or one or more pages).**

   If you're using the Page Borders card, your main choices are Whole document, This Section – First Page Only (translation: page 1 of your document), and This Section – All Except First Page (translation: all pages *but* page 1). (In most of this book, since I don't discuss sections much, I assume your entire document is a "section.")

7. **Click OK in the dialog box.**

Making shady paragraphs

If you have a really red-hot paragraph, you can draw the reader's attention to it by putting it in the shade. By selecting multiple paragraphs, you can create one continuous block of shade for them all to lounge in. Here's how:

1. **Select your target, then choose Choose Format⇨Borders and Shading.**

   You should now be looking at the Borders and Shading dialog box.

2. **Click the tab of the Shading card if it's not already displayed.**

3. **For a solid background, click one of the shades of gray or a color in the Fill area of the Shading card.**

4. **For a patterned background blended from two colors (including black and white), choose the first color in the Fill area, choose a percentage in the Style box, and then choose the second color in the Color box. Observe the effect in the Preview area.**

5. **Click OK in the dialog box.**

Keep your eye on the Preview box as you go to make sure that you aren't creating something hideous. Hideousity happens — there's a little Dr. Frankenstein in all of us.

Columns

You can't have a newsletter, newspaper, or magazine without columns. I don't know why that's true, particularly, but there it is: a fact of life. So if you're pursuing a career in self-published journalism, you need to know how to put your text into columns.

You can either put the entire document into columns, or start columnizing (columnifying?) — well, change the number of columns, then — from your insertion point forward.

1. Choose Format⇨Columns.

The Format Columns dialog box appears, as shown in Figure 13-4. (If you are not already working in Layout view, Word — or its paper clip guy, who squawks and clinks first — asks if you want to switch to that view; click Yes.)

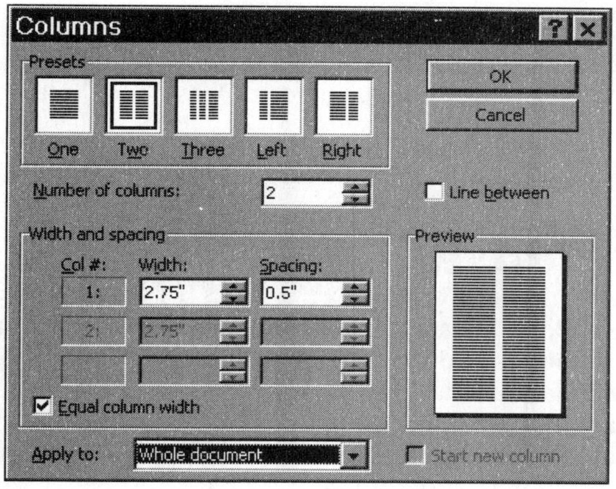

Figure 13-4:
Getting
columnar.

2. Click the number of columns you want in the Presets area, or enter a number in the Number of Columns box.

3. If you don't want columns of equal width, click to clear the Equal Column Width check box.

4. Enter how wide you want your columns in the Width box(es).

If your columns are of equal width, the width you enter in the Col # 1 row applies to all columns.

5. Enter the amount of space you want between the columns in the Spacing box.

6. **Click the Line Between check box if you want a vertical line between your columns.**

7. **Click Apply To and choose This Point Forward if you intend to affect the column only from the insertion point forward.**

   You probably want the following text to begin a column. If so, click to enable the Start New Column check box.

8. **Click OK.**

Here are a few tips to deal with Word quirks when using columns:

✔ If you're using columns to make a newsletter, you probably want a banner at the top of the newsletter, spanning all columns. Create the banner using a single column, then in the subsequent paragraph, switch to multiple columns.

✔ Text flows automatically through the columns. To force a particular piece of text to wrap to the top of a column, insert a column break: Choose Insert⇨Break, then in the Break box that appears, choose Column Break.

✔ To create *balanced columns* (in which every column has equal length), click at the end of the text, choose Insert⇨Break, then in the Break box that appears, choose Continuous.

The Envelope, Please!

May we have the envelope, please? And the winner is . . . you! You win because printing envelopes and labels is one of the dirty little jobs that Word makes easier than it used to be. In the dark ages of word processing (seven or eight years ago), printing envelopes or labels was a job that took a squadron of software engineers, five phone calls to the printer and software vendors, four Tylenol tablets and, ultimately, a ballpoint pen. (Another tale I can bore young people with when I get old.)

Don't toss out the ballpoint pen yet. Some days, turning on the PC and printer to address an envelope is just not worth the effort!

Creating and printing an envelope

Printing a single envelope is usually a pretty fast job in Word. Word knows all about your printer and makes all the right choices about sending the address to it. Usually. So, usually, the following steps go quickly, despite the length of this section. The reason these instructions are as long as they are is so that you can check all of Word's choices. When envelope printing doesn't go well, the result is a lot of frustration and expense as you chew up envelope after envelope. Here's what to do to minimize hair-pulling:

1. **If your document is a letter and already has the recipient's name and mailing address in it, select (highlight) the name and address portion.**

   Otherwise, move on to Step 2.

2. **Choose Tools⇨Envelopes and Labels.**

   The Envelopes and Labels dialog box makes the scene.

3. **Click the Envelopes tab and examine the Delivery Address text box.**

   If, in Step 1, you initially highlighted the recipient's name and address in your letter, it appears in the Delivery Address text box. You can edit the recipient's address now if you like. If you didn't select an address, this text box is blank, and you can fill it in by clicking the text box and typing.

4. **Click the Return Address text box.**

   If you have never printed an envelope before, the Return Address text box is empty. Type in your name and address. If you have printed an envelope before, and saved the return address as the default return address, the default address is displayed here; edit the return address if you need to.

5. **Click the Options button tab to check or change settings.**

   You probably don't need to change anything, but checking is a good idea. The Envelope Options dialog box appears with two cards: Envelope Options, and Printing Options. These cards give you the chance to make sure you're printing on the correct size envelope, or make adjustments to the way the envelope is printed. Click OK when you're done.

   On the Envelope Options card, click the Envelope Size box and choose a size from the list. If your envelope doesn't match any of the standard sizes listed, choose Custom size from the list and enter your envelope's dimensions in the Envelope Size dialog box that appears.

   Other frequently useful options on this card are:

   - **Add a bar code for the Zip code.** Click Delivery Point Barcode.

   - **Change the font for the delivery or return address.** Click the Font button for Delivery Address or Return Address to use the usual Font dialog box.

- **Reposition the addresses.** The From Left and From Top boxes adjust the position of the delivery and return addresses from the upper-left corner of the envelope. Auto uses standard settings for standard envelopes.

Click the Printing Options tab, to see the card shown in Figure 13-5. This card tells Word how you're feeding envelopes into your printer. (Check your printer manual to make sure *you* know how you're feeding envelopes into your printer!) If Word thinks you're using a different printer than you actually are (or a fax modem!), you need to click Cancel to exit the Envelope dialog boxes, then use File⇨Print to choose the correct printer.

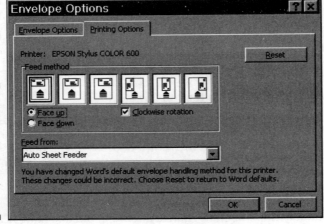

Figure 13-5:
Make sure
Word
knows how
you're
inserting
your
envelope.

Check three settings on the Printing Options card:

- **Feed method:** In the pictures in the area labeled Feed Method, Word chooses (with a blue frame) the most likely way for you to orient and position the envelope in your printer's feed tray. Look very closely at the selection and click a different way, if necessary. Certainly make sure that your envelope's left or right edge is aligned with the tray's edge as the picture shows. An arrow shows how the envelope moves when it's fed into the printer. Make sure you're not thinking that the envelope will feed the other way! If you feed your envelope sideways, but not the way shown, click the Clockwise Rotation check box.

- **Face Up/ Face Down:** Most printers print envelopes face up, but check your manual and choose the proper selection.

• **Feed From:** Most small home or office printers feed envelopes from the standard paper tray, but some have a special manual feed option (probably already chosen by Word). Click the Feed From box and choose the correct feed tray.

Click OK in the Envelope Options dialog box to return to the Envelopes and Labels dialog box.

6. **Click the Print button to actually, physically commit ink to paper.**

Word may pop up a dialog box, asking whether you want to save the return address you entered as the default return address. If you intend to use this same address for the next envelope you create, click Yes. Otherwise, click No.

After a few seconds, your printer is ready to print. Your printer may wait for you to put an envelope in it manually, unless it has a stack of envelopes already in an envelope feed. Every printer handles envelopes differently; insert a blank envelope the way the printer manual tells you to. Your printer's software may also pop up a dialog box or two, either simply to keep you informed on the printer's progress, or to remind you to do something.

7. **Click the Add To Document button to save the envelope as part of the currently open document. (Click the Cancel button if you don't want the envelope saved.)**

The envelope tool creates something called an envelope page, putting it at the top of your document. A special envelope/page break (the dotted line) separates the envelope page from the rest of your document.

Choose View➪Page Layout or File➪Print Preview to see your envelope more realistically before you print.

You can edit the envelope page or format it just like any other page of your document. If the envelope is all the page contains, you can save the file to re-use later. You can also call on the envelope tool again to edit the text, if you prefer. (If so, the Add To Document button becomes the Change Document button.) If at any time you decide you won't need the envelope again, you can delete it. Click and drag across the entire envelope page, including the page break and press the Delete key on your keyboard.

After you attach an envelope to a document, whenever you print your document, you get an envelope too — unless you tell the Print dialog box otherwise. Chapter 12 tells you how to print selected pages of a document. Use those instructions to determine what you print. To print only the envelope, for instance, click in the envelope page before choosing File➪Print, then in the Print dialog box, click the Current Page check box.

If all works well, you soon have a nicely printed envelope. If not, well, there's always the ballpoint pen.

A few things can go wrong; here's information on how to fix 'em:

- ✔ **Nothing happens when you print:** Your printer may be waiting for you to manually feed an envelope into it. If no way is available to manually feed the printer an envelope, follow these steps: Click the envelope page. Choose File⇨Page Setup from the menu bar. Click the Paper Source card, and in the drop-down menu for First Page, choose Default Tray. Try printing again.

- ✔ **The envelope jams:** After you carefully extract the smushed envelope, try printing again with a new envelope, but this time, sharpen the crease of the edges of the envelope by running a hard object across them (or by running the edge between your thumbnail and middle finger tip). If this fails, try adjusting the paper thickness control of the printer or using a thinner envelope.

- ✔ **Stuff prints in *very* wrong places, or upside-down:** In the previous instructions for "Creating and printing an envelope," Step 5 is to choose the envelope size and position. Perhaps the real envelope is not the size you specified. Or you may not be putting your envelopes into the printer as the Envelope tool depicts. Check to make sure you're not looking down on your printer's feed tray upside-down from the way the Envelope tool depicts. Also, some printers have a special manual-feed guide for you to use. Finally, check to make sure that Windows is set up for exactly the model of printer you're using (see the appendix).

- ✔ **Stuff prints in *somewhat* wrong places:** See the possible reasons given in the preceding paragraph. Another possible remedy is to click the envelope page and adjust margins by choosing File⇨Page Setup.

Printing labels

People who want to print labels typically have one of two different jobs in mind: printing pages of labels with a single address (or other text), or performing a rather complex operation called *mail merge* to print labels from an address database. Because Works includes a database tool that will, most likely, be the place you store address data, I suggest that you use the Works word-processor's Envelope wizard for mail merge. Chapter 9 tells you all about it.

To print labels, you need to buy special labels for the kind of printer you have. Unless you have a special label printer, your labels come on sheets that you use like paper in your printer. After printing, you peel the labels off the sheets. Two common label vendors are Avery and Maco, and the two most common types of labels are those for laser printers and those for ink-jet printers. Check your printer manual for its suggestions on label printing.

Don't try to use laser printer labels in an ink-jet printer, or vice-versa. Problems can include smearing, misalignment between print and labels, and sticky paper jams!

In Word, printing labels that all have the same text (or just a single label) is usually a piece of cake. Here's how to cut that cake:

1. **If your document already has the label text in it, select (highlight) that text.**

   Apply any special character formatting that you want, such as color or special fonts. Otherwise, move on to Step 2.

2. **Choose Tools⇨Envelopes and Labels.**

   The Envelopes and Labels dialog box skitters into existence.

3. **Click the Labels tab and examine the Address text box.**

   If, in Step 1, you initially highlighted text, it appears in the Address text box. You can edit this text now if you like. If you didn't select any text, this text box is blank, and you can fill it in by clicking the text box and typing.

   If your intention is to print return address labels for yourself, try clicking the Use Return Address check box. If the address is correct, proceed to Step 4; otherwise, edit the address.

4. **Check the Label area of the dialog box to see if the label part number matches your labels; if not, click the label displayed (or click the Options button) to access Label Options.**

   In the Label Options dialog box of Figure 13-6, choose the label vendor and series in the Label Products selection box, then choose the label's product number in the Product Number list. The Label Information area provides details on label and page size.

Figure 13-6:
Choose a type of label and make sure you feed it properly to the printer.

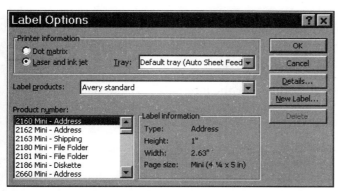

Inspect the type of printer feed listed in the Tray selection box. Click to choose a different option: Default Tray, for instance if you are printing a stack of label sheets, or Manual Feed to print a single sheet.

Click OK in the Label Options dialog box when you're done, to return to the Envelopes and Labels dialog box.

5. **If you only want a single label, click the Single Label check box in the Envelopes and Labels dialog box.**

Specify which label on the page of labels you want to print, by entering the label's row and column number in Row and Column.

6. **Keep your label setup as a document. Click the New Document button.**

A page of labels is created as a document and displayed in your Word window.

7. **Ready to print? Click the Print button, but first . . .**

. . . insert a regular piece of paper in your printer's feed tray or slot. In case anything goes wrong, you haven't wasted a sheet of labels. After printing, hold the paper over a sheet of labels and see how the text lines up with the label.

If all is well on plain paper, place a single sheet of labels in your printer's feed tray.

The Envelopes and Labels dialog box goes away after you click the Print button.

8. **You created a new document in Step 6; save it with File⇨Save now.**

9. **To print on a sheet of labels, choose File⇨Print.**

Many of the same problems that afflict envelope printing also afflict label printing. See the tips at the end of the previous section, "Creating and printing an envelope." In addition, two other problems are:

✔ High humidity can cause your labels to warp, print badly, stick together, or stick to your printer's innards. Wait for a dry day, or buy a dehumidifier.

✔ Label sheets can slip or bind in the printer's rollers. You may need to adjust the printer for the label sheet thickness.

Chapter 14

Adding Graphics, Charts, and Sidebars

- -

In This Chapter

▶ Reproducing some art for your document

▶ Hanging some pictures

▶ Making your own art

▶ Getting glitzy by adding sidebars

▶ Using art in the public domain

▶ Exploring WordArt

▶ Keeping up-to-date with charts

▶ Tweaking your art

- -

*O*ne picture is worth a thousand words, so I figure a chapter about pictures warrants several thousand words. But I'm not just talking pictures, here. Word lets you add all kinds of useful visual stuff to a document, including drawings, spreadsheets, charts, and sidebars. But I'm wasting my thousand words; read on!

Attention: Works word-processor users!

The word-processing basics of Word 97 and the Works word-processing tool are so similar that they often use the same commands. In this part of the book, if you're a Works user, the *Works for Me!* icon guides you to instructions that work for you. If the icon isn't present, the instructions are only for Word users.

If the Works For Me! icon appears at the first paragraph of a section, the whole section applies to the Works word processor. If the icon appears before a numbered list, the whole numbered list applies to Works. I call any exceptions to your attention.

Copying and Pasting Images

If you can see an image on your PC, you have a reasonable chance of being able to "copy and paste it" into a document, using the Windows *clipboard*. (See the appendix for a discussion of the Windows clipboard.) Your ability depends on the application (program) you're using to view the image. Try the following:

- ✔ If, when you click on the image, a frame (a box) appears around the image and remains after you release the mouse button, you can probably copy it. Click the image to select it for copying, and then choose Edit➪Copy from the viewing program's menu bar (or from the right-mouse menu).

- ✔ See if the image fills the program's window, and when you peek in the program's Edit menu, a Copy or Cut command is present and not grayed out. If so, choose Edit➪Copy from the viewing program's menu bar (or right-mouse menu).

In a document in Word or Works, click where you want the image to go and press Ctrl+V or choose Edit➪Paste from Word's menu bar.

To adjust position, size, or anything else about the picture, see the last section of this chapter, "Messing Around with Art in the Document."

Inserting Pictures from Files

To insert a picture from a file, just click where you want the picture to go, and use Word's rather obvious command: Insert➪Picture➪From File. The Insert Picture dialog box that appears (shown in Figure 14-1) includes a Preview feature: Click a file (like rustfris.jpg in Figure 14-1) and the image is displayed.

Here are some instructions and tips for using the Insert Picture dialog box shown in Figure 14-1:

- ✔ If the Preview feature slows down your browsing too much, click the List button on the dialog box toolbar.

- ✔ Browse through folders on your PC just as you do in the File Open dialog box. (See the appendix if browsing through folders is a new concept for you.)

- ✔ To select a picture, click its file in the left-hand window.

- ✔ To insert your selected picture into your document, click the Insert button.

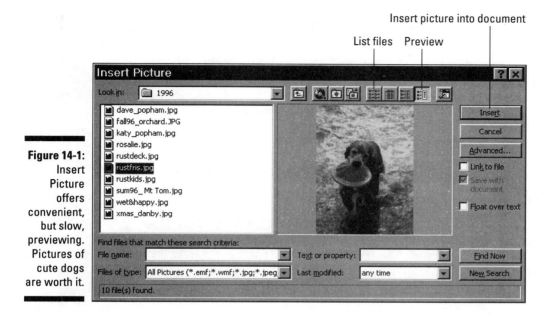

Insert picture into document

List files   Preview

Once you insert the pictures, you can size, position, or otherwise mess around with the picture. See "Messing Around with Art in the Document" later in this chapter for instructions.

Drawing "Blob Art"

Few things strike more dread into the heart of the average adult than being asked to draw something. Otherwise brave souls who daily undertake such daunting ventures as business trips, advanced courses in physics, or even (shudder) a field trip with their child's class shiver in their berets at the thought of drawing.

Fortunately, the most artistic endeavor most of us are ever called upon to do in Word is what I call "blob art." *Blob art* is the art of putting together a bunch of simple shapes with lines and text. Word gives you a convenient drawing feature for making your blob art attractive. Here are some useful factoids about using Word's drawing feature:

✓ Word lets you draw anywhere in your document — even on top of your text!

✔ To draw on your document, just display the drawing toolbar shown in Figure 14-2: Choose <u>V</u>iew⇨<u>T</u>oolbars, then click the Drawing check box in the list of toolbars that appears. The Drawing toolbar normally appears at the bottom of your Word window. Repeat these steps to remove the toolbar.

✔ The drawing tool includes a blob art feature called AutoShapes, containing pre-designed blobs of all kinds.

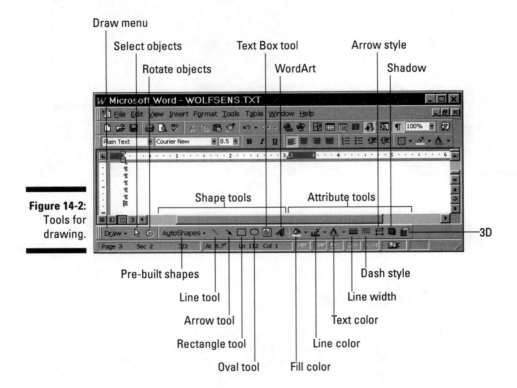

Figure 14-2: Tools for drawing.

Making shapes and text

The shapes and text you create using the drawing tools are separate, movable objects, like cutouts lying on a piece of paper. You can even stack them in any order, like paper shapes, in which case they often partially obscure each other. You can also group them for purposes of moving them or changing various attributes like color.

To use a tool, click the tool and then move your cursor into the document area. After you do that, using the tool is generally a matter of clicking at various points, or clicking and dragging. Pressing the Shift key while you click (which this book refers to as Shift+click) allows you to get certain specialized objects, such as circles and squares, from the more general ellipse and rectangle tools.

Refer to Figure 14-2 to identify these basic shape and text tools on the drawing toolbar.

- ✔ **Line:** Click where you want one endpoint and drag to where you want the other endpoint. Shift+click forces a line to be drawn at even multiples of 15 degrees (15, 30, 45, 60, 75, 90, and so on).

- ✔ **Oval:** Click and then drag in any direction to create an ellipse. Dragging diagonally makes the shape more circular. To force it to be a true circle, use Shift+click.

- ✔ **Rectangle:** Click where you want one corner and drag to the opposite corner. For a square, use Shift+click.

- ✔ **Text box:** Click where you want one corner and drag to the opposite corner. For a square, use Shift+click. Click inside the box to type text. Use the same font controls you use for document text, plus the text color button in the attributes group shown in Figure 14-2.

    Text boxes are ideal for sidebars! See "Messing Around with Art in the Document" for tips on making text flow around a text box.

- ✔ **WordArt:** See the WordArt section, later in this chapter.

- ✔ **AutoShapes:** AutoShapes are, for the most part, pre-designed shapes you simply choose in the AutoShape menu, and then click and drag in your document.

Modifying objects

Drawing objects have a variety of qualities, or *attributes,* controlled by the attribute buttons shown in Figure 14-2. To change any attribute, select the object (if it isn't selected already) and click the attribute button.

Selected objects are marked by tiny squares at various points on the shape. To select an object, click the *selection tool* (the fat arrow) in the toolbar, then click the object. You can tell when the selection tool is the active tool because your cursor becomes a four-headed arrow.

To select a group of objects, choose the selection tool and drag a rectangle to completely enclose the objects. To select a bunch of objects scattered all over the drawing, hold down both Ctrl and Shift, and click on each object individually.

Check out some of the attributes you can set using the Drawing toolbar shown in Figure 14-2:

- **Fill Color** applies the fill color displayed on that button. (A *fill color* is a solid, colored center for closed shapes, like ovals.) Click the triangular down-arrow with the Fill Color button to choose a color from a palette (or choose None).

- **Line Color** applies the color displayed on that button. (For closed shapes, "line" refers to the shape's outline.) Click the triangular down-arrow with the Line Color button to choose a color from a palette.

- **Line Width** lets you choose a line width (which, for a closed shape, refers to its outline).

- **Dash Style** lets you choose a solid or broken line (which for a closed shape, refers to its outline).

- **Arrow Style** lets you turn a line into an arrow, and choose the direction the arrow points. (Not for closed shapes.)

- **Shadow** lets you apply a shadow to an object. Choose both a direction for the shadow and a style from the graphical menu that appears.

- **3D** switches an object to a three-dimensional appearance. Choose a 3D style from the graphical menu that appears, or click No 3-D to restore a two-dimensional appearance.

Here are ways you can adjust an object (or bunch of objects). Choose the selection tool and select the object(s) before you attempt any of these actions:

- **Move:** Click anywhere on the object and drag. To move straight horizontally or vertically, hold down the Shift key and drag. (Don't forget: You can select a bunch of objects and move them all together.)

- **Copy:** Press Ctrl+C and then Ctrl+V. A copy appears somewhere nearby; click and drag it to the place you want it.

- **Stretch or shrink:** (For shapes, not text.) Click any of the squares around the shape and drag. Shift+drag constrains dragging to certain directions: Shift+drag a side square to move it straight horizontally or vertically; Shift+drag a corner square to move it at a 45-degree angle. To stretch or shrink while keeping the shape's center in place, hold down the Ctrl key.

- **On-top/Underneath:** Objects overlap each other in Draw; to change a selected object's position in the pile, click Draw⇨Order on the drawing toolbar and choose an order from the menu that appears.

✔ **Rotate or Flip:** Click Draw⇨Rotate or Flip on the drawing toolbar and choose a rotation or flip in the menu that appears. Rotate Left and Rotate Right turn the object 90 degrees. Click Flip Horizontal for a mirror image or Flip Vertical for upside down. Choosing Free Rotate (which is also a button on the drawing toolbar), puts exciting green dots around the shape. (I get excited easily.) Drag a dot to rotate the shape around its center. Hold the Ctrl key down to drag the shape around the dot on the opposite corner. If you choose Free Rotate, it stays on; choose Free Rotate again to turn the tool off.

If you realize you made a mistake (maybe you accidentally nudged something that took you a long time to get in exactly the right place), you can undo it. Choosing Edit⇨Undo or pressing Ctrl+Z works here just like it does everywhere else in Word.

If you get a few objects positioned just perfectly relative to each other, you can freeze them in their relative positions by selecting them all and choosing Draw⇨Group. Now Works considers the collection to be one single object, and anything that is done to one is done to all. If you decide later that you want to modify the objects individually, select the grouped object (by clicking any of its pieces) and choose Draw⇨Ungroup.

To apply a border, adjust position, size, or anything else about a particular blob, see the last section of this chapter, "Messing Around with Art in the Document."

Creating Sidebars (Text Boxes)

All the highest-quality magazines and books (like this one) use sidebars, right? So why shouldn't your document?

Works doesn't offer sidebars or text boxes as such, but you can use WordArt to create a pretty acceptable — or even pretty jazzy — sidebar in Works (or Word, for that matter). See the section, "Creating WordArt," later in this chapter.

A sidebar in Word is nothing more than a special piece of blob art called a *text box*. Because a text box *is*, simply, a piece of blob art, you can create a text box using the Text Box tool of Word's drawing toolbar, as described briefly in the preceding section. Or, to avoid dealing with the drawing tools, you can do the following:

1. **Choose Insert⇨Text Box.**

   Your cursor changes to a set of cross-hairs. Ready, aim, . . .

2. **In your document, click where you want one corner of the box, and drag diagonally across your text to where you want the opposite corner.**

A text box with a shaded frame and eight *handles* (tiny squares) appears, overlaying your document text, with a blinking cursor in the box.

3. **Type your sidebar text.**

Format characters and paragraphs just as you would any other text in a Word document. In Figure 14-3, I used bold text and center alignment for the sidebar heading, and bullets for the sidebar text.

4. **Click anywhere outside the text box when you finish typing and formatting your text.**

To edit your sidebar text at any later time, just click in the text box.

You're not done yet, though; your text box needs some fine-tuning to become a real sidebar. Most noticeably, your sidebar, unlike the one in Figure 14-3, is probably sitting right smack on top of your document text!

What you need to do now is to adjust how text *wraps* around the sidebar. You may also want to fine-tune the size and position of your text box in the document, the margins between the box and the text, the border *(line)* around the box, or the box's background color or pattern *(fill)*. The dialog box that controls all these features is the same for text boxes as for graphical objects, like pictures, WordArt, and blob art. See the final section of this chapter, "Messing Around with Art in the Document," for details.

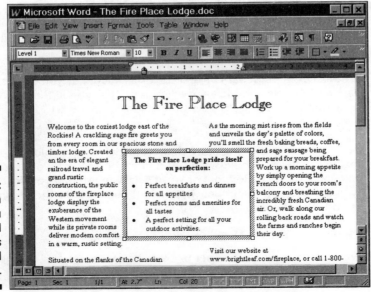

Figure 14-3: In Western lodges, you might find bullets embedded in a sidebar.

Clipping Clip Art

When your document needs a little pizzazz — not functional, industrial art like blob art or charts — use some clip art. Clip art is nothing more than a bunch of illustrations that you can use in your documents. Works Suite comes with a batch of drawings; you can add more by connecting to the Internet with Microsoft's Internet Explorer, discussed in Chapter 20.

The clip art feature that comes with Works Suite is called the Clip Gallery, designed to let you find, choose, and organize not only the artwork prepackaged with Works, but also any images, sounds, or video files you add from the Microsoft Web site.

Summon the Clip Gallery by choosing Insert⊏>Picture⊏>Clip Art (or Insert⊏>ClipArt in Works), and it appears as shown in Figure 14-4. (A reminder box may appear at first, to tell you that additional artwork is available on the CD. Click the Don't Remind Me Again check box, then click OK.)

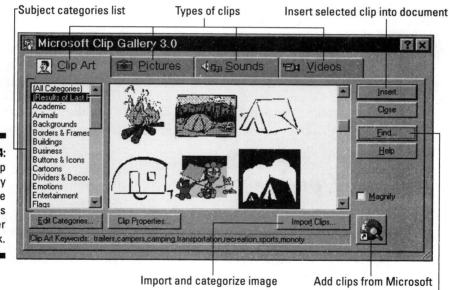

Figure 14-4: The Clip Gallery of fine drawings and other artwork.

┌Subject categories list   Types of clips   Insert selected clip into document

Import and categorize image   Add clips from Microsoft

Find clips by keyword, filename, or file type┘

Clip art often looks much better in your document than it does in the Clip Gallery, where certain types of art appear rather grainy and blotchy.

Inserting a clip into your document

To insert a clip in your word-processing or database document follow these steps:

1. **In your document, click where you want the art to appear.**

2. **In Word, choose Insert⇨Picture⇨ClipArt. (In Works, choose Insert⇨ ClipArt.)**

   You may have to wait, staring at a cursor-turned-hourglass, while Word or Works quietly builds its museum of masterpieces or reads the clips from the CD.

3. **Click a subject category list presented to you on the ClipArt tab. Or click other tabs, such as the Pictures tab, to check for clips there.**

   The Clip Art illustrations are divided by subject category for your artistic critique and selection. Scroll the gallery window to see more of the clips in any category. (Works Suite provides nothing in the Pictures, Sounds, or Videos cards of the gallery.)

4. **Click the picture you want.**

5. **Click the Insert button.**

6. **Click the Close button.**

After you insert the art into your document, you can size it and otherwise fine-tune it the same way you do your own drawings. See the final section of this chapter, "Messing Around with Art in the Document" for more information.

Creating WordArt

Oh, those madcap Microsoft engineers! First blob art, then clip art, and now word art. What's next, punctuation art? Well, WordArt is definitely fun, and it's also great for getting readers' attention (see Figure 14-5). The WordArt feature lets you create special effects for text — like you see in advertisements and brochures.

The basic procedure for getting swoopy, loopy text in your word-processing document goes like this:

1. **Click at the place you want your text art.**

2. **Choose Insert⇨Picture⇨WordArt (choose Insert⇨WordArt in Works).**

   In Word, a way-cool WordArt style gallery appears. Click any style that appeals to you, then click the OK button. You can vary or customize the style later to suit your needs.

An Edit WordArt Text dialog box appears. (In Works, an Enter Your Text Here dialog appears.) `Your Text Here` appears in the dialog box. The phrase "Your Text Here" probably doesn't quite get *your* point across, so move on to Step 3!

3. **Type your text in the dialog box, then click OK. (Click Update Display in Works.)**

   Your document displays your cool WordArt, as shown in Figure 14-5. In Word, you also get the WordArt toolbar of Figure 14-5.

   Things are a bit less jazzy in Works. You don't get a toolbar. Instead, the Works menu and toolbar changes to let you fool with WordArt.

4. **To change the shape of your WordArt, click the WordArt Shape button (marked ABC) on the WordArt toolbar.**

   In Works, click the list box in the toolbar where it currently says Plain Text.

Format WordArt Shape

Gallery of WordArt Free Rotate

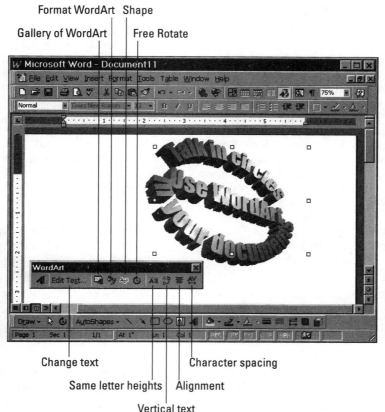

Figure 14-5: Playing with WordArt: Curved text can turn heads.

Change text

Same letter heights Alignment

Vertical text

Character spacing

5. **A gallery of weird shapes appears. Click any shape in the gallery. (Shapes with multiple lines are intended for multiple lines of text.)**

   In Works, when you choose a shape, your text may become an illegible blur in the document, as Works tries to fit the artwork in a standard-height line. To fix that, click the down-arrow button next to where it says Best Fit and click a larger type size in the drop-down list. Works may display a Size Change dialog box babbling about enlarging a frame and asking the question `Resize WordArt object?` Click Yes.

When you're happy with your WordArt, click the X in the upper-right corner of the WordArt toolbar to dismiss the toolbar. (In Works, when you're done, click the document anywhere outside of the gray-shaded frame.) If you're not yet happy with your WordArt, read on for special effects.

Inserting Charts and Other Foreign Objects

As a kid, I was always amused at the medical world's use of the phrase "foreign object" to describe the various kinds of specks I got in my eyes. (What can I say? I was easily amused as a child, and dirt was one of my favorite toys.)

Today, thanks to the wonders of software, you and I can not only get foreign objects in our eyes, we can deliberately put foreign objects in our documents. By *foreign objects,* however, I now mean stuff you make using another program — like charts, graphs, spreadsheets (entire spreadsheets or named ranges), or even other documents — that you want to use as an illustration. You have several ways to put such foreign objects into your Word (or Works) document:

   ✔ **Copy and paste the object as a graphical image.** See the first section of this chapter, "Copying and Pasting Images," for instructions. You cannot easily edit this object, so if you want to alter it in the future, you need to edit it in the other program, then copy and paste it again.

   ✔ **Paste a link to the object.** This special form of pasting allows you to keep your illustration (a chart, for example) up-to-date by incorporating the latest changes in the data. Whenever you change the chart in the other program, that change automatically shows up in the Word document.

   If you paste a link to an object, you can't move that object's file to another folder, change that file's name, or copy the document to another person's computer. If you do any of these things, you must get into editing links, which I don't have room to discuss here!

▶ **Embed the object.** This special form of pasting actually stores a copy of the object — a chunk of spreadsheet data, for instance — in your Word document. You can edit the object by double-clicking it.

Following are the steps for pasting a link or embedding an object. These steps work for objects created under many Windows programs, but not all of them. If these steps don't work for you, you must resort to copying and pasting the object as a graphical image.

1. **Create your object (a spreadsheet, chart, or drawing, for instance) using a Windows program.**

2. **Save your work in that program as a file.**

3. **Select your chart window or other object in that program, then copy the object by choosing Edit⇨Copy. Don't exit the program.**

4. **Open (launch) Word (or the Works word processor tool) if it isn't already running, click your document where you want the object to appear, and choose Edit⇨Paste Special.**

   The Paste Special dialog box appears. Within it, the As selection box offers several ways of pasting your object, with one of those ways highlighted for you.

5. **To link or embed an object, look for an *object* in the As selection box, and click that selection if it is not already highlighted. For instance, if you are copying a Works chart, look for a Microsoft Works Sheet or Chart *Object*.**

   If none of the selections offers an *object,* you cannot link or embed. Press the Esc key and resort to ordinary copying and pasting.

6. **Choose Paste Link to paste a link, or choose Paste to embed the object.**

   If Paste Link is grayed out, you cannot paste a link to this object. You can only embed it.

7. **Click OK in the Paste Link dialog box.**

   You may now exit the Windows program in which you created the object.

You can now format and edit this object like most other graphics objects. See the last section in this chapter, "Messing Around with Art in the Document" for instructions. As with other graphics objects, you can edit the object by double-clicking it. If you pasted a link to the object, you then return to the original program in which you created the object; save your work as a file in that program.

If you pasted a link, you can use the Windows program that created the file to change that file, even when Word is not running. (After changing the file, however, don't move the file to another folder or change the file's name, or the link will no longer work.) When you next open your Word (or Works word processor) document, the object in that document will be up-to-date.

Messing Around with Art in the Document

To do anything to a figure of any sort (blob art, WordArt, picture, or other object), first click the figure to select it. The figure then appears framed, as is usual when any object is selected, with eight tiny squares *(handles)* around the outside. To select a group of figures so that you can move or otherwise operate on them all together, hold down the Shift key while clicking each one.

- ✔ **To move a figure:** Position your cursor over it until the cursor changes to a four-way arrow, then click and drag the figure. (If a figure's center is transparent, click on its border.)
- ✔ **To delete a figure:** Press the Delete key.
- ✔ **To resize a figure:** Click and drag any of the handles around the figure.
- ✔ **To modify the figure:** Double-click the figure, and you return to the original tool.

To more precisely control size and position, to choose a border or fill, to control text wrapping around a figure, or to set interior margins in a text box, choose Format from the menu bar, then click the last selection on the Format menu that drops down. That selection reads Format Object, Format Picture, Format WordArt, or Format something-or-other, depending upon what sort of something you selected. A Format something-or-other dialog box appears. Do the following:

In Works, click Format and choose individual selections from the Format menu: Borders and Shading, Picture, or Text Wrap.

- ✔ **To adjust the frame around your figure:** Click the Colors and Lines card. Choose a color, line width (weight) and dashed style, if you like. If your object is a line or arrow, you can choose arrowhead size and style. (You can also access the Colors and Lines card by choosing Format➪Borders and Shading from the menu bar.)
- ✔ **To change the figure's dimensions or rotation:** Click the Size card. To adjust the figure's height and width (proportions) separately, click to clear the check mark in the Lock Aspect Ratio checkbox. You may

either enter *absolute values* (inches) in the Height and Width boxes of the Size and Rotate area, or adjust *scale* by entering percentages in the Height and Width boxes of the Scale area. Enter rotation in degrees (360 being a complete turn) in the Rotation box.

✔ **To make text wrap around the figure in the word-processor tool:** Choose Format⇨Picture and click the Text Wrap tab. Then click the Absolute button.

✔ **To position a figure:** Click the Position card. Enter Horizontal and Vertical values (which set the distance to the figure's upper left-hand corner). A bunch of options here control how the graphic moves as text is added or deleted from your document:

   • Click to clear the check mark in the Float over Text check box if you want the graphic to flow with the text around it, instead of staying at a fixed position on the page.

   • Click to enable the Move Object with Text check box if you want the figure to move vertically with the paragraph it appears in.

   • Click to enable the Lock Anchor check box to ensure that the figure stays on the same page as the paragraph it is inserted in.

   • The preceding three check boxes affect settings in the From selection boxes; you can override those settings manually, if you like. Choose Column, Margin, Page, or (for Vertical settings only, Paragraph) in those selection boxes to tell Word whether the distance you set is from the left edge of the column, the page margin, the physical edge of the page, or the upper-left-hand corner of the paragraph.

✔ **To control text wrap around the figure:** Click the Wrapping card. Choose a style in the Wrapping Style area, by clicking one of the example illustrations given. Likewise, choose which side or sides to wrap *around* by clicking a sample illustration in the Wrap To area. To adjust the space between the figure and the document text, enter distances for the top, bottom, left, and right sides of the figure in the Distance from Text area.

✔ **To crop or adjust the quality of a picture:** Click the Picture card. Enter crop distances for the left, right, top, or bottom of the picture. To adjust picture appearance, use the Image Control settings. Choose from the Color selection box: Automatic to use original colors, Grayscale to convert the image to shades of gray, Black & White to reduce the image to lines and dot patterns, or Watermark to fade the image by applying predetermined Brightness and Contrast settings. You may also adjust Brightness and Contrast yourself, using the horizontal scroll gizmos or by typing in percentages.

✔ **To adjust the space between a text box border and the text it contains:** Click the Text Box card. Set values for the top, bottom, left, and right interior margins.

Part III
Learning to Love Money

The 5th Wave   By Rich Tennant

"We were told to put our money into something that got more interest, so we started sticking it into this mason jar that's got some dang thing in it we bought from a traveling freak show."

In this part . . .

The love of money may be the root of all evil, but the love of Microsoft Money is more benign. Understandable, too, considering how nicely Microsoft Money helps you keep tabs on your expenses and income, generates reports and charts to help you understand why you aren't richer, and prepares you for tax time (to help the IRS undertand why you aren't richer).

In this part, you see how to set up your various bank and other accounts in Money, enter transactions, track your investments, and analyze the results. And if, along the way, you develop a certain fondness for Money, that's quite understandable.

Chapter 15

Setting Up Banking and Checking Accounts

• •

▶ Is Money right for you?

▶ Getting ready for Money

▶ Looking through the Money window

▶ Opening your Money accounts

▶ Changing account information

▶ Categorizing your accounts

▶ Issues with online banking

• •

So, you've got *Money,* have you? How *Suite* it is to have *Money!* And how *Suite* it *Works,* once you get the basic instructions. But before you commit yourself to this electronic bookkeeping marvel, let this chapter help you ponder the question, "Is Money good for me?"

If the answer is "*You bet* Money is good for me," the next step is to set up some accounts, and this chapter helps you do that. (After all, who wants no-account software?) This chapter also shows you how to set up categories of expenses and income so that you can analyze your finances with the planners, charts, and reports that Chapter 17 gets into.

Money is a big topic. And *Microsoft Money* is a fairly chunky topic in its own right. So chunky, in fact, that IDG Books Worldwide offers an entire book: *Microsoft Money 99 For Dummies* by Peter Weverka. If you want the big picture, the entire chunky enchilada, check out that book. I'm just going to hit the basics here. In particular, I am going to avoid much discussion of online banking or electronic transactions, except for getting security prices online.

Deciding Whether Money Is Good for You

If the love of money is the root of all evil, can Microsoft Money 99 really be good for you? You decide. Some of the most useful jobs (in my opinion) that Money can do are:

- Provide a single place (your PC) to record all payments, deposits, and transfers, to review these transactions, and see your balances. If your bank provides online services, Money can automatically get this information from your bank over the Internet; you don't have to type it in.

- Print checks (or, pay bills online — in theory), recording the transactions and adjusting your account balances.

- Remind you when regular payments are due and the amount due.

- Tell you how much you owe on mortgages and/or car loans.

- Tell you how much money you spend on various things (categories of expenses, like dining out).

- Help you plan and stick to a budget.

- Total your tax-exempt expenses, separated by categories, so you can simply enter the expenses on your tax forms.

- Record in one place all your investment holdings, your purchases, and your sales, and display the value of your investments.

- Update the value of your investments automatically by obtaining stock, bond, and mutual fund prices off the Internet.

"What's the downside?" you ask (using your best financial jargon). The downside (or disadvantage, if you prefer) is that you must:

- **Take the time to tell Money all about your accounts.** This job can take anywhere from hours to days, depending on how many different accounts you have! The more complicated the account (say, a mortgage), the more information you have to enter.

- **Take the time to enter every transaction into the computer.** If you're the kind of person who balances your checkbook every month, you won't find this too onerous. Otherwise, you may want to consider using Money's online features and your banks' online services (if available) to automatically download your transactions, because manually entering all those transactions can be a pain in the wrist.

- **Take the time to learn how to use Money.** Compared to the previous two points, this job is a snap.

In my opinion, there is also a significant downside to online banking that you should be aware of. See my warning in "Setting Up Online Banking," later in this chapter.

Preparing to Use Money

The main job facing you before using Money is to assemble your financial information; at the very least, your most recent statements from financial institutions. If you want to analyze your past expenses (say, it's April 14 and you're doing your taxes), you also need past statements. (And if it *is* April 14, you need a very large pot of coffee.) If you're entering a mortgage, you need initial amounts from the mortgage papers.

You need these records so that you can copy information from them into Money. You don't *have* to record *all* of your account information in Money. You can start with, say, household checking and savings accounts. If your main reason for using Money is to summarize tax-related income and expenses, don't bother recording any accounts where the financial institution already sends you tax summaries!

If, from the descriptions I gave in the section "Deciding Whether Money Is Good for You," you think you want to use online banking, I suggest that you get your PC online before starting to use Money. Turn to Chapter 19 in this book for instructions on getting your PC online.

If you have been using Quicken, Money can translate your Quicken account files into Money 99 files. In the Money window, choose File⇨Convert Quicken File, and in the Convert Quicken File dialog box that appears, browse to your Quicken file (it ends in .qdb). (See the appendix if browsing files is new to you.)

Starting Money, Exiting, and Saving Your Work

Just as you do for any other Windows program, you can start Money from the Windows Start button or a program icon. Do one of the following:

  ✔ On the Windows taskbar, choose Start⇨Programs⇨Microsoft Money.

  ✔ If you have an icon labeled "Microsoft Money" on your screen, double-click that icon.

To read more about starting Windows programs, see the appendix. Likewise, turn there if you're a little shaky on using the mouse or keyboard, windows, menus, or dialog boxes.

To exit the program, choose File⊃Exit. Money automatically saves your work as a file when you exit.

When you exit, Money may also ask you if you want to back up your files to a floppy disk. This is an excellent suggestion, because if your PC or hard disk fails and you have no backup file, all your work is lost and you are one very sorry person. Pop a floppy into your diskette drive and click Back Up Now. The process may take a few minutes. You may also choose File⊃Back Up at any time to backup to a diskette.

What's What in the Money Window

Figure 15-1 shows you approximately what the Money window looks like when you start the program. Your window will be different, depending on what accounts you set up, and how you customize this window, which is called your *Money Home Page,* the *Financial Home Page,* or just *Money Home*. Money has several different windows besides the Home Page of Figure 15-1, one window for each different kind of activity.

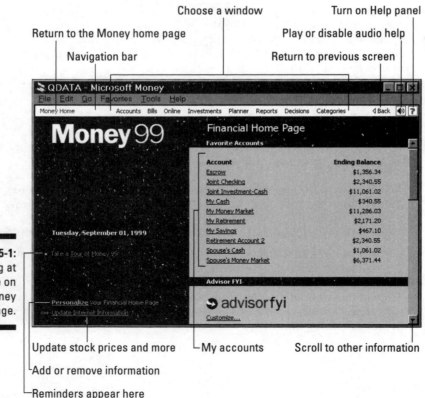

Figure 15-1: Feeling at home on the Money Home Page.

The Home page is your starting place for many different activities. Here's how to use the various controls on Money's home page:

- ✔ Click any of the navigation bar choices *Accounts* through *Categories* to move to that page. If you start hearing a voice, fear not. It's only your recorded tour guides, Eric or Carrie, speaking to you from your Money CD-ROM! To control them, see the following bullet about the speaker icon.

- ✔ Click the speaker icon (near the question mark) to control Eric and Carrie, the narrators of the audio help that your PC may play (if it is equipped for audio). In the menu that appears, you can select Turn All Audio Help Off or Replay Previous Clip. (Play it again, Sam.)

- ✔ Click the Back button to return to whatever page you were looking at previously.

- ✔ Click the red question mark icon to display or hide The Money Help panel. The Help panel occupies the right side of the Money window.

If you turn on the Money Help panel, you can get documentation on all kinds of subjects. I won't detail the controls here because it has one nice, simple way to get help. To search for a subject, first click Help's magnifying glass icon. Click the Ask Money area at the bottom of the Help panel, and type a subject you need help on. Press the Enter key on your keyboard, and the Help panel displays several topics; click any of those topics to read documentation.

Unusual behavior

Money's operation and controls are a bit different from the other Works Suite programs. The user interface (the way it looks and responds to your actions) is more like the user interface you see on Web pages. If you're not a Web user yet, here are the main distinctions from other Windows programs.

- ✔ Money uses *links* or *hot text* extensively: text that does something if you click it. You can sometimes identify links or hot text because it changes in some way as you pass your cursor over it and your cursor changes to a pointing finger icon. Links are generally entirely underlined; hot text may have one letter underlined.

- ✔ You may find that the *boundaries between windows* or areas of windows are vague;

the boundaries should clarify as you get more familiar with the program. You can detect if a boundary is movable if, when you pass your cursor over the boundary, your mouse changes to a double-arrow. That means you can click and drag the boundary.

- ✔ You can customize the Money opening screen (called its *Home Page*) like crazy, and significantly change its appearance. I don't discuss customization here, but you can fool with it yourself by choosing Tools⇨Options and clicking the Money Home tab in the Options dialog box that appears.

Setting Up Accounts

What are accounts? An account in Money is any pool of money, or any asset or liability, that you're involved with. That includes bank accounts, checking accounts, credit cards, CDs (Certificates of Deposit), stocks, bonds, mutual funds, the cash lying around the house and in your wallet, the equity in your house, loans (which are simply pools of money owned by someone else), liabilities (money you owe but haven't paid yet), and lines of credit. Microsoft Money can deal with them all.

You can begin setting up an account. I suggest you start with your checking account. To set up any account, do the following:

1. Click Accounts on the navigation bar.

Your screen displays either the Account Manager page (which lists all your accounts), or the account you looked at most recently. In the latter case, click the Accounts bar again so you can see all your accounts. Figure 15-2 shows one view of the Account Manager page.

Choose an account from a menu

Click for more useful views

Double-click to open an account

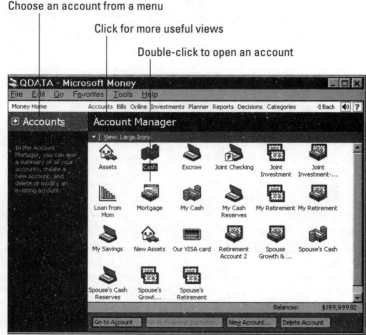

Figure 15-2:
The Accounts Manager page shows you all your accounts.

2. **Click the New Account button at the bottom of the Account Manager page.**

   A New Account dialog box (a *wizard,* or automated program) appears and step you through the process of setting up an account.

Money has a different wizard for every kind of account, and this book doesn't have room for me to take you through them all. Fortunately, Microsoft has done a good job of making its wizards self-explanatory, so you shouldn't need much help from me.

Fill out the wizard's various forms as they appear, reading the explanations. (If you have audio capability on your PC and the Money CD in the CD drive, a narrator speaks to you soothingly.) To move from step to step, click the Next button. To return to an earlier step, click the Back button. Check out these suggestions to help you along:

✔ You can change anything later that you set up in the wizard, or add information you don't currently have on hand. See the following section for details.

✔ As you set up your first accounts, avoid any options that deal with online banking.

✔ If a wizard offers to "associate" your account with another account (say, associate an asset with a mortgage or loan account) choose association if you expect to have regular transfers between those accounts, which, you do with, say, a mortgage and the account you pay it from.

✔ When you set up credit card accounts, you're given the option of adding the card payment to your Bill Calendar. Choosing this option means that you're reminded as the payment date approaches, and a payment entry form is automatically filled out. You are then given the option of paying the card from a particular account, for which you would typically choose your checking account.

When the wizard finishes, a new icon with the account name appears on your Account Manager page. Double-click that icon to view or modify the account.

Money gives you several ways to view the Account Manager page. Click View (located where Figure 15-2 indicates) and choose any of the views listed in the menu that drops down. Choose Large Icons to return to a view like the one in Figure 15-2.

Viewing and Modifying Individual Accounts

Money gives you several convenient ways to view an individual account, so you can enter data, modify the account's setup, or review recent transactions. Two ways to view an individual account are:

✔ **From the Money Home Page:** Click any account shown (they appear in the Favorite Accounts listing).

✔ **From the Account Manager page:** Double-click the account's icon, or click Accounts in the upper-left corner of the page and choose the account from the list that appears.

The first view Money presents of your account is the Register view, where you enter transactions. See Chapter 16 for details of using this view.

To modify the setup of an individual account (for instance, if you didn't know your closing balance when you first set it up), click Details on the left side of the account page, and Money displays the Details view as shown in Figure 15-3.

Click to view the setup of an account

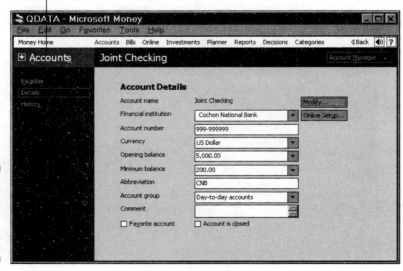

Figure 15-3:
Fine-tuning an account's details.

Click any of the boxes to edit its contents, or choose a different value from a selection list. Following are a few tips:

✔ Click to place a check mark in the Favorites check box, and thereafter you can go immediately to this account by clicking Favorites, and then the account, from the Money menu bar. The account also appears among the Favorites on the Money Home Page.

✔ To change the name of the account (or even to change the *type* of account, say savings to checking, which is rarely necessary), click the Modify button. Enter the new account name in the Modify Account dialog box that appears.

✔ To set up online banking with this institution (or modify an existing setup), click the Online Setup button.

Setting Up Categories and Subcategories

Categories are how Money lumps stuff together in reports and charts. Setting up categories is important if you want Money to tell you how much you spend on certain things (or earning from certain sources).

For instance, you probably have household expenses of various types: electricity, fuel, postage, home maintenance, home improvement, and so on. As you enter these expenses into Money, you can assign all of them to a category of "Household" and then generate a report to show you the total (by year or month, for instance) of all household expenses. (You can do likewise for entertainment expenses, education expenses, and so on.) If you want to total each kind of household expense separately, add electricity, fuel, postage, and the like as subcategories to the Household category.

While you're categorizing things, you probably also want to designate certain categories as tax-related, such as wages or tax-deductible contributions. Money can then generate a report that shows only the income and expenses that affect your taxes. See Chapter 18 for instructions on creating reports and charts.

Just to make life confusing, Money can also create "classifications." You typically use these to group together income and expenses for a particular project or investment. I don't go into classifications in this book, but *Microsoft Money 99 For Dummies* does.

Viewing Money's categories

The good news about setting up categories is that you may not need to do it! Money already includes a bunch of categories that you can use. To see Money's list of categories, do the following:

1. **Click Categories on the navigation bar.**

   The Categories & Payees page appears, displaying one of several possible views: Payees, Categories, Set up Tax Categories, Classification 1, or Classification 2.

2. **If the page is not currently displaying a list of categories, as Figure 15-4 does, click Categories on the left side of the page.**

3. **Review the list of categories by using the vertical scroll bar on the right. (See the appendix if scroll bars are unfamiliar to you.)**

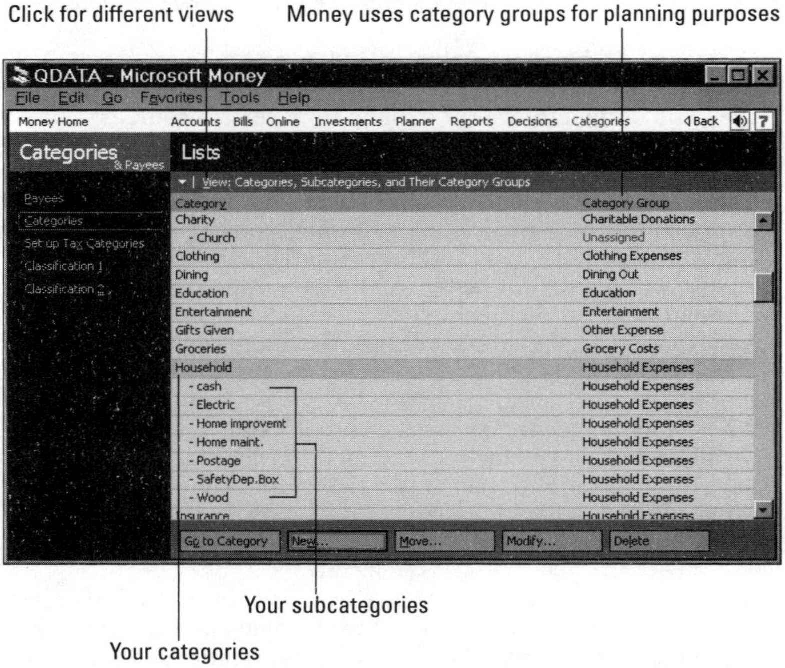

Click for different views   Money uses category groups for planning purposes

Figure 15-4:
Being
categorically
correct.

Your subcategories

Your categories

What the heck are category groups?

Money uses categories, subcategories, and something called "category groups." *Category groups* mystified me until I realized they are just Money's way of relating *my own, custom* categories (which Money doesn't really understand) to the various kinds of income and expense it *does* understand.

If I add the expense category Photographic Supplies, for instance, Money has no idea how expenses in that category fit into my life. Are they essential? Money needs to know so it can help me plan my life with its planners, reports, and other tools. If the category group for Photographic Supplies is Entertainment, money might advise me to trim that expense. The Money category groups are fixed and immutable.

The Categories & Payees page can show you categories in different views. Click View just above the Category column, and choose one of the alternatives in the menu that appears: You can simplify your view or add tax information to the view.

Adding your own category or subcategory

Money offers a fine selection of starting categories, but you may like to add your own. To add a category or subcategory, do the following:

1. **If you are adding a category, begin at Step 2. If you are adding a subcategory, first click its parent category.**

   To add Pet Supplies as a subcategory to Household expense, for instance, click Household.

2. **Click the New button on the bottom of the page.**

   The New Category dialog box appears.

3. **Click to choose a New Category or a Subcategory, and then click Next.**

4. **Type a name for your category or subcategory in the Name field, and then click Next.**

5. **Click the category group that most closely describes the nature of your new category, and then click Finish.**

   You might choose Grocery Costs for your Pet Supplies subcategory, for instance. A subcategory does not have to be in the same category group as the parent category.

To delete a category, simply click it and click the Delete button at the bottom of the page.

Adding tax info and otherwise modifying categories

You can modify your (or Money's) categories by adding comments, supplying an abbreviation to make entering data easier, or identifying the category as tax related. You can even assign categories to specific IRS forms and line numbers!

On the Categories & Payees page, either double-click the category or click the category and then click the Go to Category button at the bottom of the page. A page for that category appears with all the available settings and options, as follows:

- ✔ **Modify:** Click to choose a new category name.

- ✔ **Abbreviation:** To save typing when you enter data in an account register, type an abbreviation here. Then you can type the abbreviation in the register instead of the full category name.

- ✔ **Comment:** Type a comment to remind yourself what the category is all about.

- ✔ **Category Group:** See the sidebar, "What the heck are category groups?" for more info.

- ✔ **Include on Tax Reports:** Click to put a check mark here if this category represents taxable income or tax-deductible expense.

- ✔ **Tax Form, Form Line, and Form Copy:** These boxes are enabled if you click the check box above them. If you know what tax form, line, and copy (usually 1) this category appears on, select those details here.

To better see and set up your tax-related categories, click Set Up Tax Categories on the left side of the Categories & Payees window. As on the main Categories page, you can double-click a category to modify its setup in details. Or, click the category once, and then enter your tax choices in the check box and text boxes at the lower-right corner of the page.

Chapter 16

Doing Banking and Checking Transactions

• •

▶ Using an account register

▶ Recording your transactions

▶ Scheduling recurring bills and transactions

▶ Printing checks

▶ Balancing your checkbook

• •

*Y*ou know what a transaction is in real life, but what does it mean to "do" transactions in Money? You can do transactions in Money in one of two ways:

✔ You can *record* your real-life transactions (checks written, or funds transferred, for instance) after the fact, using your checkbook and other records.

✔ You can actually *perform* transactions in Money (check printing, electronic payment, and the like), as well as *record* those transactions. In that case, you enter the data before the fact of the check being printed (or the payment being made electronically, which this book doesn't cover.)

If you record transactions after the fact, you get your transaction information from one of two possible sources:

✔ **From your own checkbook(s), records and receipts:** For instance, sit down at your PC periodically with your checkbook, automatic teller receipts, credit-card receipts, and other tiny illegible scraps of paper and copy the information on them into Money. The benefit of doing all this copying is that Money turns your creased and scribbled-upon papers into a legible, organized record against which you can reconcile your bank's records.

> ✓ **From the bank's records:** Sit down at your PC (or, stand up; it's better for your health), and copy information from your monthly statements. If you trust the bank to record your transactions properly most of the time, this is the way to go. You can always check Money against your checkbook and credit card receipts later to discover any errors.

Recording Transactions in an Account Register

The task you spend most of your time doing in Money is entering your deposits, withdrawals, and payments of various kinds into a Money account register. The following steps show you in detail how to record those transactions for bank and checking accounts. Investment accounts are similar, but with a few differences; see Chapter 18 for details.

If you are unfamiliar with basic Windows tasks, such as filling out dialog boxes, please see the appendix before proceeding.

The following process looks long and involved, but it's really not so bad. Before entering any transactions that happen regularly (say, mortgage or insurance payments) into your account register, you should check out the next section, "Setting Up Recurring Bills and Scheduled Transactions." Otherwise, here's what you do:

1. **Open your account register.**

   Clicking Accounts on the Money navigation bar is one way to access your account register. One of the following pages appears:

   - The Account Manager page (listing all your accounts) appears — in which case, double-click your chosen account.

   - The last account register you viewed appears. If this isn't the account you want, click Accounts again on the Money navigation bar (or click Account Manager in the upper right-hand area of the account window) to see all your accounts. Double-click the account you want.

   If an account is in your list of Favorites, another way to open the account register is to click the account name in the list of Favorites on the Money home page. Or, click Favorites in the menu bar, then choose your account from the drop-down menu that appears.

   Either way, an account register page resembling the one shown in Figure 16-1 appears. Click View to get other views of the register page. Other views include: transactions sorted by check number or by date entered; unreconciled transactions only; or a register page without the data entry form at the bottom (so you enter transactions directly into the register).

Register area Double-click a transaction to edit it

Click to see other views

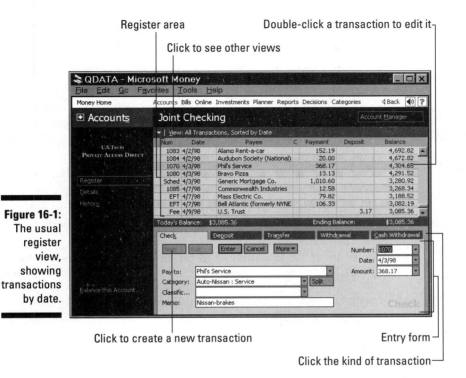

Figure 16-1:
The usual
register
view,
showing
transactions
by date.

Click to create a new transaction Entry form

Click the kind of transaction

2. **Click the New button to create a new transaction (or double-click any transaction listed in the register to edit it).**

   The form area indicated in Figure 16-1 wakes up and displays text boxes and various gizmos for data entry.

3. **At the top of the form area, click the tab for the kind of transaction you want to enter, such as Check, Withdrawal, Charge, Deposit, or Credit. (Refer to Figure 16-1.)**

   The types of transactions shown on the tabs depends on the type of account you're using: checking, credit card, loan, or other.

4. **Click the Pay To box and type the payee's name.**

   If you're making a Deposit or Credit, click the From box that Money displays instead of the Pay To box, and enter the payer's name.

   Money keeps a list of names for every payee (and payer) you ever enter. So, as you type, Money tries to match your typing to previous names, filling out the rest of the line; keep typing until Money guesses correctly. (If you're just starting to use Money, you have to type the whole name.) To choose a name off Money's list of names, click the tiny down-triangle at the right end of the Pay To (or From) box.

When making a transfer: Type your own name (or the name of whoever owns the receiving account) in the Pay To box. Click the To box to choose the receiving account (the account that gets the money).

5. Click the Category box (if it is present), then see if Money has guessed the proper category.

Unless the payee is new, Money fills out the rest of the form, using the same category and dollar amount as the last payment to (or receipt from) this payee. If Money has guessed the category correctly, skip to Step 7.

If the transaction actually includes funds in multiple categories, see the sidebar "Splitting a transaction into multiple categories."

6. To choose a category, click the tiny down-triangle at the right end of the Category box and choose a category from a list of previous payees.

(See Chapter 15 for background about categories and instructions for creating them.) To create a new category, type its name in the Category box. (Money attempts to match your typing with existing category names; keep typing.) Press the Enter or Tab key when you're done.

A New Category Wizard appears, in which you click Income or Expense to tell Money what kind of category your new category is. Click Next, and on the next wizard page, click one of Money's standard groups to associate your category with. Click Finish when you're done.

7. See whether the figure entered in the Amount box is correct. If not, click there and type a new value.

(As in any Windows text box, you can double-click to highlight the entire value, then the new value you type replaces the old one entirely.) If the value is already correct, skip to Step 8.

You can choose one of the last five dollar-amounts paid to this same payee by right-clicking the Pay To box.

8. Click the Memo box and type a memo to yourself about the transaction, if you like.

Don't bother with the Classification box unless you think you understand the concept. I don't explain classification in this book.

9. Record how you're making this payment: by check, electronic payment, funds transfer, blood, Green Stamps, or other medium.

If you are copying a check transaction from your checkbook, examine the check number Money has guessed at and placed in the Number box. If the number is wrong, click it, edit it, then press Enter or Tab.

If you're recording an ATM (Automatic Teller Machine) transaction, type **ATM** or any code (text) you choose in the Number box. Likewise, you may create your own code if the transaction is an automatically deducted fee or other special transaction that Money doesn't already provide a code for in the Number box.

To actually make a payment or transfer from Money, click the tiny down-triangle at the right end of the Number box, and choose one of the following:

- Choose Print to print a check. Money makes a kind of musical burping noise (see the joys of audio?) and places a reminder to print checks on the left side of the account window. See "Printing Checks" later in this chapter for instructions.

- Choose Epay to pay a bill online, or choose Xfer to make a funds transfer online (assuming you set up online service).

10. **Look at the Date box. If you need to change the date, click it and edit it.**

    The date you should use is the date of the transaction (although Money always puts today's date in this box). Click the tiny down-triangle at the right of the date box to choose a date from a calendar; or press + or – on the keyboard to advance or regress the date by one day. (For electronic payments, you need to use a date in the future to allow your bank time to process the transaction.)

    Click the Date box and press F1 on your keyboard to see suggestions for quick ways of changing the date.

11. **Click the Enter button or press the Enter key on your keyboard.**

    If you entered everything to Money's satisfaction, Money enters your transaction in the account's register. If not, Money pops up a dialog box to help you straighten things out.

Splitting a transaction into multiple categories

Some transactions need to be divided into two or more categories. The charges of a credit card payment, for instance, often need to be split into individual categories. To split a transaction, click the Split button adjoining the register's Category box. The Split Transaction box that appears has several rows, one row for each category.

To add or modify a category, click the Category column of a row and choose from the list of categories that appears. (The bottom half of each category row is for classifications, which I don't deal with here.) Enter a dollar amount for each row until the amounts equal the total. To divide any remaining amount among all categories, press the F6 key on your keyboard. Click the Done button when you're done.

Setting Up Recurring Bills and Scheduled Transactions

We all have recurring bills, and Microsoft is doing something about it! (No, Bill Gates is not going to pay our debts for us. In fact, he's kind of a recurring Bill, himself, with his products all over your PC.) But Microsoft Money can do two things for your recurring bills:

✔ Remind you when to pay a bill. (Again, not Bill Gates. You already paid him by buying Works Suite.)

✔ Reproduce the same transaction in Money each time, on time, so that all you need to do is verify or correct the amount and pay the bill.

I'm talking about recurring bills, but heck, the bills don't have to *re*cur; they only have to 'cur once, at some time in the future. Got a one-time payment to a bookie, due by New Year's Day? Put Mr. Armbracher on your Money calendar. And you can also set up Money to handle paychecks and other regular deposits, withdrawals, transfers, and even regularly purchased investments (generally recommended by investment advisors).

You can't always set up all the details about a transaction in advance. Paying your phone bill, for instance: Who knows how often your kids will call collect? But Money lets you review and change the details before the transaction actually happens. Fill in your best guess now to save time later if you happen to be right.

Here's how to set things up:

1. **Click Bills on the Money navigation bar.**

   Money displays the Bills & Deposits window.

2. **On the left side of the Money window, click <u>S</u>et Up Bills & Deposits.**

   The Recurring Bills & Deposits page of Figure 16-2 appears.

3. **Click Ne<u>w</u> to set up a scheduled transaction.**

   A Create New Scheduled Transaction Wizard leaps nimbly into action (despite having a rather ponderous name). Its first card asks what kind of transaction you have in mind.

4. **Choose one: <u>D</u>eposit, <u>B</u>ill, <u>T</u>ransfer, or <u>I</u>nvestment Purchase, and then click Next.**

5. **Tell Money how often the transaction happens: Click <u>O</u>nly Once or <u>M</u>ore Than Once, at Regular Intervals; if more than once, click <u>F</u>requency and choose one of the intervals listed. Click Next.**

   If you are entering a scheduled investment, skip to Step 8.

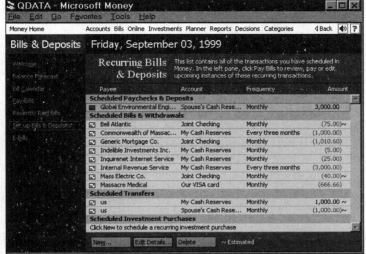

Figure 16-2:
Money
makes your
PC a star at
knowing
when a bill
is going to
come.

6. **Tell Money how you plan to pay by clicking the Payment method selection box and choosing from its menu. Then click Next.**

   You still have the opportunity to choose a different payment method before Money records or makes the transaction.

   If you're setting up a bill or a transfer, the menu displays many ways of making the transaction happen. If you're setting up a deposit, your choices are Manual Deposit (cash or check), Direct Deposit (somebody transmits funds to your account), or the mysterious Other (Money? What money? Did someone give me some money?).

7. **Tell Money if the amount will be the same each time. Click either Yes, It's The Same Amount each time, or No, The Amount Usually Varies.**

   Whichever selection you choose, you still have the ability to change any individual payment before it is recorded.

   Click Next, and a transaction form appears.

8. **Fill out the payment, deposit, or transfer form, just as would in your account register, then click Finish.**

   If you're scheduling an investment, see the "Scheduling an investment" sidebar.

Scheduling an investment

For a scheduled investment, such as a regular investment in your retirement account, fill out the investment form in the Create New Scheduled Transaction Wizard as follows:

1. In the Purchase Date box, enter the date for the next purchase.

2. Click Inv. Account to choose which of your investment accounts you will make your investment in.

3. Click Investment to type in the stock or mutual fund, or choose from existing investments.

4. Enter values for the Number of Shares you expect to buy, the Price Per Share you expect to pay (you can change it at purchase time), and the Commission (in dollars).

5. Leave Check Number blank if you expect to pay by check; choose Print if you expect to print a check. (Choose Epay for electronic payment.)

6. Click Payee and enter the name of the organization you're paying for these shares.

7. Click Transfer Account and choose the account from which you're transferring funds or writing a check to buy the shares.

After filling out this form, click the Finish button in the Create New Scheduled Transaction Wizard. Money will now keep track of your scheduled investment.

Being aware of upcoming transactions

You never have to miss another mortgage or credit card payment with Money. Money provides monitors for staying on top of your recurring bills (or other financial transaction).

One key monitoring tool is a flaming bill icon that Money places on your Windows Taskbar ten days before bills are due. The icon is on the opposite end of the Taskbar from the Start button, so you need to keep an eye out for it. (Unfortunately for me, the icon reminds me of an old Halloween prank involving placing a flaming paper bag, filled with an unsavory substance, on someone's doorstep and ringing the doorbell. Not that I ever did that.)

But I digress. Double-click that flaming icon to get a Microsoft Money Bill Reminder. (As if you needed reminding how much money Microsoft's Bill has! See? There's our recurring Bill again!) Click the Reminder's OK button to dismiss the Bill Reminder, or click the Start Money button to launch Microsoft Money. To disable reminders or change the advance warning period from 10 days, choose Tools⇨Options from the Money menu bar, and then click the Bills card of the Options dialog box that appears.

You can choose to view the other monitors by clicking the following selections on the left side of the Bills & Deposits window:

- ✔ **Balance Forecast:** Displays a graph of your finances based on scheduled incomes and payments.

- ✔ **Bill Calendar:** Displays the bills due in the current month. Click the tiny arrows on either side of Month title bar to move to another month.

- ✔ **Pay Bills:** Displays all the bills due within one month (or overdue). You can see ahead further by clicking View and choosing 2, 3, 6, or 12 months. This page is your best choice for recording bills as paid. See the following section for details.

- ✔ **Recently Paid Bills:** Displays scheduled bills paid within the last 60 days. You can sort by check number, date, payee, amount, or status by clicking on the headings for those columns.

If a bill is overdue, Money places a notice on the Money home page. Click that notice to go directly to the Bills & Deposits window.

Proceeding with scheduled transactions

When you have paid a scheduled bill from your checkbook or carried out some other scheduled transaction, you should record it in Money. Here's how to record the transaction as completed:

1. **Click Bills on Money's navigation bar.**

2. **On the left side of the Bills & Deposits window that appears, click Pay Bills.**

   The Upcoming Bills & Deposits page appears.

3. **Click the bill or other transaction to select it.**

4. **Click the <u>R</u>ecord *whatever* button at the bottom of the page.**

   By *whatever* I mean the word "Payment," "Transfer," or whatever the nature of the transaction is.

   If an earlier instance of this same transaction is overdue, Money doesn't let you record this one. You must click the earlier instance, then click either the Record or the Skip Transaction button, before proceeding to any later instance.

5. **In the form (dialog box) that appears, review the details of the transaction and make any edits necessary.**

   Money fills in the check number if one is needed.

6. **Click the Record Payment button in the form.**

Money draws a line through the transaction to mark it as recorded. Your account register now also shows this transaction.

Printing Checks

Actually, you can't print checks in Money. You *can* print *on* checks, however, which means you need to get blank, numbered checks. You probably already have checks — but you need special (and, naturally, more expensive) checks designed for Money to print on your printer. Money-compatible checks in different sizes and styles are available from several sources, including (no surprise) Microsoft. Consult a good office supply store, and bring your checkbook with you.

If you currently pay bills one at a time, you'll find that printing checks in Money is more work than writing checks. But at least Money's checks are neatly printed, and if you're recording the check in Money anyway, printing is not *that* much additional work. If you pay several bills at once, rather than singly, check printing is somewhat more worthwhile.

Setting up your printer for your checks

Windows already knows about your printer (assuming the printer is installed properly), but now you need to tell Money about your checks. Here's how:

1. **Choose File⇨Print Setup⇨Check Setup.**

   The Check Setup dialog box appears.

2. **Review the printer selection.**

   Money gets its information about what printer to use from Windows. If you have more than one printer installed on your PC, and the one you want to use is not displayed in the Printer box, click that box to choose the correct printer.

3. **Review the check info in the Type box.**

   The Type box lists a check style and size. Compare that information to the label on your check package, and if the description differs, click the Type box to choose a description closer to the one on your package. The "Laser" description is usually also okay for checks printed on ink-jet printers. A picture to the right of the Type box shows what each style looks like. Styles with white dots down the sides of the checks (representing holes) are only for printers that drive a continuous, perforated sheet of checks through the printer with sprockets.

Numbering your printed checks differently

You probably won't give up your checkbook. Your checkbook already has numbered checks; unfortunately, you can't print on them. You probably don't want to drag sheets of Money's printable checks to the store with you to write upon, either, although you could. How, then, do you keep Money's check numbers in sync with your checkbook's number series, and avoid duplicate or missing numbers? If you keep Money absolutely up-to-date by recording checkbook checks as you (and your spouse!) write them, Money uses the next check number in the series, and all you do is tear up any duplicate-numbered checks. But few humans are that organized. Instead, I suggest you number your Money-printed checks very differently: Start at, say, check number 10,000.

4. **Review the printer feed info in the Source box.**

   The Source box tells you where Money thinks you're going to feed the blank check sheets into your printer. Auto Sheet Feeder is where you normally put a stack of blank paper. Consulting your printer manual may help you figure out what Money is talking about. If you want to feed from a different place (say a manual feed slot), click Source and choose a new source.

5. **Decide if you want the payee's address on the check.**

   Money normally prints the payee's address on the check, and if the payee's address is not already on file in Money, it asks you for it when you print a check. If you don't want the address printed, click to clear the Require Address For Payee When Printing Checks check mark.

You can change the font used on the check by clicking the Font button and making selections in the Font dialog box. Click OK when you're done.

Actually printing checks

Before you can print a check, you must record the transaction (as a Print transaction) on your account register page or the bill payment page. See the earlier sections of this chapter for instructions on recording transactions in account registers and while paying bills. The transaction must have Print chosen in the Number field, if it is to result in a printed check.

After you record the transaction, the phrase Print Checks appears in a Reminders area on the left side of the account's register page, the bill payment page, or the Money home page. Then do the following:

1. **Click Print Checks in the Reminders area.**

   A Print Checks dialog box springs into action, as Figure 16-3 shows, telling you how many checks Money is prepared to print at this time.

   If you want to print only certain checks, click Selected Checks, and in the Select Checks dialog box that appears, click the checks you *don't* want to print, which *un*selects them. (Unselected checks are in white.) Click OK when done.

Partially used sheets may require special orientation

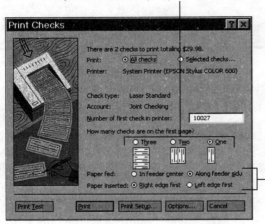

Figure 16-3: Printing checks. Sometimes you print checks sideways.

Align your check sheet to these settings

2. **Examine your sheet of checks, and type the lowest number on that page of checks into the box labeled Number of First Check in Printer.**

   If you're not printing on sheets of checks, but on continuous-form paper, skip to Step 6.

3. **If you already used one or more of the checks on the first sheet of checks, you need to tell the Print Checks dialog box how many checks remain on that sheet. Click Three, Two, or One.**

   Each selection (Three, Two, or One) displays how you should orient the first page of your check sheet.

4. **Place your checks in the printer feed area that you chose during setup.**

   Orient the top sheet the way you were given in the previous step. Align the edges as indicated by the Paper Fed and Paper Inserted buttons in the dialog box, or choose the orientation your printer manual suggests, and click the buttons to match:

   • **In Feeder Center:** Money expects you to center the checks in the feed area.

- **Along Feeder Side:** Money expects you to align the edge of the page to the left (as you face the printer's front) in the feed area.

- **Right Edge First / Left Edge First:** Choose which edge of the check, right or left (as you read the check), goes into the printer first.

5. **If you are not certain that everything is set up right, insert a plain piece of paper in place of the check sheet and Click Print Test.**

   Money prints a dummy check. Lay the dummy over the check sheet in the proper orientation and hold the two up to the light to see if everything is printed in the right place. If you need to reposition, click Options. In the Printing Alignment area of the Options dialog box, you can adjust the printing position by $1/4$-inch intervals. Two separate controls are provided for full-sheet and partial-sheet adjustment. Adding 1 to a horizontal setting moves the printing one $1/4$ inch to the right. (Adding 1 to a vertical setting moves the printing a $1/4$ inch down.) Use negative numbers to go the other direction.

6. **When you are certain the check will print correctly, click the Print button (on the bottom of the Print Checks dialog box).**

7. **If the check prints satisfactorily, click the Finish button.**

   Otherwise, click the Reprint button, and in the dialog box that appears, click the listing for the check you want to reprint. You need to reinsert, and possibly reorient the top check sheet (as in Step 4) because one of the checks has been used. Then click the OK button.

Reconciling Accounts

Do your records and the bank's records agree? You can find out by using Money's reconciliation feature. Personally, I hate *reconciling,* otherwise known as balancing one's checkbook, because I simply end up wasting hours tracking down some stupid typo I made. I prefer to enter data into Money directly from the bank statement, so the two must agree! I review for errors by comparing Money's register to my checkbook register. But then, I suspect I am morally deficient in my banking practices.

If you feel morally bound to reconcile your account, begin by making sure you entered all the transactions from your checkbook, ATM receipts, and other records into the Money register. Then take your monthly statement firmly by the hand and do the following:

1. **Open Money to the account register page: Click Accounts in the navigation bar (click it again, if necessary, to see the list of all accounts), then double-click your account.**

2. **Click Balance This Account at the bottom of the left side of the screen.**

   The Balance Wizard, shown in Figure 16-4, strides onto your screen in a well-balanced fashion.

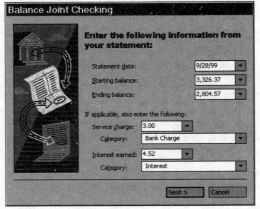

Balance Joint Checking

Enter the following information from your statement:

Statement date:	9/28/99
Starting balance:	3,326.37
Ending balance:	2,804.57

If applicable, also enter the following:

Service charge:	3.00
Category:	Bank Charge
Interest earned:	4.52
Category:	Interest

Next >   Cancel

Figure 16-4:
Copy information from your account statement into Money.

3. **Enter the statement date and ending balance from your bank statement.**

   Money obtains the starting balance from your last reconciliation.

4. **Enter any service charge(s), and click Category to categorize that expense.**

5. **Enter any interest earned, and click Category to categorize that income.**

6. **Click Next, and Money displays a reconciliation window for your account. The panel in the left side of the window describes the three steps you need to take next:**

   • Review each transaction listed and click the skinny C column for each transaction that matches the bank statement. ("C" stands for Cleared.)

   • To add or edit transactions (for instance, your statement may show ATM fees), click the Click Here to Add or Edit Transactions check box. A data entry form appears, which works exactly like the one in your account register.

   • By clearing, adding, and editing transactions, you reduce the Difference figure (shown in step 2 of the instructions on the left panel of the window) to zero. Click Next.

Reconciling an account with online reports from your bank

Money can (in theory) automatically reconcile your account with an online report that — if your bank offers this service — Money downloaded from your bank when you last went online. Click Online on Money's navigation bar to go to the Online window, click Online Financial Services at the top, left side of that window, and choose your bank or other financial institution from the list that appears. If more than one account is shown, click the account you want.

A Read Statement button appears at the bottom of the page; click it and follow the instructions of the wizard that appears. Click the wizard's Postpone button if the process seems unwise at any point.

If you finally give up in frustration, as I do, you can click Postpone instead of Next to return later. Or, click Next anyway to try Money's reconciliation features.

7. **If your account doesn't reconcile, Money tells you so with a new dialog box, in which you can choose to: Return to balancing the account; try the Money AutoReconcile thingy; or have Money change (technically, *fudge*) the account balance by adding or subtracting a correction amount.**

   If you choose the AutoReconcile thingy, Money displays a Possible Error dialog box if it finds anything fishy, with a suggestion for correcting the fishiness. Click Yes in that box if you like the suggestion; click No otherwise.

   If you choose to fudge the balance, you need to categorize the fudge value. Type a special category called, say **Fudge,** into the Category box, and Money helps you create the category. Make it an Income category, in the Other Income group.

8. **On the last page of the reconciliation wizard, click the Finish button.**

Types of Electronic Transactions

Money allows for a variety of electronic transactions, including the following:

- ✔ **Epays:** electronic payments that you make, one at a time.

- ✔ **Apays:** automatic payments of the same amount, made regularly, that you instruct your bank's computer to make.

> ✔ **Web payments:** bill paying and other transactions such as statement downloading that use your bank's Web page.
>
> ✔ **Xfers:** transfers between two accounts at the same bank or other institution.
>
> ✔ **E-bills:** electronic bills delivered to you through a Web site.

In the spirit of not belaboring the online part of Money in this book, I refer you to Money's help files for full information on these transactions. Choose Help⇨Help Topics. In the Help panel that appears, click in the bottom area labeled Ask Money, and type this text: Learn about Epays, Apays. The Help panel displays the text, "Learn about Epays, Apays, Web Payments, Xfers, E-bills, and automatic transactions." Click that text to view the help file. Click the X in the upper right-hand corner of the Help panel to remove the panel.

Chapter 17

Budgeting, Reporting, and Analyzing

● ●

▶ Cleaning up your categories for easier budgeting

▶ Running the Money Budget Planner

▶ Entering income, savings, expenses, and debt

▶ Automatic budgeting

▶ Entering debt into the Debt Reduction Planner's plan

▶ Viewing your monthly and yearly budget

▶ Viewing a forecast of savings

▶ Choosing reports or charts in Money

▶ Getting useful reports for tax time

▶ Customizing reports and charts

▶ Printing reports and charts

● ●

*H*aving all your transactions neatly organized and displayed in Money is lovely, but it doesn't pay the bills. Well . . . actually, it *does* pay the bills, I guess, but what I mean is that neatness and organization aren't everything.

One of the benefits of entering all your transactions into a computer program and categorizing them is that the program can help you summarize and analyze your finances, and do some planning. It can also help you prepare reports and charts of financial information for the people nearest and dearest to you, like your spouse, your accountant, or the Internal Revenue Department.

Money does all this work with the aid of *planners* (in Money's Planners department) and with reports and charts (in Money's Reports department). In this chapter, I focus on the tools I think most people want to use: the Budget Planner, and the report and chart features. The report and chart features are particularly useful for that most popular pastime, paying taxes, where you need to separate the wheat from the chaff. (And pay taxes on the wheat.)

How to really clean up

Money's planning, reporting, and charting features need a clean set of categories to work well. (Oh — you thought I was going to give you my secret stock market tips to "really clean up" with? Given my financial expertise, you should be glad I'm not!) No, fortunately for you, I'm just suggesting that you clean up your categories, so that using Money's planners and decision tools is easier.

Click Categories on Money's navigation bar, and make sure your categories make sense. (See Chapter 16 for more details. You're okay if you haven't added any to Money's original set.) Problem spots are:

✔ **Categories with different names but which mean the same thing:** Dividends, for instance, and Dividend Income. To fix the problem, click one (say, Dividend Income) and click the Delete button. Money asks you what category to reassign its transactions to. (Choose Dividend in this example.)

✔ **Categories unassigned to groups:** Double-click the category and in the window that appears, click to choose a Category Group. Click the Back button on the navigation bar to return to the Categories window.

✔ **Categories that should be subcategories:** Fred's Dividend Income should be a subcategory of Fred's Income, for instance. To make Category X a subcategory under Category Y, click Category X, click the Move button at the bottom of the window, and enter Category Y in the Move Transaction dialog box that appears. The category can keep its old name.

Budgeting

Ugh. Budgeting. Nothing is more depressing than trying to stick to a budget. But I'm not talking about *sticking* to a budget, here, I'm talking about *making a budget!* Totally unrelated. Much more fun.

Money makes building a budget interesting by automatically adding up all the many picky details about your various types of income, savings, bills, and debts, then showing you how well you can expect to do monthly or yearly. Money can also *autobudget:* create a budget for you based on previous transactions. The Budget Planner's reports and forecast chart can help you see where you may have budget problems, and how fast savings will increase under your plan.

Even with the raw, untamed excitement of using Money, budgeting can be a bit tedious, so get yourself a large box of cookies and a pot of coffee. Remember, budgets are good for you.

Getting started

1. **Click Planner on the Money navigation bar, and then click Budget Planner on the screen that appears.**

   The Getting Started screen appears.

2. **Click Group Your Accounts to enter the Organize by Accounts dialog box.**

   Here you review and/or change how you want Money to think of your various accounts: which ones are for day-to-day expenses, and which ones for long-term savings, for instance. Click an account, and then click a purpose. Money uses these purposes to help you plan.

   Click Close at the bottom of the dialog box when you're done.

3. **Click Next in the top-right corner of the Getting Started screen.**

   The Budget Planner begins to step you through a series of windows for each kind of budget item. This chapter has a subsection for each planner window.

You can move directly to any budget planner page by clicking its name (Debt, for instance) on the left-hand panel of the planner window.

Have a cookie.

Income

You know that as you record your deposits in Money, you associate them with categories, right? (Oh, come on. I'm sure you do. But, if not, check out Chapter 15.) Money uses the total deposits you have associated with each category to estimate an initial income budget. Figure 17-1 shows the Income window.

The task here is to include all important income categories in the plan and to establish a reasonable budget amount for each category. To remove a trivial, incorrect, or otherwise insufferable category, click it and then click the Remove button.

To add a category of income, you click Add Category. A dialog box politely asks you to choose the category (or subcategory). If you choose a category, when you click Next, a second screen appears. Despite its tedious explanation, it merely wants to know if you wish to include all the category's subcategories. Click Yes if so, No if not, and then click Finish.

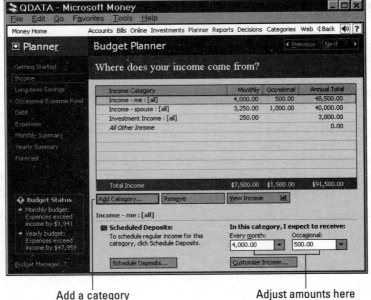

Figure 17-1:
Use income
categories
to budget
income.

Add a category   Adjust amounts here

You don't have to live with the amounts shown. Click the category and you can adjust the amounts. Figure 17-1 shows you where. ("Occasional" income is added income, by the way, not an alternative to monthly income.)

Is your income seasonal? If you're a ski instructor or house painter, click Customize Income, click Custom in the dialog box that appears, and you can enter a separate figure for each month.

Click Next in the window's upper right-hand corner (or click Long-Term Savings in the window's left panel) to proceed to the Long-Term Savings window.

Have another cookie.

Long-term savings

The Money philosophy (if software can have a philosophy — a matter for philosophers to decide) is that you should consider saving money to be "paying yourself first," and give it an appropriately high priority compared to spending it (paying other people). That philosophy is why savings occurs before expenses in this planner, as I'm sure it does in your life.

On the Long-Term Savings window, the planner thoughtfully suggests a budgeted monthly contribution for you to save for long-term goals — like hiring someone else to do this budgeting stuff. You can change the amount suggested by double-clicking the contribution shown. In the Custom Contribution dialog box that appears, either enter a monthly and (optional) occasional value, or (if your savings contributions will be seasonal) click Custom and enter a contribution for each month.

You can also add specific, scheduled deposits into any account to which you gave the "purpose" of long-term savings (back on the Getting Started screen). Click New Contribution, and a wizard-like series of dialog boxes asks you nosy questions, culminating in a data entry form. Fill out this form as you would for a transfer transaction in an account register (see Chapter 16 for details), and then click Finish.

Click Next in the window's upper right-hand corner (or click Occasional Expenses in the window's left panel) to proceed to the Occasional expenses window.

Put a cookie under the sofa for long-term savings. Or for the dog. Whoever gets there first.

Occasional expenses

Money's "occasional expenses" are for those very special occasions, like a vacation, a romantic dinner, or your car's exhaust system falling off on the turnpike. Here you budget for a certain periodic contribution, to save for your muffler guy's kid's college education.

Use this page like you do the Long-Term Savings window.

Click Next in the window's upper right-hand corner (or click Debt in the window's left panel) to move on to the Debt and Loans window.

(Now, pour a cup from that pot of coffee I recommended at the start. I know *I* need a cup!)

Debt and loans

Whatever happened to "neither a borrower nor a lender be?" We're all in hock up to our ears! So much so, that Money provides a Debt Reduction Planner, a close neighbor to the Budget Planner.

The Debt window shows you the debts the Budget Planner is currently aware of. If the Debt window doesn't display a mortgage, loan, or other debt account that you set up, and you want to add that debt, you must make the debt part of a *debt plan,* using the Debt Reduction Planner.

A quick trip to the Debt Reduction Planner

You find a link (underlined text) to the Debt Reduction Planner at the top of the the Debt window of the Budget Planner. You can also find a Debt Reduction Planner link in the top-level Planner window: Click Planning on Money's navigation bar to go to that window, then, whichever way you get to it, click the link.

Using either link gets you to the Debt Reduction Planner. It displays a Debt Plan window like the one in Figure 17-2.

Note: Figure 17-2 shows a mortgage in the plan, which is not really the high-interest kind of debt that the Debt Planner is normally concerned about. Mortgages are not usually high-interest debts. Remove such debt from your Debt Plan. Click the debt, and then click the Move out of Plan button.

To bring a debt into the plan, click the debt in the lower portion of the window, and then click the Move into Plan button at the bottom of the window. (The Debt Planner may ask you a few questions at this point.)

To edit anything about the debt, click the debt, and then click the Edit Debt Info button. You can also add a new debt account by clicking New Account and following the instructions of the New Account Wizard.

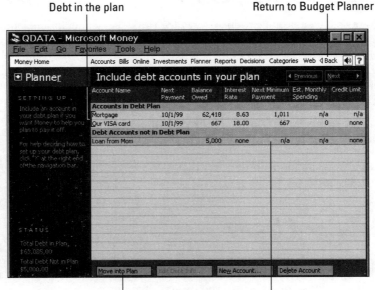

Debt in the plan   Return to Budget Planner

Figure 17-2:
You and
Microsoft
Money will
feel better
when your
debt is in
a plan.

Click to move loans into the plan   Debt not in the plan

Going back to the Budget Planner

To return to the Budget Planner, don't click Next in the Debt Reduction Planner, as you may do out of habit. Click the Back button on the Money navigation bar instead.

If debt reduction is a serious goal of yours, *do* click Next in the Debt Reduction Planner and continue in this tool until its end. I don't have the room in this book to do justice to this tool, but read the planner's instructions carefully and you just may save some money in the end. To return to the Budget Planner, click Planning in Money's navigation bar and then click the link to the Budget Planner.

Have two cookies.

Click Next in the Budget Planner's upper right-hand corner (or click Expenses in the window's left panel) to proceed to the Expenses window.

Expenses: Spending by category

In the Expenses window, the Budget Planner asks you to review each of your expense categories and set a monthly budget amount for each category. The Planner suggests amounts, and you can change them. Here's how to do it:

✓ **Autobudget:** If you already entered one month or more of categorized expenses into Money, click the Autobudget button to have the Budget Planner estimate a budget for you. In the Autobudget dialog box that appears, click to clear the check marks of categories you want to omit from your budget, and then click OK.

✓ **Enter budget amounts:** Click an expense category, and two text boxes at the bottom right of the window appear. Click the Every Month box and enter whatever you think you'll spend monthly. If you think you may occasionally spend more (or if an expense is paid annually), click the Occasional box and type that amount, to be added to your monthly expense. Click Customize Spending to vary spending seasonally.

✓ **Add or remove categories:** To add a category not listed here, or to create a new category, click the Add Category button to use the New Category dialog box described in Chapter 16. To remove a category from your budget, click it and then click the Remove button.

✓ **Budget for scheduled bills:** Categories that include scheduled bills display an envelope icon, and if you click that category, you can review the bill summary in the lower left-hand corner of the window. Click the Edit Bills button there to display a dialog box where you can edit, delete, or add scheduled bills to the category. Click the Additional Spending button to add other monthly or seasonal expenses to this category.

✓ **Check your spending:** Click the View Spending button to see a report of your past six months' spending.

Now go to the Monthy Summary window. Click Next in the window's upper right-hand corner (or click Expenses in the window's left panel). Yawn. Have a cup of coffee.

Monthly or yearly summary

This is the moment of truth. The Budget Planner takes the monthly amounts you budgeted for income and outgo, and puts them all together in the Monthly Summary window. If monthly savings, expenses, and debt payments exceed monthly income, the planner lets you know here. Have a nice, stiff cup of coffee and ponder whether you can rent out that spare room for extra income.

If you have income left over, choose whether to place the extra in your savings (click Save It in My Occasional Expense Fund), or spend it (click Spend the Money). Surprisingly, Money does not suggest where you should spend your money — an admirable show of restraint from Microsoft.

For a yearly summary, click Next in the window's upper right-hand corner (or click Yearly Summary in the window's left panel). The yearly summary combines both monthly and occasional amounts into a single report. If you have a lot of once-a-year payments, this summary may hold some additional surprises for you. Consider having some more cookies.

Forecast

Click Next in the upper right-hand corner of the Yearly Summary window, or click Forecast on the left side of the Budget Planner window, and you get a chart showing the gradual rise (or fall) of your fortunes.

Click the Interpret the Forecast link for tips on interpreting the graph. The tips appear in the Money Help panel. Click the X in its upper-right corner to remove the tips when you finish reading them.

Click the Customize link to change the chart. In the Customize Report dialog box that appears, you may do the following activities. Click the Apply button to see the result of your choice, or click OK if you are done fiddling.

- Click the Show Next selection box to choose a time period for the forecast.

- Click Level of Detail to change the time interval on the bar from weeks to months — or to another time interval.

- To make your unscheduled expenses appear either at the beginning or end of the month, click the Unscheduled Monthly Expenses Happen selection box, and choose one of those options.

> ✔ To do the same for annual expenses, click the Unscheduled Annual Expenses Happen selection box.
>
> ✔ Click the chart tab for chart options. By clicking to clear the Stacked check mark, you can un-stack the Monthly Expense Fund (blue) from the Occasional Expense Fund (yellow). Enable the Show in 3D check box for bars with depth, or clear the Show gridlines check box to eliminate the horizontal lines on the chart.

You're done! That's everything the Budget Planner can tell you, budget-wise. Click Finish at the upper right-hand corner of the window, and finish off that box of cookies!

Analyzing with Reports and Charts

Money's reports and charts help you summarize and visualize your expense and income categories. Or, in more practical terms, they can help you:

> ✔ Make gee-whiz color charts and reports to justify all the time you're spending with this program to your spouse, boss, or accountant.
>
> ✔ Find all your tax-related income and expenses by category.
>
> ✔ See who is getting all your money.
>
> ✔ Compare your current income to your current spending.
>
> ✔ Find out whether or not you are living within your budget.
>
> ✔ See your net worth, or watch how your accounts change over time.
>
> ✔ See how your investments are doing.
>
> ✔ Display price trends of your stocks and schedule your bankruptcy.

Choosing and using report and chart windows

To perform any or all of the marvelous Money chart and report functions, stroll Money's fabulous gallery of reports and charts and pick one that fits right over the living room couch. Do the following:

1. Click Reports on the Money navigation bar.

Money's Report & Chart Gallery rushes to your aid, listing various groups of charts down the left panel of the Gallery.

Tools for taxes

If you are diligent about putting your tax-related expenses into Money's tax categories (and marking any new categories you create by checking Include on Tax Reports), the Money Tax Software Report can be very useful — even if you don't have tax software! Click Taxes on the left of the Report & Chart window, and then click Tax Software Report in the gallery that appears.

You can export this report to your tax software by choosing File⇨Export to Tax Software. In the Export Tax dialog box that appears, type a filename in the File Name box. If you want to give this report to your accountant on a diskette, put the diskette in your A: drive, click the Save In selection box, and choose 3½ Floppy (A:). Click OK when you're done.

2. **On the left side of the window, click to select a category of reports and charts.**

3. **On the right side of the window, click to select a specific report or chart.**

4. **If any selection boxes appear at the bottom of the window, click them to make selections that adjust the focus of your report or chart.**

   Depending on the specific report or chart you choose, you can click a selection box and choose to focus on general categories (such as taxable transactions), specific income or expense categories, accounts, or date ranges.

5. **Click the Go to Report/Chart button to view your selected report or chart.**

   If you choose a chart, it may appear in any of several forms: bar, line, or pie chart. Depending on what other forms of chart are available, you can change the form.

Pie charts are useful for seeing proportions: what portion of your spending is on dining out, for instance. Line charts are useful for trends or things that vary over time, like spending in a particular category. Bar charts are useful for comparing values.

Figure 17-3 shows a bar chart and the controls for changing to a different form of chart. If a form of chart is not available, that button is grayed out.

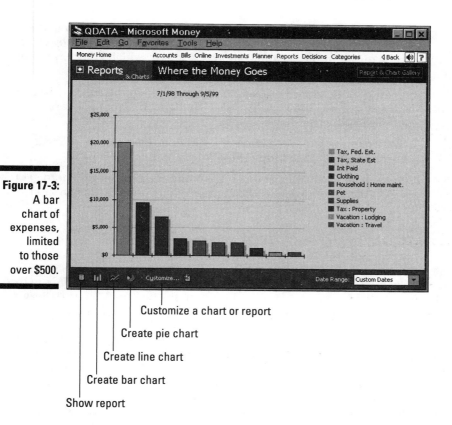

Figure 17-3:
A bar
chart of
expenses,
limited
to those
over $500.

Customize a chart or report

Create pie chart

Create line chart

Create bar chart

Show report

In Money, you can turn many charts into reports, and vice versa. Simply click the Report button or one of the Chart buttons shown in Figure 17-3 to make the transformation.

Here are a few tips for chart and report windows:

✔ Most charts and reports need some customization to be useful. For instance, I limited the chart in Figure 17-3 to high values to avoid squeezing dozens of bars illegibly into the chart. See "Customizing reports and charts" later in this chapter.

✔ Pause your cursor over any bar, pie segment, line, or legend entry (in the list on the right side) to see the dollar value of that item. Double-click that item to see what categories, accounts, or transactions it includes.

✔ To choose new dates, either double-click the dates at the top of the chart or report, or click the Date Range selection box at the lower right. Both take you to the Customization dialog box, which I discuss in the next section.

✔ To view the details of a transaction in a report, double-click it. To edit the transaction in the View Transaction dialog box that appears, double-click the transaction.

✔ To return to the gallery to choose a different report or chart, click Return to Gallery at the top right of the report or chart page.

✔ Reports tend to be long, and you generally need to print them to get the big picture. See "Printing your report or chart" later in this chapter.

Customizing reports and charts

Money's pre-designed reports and charts are great, but most need some customization to be useful to you. You can customize a report before you display it by clicking the Customize button in the Report & Chart Gallery, or by clicking Customize at the bottom left of the chart or report window.

The Customize Report dialog box then appears, displaying several tabbed cards, like index cards. Click a tab to select that card. Each of the most important of those cards is described with a heading in the following text. (The trivial cards, Text and Font, I'm sure you can figure out on your own.)

To see your customizations applied to the chart or report currently displayed, click the Apply button in the dialog box. You probably need to drag the dialog box by its title bar to get it out of the way. Click the OK button after you make all the customizations you want.

One of the most useful customizations you can perform is to limit the amount of data displayed. Money has a tendency to show you too much: too many categories, too many accounts, too many payees, or too many transactions. To limit the data, use the cards I describe in the following sections. In particular, see how the Rows and Columns card can create an "all other" category containing all the tiny, floor-sweepings data you don't want to show separately.

Unfortunately, you can't undo changes. But you can use the Reset button to undo all your customizations and return to the pre-designed settings that were in effect when you first chose this report or chart from the Gallery.

To save your customized chart or report, add it to Money's Favorites. Click Favorites on the Money menu bar, and in the Add to Favorites dialog box that appears, type a report name. Click OK, and your report is listed as a link on the Money Home Page. Click that link to return to the report or chart, or choose Favorites⇨Favorite Reports, and then your report's name.

Date

The Date card is pretty obvious, I think. It limits your display to data between certain dates. Click Range to choose pre-set ranges, like Previous Year, or click in the From or To text boxes to enter custom dates.

Account

The Account card limits your chart or report to certain accounts. Click to clear an account's check mark and remove it from the display. Click Select All to put check marks in all accounts, or click Clear All to remove all the check marks.

If you need to select just a handful of accounts, click Clear All first to remove all check marks. If some accounts are closed, you can limit the display to just the open ones by clicking All Open Accounts.

Category

The Category card limits your chart or report to certain categories or subcategories. As in the Account card, click to clear a category's check mark to remove it from the display. If you need to select just a handful of accounts, click Clear All first to remove all check marks. Click one of the Select buttons to select various types of categories: All categories, Income, Expense, or Tax-related.

Click to clear the Show Subcategories check mark to eliminate subcategories from the list.

Payee

The payee card works just like the Account and Category cards, but for payees! Clear the check marks for payees you want to eliminate. (From the report/chart that is.)

Amount

The Amount card lets you restrict the display to certain exact amounts (click Search on This Amount) or a range of amounts (click Search on This Range).

To specify a range of amounts, click the From box to enter the low end, and then click the To box to enter the high end. For an open-ended range (say, above $500), leave the other value (To, in this example) blank.

Details

The Details card enables you to limit the chart or report by type of transactions you want (click the Type box to choose), and/or the transaction's reconciliation status (click the Status box to choose), and/or the check number.

You can limit the display to a particular check number (click Find This Check Number and enter a check number in that box), or to a range of check numbers (click Find This Range, and enter the lowest and highest check numbers in the From and To boxes, respectively).

Rows & Columns

The Rows & Column card is intended to let you specify what appears in the rows and columns or reports (as its name implies), but it also affects charts.

A very useful option in this card is to create an *all other* category into which you sweep stuff whose amount is under a certain percentage of the total: all categories, for instance, where the amount is under 2 percent of the total. Click the Combine All Values Under __ % of Total box, and enter the percentage. This choice helps reduce clutter in your report or chart.

Click Rows to choose what each row of the report (or bar or pie slice of a chart) displays: a category, an account, a particular week, or a particular month.

Click Columns to choose what each column of the report displays (or what the horizontal axis of a chart displays). You can have a column for each month, for instance, to create a spreadsheet-like report.

Click to enable the Sort by Amount check box to have rows appear in descending order of amount. Otherwise, rows appear in alphabetical order.

Chart

The Chart card lets you add features to charts, change the form of a chart (pie, bar, or line) or switch between chart and report form. Among the features you can add are labels to pie segments in a pie chart, 3D-looking bars, lines, or pies, and horizontal gridlines. You can also position the chart's legend (the text that says what color means what) to the right or below the chart, or turn it off.

Printing your report or chart

Printing a report or chart is straightforward. In a report, you have the option of printing specific page numbers. In a report or chart, you can print vertically (Portrait) or sideways (Landscape). Choose File⇨Print.

If you are printing a report, the Print Report dialog box appears. To print the whole thing, just click OK. To print just certain pages, print the entire report once to find out where the page breaks are. Then choose File⇨Print again, click Pages, and enter the starting page and ending page numbers, respectively in the From and To text boxes. For multiple copies, double-click in the Copies text box and enter the number of copies you want. When printing multiple copies of multipage reports, click Collate Copies to avoid having to collate yourself.

If you are printing a chart, the Print Chart dialog box appears. Choose the number of copies and the print quality, and then click OK.

In either the Print Chart or Print Report dialog box, you have the setup options that nearly every Windows program provides. To use a different printer, use sideways printing, funny-sized paper, or your printer's manual insertion slot, click the Setup button. The Report and Chart Setup box appears. To choose another printer installed on your PC, click the Printer selection box. For sideways printing (for reports with many columns, for instance) click Landscape. Choose a new paper size by clicking Size, if necessary, or a manual feed slot by clicking Source. (Click Options to fiddle with printer settings, like quality of printing.) Click OK when done.

Making Decisions with Money

Money includes a set of calculators and worksheets for helping you make financial decisions. Click Decisions on Money's navigation bar to see a gallery of them.

I think these tools are sufficiently well-written that you can figure them out for yourself. Just click the one you want and follow the directions given.

One peculiarity of some of these tools is that they run in a special Web view of Money. This view is not a problem, but it does look unusual and may be a bit slow. To return to Money when you're done, click the Return to Money button at the top of the screen.

Chapter 18

Investing with Money

● ●

In This Chapter

▶ Starting your investment accounts

▶ Buy! Sell! Enter Data!

▶ Getting good and bad news online

▶ Figuring out what to buy or sell next

● ●

*I*nvesting with money is a good idea. Traders (despite the name) are notoriously unwilling to accept livestock and other hard goods.

Investing with Microsoft's *Money* (Microsoft's software, not their cash) is a similarly good idea. Not only does Money then include your investments in its reports and planners, but it also gives you useful graphs and views for comparing and evaluating your investments. It even offers a very simple way to obtain price histories and current trading online, so you can be up-to-date. Grab your portfolio's statements and prospectuses *(prospecti?)* and fire up Money. Even if you currently have no investments, Money lets you track whatever securities look attractive to you.

Setting Up Investment Accounts

Before you set up an investment account, make sure you understand that an investment *account* is not the same as a specific *security:* a stock, bond, fund, or certificate of deposit (CD). An investment *account* in Money matches your account with a broker, bank, or investment firm: It's a pool of money or value with your name attached to it. Some accounts involve only a single security; others involve many different securities. If you simply want data on a prospective security, see the tip in the later section, "Viewing Current and Prospective Investments."

You set up an investment account much the same as you set up a bank account. (Chapter 15 discusses setting up such accounts.) Here is a quick review:

- First, click Accounts on the navigation bar. (Click Accounts again if the screen does not initially display all your current accounts.)

- Second, click the New Account button at the bottom of the page. A New Account dialog box (a wizard) appears and takes you through the process of setting up an account. Fill out the forms and click the Next button to proceed.

You can use Money to get stock prices from the Internet without setting up online services. The phrase *online services* in Money refers to private account services such as making transactions or downloading statements that this book does not get into.

Recording Your Buying, Selling, and Dividends

Recording your investment transactions is very similar to recording bank and checking account transactions in Money. (See Chapter 16.) The procedure for investments goes like this:

1. **Click Investments on the navigation bar.**

   The Investments window appears, displaying the Portfolio page. Accounts are displayed in bold; individual investments in each account are indented under that account.

2. **Double-click your investment account (shown in bold text).**

   The investment's register opens, as shown in Figure 18-1.

3. **Click the Date text box and enter a date.**

4. **Click the Investment selection box and choose an investment.**

   If you haven't invested in this security before, Money launches an inquisitive little wizard. The wizard's questions include what kind of investment it is, its tax status, and its *ticker symbol* — the symbol that represents it in the stock market. Refer to your broker or the security's prospectus for this symbol. Only by entering the symbol can you get online quotes and history for this security.

View price history

Account setup details

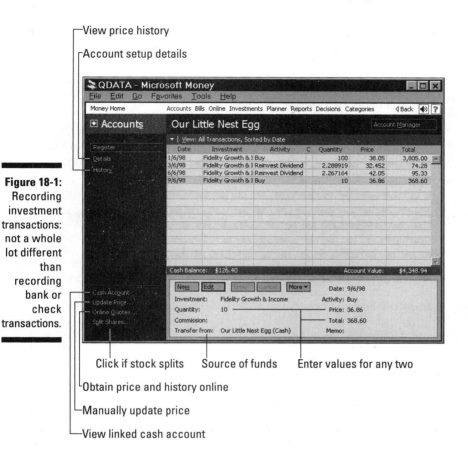

Figure 18-1:
Recording
investment
transactions:
not a whole
lot different
than
recording
bank or
check
transactions.

Click if stock splits   Source of funds   Enter values for any two

Obtain price and history online

Manually update price

View linked cash account

You can also find symbols online. Using Internet Explorer, go to the address home.microsoft.com (the page IE normally starts with), look for the Microsoft Investor area, and click the Find Symbol link.

5. **Click the Activity selection box, and choose Buy, Sell, or other activity.**

6. **Click and enter values into any *two* of the following text boxes: Price (price per share), Quantity (how many shares), or Total (how much money you spent or received).**

   Money computes the third value that you leave blank. Check it against your statement.

7. **Click Commission and enter a commission, if any.**

8. **Click Transfer To (or Transfer From) and choose the account supplying the cash (for a buy) or receiving the cash (for a sale or unreinvested dividends).**

   This account is usually an associated cash account.

9. **Add a memo if you like, then click Enter.**

You must fill out the data entry form before you can go to any other window in Money. Or, click Cancel if you need to go to another window, but the data you have entered in the form so far will be lost.

Tracking Securities Using Online Data

One of Money's most solid online features is its ability to obtain prices and price histories of stocks, funds, and other investments online. The process is free, easy, and you don't need to set up "online services" with your financial institution. You must have your PC set up for online communications on the Internet however, and have a Web browser (such as Internet Explorer, which comes with Works Suite) installed. (See Part V of this book for instructions.) Then do the following:

1. **Click Investments on Money's navigation bar.**

   You're viewing the Investments window's Portfolio page.

2. **Click the Online Quotes button at the bottom of the page.**

   If the button is not shown, click Holdings View on the left side of the page to go to a page where the button appears.

   The Get Online Quotes dialog box appears, listing all the securities you told Money to invest in.

3. **Click to clear the check mark for any security you don't want to download quotes on.**

4. **Click the Call button in the Get Online Quotes dialog box.**

   Your PC goes online in its usual fashion. Eventually, you get a Call Summary dialog box. Click Close.

Money now knows the current value of all the securities you updated! It also downloaded the most recent day's high and low prices, and a history of the security's performance for the past 12 months! See the next section for instructions on viewing and making use of this information.

Viewing Current and Prospective Investments

Money gives you six different ways to examine your investments, plus a price history graph for individual investments. The price history graph even lets you visually compare one investment to other investments!

Portfolio views

Click Investments on Money's navigation bar, and choose one of the six different views down the left side of the Portfolio window that appears. Here's where to look for what:

Money does not know the value of *anything,* right at this minute. All views showing "current" values, changes, or high/low figures can at best use only the most recently downloaded figures. Even the most recently downloaded market values are delayed from actual market values according to trading laws.

- ✔ **Holdings View** gives a current status report of all your accounts and holdings, how many shares you hold, their prices, and the total value.

- ✔ **Performance View** shows how your investments have been doing: current price, most recent change in price, and 52-week estimated percentage return for each security.

- ✔ **Quotes View** shows recent trading history: last value, change, hi/lo values, and trading volume.

- ✔ **Fundamentals View** helps you review the basics of a security: 52-week high and low, and current P/E (price/earnings) value.

- ✔ **Positions View** displays all the securities you hold listed in alphabetical order (without regard to accounts), with most recent price and total value of your holding.

- ✔ **Investment Allocation** shows a pie chart of your investments by type: mutual funds, stocks, CDs, whatever.

You can monitor the prices of securities you don't even own. Choose the Quotes, Fundamentals, or Positions View listed on the left of the Portfolio window. Click the New button on the bottom of the page. In the wizard dialog box that appears, choose A New Investment. Follow the wizard's instructions. When you're done, the investment is shown in all three views, and can also be viewed graphically as the next section describes.

Graphically viewing and comparing security prices

Money's Price History view is a great way to see how a security's price has been doing. You can also compare a security to a standard index or another security. Here's how:

1. **Click Investments on Money's navigation bar.**

   You're viewing the Investments window's Portfolio page. (Choose any view but Investment Allocation.)

2. **Double-click any security listed to display the details of that security.**

3. **Click Price History on the left side of the window.**

   You now get a very nice graph of the past 52 weeks' prices, as Figure 18-2 shows.

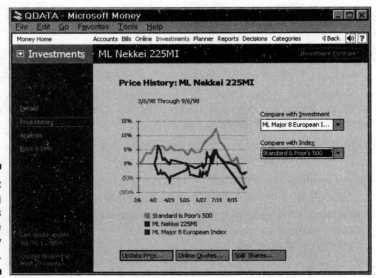

Figure 18-2: Comparing investments in a Price History graph.

To compare price history to that of other securities, click the Compare with Investment selection box and choose a security. That security's price history is overlaid on the graph, as Figure 18-2 shows. Similarly, click the Compare with Index selection box and choose the Standard and Poor, NASDAQ, or Dow Jones Industrial Average to overlay the graph.

Part IV
'Netting Ventured, 'Netting Gained

The 5th Wave   By Rich Tennant

"SINCE WE GOT IT, HE HASN'T MOVED FROM THAT SPOT FOR ELEVEN STRAIGHT DAYS. ODDLY ENOUGH THEY CALL THIS 'GETTING UP AND RUNNING' ON THE INTERNET."

In this part . . .

If, to you, *online* is where the laundry goes after the clothes dryer breaks, take heart! No, Works Suite can't fix your dryer. But it *can* take your PC online — connecting you to the Internet and then to your dryer manufacturer's online disclaimer of responsibility or even to a fellow launderer in Fort Lauderdale.

In this part, see how Microsoft Internet Explorer can get you out of the laundry room and onto the Internet's World Wide Web — the ultimate online wilderness. A special Internet Connection Wizard makes sure that you can get online without getting hung out to dry.

Also in this part, whether your goal is telecommuting or sending files to your accountant in Aruba, you find out how to use Microsoft Outlook Express to send and receive e-mail. This part also shows you how to use Outlook Express to get the latest news and gossip in your profession or hobby from Internet newsgroups — public forums on anything from raising aardvarks to touring Zanzibar.

Chapter 19

Gearing Up for the Internet

● ●

In This Chapter

▶ Discovering what things you can do online

▶ Finding the best connection for you

▶ Getting the information you need

▶ Finding an Internet service provider

▶ Getting online using the Internet Connection Wizard

▶ Dialing and disconnecting

● ●

*O*kay, just what is all the noise about, anyway? What is "being online," and why has the whole world gone wild over the Internet? Good questions, pilgrim — questions best answered by plugging in and going online yourself. This chapter explains how and why to get yourself to the Internet.

Ways and Whys of "Going Online"

Being (or going) *online* means different things to different people, but the broadest definition of being online is that your PC is communicating in some way with another computer. To Windows and to most people, the word *online* means connected to the Internet. The Internet is a global network of computers in which, if you connect your PC to one of those computers, your PC can talk to *any* of those computers.

But why on earth would you want your PC to talk to any other computer? Doesn't it get into enough mischief by itself? Read on to find out.

Things to do online, and why

Here are the various online activities you can do, in order of popularity, and why you may want to do them:

- ✔ **E-mailing:** Exchange typed messages or files with other people. Often you can exchange pictures or other files (such as Works, Word, or Money files) with other people, too, by electronic mail. The Works Suite e-mail software is Outlook Express.

- ✔ **Web browsing:** Look up something in the vast heaps of information publicly available on the World Wide Web (or just *Web*) on nearly any topic you can name. The Web is a collection of public electronic documents, with text, illustrations, animations, audio, and even video. Web documents are placed on a computer that runs a *Web server* program at a particular address on the Internet. A collection of such files is called a *Web site,* and each document has its own address at that site. You tell your Web browser the address of the document you want, and it delivers the document to your screen. Your Web browsing software in Works Suite is Internet Explorer.

- ✔ **Downloading:** Obtain software and information from the Internet (usually from the Web). Works Suite's downloading software is also Internet Explorer.

- ✔ **Joining newsgroups:** Read and publicly exchange typed messages with a group of people about a particular topic. Works Suite's newsgroup software is Outlook Express.

- ✔ **Chatting:** Spend large sums of money and time exchanging messages in a live, but often sophomoric, public dialog on a subject. Everyone in the group (called a "chat room") types lines of text to each other, and the lines appear, one after the other, in a single window. Works Suite provides no specialized chat software, but chat groups increasingly use the Web.

Finding the best way to connect

To do any of the activities I mention, you need to be connected. No, I don't mean you need highly-placed friends — although that always helps. You need a computer connection to the Internet.

You can get a connection to the Internet in any of three ways: through your company's or university's network (often called an in*tra*net), which in turn connects you to the Internet; through joining a private network like America Online or CompuServe that includes Internet service; or by connecting directly to the Internet through an Internet service provider (ISP). Except for some kinds of corporate or university connections, your connection is through your phone line (called a *dial-up* connection).

This chapter focuses on that last (and most common) way of connecting to the Internet: through an Internet service provider. If you connect through your company, a university, or an online service that supplies its own software, you must get special instructions — and perhaps, special hardware — from that organization.

Gathering What You Need

If you want to connect to the Internet, you need to get and do a few things. (Don't panic as you read these tasks — your PC has an Internet Connection Wizard that can help you do the hard stuff):

✔ **Get a modem, if you don't already have one:** A *modem* is a PC hardware accessory that connects your PC to another computer (and its modem) via a phone line. If your PC has a modem you can find a standard phone jack on the back of your PC (for an internal modem) or on the modem case for you to connect your phone line. If you must buy a modem, I suggest buying one rated for 56,000 bits per second (often stated as *56 Kbps*). Follow the installation instructions that come with your new modem.

✔ **Make sure Internet Explorer and Outlook Express are installed:** This software may already be installed on your PC, or you may need to install it from Works Suite. Check out the "Making Sure Your Software Is Installed" section in this chapter for more info.

✔ **Get an account with an Internet service provider (ISP):** An ISP has a big computer permanently connected to the Internet that your PC can connect to by calling on the phone line. The big computer "speaks Internet speak" (called *TCP/IP*) to your PC and the rest of the world. See the sidebar, "Finding an Internet service provider yourself" for more info.

✔ **Set up your PC to go online:** Your PC needs software that works with your modem to call your ISP's computer by phone and "speak Internet speak" to that computer. Windows comes with dial-up networking software, and in fact, your PC may already be set up to use the software. If not, the Internet Connection Wizard will set it up.

✔ **Set up your e-mail** (or *mail*) **and newsgroup** (or *news*) **service:** Your mail and news software, Outlook Express, must communicate with special computers called mail and news *servers,* named and managed by your ISP. You have to give your PC the names of those servers, plus your personal identification and password, before you can use those servers to get mail or news.

Whew! Sounds like a lot of effort, right? It would, indeed, be a lot of effort, except that the Internet Connection Wizard helps you get an ISP, sets up your PC to go online, and guides you through setting up e-mail and news. See "Running the Internet Connection Wizard" section later in this chapter.

Note: You may need the Windows installation diskettes or CD if your PC isn't set up for networking. The wizard lets you know. If you do need the Windows installation program, and don't have it, you need to have a very forceful conversation with the person who supplied your PC.

Finding an Internet service provider yourself

The Internet Connection Wizard can help you find an ISP, if you like, but it typically offers only major, nationwide companies. You can find local ISPs by looking in the yellow or commercial pages of phone books or in the business pages of your newspaper. Colleges and universities sometimes offer access for alumni or local people, as well.

What sort of ISP should you look for? Local ISPs sometimes offer more bang for your buck, with better help services, lower rates, or more local phone numbers for your PC to call. National ISPs are good if you travel, because your chances are high of getting a local number to call for access from wherever you are. Some smaller ISPs compete by offering reciprocal arrangements with other ISPs when you need remote access.

ISP attributes to look for include local phone numbers, a good reputation for patient and accessible customer service, reliable dial-up access (few busy signals or other connection problems), and low cost. You are better off if you ask other users before you buy. Charges typically range from about $6 to $25 per month. If you discover that you don't like your ISP, switching to another is easy — until you start using e-mail. After you have e-mail, you have to notify all your friends about your e-mail address change if you change your ISP.

No matter how you get your PC on the Internet, you need at least the following information from your ISP: your username (or login ID), your password, and the number your PC should dial to go online. That minimum at least allows you to use Internet Explorer. For mail and news, you also need the names of the ISP's mail and news servers.

Making Sure Your Software Is Installed

On a new PC, chances are pretty good that your most important Internet programs — Internet Explorer and Outlook Express — are both already installed. On the Windows taskbar, click Start, then click Programs, and look for Internet Explorer and Outlook Express in the menu that appears. If the programs appear in that menu, they are already installed. Or, if you see icons labeled Internet Explorer and Outlook Express on your screen, those programs are already installed.

If Internet Explorer and Outlook Express are not already installed, put your Works Suite CD-ROM #1 in your CD-ROM drive. The Works Suite setup program runs automatically and displays buttons for you to click to install Internet Explorer and Outlook Express. (The setup program may display a separate button for each program, or a single button for both programs. I can't tell you exactly what you will see because the installation program isn't final as of this writing.)

When Internet Explorer is installed, the all-powerful Internet Connection Wizard gets installed, too. Read about him next.

Running the Internet Connection Wizard

The easiest way to set up your PC to go online is to use the Microsoft Internet Connection Wizard. You should also run the wizard if you change ISPs (Internet service providers) or if your ISP tells you to use different settings.

If your PC uses Windows 98, the wizard already lives on your PC and is lurking in every corner, eager to set up your PC to go online. In fact, using Windows 98 without at some point running this wizard is nearly impossible! If your PC runs Windows 95, the wizard is installed when you install Internet Explorer from your Works Suite CDs.

Unless it has already been run (by you or someone else), the Internet Connection Wizard launches when you do any of the following:

 ✔ **Run Internet Explorer or Outlook Express.** Double-click the Internet Explorer or Outlook Express icon on your Windows screen. The first time you run these programs or just about any other online program (or an online feature of a program) the wizard awakens.

> ✔ **In Windows 98, double-click the Connect to the Internet icon if you see it on your screen.** (In Windows 98, if you *don't* see this icon, your PC is at least ready to connect to your ISP, if not ready to do e-mail or news.)
>
> ✔ **In Outlook Express, choose Tools⇨Accounts.** The Internet Accounts dialog box pops up on your screen, displaying several tabbed cards, like an index card file, with the All card on top. Click the Add button, then Mail or News, depending on which service you want.

If the preceding actions fail to awaken the wizard, or if you are running the wizard a second time to add or change your online settings, use whichever one of the following set of choices is available on the Start menu of your PC:

> ✔ **Start⇨Programs⇨Accessories⇨Internet Tools⇨Get On The Internet**
>
> ✔ **Start⇨Programs⇨Internet Explorer⇨Connection Wizard**

Like all wizards, the Internet Connection Wizard is a series of dialog boxes that ask a lot of questions and ask you to fill out forms in response. After you fill out each form, click Next to advance to the next question or form. Click Back to return to an earlier screen or form. When you're done, click the Finish button.

The wizard's initial starting screen: Do you need an ISP?

When the Internet Connection Wizard first starts, it displays a screen that (when translated from technobabble) asks, "Do you need an Internet service provider?" Figure 19-1 shows the actual screen.

Here's how to respond to this screen:

> ✔ If your answer is, "Yes, thank you. I do need an ISP (or a new ISP), and I want you to help me choose one," click the first option button ("I want to sign up and configure my computer . . .").
>
> ✔ If your answer is, "No, thanks, I have an ISP. I'm talking to you because I need to change or add online settings, such as adding e-mail or news, or entering an alternative telephone number for my ISP," click the second option button ("I have an existing Internet Account . . .").

If you need an ISP, but would rather get one yourself than use one pre-screened by Microsoft, see the sidebar, "Finding an Internet service provider yourself," in this chapter. In general, the wizard does not list smaller, local ISPs in your area, some of which may be excellent choices.

Click to change or add features

Click to get an ISP

Choose the third option (which, translated, says, "Get lost, you silly wizard!") if the wizard appears and you don't want it. Although the third option promises the wizard will never return, you *can* get the wizard back if you need it. See the preceding section, "Running the Internet Connection Wizard," for instructions.

Yes, I need an Internet service provider (ISP)

If, on the wizard's opening screen, you chose the first option, "I want to sign up and configure my computer . . ." the wizard dials into a Microsoft "referral service." It then downloads a list of ISPs covering your area that Microsoft made special arrangements with and displays the list on the left side of a two-panel window. To read about an ISP, click that ISP in the left panel and read the rates and features in the right panel. To sign up, click your preferred ISP and then click Next.

One or more additional screens follow, depending upon your choice of ISP, asking many questions and requesting a method of payment. After you finish with these screens, you're given (or told how to get) certain information you need to fill out additional forms in the wizard. That information includes at least:

✔ The telephone number your PC should dial to go online. (Your ISP may list several numbers for you to choose from.)

✔ Your account name, also called your *login ID, logon ID,* or just *ID;* this name is typically derived from your first and last names and/or initials, such as `billgates`.

✔ A password (which you choose in consultation with your ISP, online or on the phone). To create the most secure password, mix letters and numbers together, like `i8newyork` (Godzilla's password).

✔ Your e-mail address, which typically looks something like `billgates@msn.net`.

✔ The names of things called "servers" for getting mail and newsgroup service, like `mail.someISP.net`.

You may also be given other advanced stuff, such as IP addresses, DNS numbers, and so forth. Just write it all down for later use.

If you choose MSN (Microsoft Network) for your ISP, you may be prompted to double-click the MSN icon on your screen labeled, "Set Up the Microsoft Network." Do so, if MSN is indeed your choice.

If you don't succeed in getting online by using the wizard, take a look at the instructions in the "Finding an Internet service provider yourself" sidebar earlier in this chapter.

No, thanks, I have an existing Internet account

If, on the Internet Connection Wizard's opening screen, you chose the second option, "I have an existing Internet Account . . ." the Wizard now presents a second screen and wants to know what *kind* of ISP you have. (Nosy, nosy.) It instructs you to "Select an option, and then click Next."

The options are fairly self-explanatory (if wordy). On this screen, you should choose the second option only if you will be using America Online (AOL), Compuserve, the Microsoft Network (MSN) or another "value-added" provider. The wizard prompts you about what to do next.

Choose the first option on this screen if you are using any other ISP. (Or, choose this option if you are using your company or university's LAN — Local Area Network. You should, however, get your instructions from your local network guru, at this point. Stop reading my instructions.)

If you choose the first option, click Next, and the next screen asks how to make the connection. On that screen, just click Next (which automatically chooses the first option, "Connect using my phone line"). Read on.

Dial this number: Creating a dial-up connection

Unless you're connecting to the Microsoft Network, AOL, or another fancy service, Windows needs to know what telephone number (or numbers) your PC should dial to connect to your ISP's computer. When you arrange for your account with your ISP, your ISP should give you one or more local telephone numbers to choose for this *dial-up connection*. The Internet Connection Wizard displays a Dial-Up Connection screen so you can create or change such a connection.

Choose the first option in this wizard screen, Create a New Dial-Up Connection, if you have never before given the wizard a telephone number to call. Choose the first option, too, if you already have a dial-up connection and are returning to this page of the wizard to add an alternate phone number.

(If you are returning to this page of the wizard to change settings for an existing dial-up connection, choose Use an Existing Dial-Up Connection, then click the existing connection listed in the white selection box of the wizard screen. When you click Next, the next page asks you if you want to change the settings. Of course you do! Click Yes.)

Click the Next button on the current screen, and the following screens (with their names shown in bold) that the wizard takes you through to create or change your dial-up connection appear; click Next between each step:

1. **Phone Number:** Enter one of the local phone numbers your ISP gave you, complete with area code, even if the area code is your own.

2. **User Name and Password:** Enter the username (also called an *ID, logon ID, login ID,* or *account*) and the password your ISP told you to use in the boxes provided. When you type the password, each character appears as an asterisk on your screen, just in case someone is looking over your shoulder!

3. **Advanced Settings:** Just click Next (which automatically selects No) — unless your ISP tells you to fiddle with advanced settings. If you choose Yes, follow your ISP's instructions from there.

4. **Dial-Up Connection Name:** Enter your ISP's company name or anything you like here; this name is just for your own reference.

The Internet Connection Wizard may ask you if you want to set up your Internet Mail account now. If it does ask, click Yes, and the wizard begins to usher you through the setup of mail or newsgroup reading services as the following section describes. Click No, and you're done for now! You can now use Internet Explorer, if you like; move on to Chapter 20 for instructions.

If, for mysterious wizardly reasons the wizard does *not* now ask if you want to set up your Internet Mail account, you can do the setup yourself. See the following section, "Setting Up Your Internet Mail and News Accounts with the Wizard."

Setting Up Your Internet Mail and News Accounts with the Wizard

After you arrange to have an account with an Internet service provider (ISP), you need to set up your PC so it can send or receive electronic mail. As the preceding section describes, the Internet Connection Wizard keeps running (unless you tell it not to) after it finishes setting up your ISP account and dial-up connection: It begins to set up Windows to handle your e-mail and news accounts.

If you previously ran the wizard but chose not to set up e-mail at that time, just run the wizard again. Follow the instructions in "Running the Internet Connection Wizard" for re-running the wizard. Or, launch Outlook Express, and the wizard should run automatically.

No matter which way you run the wizard, you eventually end up at the screen entitled Set Up Your Internet Mail Account. The screen asks, Do you want to set up an Internet mail account now? Follow the steps below, clicking the Next button on the wizard screen after each step:

1. **Choose whether you're setting up mail service at this moment or newsgroup (news) service:**

   To set up mail, click Yes, then click Next, and the Internet Mail Account screen appears.

   To set up news, click No and skip to Step 8.

2. **Click Create a New Internet Mail Account.**

   (If you already set up an Internet mail account and are running the wizard again to change the account's settings, choose Use an Existing Internet Mail Account, then click the account name in the white selection box on the wizard screen. In the Confirm Settings Import dialog box that appears, click Change Settings, then click Next.)

   In the following steps, wizard screens appear in sequence. To save your eyeballs and sanity, only the name of the wizard screen is given (in bold) followed by the instructions.

3. **Your Name:** Type your name.

4. **Internet E-mail Address:** Type the e-mail address your ISP gave you.

5. **E-mail Server Names:** Enter the server names your ISP gave you.

   You don't have to understand what the terms mean, just check the information from your ISP for the same terms. To help you identify the correct terms, here are some entries typical of what ISPs give you (where *yourISPname* is the name of your ISP):

   - A typical "incoming mail (POP3 or IMAP) server" is `pop.yourISPname.net`.
   - A typical "outgoing mail (SMTP) server" is `mail.yourISPname.net`.

   Don't literally use the server names I've listed, and don't try to make up names yourself! Ask your ISP if you have any questions.

6. **Internet Mail Logon:** Enter the e-mail account name and password that your ISP gave you.

   If your ISP tells you to use Secure Password Authorization (SPA), click Log On Using Secure Password Authentication (SPA), instead.

7. **Friendly Name:** Type any nickname you like for your e-mail account, like "My Mail" or accept the name the wizard suggests.

   The wizard now moves on to setting up your News account on your PC.

8. **Set Up Your Internet News Account:** Click Yes to set up a news account now. Click No if you don't want to set up a news account now, and skip to Step 14.

9. **Internet News Account:** Click Create a New Internet News Account.

10. **Your Name:** Type your name.

11. **Internet News E-mail Address:** Type the e-mail address your ISP gave you.

12. **Internet News Server Names:** Enter the server name your ISP gave you.

   A typical "news (NNTP) server" looks something like
   news.*yourISPname*.net.

   Occasionally, a news server requires you to log on. If so, your ISP or the owner of the server will give you a special server logon ID and password, and you must check the My News Server Requires Me to Log On check box. A subsequent wizard form requests the special ID and password.

13. **Friendly Name:** Type any nickname you like for your news account, or accept the name the wizard suggests.

14. **Set Up Your Internet Directory Service:** Click Yes only if you arranged for "white pages" or directory services at your ISP. Otherwise click No, then Next.

   Finally! You're done, and the Complete Configuration screen appears. Click the Finish button.

Going Online: The Dialing Process

When you launch an Internet program like Internet Explorer or Outlook Express, or when you use the online features of Microsoft Money, Windows begins a process of *automatic dialing*. No, it's not surreptitiously dialing Bill Gates with your credit card number. Windows is dialing your Internet service provider (ISP) so that you can go online to the Internet. To go online by using a dialup connection, take the following steps:

1. **Launch any online application (like Internet Explorer) or feature (like Microsoft Money's online stock quotes feature).**

   Double-click either the Internet Explorer or Outlook Express icon on your Windows screen to launch one of those programs. Or, on your Windows taskbar, click Start➪Programs➪Internet Explorer➪Internet Explorer.

2. **A dialog box entitled either Connect To or Dial-Up Connection may appear — at least the first time you go online.**

   If for some reason that dialog box does not appear when you first try to go online, you may have to connect "manually." Double-click the My Computer icon on your screen, double-click the Dial-Up Networking folder in the window that appears, and then double-click the icon for your ISP in the next window that appears.

3. **When the Connect To or Dial-Up Connection dialog box appears, enter the account name (your "ID") in the User Name box (unless it's already filled in) and in the Password box enter the password assigned to you by your ISP.**

   As you type the password, asterisks (****) appear in place of the characters you type, to thwart any spies who may be looking over your shoulder.

   To avoid having to type the password in the future, if the Save Password check box is not grayed-out, click to place a check mark there. (In Windows 95, for strange and complicated security reasons, this check mark is grayed out unless Windows is set up to request a Windows password when you start your computer.)

   If the dialog box you're viewing is entitled Dial-Up Connection box, you can avoid having to see it ever again by clicking its Connect Automatically check box.

4. **Check to see that the phone number is correct.**

   The Connect To dialog box shows the number as it will be dialed. The box will not dial a long-distance prefix (1 plus the area code) if the area code is the same as your own. But, if the number is distant enough *within* your area code, that prefix may still be necessary! If the prefix *is* necessary, click the Dial Properties button in the dialog box, then (in the Dial Properties dialog box that appears) click to enable the Dial As Long Distance Call check box (near the bottom). Click the OK button.

5. **Press the Enter key or click Connect.**

   A dialog box (entitled Connecting To or Dialing Progress) appears as your PC begins the process of dialing out. In Windows 98, you may see a Connection Established dialog box; if so, click the check mark Do Not Show This Dialog Box in the Future, then click Close. Windows tries dialing several times if the line is not answered at first.

If your PC succeeds in connecting, an icon (or button with an icon in Windows 95) appears on the Windows Taskbar. The icon features two PCs with a line (or a line and telephone) between them.

To disconnect, scrutinize your Windows taskbar for this icon or button and double-click it. (In Windows 98, the icon may be tiny and lurk at the opposite end of the Taskbar from the Start button.) In the dialog box that appears, click Disconnect. Some programs, like Outlook Express, ask whether you want to disconnect when they are done.

If you click the Save Password and Connect Automatically check boxes in Step 3, the Connect To dialog box doesn't bother you again when you launch any Internet program or feature. Your PC simply goes online.

If everything worked, you're now online! See Chapter 20 for details of using Internet Explorer, or Chapter 21 for Outlook Express.

If you don't seem to have gone online, call the customer service number of your ISP. Most customer service specialists are intimately familiar with the online features of Windows and will be able to help you fix your setup. Being experts, they generally don't need or want to use the Internet Connection Wizard, and so may direct you to use more technical features.

Chapter 20

Exploring with Internet Explorer

● ●

In This Chapter

▶ Browsing

▶ Searching

▶ Printing

▶ Downloading

▶ E-mailing and other Internet activities

▶ Minimizing warning messages

▶ Disconnecting

● ●

*I*nternet Explorer is your Microsoft-built, Microsoft-tough sport utility vehicle for a safari on the World Wide Web (or just the Web). If you have followed the instructions in Chapter 19, Internet Explorer is now gassed up and ready to roll.

Internet Explorer isn't hard to drive, and this chapter gives you basic instructions and tips for navigating the Web. Double-click the globe icon labeled Internet Explorer on your Windows screen to start your Web-surfing safari. Your PC goes online, and you're ready to start browsing.

Note: I, and many other computer writers, get tired of typing Internet Explorer all the time, so we use the abbreviation IE (or add the version number, such as IE4.1) instead. I use the abbreviation here so you get used to seeing it elsewhere.

Ready to roll? Double-click the Internet Explorer icon on your Windows screen, or, in Windows 98, click the *e* icon on the Windows Taskbar. Or, on your Windows taskbar, click Start➪Programs➪Internet Explorer➪Internet Explorer.

When you launch IE, the Dial-Up Connection dialog box offers a Work Offline button. Click that button and you can review, without needing to dial out, any pages among your Favorites that you have viewed in the last 20 days.

Home, Sweet Home Page

Each time you start up Internet Explorer, it displays a Web page located somewhere on the Internet. The page that Internet Explorer turns to first (no matter where it is) is called *Internet Explorer's home page. Home page* just means "starting page."

The very first time you fire up IE, you probably see an introductory page about MSN.COM, or the Microsoft Network. Microsoft set up Internet Explorer so that it initially reads this page from the Microsoft *Web server* (a computer that transmits Web stuff).

The next time you use IE, its home page is set to either the MSN.COM home page or the home page of your Internet service provider (ISP). If IE goes to the MSN.COM home page, browse the offerings of that page to find useful programs and enhancements to download, plus software information, news, investment information, sports, and weather.

The MSN.COM page may suggest that you sign up for e-mail at a service called Hotmail. Don't sign up for Hotmail if you intend to use Outlook Express for e-mail. Hotmail uses the Web to deliver e-mail to you.

The MSN.COM home page has many useful features. In the long term, however, you may ask yourself, "Do I mind that a giant corporation with vested interests in my software decisions is making choices for me about which Web sites are on my home page, and therefore most convenient for me to explore?" (You probably wouldn't be quite so wordy, though.) If you prefer to have IE go first to another page on the Internet, such as a search engine or your company or university's home page, first browse to that page. Then in IE, choose View➪Internet Options, click General on the Internet Options dialog box that appears, and click the Use Current button.

Knowing who you're looking at

Although some things that you click on the MSN.COM page take you to another Microsoft page, sometimes they go to someone else's page. You can very easily get confused about whose Web site you're looking at. Read the title bar (the top bar) of the IE window to see the title of the page you're reading, and see if you can discern a company name in the Address box at the top of the IE window. To return to the IE home page, click the Home button in the toolbar.

Browsing the Web

Browsing is the trendy activity of the late 1990s, whether you're into computers, shopping, or eating. Applied to the Web, *browsing* means viewing the documents (together with their graphics and sounds) located at various Web addresses around the world.

Viewing a distant Web document isn't quite like viewing a distant mountain through a telescope; it's more like having a copy of the distant mountain shipped to your doorstep piece by piece. The entire document is transmitted to your Web browser, and this transmission can take a while.

Browsing by typing an address

One way to browse the Web is to specify a document's address, which is called an *URL* (and pronounced either "earl" or You Are Ell). Addresses on the Web are a bit cryptic; you've undoubtedly seen them on TV and elsewhere. They can look like the following addresses:

- ✔ http://www.snoggle.com
- ✔ www.snoggle.com
- ✔ home.snoggle.net/users/barney.html

Technically speaking, all Web addresses should begin with http://, but typing that code is boring and tedious, so the newer versions of the popular Web browsers, such as Internet Explorer 4.0, don't require it (a feature called *friendly URLs*). You may omit it and just type the rest of the address: www.brightleaf.com/tracking, for instance, or home.microsoft.com. A slash (/tracking) indicates folders under the main address (brightleaf. com). Individual Web documents typically end in .htm, .html, or .shtml. Any URL that ends in a slash (a folder address) is actually pointing to a special index document in that folder that is supposed to list the folder's contents.

TIP

Browsing versus snoozing

Using the World Wide Web is sometimes so slow that the experience is called the World Wide Wait. To speed up your browsing, turn off the graphics: Choose View⇨ Internet Options, and then click the Advanced card in the Internet Options dialog box that appears. Scroll down to the Multimedia category, and click to clear the check mark labeled Show Pictures. On most Web sites, you now find text where the graphics were.

If you know the URL of the Web site you want to see (for instance,
www.dummies.com), you can enter that address in one of two places:

✔ **Click in the white area (text box) of the Address bar, and type in the
address.** If an address is currently present, you replace that address
with whatever you type. Press Enter when you're done.

✔ **Choose File⇨Open (or press Ctrl+O), and in the Open dialog box that
appears, type the address.** Press Enter when you're done or click OK.

After the Web page is loaded, its title appears in the title bar of the Internet
Explorer window, and its full address (URL) appears in the Address text box.
(See Figure 20-1.)

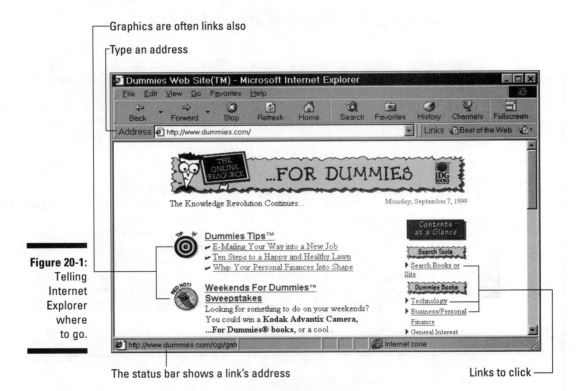

Graphics are often links also

Type an address

Figure 20-1:
Telling
Internet
Explorer
where
to go.

The status bar shows a link's address

Links to click

Browsing with buttons

The toolbar of IE gives you some helpful controls for browsing and other
jobs. Figure 20-2 shows what each button does.

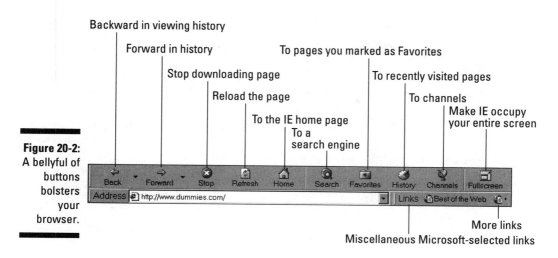

Backward in viewing history

Forward in history

Stop downloading page

Reload the page

To the IE home page
To a
search engine

To pages you marked as Favorites

To recently visited pages

To channels

Make IE occupy
your entire screen

Figure 20-2:
A bellyful of
buttons
bolsters
your
browser.

Miscellaneous Microsoft-selected links

More links

I explain what is meant by *history, home pages, search engines, Favorites, channels,* and *links* in the other sections of this chapter. The Fullscreen button not only expands the IE window to fill your screen, it cleans off all vestiges of Windows controls, leaving you with only a tiny version of this same toolbar to control the program with. Click the Fullscreen button there to return the IE window to its previous size.

Browsing by clicking links on Web pages

If you're currently viewing a Web document, you can click buttons, specially marked text, or certain graphics on the page to view a different document. That other document may be at the same general address (say, www.dummies.com, which is run by IDG Books Worldwide, Inc.) or may take you somewhere else altogether (say, net.gurus.com, run by a friend of mine). The item you click to view a different document is called a *link* by most people, and sometimes called a *shortcut* by Microsoft.

The best way to tell whether a word, a graphic, a button, or some other element on the page is a link is to move your cursor over that element without clicking. The cursor changes from an arrow to a little hand if the element is a link.

Text links are easy to spot. They're usually underlined and often appear in a distinctive color (typically, bright blue). If you've already visited a page that a text link connects to, the color of the text usually changes to a darker or fainter color so that you know you've already visited that link. (In Figure 20-1, Dummies Tips has already been visited, but I doubt you can see the color difference in that black-and-white figure!)

How to treat panes in your window

Sometimes, your Internet Explorer window gets divided into multiple panes, called *frames*. When a Web page uses frames, part of the page stays still while the other part changes when you click a link.

Depending upon how the page designer created the page, you may be able to scroll the contents of a frame independently of the other frames. You may also be able to click and drag the borders that appear between the frames.

Frames can also be printed independently. (See "Printing Web Documents" later in this chapter.)

Sometimes, you even get a new (usually small) window! The window may contain a special message or some controls for playing audio or video. To clear this window off your screen, click the X in the upper-right corner of the window.

Clicking some links starts downloading a file instead of taking you to another Web page. If that happens unexpectedly, simply press the Esc key to exit from the File Download dialog box that appears. See "Downloading Programs and Other Files from the Web," later on for more information.

Returning to a page in History

Don't know much about History? Well, Internet Explorer does. Each time you use IE, it keeps a record of the Web pages you've visited so that you can return to them. Several buttons on the toolbar can help you travel through time:

- ✔ **Back:** To return to the last Web page you visited, click the Back button on the toolbar. Keep clicking the Back button to move backward in History.

- ✔ **Forward:** After moving back in History, you can move Forward again by clicking the Forward button.

- ✔ **Down arrows:** To go back to any recently visited page in History, click the tiny down arrow adjoining the Back button, and choose a page title off the list that appears. Likewise, to move forward in History, click the tiny down arrow adjoining the Forward button. Click the down arrow at the far right of the Address bar, and you can revisit a previously visited site by clicking its address in the drop-down list.

- ✔ **History:** To revisit any Web page you visited in the past 20 days, click the History button. (You can change this time frame by choosing View⇨Internet Options, and on the General card of the Internet Options dialog box that appears, entering a new value less than 99 in the Days to Keep Pages in History box.)

If you click the History button, a History menu appears on the left side of the IE window, as shown in Figure 20-3. Any pages you've visited are underlined. The pages you visited today are in a Today category. Earlier sites are categorized by week.

View earlier sites

Remove History panel

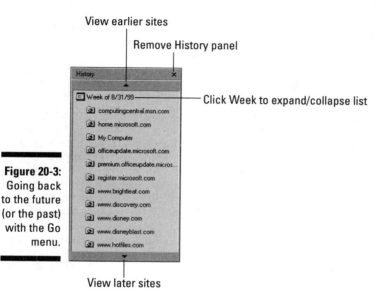

Click Week to expand/collapse list

Figure 20-3:
Going back
to the future
(or the past)
with the Go
menu.

View later sites

Here's how to use the History panel:

- ✔ **To return to any page listed:** Just click it. That page appears in the remainder of the IE window on the right side.

- ✔ **To view sites visited during the last 20 days:** Click the icon for the week that includes that day (such as Week of 8/31/99 in Figure 20-3). The icon spews forth (*expands* into) a list. To *collapse* the list (stuff it back into the icon, so to speak), click the icon again.

- ✔ **If the page name or week icon that you want isn't visible in the History panel:** Try clicking the tiny up or down arrows at the top and bottom to scroll in history.

- ✔ **To remove the History panel altogether:** Click the X in the upper-right corner of the panel.

Returning to your favorite pages

Now, just where was that recipe for tripe soufflé? The Web is so vast that you may never find it again, much to the dismay (or joy) of your dinner guests. The Favorites feature helps you rise above absentmindedness.

Adding to Favorites

When you view a Web page that you think you may want to revisit, tell IE to add it to your list of favorites.

Don't try to use Favorites as a way to store a page containing account and password information, or an order form for a purchase you have made. The page won't be there when you return. Save the page as a file instead. See "Saving Text and Graphics from Web Pages," later in this chapter.

Choose Favorites⇨Add to Favorites from the menu bar. The Add to Favorites dialog box appears, offering some nit-picky options.

I suggest you choose No, Just Add the Page to My Favorites. This choice simply adds the page to the Favorites list that Internet Explorer keeps, so you can return to it at any time. The other choices *subscribe* you to a Web site, and may be helpful if you're really, seriously interested in keeping up-to-date on the page. Subscribing tells IE to check those sites, which it does invisibly, whenever you go online, and either simply notify you of a changed page or notify you and save the page for later viewing. Many page changes can be so trivial or predictable, however, that I find these choices annoying.

Then, make sure that the text in the Name box (which is the title of the Web page) is descriptive enough that you can recognize the page by that text. If not, type new text. Then click OK or press the Enter key to enter the page in the basic Favorites list.

You can keep your favorite pages in various folders, too. The Favorites list already has several folders. To enter the page in a folder, click the Create In button in the Add Favorite dialog box. A conventional Windows tree of folders appears in the dialog box. Click to open a folder, or click New Folder to create your own folder. When you click OK, your favorite goes into that folder.

Returning to Favorites

To return to a favorite page, click the Favorites button. A Favorites panel opens up on the left side of your window. Click your favorite's name in the panel. Click a folder to see additional favorites in that folder.

Click the folder to close it again. Click the X in the upper-right corner of the Favorites panel to make the entire panel go away.

You can return to a page without even going online! Choose File⇨Work Offline. When you choose a Favorite, Internet Explorer retrieves the page from your PC's hard disk instead of the Internet. The page isn't up-to-date, but many pages don't change that often, anyway, or you simply may not care about updates.

Organizing Favorites

After you have a dozen or so favorites in this list, you may want to add folders so that you can organize them or change the names of your existing favorites. Choose Favorites⇨Organize Favorites to get into the Organize Favorites dialog box.

To move a favorite to a folder, you can drag it. You can rename or delete favorites and folders or create new folders just as you would in an Open or Save As dialog box, as described in the appendix. Or you can click the favorite or folder, and then click the Move, Delete, or Rename button.

Searching the Web for Information

Don't know something? Check the Web. The Web is turning into a vast library of information. But unlike your town library (or so I hope), the librarians of the Web are computer programs, and the quality of information ranges from timeless and irrefutable truths to complete and utter Biscuit Sauce (BS). Only you can determine which is which.

Deciding what kind of search engine to use

What I call librarians are called *search engines* by most people. These search engines all live at different addresses (URLs), and they all have different strengths and weaknesses. Although they differ in the details, in general they enable you to choose a subject, and then they present you with a page of links to various pages on the subject. Each link is accompanied by a brief excerpt from the page so that you can tell if the page may be of interest to you.

One of my favorite librarians is AltaVista (which means, I believe, "high view"), at the address www.altavista.digital.com. AltaVista is truly a search engine, which means that you type one or more terms for which you want the engine to search and then click the Search button on that page.

 If you understand and enjoy using combinatorial logic, like *and, near,* and *or* to combine search terms and construct a more precise search, try AltaVista's Advanced search page. Go to the Alta Vista home page and then click Advanced.

The most famous of the Web librarians is Yahoo!, which lives at www.yahoo.com. Yahoo! is, technically speaking, not a search engine but a Web guide. A *search engine* searches for a subject you name; a *Web guide* presents you with subjects to choose from, although it may also offer search capabilities. Yahoo! presents you with a list of broad topics and subtopics.

Click on topics or subtopics to see additional subtopics. Keep on drilling deeper into your subject in this way until, at the bottom of the page, you see individual Web pages that may be of interest to you. You can also search for terms as you do at the AltaVista site.

The Internet Explorer Search button and Search panel

Microsoft lists certain popular librarians (search engines) on a page on the Microsoft Web site. The first time you click the Search button on the toolbar, this Microsoft-maintained listing appears in the right-hand side of the IE window. Pause your mouse cursor over any of the search engines Microsoft lists for a quick introduction. Click any of the search engines listed there, and in the future, whenever you click the Search button, that engine appears in a Search panel on the left side of the IE window for your use.

To return to Microsoft's listing of search engines to use or to choose a different search engine, click the Choose a Search Engine button near the top of the Search panel, and then choose List of All Search Engines from the drop-down menu. The Search button maintains a list of engines that you've used in the past; just click the button to choose from that list.

Searching successfully requires some care. Simply typing **duck web recipe** may get you a list of a million or so pages mentioning the World Wide Web, ten thousand pages mentioning recipes, and a thousand pages discussing spider webs, ducks, or duck feet. Most search engines have Help pages that you need to read to be successful in your search. Click the Help button on the search engine page, and then read the instructions on how to make a search. Click the Back button on IE to return to the search form.

Subscriptions and channels are two new ways to use the Web. Instead of you browsing certain Web sites to see if anything is new, IE checks the Web every so often, tells you if any pages change at the Web site you specify, and downloads the information. As a result, you can see the latest stuff on your PC at any time without going online.

Subscription doesn't imply sending anyone money! Subscriptions are simply a feature of Favorites in which IE checks any Web site or channel site that you subscribe to, either on a schedule or when you manually command it to do so. If IE finds that the site has changed, IE places a red sparkle (gleam) on the site's listing in your Favorites list. Optionally, if you set up your subscription properly, IE also downloads one or more documents from that site to your PC. To see the new material, you go to that site as you would any other Favorite, but you can do it offline (choose File⇨Work Offline).

To subscribe to a Web site, you add it to your Favorites, but with a twist. Browse to the page, and choose Favorites⇔Add to Favorites from the menu bar. The Add to Favorites dialog box appears. Click either of the two lower selections in that box (whichever you prefer), both of which begin with "Yes." (You can change your choices later.) A subscription wizard guides you through various options, including being notified of changes by e-mail, manual or scheduled updates, and entering any identification or password if this site usually requires it.

To subscribe to a channel, click the Channels button on the toolbar, and then click one of the channel categories (such as Business or Sports) that appear on the left side of the IE window. Click any of the channels listed. (Channels have logos.)

On the channel page that appears, you subscribe by clicking the Add Active Channel button. The process of subscribing to a channel is almost identical to the process of subscribing to a Web site: A wizard takes you through the process.

If you don't schedule your subscription updates, you must update manually. Choose Favorites⇔Update All Subscriptions to update your subscriptions.

To change or review how a Web or channel subscription is set up, or to delete the subscription, click Favorites⇔Manage Subscriptions to view the Subscriptions folder window. To delete a subscription, click it and press the Delete key. To change its setup, right-click it and choose Properties off the drop-down menu. In the Properties dialog box that appears, click the Receiving or Schedule tabs to change settings.

Saving Text and Graphics from Web Pages

Internet Explorer automatically saves the documents you browse — for a while, anyway, usually at least 20 days. (How long IE saves the document depends on a variety of technicalities.) You can view those documents by choosing File⇔Work Offline in Internet Explorer and then clicking Favorites and choosing the page.

If you want to keep a document permanently, saving its text or graphics as a file is an option. To save the text of a page as a file, choose File⇔Save As File. The dialog box that appears works exactly like the one you use in Word or Works, except that it saves a different type of file: HTML (which stands for HyperText Markup Language, but who cares?) — or, you can choose plain text.

TIP

Copying from Web pages to other documents

You can copy any text or graphic from the IE window, using the Windows clipboard (described in the appendix). To copy a graphic, right-click the graphic and choose Copy from the drop-down menu. To copy text, select the text first (click and drag your mouse cursor across the text), and then right-click and choose Copy. To paste, open Word, Works, or another Windows program and choose Edit⇨Paste from its menu bar.

HTML is formatted text that can be viewed in Internet Explorer (or any other Web browser) and many modern e-mail programs, and read by Microsoft Word. To save a document as plain text, click the Save As Type box and choose Plain Text (*.txt). (Internet Explorer adds the three-letter extension .txt to the file.) Plain text has no formatting apart from tabs, spaces, and line breaks, and any word processor can read it.

When you save a page as a file, Internet Explorer doesn't save the graphics (or other media, like sound) that go with the document. You can, however, save graphics as separate files. Right-click the graphic, and choose Save Picture As from the menu that appears.

Printing Web Documents

You can print most Web documents just as easily as you print Works or Word documents. In fact, the print command (File⇨Print) is the same in all those programs, and the associated Print dialog box is very similar. The printed page includes graphics and, if you have a color printer, color. (Colored backgrounds are, however, not printed. Thank goodness, or your ink cartridge would be depleted in about a minute.)

Page setup works about the same for Internet Explorer as it does for Works or Word: Choose File⇨Page Setup. Page size, orientation, and margins are all together on a single card in the Page Setup dialog box. I suggest you use the paper size of Letter $8\frac{1}{2}$ x 11 inches. The Headers and Footers text boxes are full of gibberish, apparently, but it all means something, as you see when you print. To interpret the gibberish or type your own, click in the Header or Footer text box and press F1.

Some pages on the Web use frames, which complicate the printing process slightly. If you want to print a single frame, click in that frame before giving the print command. If you want to print just selected text, drag your mouse cursor across that text. Then choose File⇨Print, as usual, and at the bottom of the Print dialog box, you see several choices for printing:

- ✔ **As Laid Out on Screen:** Your printout looks like your screen, except that any documents in any frame that go below the screen are included as well.

- ✔ **Only the Selected Frame:** The entire document of the frame that you clicked in or in which you selected text prints.

- ✔ **All Frames Individually:** Each frame prints separately, as a full document.

Click one of the preceding choices. If you want to print only selected text, choose Selection in the Print dialog box.

Downloading Programs and Other Files from the Web

A Web browser such as Internet Explorer enables you to acquire (download) all kinds of stuff. Many companies and individuals make programs available for free on the Web. From Microsoft, you can download enhancements to Windows or to Internet Explorer itself. Various companies offer add-on software or special viewers for special purposes. You can also download graphics files, music, audio, and video files that can play on properly-equipped PCs!

If you look around carefully, you can find one or more download areas on the Web sites of Microsoft and most other PC software vendors. Use search engines to find free graphics (also called "clip art"), music, and video files. Follow the links and instructions, and eventually you click a link that causes Internet Explorer to download the file you choose.

To avoid computer viruses, be careful to download files only from reputable sources. If you have a virus-scanning program, scan any file that you intend to double-click or otherwise open.

After you click a link that starts a download, a File Download dialog box briefly appears and then an Internet Explorer dialog box asks what you want to do with the file: Depending upon the type of file, you have two or more choices:

- ✔ **Open this file from its current location:** This choice isn't for downloading files, just for viewing them using associated programs (programs linked to IE for viewing special kinds of files).

- ✔ **Save this file to disk:** Click this button and a Save As dialog box appears so that you can choose where you want to save the file. (Saving to Download folder, as IE suggests, is fine.) Click the Save button.

- ✔ **Run this file from its current location:** A risky choice, unless you trust the Web site owner. This choice actually runs a program, typically an installation program of some sort — but it could be anything, including a virus-contaminated program.

The File Download box reappears, usually giving you an estimate of how long the downloading process can take. To stop the download, click the Cancel button. You can browse to other locations while a file is downloading; you can also use other programs or do other Internet tasks like checking for e-mail — but expect your PC's response to be slower.

The software you download is typically in the form of a *compressed file* (a ZIP file, usually), which saves downloading time but adds a step to the normal Windows installation process. If you have virus-scanning software, use it now on the file that you downloaded. Then, to begin installing the software, double-click the downloaded file. Sometimes, double-clicking the downloaded file only uncompresses the installation files. In that case, find the file named install.exe, which you need to virus scan, and then double-click to install the software.

Secure and Insecure Sites

What about doing business on the Internet? Increasingly, businesses that accept orders and credit card numbers over the Web use secure sites. *Secure* sites work with Internet Explorer to encrypt the data between your PC and their site in a very secure way. The risk of doing business over a secure site is generally considered to be less than that of using a credit card in person.

If you're browsing a secure site, Internet Explorer displays a lock icon on the status bar at the bottom of its window. When you move from a secure site to an insecure site, Internet Explorer warns you.

Disconnecting and Quitting

If you're done Web browsing — or if you're simply reading a document and not planning to click any of its links — disconnect. You save connect-time fees by disconnecting yourself from your ISP when you're not actively browsing the Web or downloading software.

To disconnect, find the icon (or button) on your Windows Taskbar that shows two PCs linked together. (In Windows 98, the icon is probably very small and is located at the opposite end of the Taskbar from the Start button.) Double-click that icon (or click that button), and then choose Disconnect from the dialog box that appears.

While you're offline you can browse among IE's stored documents. (See the "Returning to a page in History" section in this chapter.) To browse the stored documents, tell IE that you're working offline intentionally: Choose File⇨Work Offline. Otherwise IE attempts to go online again as you browse.

To reconnect, click the Refresh button in Internet Explorer's toolbar. (Your PC goes online automatically when any program demands information from the Internet. The Refresh button demands fresh information.)

To quit Internet Explorer, choose File⇨Close or click the button with the X in the upper-right corner of the Internet Explorer window.

Chapter 21

Jungle Drumming: E-Mail and News

● ●

In This Chapter

▶ Communicating by e-mail and newsgroups

▶ Starting Outlook Express

▶ Knowing when to connect to the Internet

▶ Using the Outlook Express window

▶ Creating outgoing mail

▶ Reading incoming mail

▶ Joining and enjoying newsgroups

● ●

*H*ear that distant drumming? It's the sound of e-mail and news messages being pounded out on PCs and wafting their way across the Internet wilderness. Now it's your turn to join in the fun, using Outlook Express.

Send e-mail to family members, maybe even attach a greeting-card file from Microsoft Greetings. (See Chapter 23.) Subscribe to a newsgroup of fellow newt breeders (or whatever your vocation or hobby might be), and catch up on the latest news. You can do it all using Microsoft Outlook.

If you haven't yet set up your PC to cruise the Internet or deal with e-mail and newsgroups, you'll encounter a wizard if you try to use Outlook Express. You may as well initiate the encounter yourself by following the instructions in Chapter 19 first.

Understanding E-Mail and Newsgroups

Outlook Express is Microsoft's cheap version of its Outlook software for e-mail and news. Your copy of Outlook Express either came installed with Windows 98 (if that's what your PC runs) or it was installed when you first loaded Internet Explorer from the Works Suite CD.

Launching Outlook Express

Just as you do for any other Windows program, you can start Outlook Express from the Windows Start button or a program icon. To start Outlook Express, do one of the following:

✔ On the Windows Taskbar, choose Start➪Programs➪Internet Explorer➪ Outlook Express. In Windows 98, look for an "e-with-envelope" icon on the taskbar and click it.

✔ If there is an icon labeled Outlook Express on your screen, double-click that icon.

To read more about starting Windows programs, see the appendix. Likewise, turn there if you're a little uncertain about using the mouse, keyboard, menus, or dialog boxes.

When you first launch Outlook Express, it displays a Browse for Folder dialog box and asks you to choose a folder to keep your messages in. Just click OK, and your folder will be C:/Windows/Application Data/Microsoft/ Outlook Express.

Going Online — or Not

When you launch Outlook Express, it displays an Outlook Express dialog box that asks you to Select the Connection You Would Like to Dial from a selection box. Here are your choices:

✔ To go online to the connection listed press Enter or click the OK button.

✔ If you have several possible dial-up connections (different phone numbers in case one is busy or different ISPs), click the selection box and choose your connection.

✔ To avoid seeing this dialog box again and to always use the same dialup connection, click the Set As the Default Startup Connection check box.

✔ To create a new message offline or to review stored messages offline, click the selection box and choose Don't Dial a Connection. This choice saves connection time (which you're probably paying your ISP for).

After making your choice, click the OK button in the dialog box or press Enter. To change your choices later, choose Tools➪Options and then click Dial Up to access all of your dialing options.

How do you go offline? Outlook Express asks if you want to go offline when you choose File➪Exit. Or click Outlook Express in the left panel of the Outlook Express window and click the Hang Up button that is on the toolbar.

What's What in the Outlook Express Window

Figure 21-1 shows the Outlook Express window. The window looks like Figure 21-1 most of the time — except when you first start Outlook Express. When you start Outlook Express, the right-hand window contains jazzy icons you can click to do the same tasks as many of the buttons and menu choices described in this chapter. To see the window with jazzy icons at any time, click the highlighted text, Outlook Express, at the top of the left-hand panel.

Various message boxes and folders are listed on the left side of the window. Click a box or folder to view its contents on the right side of the window. (In Figure 21-1, I clicked the Inbox and then I clicked a message from me, Dave Kay, to myself.) The bold type indicates unread messages.

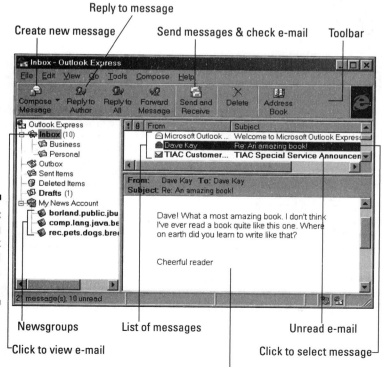

Reply to message

Create new message / Send messages & check e-mail Toolbar

Figure 21-1: Checking my Inbox for e-mail from readers.

Newsgroups   List of messages   Unread e-mail

Click to view e-mail   Click to select message

Read selected messages

Creating E-Mail Messages

To send an e-mail message to someone, you need that person's address, usually in the form *name@organization*.com (or .edu, .net, or .org). Be careful to get all characters *exactly* right or your message probably won't go through.

To create an e-mail message, do the following:

1. **Click the Compose Message button at the far left of the Outlook Express toolbar, and a New Message window appears.**

   If the Compose Message button is grayed out, click Inbox in the left panel.

2. **Click the To line and type your recipient's e-mail address.**

   To send e-mail to several people, type their e-mail addresses one after the other, separating each address with a comma or semicolon.

3. **To send a copy of your message to someone else, click the Cc line and enter an address as you did in Step 2.**

   To send a copy without informing your e-mail's recipient (the person(s) in the To line), use the Bcc: (blind carbon-copy) line instead.

4. **Click the Subject line and type a short description of your message subject.**

   That subject line is the title of your message window.

5. **Click the message area and type your message. You don't need to press Enter at the end of a line, just keep typing.**

6. **Click the Send button in the message window to send the message now, or choose File⇨Send Later to place the message in your Outbox.**

   The Outbox is one of the message boxes on the left-hand side of the window. It's the place where your messages reside until you send them.

You can send a file of any kind (an image, a document, a Microsoft Greetings file, and so on) by *attaching it* to an e-mail message. In the message window, click the button with the paper-click icon, or choose Insert⇨File Attachment. In the Insert Attachment dialog box that appears, browse through the files as the appendix of this book describes, or choose the file you want to send and then click the Attach button.

Sending and Receiving E-Mail Messages

To check your e-mail — and, at the same time, send any messages you've written but not yet sent — click the Send and Receive button on the Outlook Express toolbar. (If the Outlook Express button isn't visible, click Inbox in the left panel of the window.)

If you aren't already online, Outlook Express connects online now. If any dialog boxes appear, just click OK or Connect. If a Logon dialog box appears, click the Remember Password check box and then the OK button.

You remain online until you exit Outlook Express, or until you click Outlook Express at the top of the left panel and then click the Hang Up button that appears in the Outlook Express toolbar.

Messages are stored in boxes and folders, which are displayed in the left-hand panel; click a box or folder to open a message. Any messages that you receive go into the Inbox. Any messages that you have sent are stored in the Sent Items box. Your Outbox is empty at this point.

If someone sends you an attached file, a paper-clip icon appears at the top right corner of the panel displaying the message text. Click that icon, and in the Open Attachment Warning dialog box, choose Save It to Disk. A dialog box also appears that lets you choose a folder for the file. (It works just like a Save As dialog box — see the appendix for details.)

Reading, Deleting, and Replying to E-Mail Messages

To view the e-mail you've received, click Inbox on the left panel of the Outlook Express window. Outlook Express lists your new, unread messages (distinguished by bold type and a sealed-envelope icon) in the upper right-hand panel of the Outlook Express window, as shown in Figure 21-1. Click any listed message to view its contents in the lower right-hand panel.

To reply to a message, first click the message to open it. Then click the Reply to Author button on the Outlook Express toolbar. The Reply to Author button opens a message window just as if you were creating a new message, but with the text of the original message already included. Just type and send as you would any new message.

To move a message to the Deleted Items box, click the message in the upper right-hand panel and then press Delete on your keyboard (or click Delete in the Outlook Express toolbar). To permanently delete the message, click the Deleted Items box, click the message (or Ctrl+click to choose several messages) and then press Delete.

Listing and Subscribing to Newsgroups

Newsgroups cover thousands of topics, so your first task is to decide which newsgroups to subscribe to. To get your very first list of all the newsgroups available on your ISP's news server, choose Go⇨News. (In the future, you will simply update this list, as I tell you a bit later in this section.)

The Newsgroup dialog box appears and Outlook Express asks if you want to view a list of newsgroups; click Yes. The Newsgroups dialog box then lists all the groups by name. To trim the list, try typing a word you are interested in ("dog," for example) in the Display Newsgroups Which Contain text box.

To read or contribute to the messages in a newsgroup, you must first subscribe (sign up). Click a newsgroup name, and then click the Subscribe button. Subscribe to as many newsgroups as you like. To see which ones you are subscribed to, click the Subscribed tab at the bottom of the Newsgroups dialog box.

To quit the Newsgroups dialog box, click its OK button. To return to the Newsgroups dialog box, choose Tools⇨Newsgroups or click News Groups if it appears on the Outlook Express toolbar. (The button only appears when you are viewing news.) To update the list of newsgroups, click the Reset List button.

Downloading and Reading Newsgroup Messages

To download and read newsgroups, choose Go⇨News, or simply click your news account at the bottom of the left-hand panel in the Outlook Express window. (In Figure 21-1, the news account is entitled My News Account.) Here you see your subscribed newsgroups in a list and indented under your news account.

To download all of the latest messages, click your news account and choose Tools⇨Download This Account.

In the same way that you click the e-mail Inbox to list mail messages, you click a newsgroup to list its messages in the upper right-hand panel. Click a newsgroup message to read its text in the lower right-hand panel.

If Outlook Express tells you to "connect to your server" to read a message, choose Tools⇨Download This Newsgroup. Click the Get the Following Items check box in the Download Newsgroup dialog box that appears, and choose New Messages or All Messages.

Unlike e-mail messages, newsgroup messages are organized into *threads*. When someone *posts* a reply (sends a response) to a message, that reply is grouped with the original message and a plus sign (+) appears to the left of the original message. Click the plus sign to display the replies, which are indented underneath the message.

Posting Newsgroup Messages

Posting (sending) and replying to newsgroup messages is very similar to sending and replying to e-mail — just click the magical buttons on the Outlook Express toolbar, as follows:

> ✔ **To create a message on a new topic for the newsgroup,** click the newsgroup that you want to post to; then click the Compose Message button.

> ✔ **To reply to a previously received message,** view that message and then click the Reply to Group button.

> ✔ **To reply by private e-mail to the author of a newsgroup message,** click that message and then click the Reply to Author button.

Fill out the message window that appears after you hit the Reply to... button, just as you would for an e-mail message. Be sure to type a subject line for messages on new topics, but not for replies. You don't need to fill out an address; the message is already addressed to the newsgroup.

Click the Post button in the message window to send the message now or choose File⇨Send Later to place the message in the Outbox. If you send the message now and you aren't already online, Outlook Express goes online now. (If you have any questions about dialog boxes that appear while Outlook Express goes online, see the discussion of dialing out at the end of Chapter 19.) If you choose instead to send the message later, the message goes into the Outbox and is sent the next time you go online.

Part V

Entertaining Enlightenment

In this part . . .

1f you've been falling asleep on your keyboards, suffering those nasty, rectangular, telltale head wrinkles, help is on the way. Wake up your head by researching caffeine in Microsoft Encarta 98 Encyclopedia and then take related links to articles on coffee, tea, India, the British Empire, General Montgomery, and the real meaning of the phrase "The Full Monty." (You may need to follow links to the Web to complete *that* particular trek!)

If that sort of random walk through geography, history, science, and culture doesn't get your neurons jingling, this part also shows you how to entertain your friends with cards, posters, banners, and other colorful projects that you can make by using Microsoft Greetings.

Chapter 22

Encyclopedic Enlightenment: Encarta

• •

In This Chapter

▶ Starting up Encarta

▶ Understanding Encarta features

▶ Finding and reading articles

▶ Researching using multimedia tools

▶ Controlling multimedia players

▶ Navigating between features

▶ Getting more information from the Internet

▶ Printing and copying to the Windows Clipboard

▶ Controlling Encarta's behavior

• •

*T*he Microsoft Encarta 98 Encyclopedia is ready to enlighten you in a most entertaining way. Although it's not clad in fine Corinthian leather like a good printed encyclopedia, the Encarta Encyclopedia CD-ROM has its advantages: interactive graphics and sound, the ability to search for topics and keywords, and availability right on your PC, where you're, perhaps, writing your research paper. Besides, Encarta sings and dances enchantingly. Try to get your fine-Corinthian-leather-bound encyclopedia to do *that!*

Launching Encarta and Gazing at the Home Page

You can start Encarta from the Windows Start button or a program icon (if you have one on your screen), just as you do for any other Windows program. But first, pop one of the Encarta CDs in your PC's CD-ROM drive. Encarta doesn't work without the CDs. Then do one of the following:

✔ On the Windows Taskbar, choose Start➪Programs➪Microsoft Reference➪Encarta 98 Encyclopedia.

✔ If you see an icon labeled Microsoft Encarta on your screen, double-click that icon.

Encarta swoops onto your screen with a fanfare, almost literally. If you have audio and speakers on your PC, Encarta treats you to some ethereal music while it assembles its *home page* (the starting screen). Here you have several choices:

✔ **Encyclopedia Articles:** *Articles* are the main body of knowledge that the encyclopedia offers. See "Finding and Reading Articles" in this chapter.

✔ **Media Features:** *Media Features* are mainly alternative, graphical ways to browse articles by subject, geography, or time in history. See "Mucking with Media" later in this chapter for details.

✔ **Online Features:** Encarta is intimately linked to the Web, offering links to Web sites on various topics, an online library service for researching news articles and other stuff, and updates to the Encarta knowledge base.

✔ **Mindmaze:** An educational game of the so-called "adventure" variety.

✔ **Overview:** A tour of Encarta Encyclopedia features. Choose this selection, and when the Overview page appears, click the yellow Next button. Click Next to progress at each step of the tour.

Many of these choices place you in windows with somewhat obscure navigation controls. See "Help, I've Moved, and I Can't Get Back!" for tips for when you get stuck in one place.

Finding and Reading Articles

To read articles, choose Encyclopedia Articles on the Encarta home page. The Pinpointer tool appears and is ready to help you locate a topic. The entire screen looks like Figure 22-1, where callouts show you what's going on — and a lot is going on!

Finding articles with the Pinpointer tool

The Pinpointer, shown in Figure 22-1, is your tool for finding articles in Encarta. It appears when you first go to the articles screen or click Find on the menu bar. Here's how to use it:

✔ **To see an article:** Click any subject listed in the big Pinpointer window. I clicked Opera in the Pinpointer window that you see in Figure 22-1.

✔ **To see more subjects:** If the list is long, use the Pinpointer's scroll bar that appears. (Click the down-arrow at the bottom of the scroll bar.)

✔ **To specify a subject by title:** Click where the Pinpointer says "Type in an article title," and start typing a subject. The list suggests articles that match your typing.

✔ **To find specific subjects or media:** Click Category and other icons on the right for special *filters,* or click Wizard at the bottom to set up filtering by means of a more prosaic dialog.

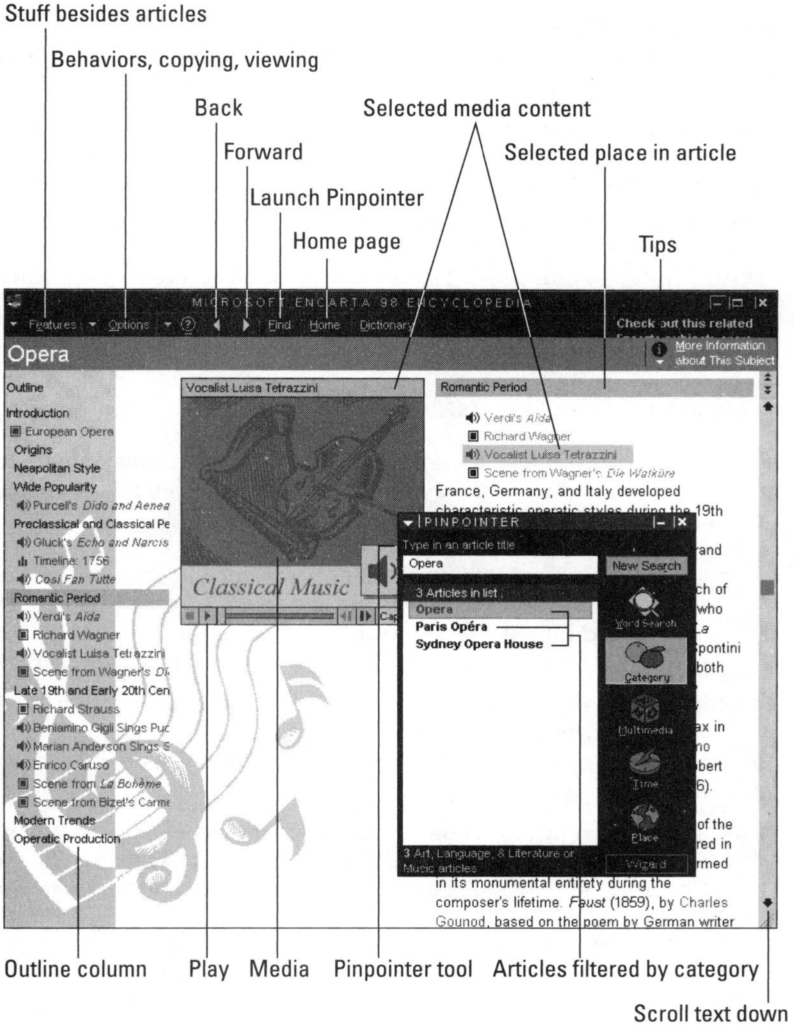

Stuff besides articles

Behaviors, copying, viewing

Back

Forward

Launch Pinpointer

Home page

Selected media content

Selected place in article

Tips

Figure 22-1: Pinpointer takes you to the opera.

Outline column   Play   Media   Pinpointer tool   Articles filtered by category

Scroll text down

Filters (the icons or buttons down the right side of the Pinpointer) help you trim the Pinpointer's list of subjects to those containing a certain word or phrase (click Word Search); or those in a certain category (click Category), time period (click Time), or place (click Place); or those addressed by Encarta multimedia (click Multimedia).

Always click New Search first to clear all the previous filters, unless you want to *add* to your previous filter choices.

Click a filter button to open a filter panel, click to make choices, and follow the instructions there. When you choose a filter, its button looks brighter.

As you click your choices in each filter panel, you're *adding* filters. (Even *within* some filters — the Category and Multimedia filters — you can combine choices. Chosen filters are shaded.) Within a panel, click a choice again to clear it, or click the Reset button in a panel to clear the choices there. (Click the ◀◀◀ button marked with three triangles in the filter's upper-right corner to retract the filter panel again.)

Your filter choices add together until you clear them all by clicking New Search. For example, click Category and choose History: European History. Then click Multimedia and choose Animations. Then click Time and drag across the time line shown, from roughly 1050 to 1700. The Pinpointer then lists an article containing an animation for the Spanish Armada.

Reading articles

Encarta articles appear on a three-column page, although the columns aren't obvious because they display no dividing lines. From left to right, the columns are as follows:

- ✔ **Outline:** This column appears only for certain large articles, such as "Opera." Click a topic in this outline to view that portion of the article. Stuff in red includes audio or other media. This column has its own scroll bar on the left; click the down- or up-arrow to scroll.

- ✔ **Illustrations:** If the article contains illustrations or other media, they appear in the center column. See "Mucking with Media" for instructions on zooming, playing, or otherwise making the media do whatever it does.

- ✔ **Text:** The rightmost column contains the article's text. It has its own scroll bar along the right side. To widen the text column, choose Options⇨ Views⇨Text. To choose larger or smaller text, choose Options⇨Text Size.

And, oh, the places you'll go from here! You can get additional information on a subject in the text that's colored a subtle red: Just click the text. (If you have trouble seeing the red, your cursor also changes to a pointing hand when you pause over such text.) To see the Encarta Dictionary definition of any word in the text, double-click that word. To view a related article, click More Information about This Subject in the upper-right corner and click an article in the drop-down list.

Mucking with Media

Curmudgeonly writers like myself (who enjoy $10 words such as *curmudgeonly*) grumble at nontext forms of information (*and* at these forms of information co-opting the word *media*); nonetheless, Encarta is full of it. Media, I mean. Or, specifically, animations, videos, sound recordings, and other fun, lively stuff that's also called *multimedia*. Hmphh. Since when are encyclopedias supposed to be fun!?

Media in Encarta may refer to one of two different things:

- ✔ **Content,** which appears in media *players:* the boxes in articles and elsewhere that have buttons, sliders, and other controls.
- ✔ **Media Features,** which (for the most part) are tools for exploring the content in Encarta by geography, history, and topic.

Media content and players

The multimedia (nontext) content in Encarta includes illustrations, animations, slide shows, sounds, video, charts, maps, tables, and 360° views. These media may appear within an article, or you can view them on their own in the Media Gallery. Wherever they appear, they're contained in a *player,* or a separate window with specialized controls. Here are some tips for operating media players:

- ✔ In an article, a single player box in the center column may serve for displaying several possible media clips in that article. Your media choices are listed next to the box in the text column. Click your choice.
- ✔ To play a video, click the Play button. See Figure 22-2 for more information.
- ✔ To view a video or illustration in a larger window, click the Expand button.
- ✔ To view a caption, click the Caption button.
- ✔ To view an animation or chart, click the Open button. Another window appears, and a control bar appears along the bottom of the animation (or, in Media Player, at the bottom of the screen). Click the Play button to play.

✔ To stop, click the Stop button.

✔ To fast-forward, click the Fast-forward button and hold the mouse button down.

✔ To rewind, click the Rewind button and hold the mouse button down.

✔ To pause, click the Pause button. In Figure 22-2, I've paused Fluffy as he's about to land on all four feet. Bravo, Fluffy! (The pause symbol is replaced by the play symbol during a pause.)

✔ To close a media window, click the X in its upper-right corner.

✔ To copy an illustration or caption to the Clipboard, click the down-arrow in the upper-left corner of the window and choose from the menu.

Figure 22-2:
Fluffy takes a fall for our education.

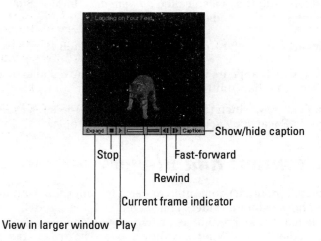

Show/hide caption

Stop

Fast-forward

Rewind

Current frame indicator

View in larger window   Play

Media features

The media *features* in Encarta are a mix of interactive presentations *(interactivities)* that stand alone from the articles, plus various aids for browsing through articles *(Collages, Topic Treks, Timeline,* and *World Maps)* and multimedia *(Media Gallery)*. From any article window, choose Features⇨Media Features, and choose one of the following:

✔ **Interactivities:** Click any subject listed. These interactive tools spring up in their own windows, and those windows create windows. All interactivities are different, so look for an Instructions button to click.

✔ **Collages:** A collage is a way of browsing related articles on a subject. Click any collage listed, and you get a continuous panel of images and captions that extends off the right of your screen. When the opening music stops, a control bar appears at the top. Click ▶ to jump to the right, or click on a ▶▶▶ forward button and hold down the mouse button to scroll smoothly. Back and forward buttons are at either top corner. Pause your mouse cursor over illustrations to activate them, and then click to expand the subject into a new window. In that window, view any related articles listed by clicking those article titles, or click the Caption button on illustrations for explanatory text.

✔ **Media Gallery:** This tool is a browsing window that works like the article window, but restricts itself to multimedia content only. The Pinpointer in this instance shows only pictures, audio, video, and animations.

✔ **Topic Treks:** Topic Treks are a way of paging (trekking?) through articles that relate to a given subject. Click any subject. At first, you appear to be viewing just an article. But a small, black topic treks control box is present in which you click Next or Back to see the next or previous article. Click ▶▶▶ in that box to see your itinerary of "stops" (articles) along the trek. Click New Trek to return to the trek selection (starting) page. Click the X in the control box window's upper-right corner to exit a trek.

✔ **Timeline:** The Timeline is a way to explore articles by history. Click the right or left arrows on the ends of the bottom scroll bar to move forward or backward in time. Click any listed event for information. The box that appears works like a miniature article page, with scrollable text on the right, media in the center (if any), and clickable article subheadings outlined on the left. Click red text to teleport to an article.

✔ **World Maps:** The World Map window enables you to explore Encarta articles by geography or view maps. Rotate the globe shown by clicking the corners of the Rotate control on the lower right. Click an area of the globe, and then choose (from the drop-down menu) Zoom In for a map or Go to Article. Or get a map by clicking Find a Place on the lower left, typing a place name in the box that appears, and clicking any place listed.

✔ **Mind Maze:** Mind Maze is an "adventure" game in the form of a medieval castle. Wander around by clicking doors. Provoke characters and objects by clicking them. Get points for answering questions. Take naps. Press the F1 key for help.

Help, I've Moved, and I Can't Get Back!

Encarta sometimes leaves you on a screen without any apparent way to get anywhere else! Here are the secret controls:

- Try pressing the Esc key to get out of whatever you're into.

- To exit a window, click the X in any window's upper-right corner. If two Xs are present, click the inner of the two. (The outer X is for Encarta itself; clicking that X exits the program.)

- To return to the starting screen (home page), click Home on the menu bar of an article window.

- To return to the previous screen, click the back symbol in a window's top bar.

Encarta is very literal about going back, so if you made many wrong turns in getting to the current screen, you'll go through them all again!

The down-arrow in the upper-left corner of a window contains various goodies, depending on what kind of tool is running: printing commands; links to related subjects; a different view of a subject; commands to copy Encarta graphics or text to the Windows Clipboard (for pasting into some other document). See the appendix for more on using the Clipboard.

Printing, Copying, and Options

You can copy or print nearly any image or text in Encarta. By *copy* I mean copy stuff to the hidden Windows Clipboard (discussed in the appendix), from which you can paste that stuff into documents in Word, Works, or other programs. (Click in that document and choose Edit⇨Paste.) Here's where to go in Encarta to copy or print:

- **In articles:** On the menu bar, choose Options, and then either Print or Copy; then choose (if not grayed out) Text Selection, Whole Article, Image/Frame, or Caption. To print a chunk of text, drag across the text to highlight it before choosing Options⇨Print⇨Text Selection. An image or a frame of a moving image must be visible in order to be printed or copied.

- **Elsewhere:** In nearly any window displaying text or graphical content, click the down arrow in the upper-left corner, and choose the appropriate Copy or Print options from the drop-down menu. (To copy a frame of a video or animation, pause the presentation first.)

In an article window, you can also choose Options⇨Settings, and by clicking to clear or place check marks in the list of behaviors displayed, you may improve how Encarta behaves in various ways:

- Get rid of the opening theme music on the home page.

- Get rid of the button swishing sounds.

- Go directly to the screen last viewed when Encarta starts again.

- Open (randomly) to an article page instead of the home screen.

Chapter 23

Entertaining Your Friends: Greetings!

*I*n today's business world, you never know what partnerships may form next, and what can result: Alcoa Aluminum and Fruit of the Loom? Disney and the Louvre? Hallmark and Microsoft? Well, wonder no more about the fruits of that last partnership. You've got it: the Microsoft Greetings Workshop, one of the cutest chunks of clicking, whistling, clanking, and barking software to ever acquire real estate (and lots of it) on a disk drive.

With Greetings Workshop (*Greetings* to its pals), you can create cards, banners, certificates of achievement, calendars, posters, signs, framed photos, and (with special paper) stickers and labels. Then you can print 'em, e-mail 'em, or stick 'em up on a special Microsoft Web page for friends to see! Greetings can even remind you a few days before someone's birthday or anniversary.

Getting Started

As with any Windows program, you can start Greetings by either double-clicking its icon on the screen or by choosing it from the Start button of the Windows taskbar. Look for an icon on your screen labeled Greetings Workshop; if you find it, double-click it. If you can't find the icon, go to the Windows taskbar (usually located across the bottom of your screen) and choose Start⇨Programs⇨Greetings Workshop⇨Greetings Workshop.

When Greetings starts, it first asks you to sign in. Click Guest, or you can click Add a Name, which calls up a dialog box that asks your name and experience level. Type your name, and if you're at all unsure about using Windows, choose Beginner. When you next launch Greetings, click your name in the list that appears.

The opening screen of Greetings, shown in Figure 23-1, gives you an idea of the program's overall cute-osity. Rocky, the dog in the corner, gives you help and command menus as you go!

Here are the things that you can do from the opening screen:

✔ Start a new project by clicking one of the many types of projects displayed on the shelves: announcements, cards, invitations, and so on.

✔ Open a project that you've created before by clicking Open an existing Project (in Rocky's voice balloon) or the Saved Projects file drawer.

✔ View stuff on the Greetings Web page by clicking either the phone or Visit Greetings Workshop on the World Wide Web in Rocky's voice balloon. (Internet Explorer starts up.)

✔ Click Create or Delete a Reminder or Reminders on the bottom shelf to program Greetings to remind you in advance of my (or anyone else's) birthday!

Figure 23-1:
The opening screen shows what happens when Hallmark meets Microsoft.

> ✔ Pet Rocky by clicking him.
>
> ✔ Click Hallmark Papers to tell Greetings that you've purchased special Hallmark paper (available through the Greetings Web page) and want to design your own card. This choice is the only way to do a project on anything except standard letter-sized 8½ x 11 paper.

Starting a New Project

In Greetings, you do many things step-by-step, following detailed instructions that appear in a series of dialog boxes. Just click your choices, or click and type text as directed, and then click the Continue button in each box until you're done. Click the Back button to return to an earlier box, or click the Cancel button to cancel whatever task you started.

Eventually, you run out of the dialog boxes with Continue buttons and end up at the editing screen described in the next section. From that screen, you can simply print your work or do more customizing.

Greetings is pretty self-explanatory as it guides you through the creative process, but following are a few helpful tips:

✔ If a dialog box asks, "How do you want to get started?" click one of the pre-designed projects listed, instead of clicking Start with a Blank Project.

✔ Some dialog boxes are full of confusing areas. Look for numbered steps to guide you.

✔ As you click pictures of greeting cards or other projects, Greetings may display the card's message. Don't worry if the text isn't right. You can change the text (or anything else) later. In some projects, Greetings gives you two standard message choices. Click the left- or right-arrow buttons alongside the word Select to switch between the messages.

✔ Some Greetings dialog boxes mention the size and fold. A *French-fold* card is folded like the ones you usually buy in the store: in four parts. (It only needs printing on one side.) A *single-fold* card is a sheet of paper folded in half. (Greetings must print on both sides of the paper to create the inside and outside of the card.) Greetings uses only standard 8½ x 11-inch paper for its pre-designed projects, so French-fold cards are small.

✔ Greetings prints cards nicely, but it can't do much about envelopes. Buy some 4 ¾ x 6 ½ envelopes for your French-fold cards!

Working on Your Own in the Editing Screen

The most versatile feature of Greetings is its main screen, which I call the editing screen. Figure 23-2 shows the editing screen.

On the editing screen, you can customize the heck out of whatever project you're working on: Change, resize, rotate, or move images; add, move, remove text; contour text to various shapes, add borders and colors — you name it.

You arrive at the editing screen in any of several ways:

- You reach the end of a new project.
- You open an old project.
- You click the Work on My Own Now button in one of the initial dialog boxes of a new project.
- You start a new project by choosing Start with a Blank Project from the opening screen.

If you don't want to do any more work on your project, you can print it or send it electronically, or you can save it for later. (Greetings automatically prompts you to save your work before you exit the program or start another project.) See the sections "Printing" and "Sending Projects Electronically" later in this chapter for more information.

You edit your project by clicking either the buttons along the top of the editing screen or the menu choices in Rocky's speech balloon. (Buttons and menu choices do basically the same things.) The editing screen changes its buttons and its menu choices according to whatever part of the project you click. The screen offers more editing options than I can possibly discuss here, but here are some basics for editing your project:

- **To add text or graphics to another page of your project:** First view that page by clicking one of the view control buttons along the left side. (Click Inside Left, for instance, to view the inside-left page of a greeting card. Click Inside Spread to see both inside pages at once.)
- **To get a hint about what a button does:** Pause your mouse cursor over the button until a description appears.
- **To select an object (text box or image) for editing:** Click it or repeatedly click the Select Next Object button until the object you want gets selected. The currently selected object has a rectangle around it. (The rectangle doesn't print.)

Copy

Paste

Adjust text

Start a new project

Add text

Open an old project

Add shaped text

Save project

Add clip art

Print

Add image

Check spelling

Draw a shape

Email this project

Draw a line

Cut

Rotate

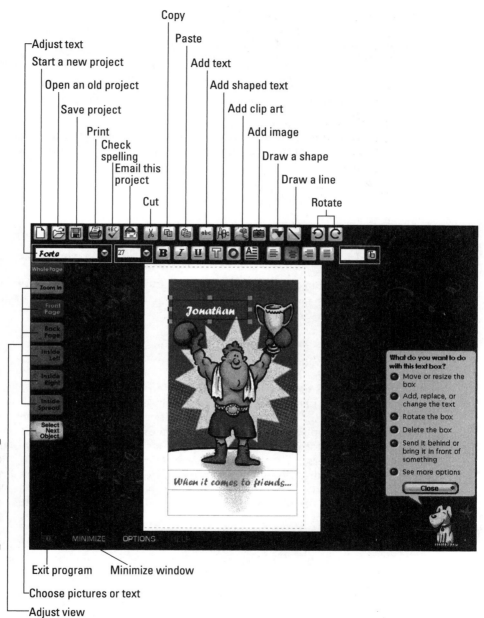

Figure 23-2:
The editing
screen
makes you
a champion
artist.

Exit program   Minimize window

Choose pictures or text

Adjust view

✔ **To add a block of text:** Click the Add New Text Block button (with "abc" on it). For a block of text in a swoopy, shaped outline, click the Add New Shaped Text button (with the capital "ABC" on it).

✔ **To add clip art (small images):** Click the Add New Picture button (with the tree on it).

✔ **To replace text:** Click the text and type. Press Backspace or Delete to delete.

✔ **To change the appearance of a specific chunk of text:** First click and drag across that chunk to select it, and then click buttons or menu selections.

✔ **To move an object:** Slowly move your cursor over it until the cursor changes to a four-headed arrow. Then click and drag the object to where you want it.

✔ **To change an object's size:** Drag a side or corner of the object.

✔ **To undo a change:** Press Ctrl+Z; repeat to undo even earlier changes.

Choosing from a menu rather than a button bar sometimes offers more control.

Printing

Printing in Greetings is somewhat limited by a very nonelectronic technology: paper. The pre-designed projects are for printing only on standard letter-size paper (8^1/$_2$ x 11). Check your printer manual, however; you may be pleasantly surprised to discover that you can print on heavier stock (nice for certificates) or continuous form paper (nice for banners). Some printers can even print iron-on templates so that you can create custom T-shirts, tote bags, or other fabric items. For differently sized projects, you can buy special Hallmark paper by going to the Greetings Web page. (Click the phone on the Greetings start page.) But you must design those projects entirely by yourself.

To print your project, you must be viewing it in the editing screen. (See the previous section for ways to get to that screen.) Then either click the Print button at the top of the screen or choose Print My Project in Rocky's speech balloon menu.

Greetings initially runs a special printer test to make sure it understands how paper goes through your printer. In that test, Greetings asks you to choose a picture that looks most like your printer. Pictures can be misleading, so I suggest that after you click your choice of pictures, you also read the text description that appears. If the description doesn't sound correct, try another choice. After Greetings understands your printer, it won't need to run the test again.

Sending Projects Electronically

Microsoft gives you three ways to send projects electronically: by e-mail, by Web site, and by diskette. To view your greeting in these various forms, your recipient has to have e-mail software for e-mail, or a Web browser for Web site or diskette viewing.

Sending to the Greetings Workshop Web Post Office

You don't even need to have your own Web site to publish your greeting on the Web! Microsoft lets you put your Greetings project on their Web site. Make sure you know your recipient's e-mail address, then click Other Options in Rocky's menu on the editing screen, and choose Send My Project.

The How Do You Want To Send? dialog box appears. Click Send to Greetings Workshop Web Post Office, then click the Continue button. After a bit of a delay, the Ready To Visit The Greetings Workshop Post Office dialog box appears. Click Post My Greeting.

Internet Explorer launches and goes online to the Greetings Web Post Office, which guides you through a series of forms to fill out. At the end, it gives you the Web address and a special access code for viewing your project on the Web. It also sends your recipients e-mail with the same information. In many e-mail programs, your recipient can just click a link in the e-mail message to view your project.

Sending by e-mail or diskette

To send a greeting by e-mail or diskette, click Other Options in Rocky's menu on the editing screen, and choose Send My Project. (If you haven't yet saved your project, Rocky asks if you want to do so. You can choose Yes, or No, and your choice doesn't affect the sending process.)

In the The How Do You Want To Send? dialog box that appears, click either Send via E-mail or Save to Diskette That I Can Send by Regular Mail, then click Continue. If you chose to send via e-mail, a Ready To Send dialog box appears. Click Send Greeting via E-mail Now, and Outlook Express opens, with a message prepared for you to send.

If you chose the Save to a Diskette option, a series of simple dialog boxes follows, ending in a Save dialog box that works like the commonplace Save As dialog box described in the appendix. Click Save In to choose a diskette drive, put a diskette in the drive, then click the Save button.

Part VI
The Part of Tens

The 5th Wave   By Rich Tennant

It started as a wrap-around porch, and then Stuart found a section on medieval architecture on the Internet.

In this part . . .

As on *Sesame Street,* this part comes to you courtesy of the Number 10 — ten nifty tricks and ten editing exhortations, that is. If you don't find what you want in the rest of this book, you may just find it here.

If you don't find it here, I didn't have room to put it in this book. So visit www.dummmies.com on the Web and check out some of the following related titles from IDG Books Worldwide:

- ✔ *Windows 95 For Dummies*
- ✔ *Windows 98 For Dummies*
- ✔ *Microsoft Works 4.5 For Windows For Dummies*
- ✔ *Word 97 For Windows For Dummies*
- ✔ *Microsoft Money 99 For Dummies*
- ✔ *Internet Explorer 4 For Windows For Dummies*
- ✔ *Microsoft Outlook For Dummies*

Chapter 24
Ten Nifty Tricks

*R*emember those great ads for magic tricks in the back of comic books? Well, continuing in that tradition, here at the back of this book is a bunch of nifty, almost-magic tricks. You probably won't amaze your friends with these tricks, but you may actually begin to enjoy your PC, which is magic enough.

Cut, Copy, and Paste to or from E-Mail

The number-one, all-time most frequently asked question I receive is, "How do I move text between an e-mail message and another program?" The secret is to use the Windows invisible Clipboard, described in more detail in the appendix. Just click and drag your mouse across text in any window to select that text, and choose Edit⇨Copy in the menu bar of that window (or press Ctrl+C) to copy the text to the Windows invisible Clipboard. Then click in the window where you want the text, and choose Edit⇨Paste from the menu bar of that window (or press Ctrl+V) to paste.

Clean Up Ragged Text

When text is ragged-looking, with some lines too long and others too short, you are looking at text with "hard" line breaks: invisible characters that force the line to wrap. (They occur either because of e-mail quirks, if you're looking at an e-mail message, or because someone pressed Enter at the end of a line instead of letting the line wrap.) To remove these characters one at a time, click at the beginning of the line *after* each too-short line, then press the Backspace key on your keyboard.

If you have a big document — say, you copied a big message into Word or Works — you need a way remove all these hard line breaks automatically. In Word and Works, use the replace feature. Choose Edit⇨Replace. In Word's Find What text box, type the magic incantation ^p; in Works, click the ¶ button. Leave the Replace With text box blank. Click Replace All if you're feeling bold, or else find and replace each incidence of the character.

The Replace feature works just as well for getting rid of those > and >> characters that occur in e-mail replies.

Change Annoying Program Behaviors

The more modern and "full-featured" a program is, the more annoying behaviors it seems to have. Contemporary word processors, in particular, have many automatic behaviors that can drive you nuts. One secret to changing such behaviors is to figure out where the program's options, preferences, or auto-whatevers are hiding.

In most programs, look for a menu choice of Tools⇨Options to access key controls. In Microsoft Word, also check out Tools⇨AutoCorrect.

In either case, the dialog box that appears has lots of check boxes for the various automatic options; if a check mark is present that automatic option is turned on. Click to clear any check mark to turn an option off. Click the various tabs in the dialog box to see other options.

If you are uncertain about what a particular option does, see the suggestion for right-clicking dialog box thingies in the "Try the Other Mouse Button" section at the end of this chapter.

Drag and Drop Document Files

This is a trick that nearly every Windows program can do. Open a My Computer window (or Windows Explorer window). When you want to work on a document file, just drag that file from the My Computer window over to the Works title bar. Release the mouse, and Works opens the file. Even if the file is not a Works file, Works tries to import it.

Freeze-Dry or Customize the Works Workspace

If you work on pretty much the same documents all the time, you can preserve your workspace; that is, tell Works to remember what documents you're using and reopen those document windows automatically when you start the program again. First, set up your workspace the way you want it. Then choose Tools➪Options and click the View tab in the Options dialog box. Click Use Saved Workspace at Startup; then click the Save Workspace button. The next time you start Works, it reloads those documents.

The Options dialog box holds all kinds of possibilities for customizing Works behavior. One of my favorite changes is getting rid of the Help screen that appears at startup: On the View card, click Show Help at Startup to clear the check mark. Another change is to get rid of the jerky word-at-a-time high-lighting in the word processor: Click the Editing tab and clear the Automatic Word Selection check mark.

Import and Export Documents

Many programs can read files from other programs or create files that other programs can read. When you open a file with File➪Open, the Open dialog box offers a Files of Type list box. Click that box, and you find a list of file-types that the program can read.

Click one of those file types, and the File Name box lists files of that type in the directory you select. Choose a file to import, and your program converts it.

Exporting a file works similarly: Use the File➪Save As command and choose a file type in the Save As Type list box. If you don't see the exact file type listed for the program to which you want to export, try either Text, Text & Tabs (called *tab-delimited*), or Text & Commas *(comma-delimited)*. Many programs can import those types of files.

When you go to save a document after importing it, use File➪Save As, not File➪Save, to make sure you save the document in your program's native format. Click the Save As Type list box, and choose the native file type of your program from the list that appears.

Wrap Text in Small Windows

When you're working on a word-processor document in a tiny window, where lines extend beyond the window's edge, it's a pain to have to scroll left and right to be able to read. Instead, choose Tools⇨Options; then, in Word, click the View tab in the dialog box that appears. (In Works, choose the Editing tab.) Click the Wrap to Window check box. The document doesn't appear this way when you print; this trick just helps you read it.

Split a Works or Word Window

In Works or Word, to work on two different parts of a document at once, you can split the window. At the very top of the vertical scroll bar, above the up-pointing arrow, is a microscopic, obscure, shy little rectangle. Click that guy and drag him downward. This action splits the document into two windows that you can scroll independently. It's still only one document, though. Click in either half to do your editing. To put the split away, drag the horizontal line that separates the two halves back up to the very top or bottom of the document window.

Try the Other Mouse Button

The *other* mouse button (the one on the right side of the mouse, unless you're a lefty and you reconfigured your mouse) has a surprising amount of power. In any Windows program — or on the Windows screen itself — try clicking something using that other mouse button and see if a menu appears. Or, try highlighting (selecting) something — text or graphics — the usual way and then clicking with that other mouse button.

You often get editing commands such as Copy, Cut, and Paste, formatting commands, or other useful commands. Use them just as you do commands from the regular menu bar. To change how some object (represented typically by an icon of some sort, such as a program icon) works, choose Properties from such a menu. You can discover all kinds of amazing and useful properties to change in the dialog box that appears.

But wait, there's more! If a dialog box presents you with a thingy (check box, button, whatever) that you don't understand, click the right mouse button on that thingy. In many programs, a brief explanation appears, and occasionally is even helpful! (The explanation is the same one that appears if you click the "?" symbol in the upper right-hand corner of the dialog box and then the thingy.)

Chapter 25
Ten Things NOT to Do

In This Chapter

▶ Avoid using multiple white-space characters

▶ Refrain from pressing the Enter key repeatedly

▶ Desist from terminating every line yourself

▶ Don't type your own file extensions

▶ Forego numbering your pages manually

▶ Abstain from turning off your PC before exiting

▶ Shun using spaces for blank cells

▶ Renounce working in tiny windows

▶ Refuse to stuff all your files in the same folder

▶ Forswear typing in all capitals

*E*veryone has an idea about how things ought to work. Unfortunately, computers don't usually work that way. You can easily fall into old typewriter habits or form a mistaken impression that Works, Word, or some other program makes you do something that you don't really have to do. Here's my list of the top ten errors, misconceptions, or just plain boo-boos that you should avoid.

Do Not Use Extra Spaces, Lines, or Tabs

If you're using multiple, consecutive spaces or tabs in a word-processing document, you're probably making your life difficult. If you're using multiple tabs in every line, it's probably because you haven't set your tab stops or you've forgotten that you can indent a paragraph with a toolbar button. If you are using blank lines to separate paragraphs, try pressing Ctrl+0 (that's a zero, not the letter O) to put space above the paragraph instead. See Chapter 6 for additional better ways to do things.

Do Not Keep Pressing Enter to Begin a New Page

This trick may have worked nicely on your Royal typewriter, but in word-processing documents, it creates a royal mess. Press Ctrl+Enter to start a new page.

Do Not Press Enter at the End of Each Line

I know, I've said this before, but it pains me greatly to see people fighting their word processor. If you press Enter at the end of every line in a word-processing document, Works can't word-wrap for you. As a result, every time you edit a line, you have to manually readjust every line! AAAAAGGGH!! JUST DON'T DO IT, YOU HEAR ME?!! (Notice how annoying text is when it's all in capital letters? If you want to know why adults shouldn't shout at each other like this, see the tenth thing not to do in this chapter.)

Do Not Type Your Own File Extensions When Saving Files

When you save a file, just type the filename, not the .wks or any other extension. Windows programs automatically put the proper extension on. If you use your own special extension, Windows and your programs will get very confused.

Do Not Number Your Pages Manually

Works can automagically number your word-processing pages, positioning the numbers where you want them. What more could you want? If you try to number your own pages by simply typing a number on each page, you'll be continually adjusting them as you edit the document. See Chapter 13 for instructions on numbering pages in Word, or Chapter 8 for Works word processor.

Do Not Turn Off Your PC before Exiting

Hey! It's time for dinner! But don't just flip the power switch on your PC. Exit your program and exit Windows first. (If your PC is one that suspends the state of all your programs — and of Windows — as you turn the PC off, you don't need to exit your program and Windows first. Some laptops also have a "suspend" feature.) If you don't exit before you turn off your computer, Windows and your program can become confused the next time you try to do things. At the very least, your hard disk fills up with little Windows temporary files.

Do Not Use Spaces for Blank Cells

In your spreadsheet documents, when you want to remove an entry, don't type a space; press the Delete key instead. If you put a space in the cell and use a COUNT, AVG, or other statistical function, the cell will be counted.

Do Not Work in Tiny Windows Unnecessarily

Just because a program starts out with a smallish window, you don't have to stay with it. Click and drag a corner or side of the Works window and enlarge Works. Do the same with your document windows. Better yet, maximize the Works or document window. See the appendix for a refresher on doing this.

Do Not Stuff All Your Files in the Same Folder

See the appendix for ways to make new folders. When you save files, put them in different folders. If you stuff them all in the same folder, like the Windows 98 My Documents folder, you will eventually get very confused.

Do Not Type in ALL CAPITALS

Particularly when you're using the Outlook Express to send mail to somebody, don't type in all capital letters. It's considered shouting. In other tools,
using all capitals (uppercase letters) makes your documents harder to read.

Appendix
Clues for the Clueless: PC Basics

. . . .

In This Chapter

▶ Getting keyed up about your keyboard

▶ Mastering mouse anatomy and behavior

▶ Understanding why nothing falls off the Windows desktop

▶ Getting programs to run, shrink, and go away

▶ Putting things away in folders and on disks

▶ Reorganizing and relabeling your stored items

▶ Placing your order at the menu bar

▶ Getting quick service at toolbars

▶ Having a meaningful dialog with dialog boxes

▶ Locating your stuff

▶ Begging for Help

▶ Quitting and going out for some fresh air

. . . .

*L*ots of software books jabber away about keyboards, mice, files, disks, folders, and directories as if you spent your childhood with a mouse in your hand and used a keyboard for a pillow.

The *...For Dummies* books are for the rest of us: the few, the brave, and — in computer matters — the clueless; hence this appendix. If you are utterly new to the world of the PC, this is your starting point. I can't do as complete a job of preparing you for Windows as, say, *Windows 95* (or *Windows 98*) *For Dummies* by Andy Rathbone (IDG Books Worldwide, Inc.), but I can try to keep you out of trouble.

What is Windows, and how is it different from Works Suite? Windows is the *foundation software* upon which your programs (or *applications*), such as the programs of Works Suite, rely. It's the software that glues together all the parts of your computer into a working system and lets you run one or more programs at a time. Windows not only serves as a foundation, it also includes certain programs, called accessories or utilities, that do basic jobs such as display text or play music. Programs that run under Windows work in very much the same way as each other, behavior that is part of what this appendix is about.

Cozying Up to Your Keyboard

PC keyboards differ from typewriter keyboards. Following are some of the keys you're likely to find on your PC keyboard:

- ✔ **Function keys:** These keys are usually located along the top of the keyboard and are labeled F1 through F12. They do different things in different programs. Pressing a function key is one of many ways a program enables you to give a command.

- ✔ **Typewriter keys:** Your old typewriter had most of the same character keys (*characters* being letters, numbers, and punctuation marks). The computer people added a few new ones.

- ✔ **Navigation keys:** These keys are to the right of the typewriter keys. You can use the four keys with arrows on them to move the *insertion point* (a typing cursor). The other navigation keys, marked Home, End, PgUp (or Page Up), and PgDn (or Page Down) are keys that move you around in a document in large gulps. Nearby is a Delete key, which deletes text following the insertion point, or any item you *select*. (See "Selecting with Mouse or Keyboard," later in this appendix.) Also nearby is an Insert key that I recommend you avoid: If you press it, it makes you type over existing text. Press that key again to resume typing normally.

- ✔ **Numeric keypad:** This keypad at the far right of your keyboard duplicates the number keys and math symbols that appear across the top of your keyboard, plus another Enter key. If these don't appear to work properly, press the NumLock key once.

- ✔ **Enter key:** This key is generally labeled Enter, or it is marked with an L-shaped arrow. You use the Enter key to signal that you're finished typing a paragraph or entering some data or instructions.

- ✔ **Esc key:** Called the Escape key, this little guy lets you back out of commands that you started but don't want to finish. Pressing Esc does the same thing as clicking the Cancel button that programs sometimes display.

- ✔ **Shift, Alt, and Ctrl ("Control") keys:** These guys don't do anything by themselves: They only work when pressed at the same time as other keys. The Shift key, if you use it as you're typing on the regular keyboard, produces the upper character on a key — just like the Shift key on a typewriter. Otherwise, you use Shift and its fellow keys for *keyboard shortcuts.*

Keyboard shortcuts are alternative ways to give commands to programs, and are written in this book and in all Windows programs like these examples:

- ✔ Ctrl+S
- ✔ Alt+Shift+F1

These descriptions mean that you need to hold down Ctrl (or Alt, or Shift), then press and release the other key listed. Ctrl+S, for instance, means hold down the Ctrl key, then press and release the S key. When two keys are listed (as in Alt+Shift+1), hold down both keys while you press and release the third (1 in this example).

Moseying Around with Your Mouse

The strange, rodent-shaped object with push buttons on the top, plugged into your computer by its tail, is called a *mouse.* If you don't have such a thing, you may have some other *pointing device,* all forms of which are intended to be wiggled side-to-side or front-to-back. One such device is a *trackball,* a device where a ball sticks out for you to wiggle. On a laptop computer, you may have a tiny joystick-like lever to wiggle, somewhere near the G and H keys in the center of your keyboard. Or, you may have a flat pad near your thumbs that you drag your finger across.

Your PC accommodates rodents and other wiggling critters so that you can point at control buttons and menus instead of having to type commands with your keyboard. Pointing also lets you indicate what stuff you want to work on.

Mouse behavior

As you wiggle your pointing device it moves a *pointer* (typically an arrow, although that symbol changes) or *cursor* (a vertical line) that appears on your screen.

Regardless of the device, to either side of the device are *buttons*. Usually, a pointing device sports only two buttons (to the left and right); really snazzy dressers may have three. In most Windows programs, the left button is the most important one. The right button usually brings up a set of editing commands, such as Copy and Paste. But, you can find the same commands elsewhere in the program (such as in the menu bar); getting menus from right-clicking the mouse is simply a convenience.

Mouse skills

The first mouse skill you need in order to control a Windows program is the ability to point and click. Here's exactly what this term and related terms mean:

✔ **To point:** Push your pointing device to move the mouse pointer or cursor. Position the pointer or cursor so that its tip is anywhere on top of or within the thing you are pointing at.

- ✔ **To click (also called *clicking on*):** Point to something, and then press and release the left mouse button.

- ✔ **To double-click:** Like clicking, but press and release the (left) button twice in rapid succession.

- ✔ **To click and drag (also called simply *dragging*):** Press the (left) button down and hold it down while moving the mouse. This action *drags* something, such as the edge of a highlighted area, around on the screen. When you're done dragging, release the button. Sometimes, when you drag, the object itself doesn't move, only a shadow of it. The object itself will move after you finish dragging it and release the button.

Selecting with Mouse or Keyboard

Pointing out something in a program is called *selecting* it. To select something, drag across it (if it is text in a document) or click it (good for graphics, icons, or things in a list or menu). To select multiple things with a mouse, imagine a rectangle completely surrounding all those things and drag from one corner of that rectangle (say, upper left) to the opposite corner (lower right). When you select something, it changes color or is enveloped in black or some other contrasting color.

In many programs, you can also select something by holding down either one of the two Shift keys and pressing your navigation keys. Exactly how the selection occurs depends entirely on the program you use, so I can't describe the process precisely here.

Cutting, Copying, Pasting, and Dragging

Nearly all Windows programs offer a common set of features that make editing easy: the cut, copy, paste, and drag features. The cut, copy, and paste features employ a Windows feature called the *Clipboard*. The Windows Clipboard is a temporary and hidden storage area.

Copy or cut and paste

To move something, you can cut and paste it. This procedure is exactly like copying and pasting, except that the original text is removed from your document. Here's the procedure for copying or cutting and pasting:

1. **Select the text or illustration that you want to copy or move.**

2. **To copy something, press Ctrl+C, or Choose Edit⇨Copy (or right-click and choose Copy), or Click the Copy button on the toolbar.** (The Copy button normally shows two overlapping documents.)

   To cut something instead of copying it, substitute any of the following: Press Ctrl+X, choose Edit⇨Cut, right-click and choose Cut, or click the Cut (scissors) button in the toolbar.

   This procedure copies the selected stuff onto the Windows Clipboard.

3. **Click where you want a copy to appear.**

   This spot can be in the document that you're working on, or in some other document. You can take your time opening documents, launching programs, or whatever you need to do.

   Whatever you copy stays on the Clipboard only until you copy or cut something else or turn off your computer.

4. **Press Ctrl+V, or Choose Edit⇨Paste (or right-click and choose Paste), or Click the Paste button in the toolbar.** (The Paste button shows a clipboard with a document.)

   This procedure copies stuff from the Windows Clipboard and pastes it into the new location.

You can repeat Steps 3 and 4 as many times as you like, until you put something new on the Clipboard.

Drag

Dragging is an easy way to move or copy text, an illustration, or a file to a different place within a window, or even to another window. See "Controlling Program and Document Windows" in this appendix if windows are new to you.

Here's how to move or copy something by dragging it:

1. **Select the text, illustration, file, or other object that you want to move.**

2. **Place your mouse cursor over the highlighted area.**

3. **Press down the mouse button (don't let go) and drag the selected text or illustration to where you want to move it.**

   If you want to copy, not move, the selected text, press and hold the Ctrl key down at this point.

   If your destination is not visible in the document window, drag to the window's edge in the direction you want to go. When your cursor hits the edge, the window scrolls.

If your destination is in another window, just drag the object to your destination in that window.

4. **Release the mouse button at your final destination.**

Viewing the Windows Desktop

A short while after you turn on your PC, you should see something like Figure A-1: the Windows *desktop*. (In some PCs, you may first be asked for your name and a password. Try simply pressing the Enter key if you haven't been told what to do about this query by the person who sold or gave you your PC.)

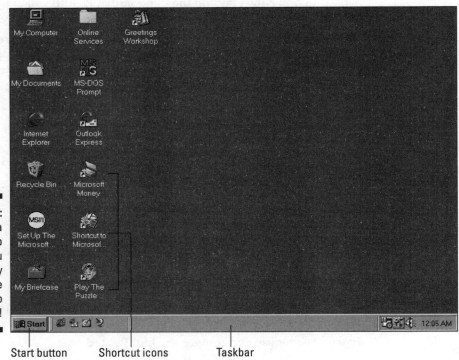

Figure A-1:
Finally, a desktop where you can't easily leave coffee-cup stains!

Start button   Shortcut icons   Taskbar

Here are a few tips for using the Windows desktop:

- ✔ **Icons** are pictures, usually labeled. You double-click icons to do something (usually, to start a program). *Shortcuts* are icons on your screen that start a program or open a window, and have a tiny arrow in one corner.

- ✔ **The Taskbar,** that large gray band along the bottom (or side) of your screen, contains one or more things that look like buttons. You only need to click a button once to use it — don't double-click it. The Start button can help you run programs, as I describe in the next section.

- ✔ **The My Computer icon** lets you open up *windows* where you can view *folders* and *files* on your computer — all you do is double-click it. It also lets you access the same standard Windows features (Setup, Help, Find) as the Start button, described in the next section.

- ✔ **The Recycle Bin icon** is a sort of trash can. Drag files or folders to this icon when you want to delete them. The files and folders are not deleted yet, just in case you change your mind. Double-click this icon to see what's in the bin. Then, to *really* delete files (which frees up additional disk space on your PC), choose File⇨Empty Recycle Bin. To restore a file to its original folder, click that file (listed in the Recycle Bin window) then choose File⇨Restore.

Finding, Starting, and Exiting Programs

Windows gives you several ways to start a program (also called *launching* a program):

- ✔ Click the Start button to browse through an extensive menu of programs, and choose one to run. (Step-by-step instructions follow.)

- ✔ Double-click a *shortcut* — an icon (symbol) on your screen, labeled with the program's name.

- ✔ Click a program icon on the Windows Taskbar.

- ✔ In any *window* (a rectangle on your screen), double-click a file that displays a program's icon.

The fastest way to start (launch) a program is with a shortcut or an icon on the Taskbar. Not all programs have shortcuts, but — don't worry — you can always start any properly installed program using the Start button. Do the following:

1. **Click the Start button on the Windows Taskbar (shown in Figure A-1).**

2. **In the menu that appears, click Programs.**

   Another menu appears next to the first one.

3. **Move your cursor horizontally until it is on the new menu. Then move the pointer vertically until it points to the program name you want, and click.**

Yet another menu appears. At this point, your screen begins to resemble Figure A-2.

As Figure A-2 shows, a black rectangle envelopes (highlights) whatever you point to in a menu.

If a triangular arrow appears to the right of the program name, and a folder icon to the left, your pointer is on a folder. You aren't at your destination yet! Repeat Step 3 until your pointer highlights the program name you want, *and* an icon appears to the left of that name, as for Microsoft Works in Figure A-2.

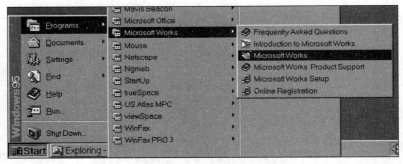

Figure A-2:
Where
Microsoft
Works
lurks.

Now you're off and running. Your program appears in a window on your screen or fills the entire screen. You can run several programs at once, if you like. For instance, if you need to copy something from your e-mail program to your word-processor program, you can run both programs.

To *exit* a program, choose File⇨Exit from the menu bar or click the X in the upper right-hand corner of the program window. If you haven't yet saved your work as a file, the program may prompt you to do so.

Understanding Disks, Folders, and Files

One subject that always confuses beginners is figuring out the basics about software: What and where is a program; a file; a document? Here's an overview of what and where those things are:

✔ **Files:** Files are what a computer uses to store anything and everything: programs, documents, pictures, you name it. Files reside on a *disk* of some kind and on most disks can be moved, copied, or erased. Each file has a *filename,* and when Windows lists files, it usually displays an *icon* (symbol) that tells you what program the file is associated with.

✔ **Filenames:** Whenever you create anything on a PC (say, a document in Word) you save it as a file and give the file a name. The name can be up to 256 characters long and include spaces. Word, or whatever program you use, adds a period and three letters to the end to create an official Windows *filename.* These three letters are the filename *extension,* and indicate what program the file is associated with. (Files ending in .doc, for instance, are Microsoft Word files.)

✔ **Folders:** *Folders* serve the same purpose as paper file folders in a file cabinet. (The "cabinet" in this case is a disk drive.) Folders (also called *directories* or *subdirectories*) group and organize files. Folders may contain additional folders, and those additional folders can contain more folders, *ad nauseum.* You can make, move, copy, delete, and rename folders.

✔ **Disks and disk drives:** Disks have one job: to store files. *Hard disks* are disks that are permanently installed in your PC. Your programs — and Windows itself — are installed (stored) as files on a hard disk. *Disk drives* (the electronic boxes which contain, read, and write disks) are referred to by letters with colons, as in C: (which is the name of your main hard disk drive). You probably have additional disk drives of different kinds.

✔ **Diskettes and floppies:** *Diskettes* (often simply called disks) are floppy little plastic disks sealed within hard, flat plastic rectangles that can be inserted into and removed from diskette drives on your PC. Windows calls a diskette a *3¹/₂-inch floppy.* Diskettes are used for *backup* (keeping a copy of your files in case your hard disk breaks, or *crashes*) or to give files to other people. The disk drives for diskettes are nearly always referred to as A: (and, if you have a second one, B:). To insert a diskette into its drive, orient the diskette's metal tab towards the drive, and the diskette label up. To remove the diskette, press the button adjacent to the drive's slot. Diskettes must be removed from the A: drive to start your PC.

✔ **CD and CD-ROMs:** *CDs* (also called CD-ROMs, where ROM stands for Read-Only Memory) are disks that cannot be altered or erased. Software vendors use CDs to distribute their programs. CDs go into special CD-ROM drives on your PC. To open a CD-ROM drive, press the button that protrudes from the drive, and a tray emerges. Place your disk label-side up on the tray and press the drive's button again. Some CDs automatically run a program when you insert them.

Viewing, browsing, and opening disk drives, folders, and files

The easiest way to view lists of your disk drives, folders, and files is to double-click the My Computer icon on your Windows screen. A window opens. (See the section, "Controlling Program and Document Windows" if windows are new to you.) I call all windows that spring from the My Computer icon "My Computer windows."

In the first My Computer window, double-click any disk drive to display the files or folders on the disk in that drive. Double-click a folder to see what files or folders are within that folder.

To view the contents of a file you created (which in this book I call a *document file*), you need to start (launch) the program that made it, then open the file (using, for instance, the File⇨Open command in that program). An easy way to do both actions at once is to double-click the document file.

The process of looking in various disk drives and folders for files is called *browsing*. The technique for browsing is basically the same throughout Windows (including any My Computer window and the Open and Save dialog boxes of all Windows programs). Here are the basic browsing techniques, using the Works Open dialog box as an example, shown in Figure A-3:

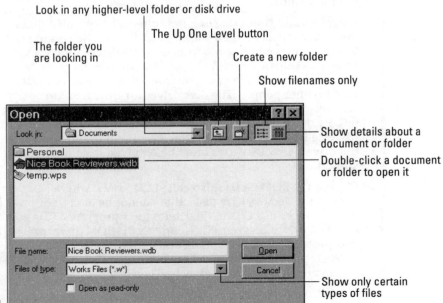

Look in any higher-level folder or disk drive

The folder you are looking in

The Up One Level button

Create a new folder

Show filenames only

Show details about a document or folder

Double-click a document or folder to open it

Show only certain types of files

Figure A-3: Typical controls for browsing files and folders.

✔ The window or dialog box shows only one folder's contents at a time. The folder's name is displayed at the top of the window or dialog box. (I call this folder the "currently displayed folder" in the bullets following.)

✔ To open a folder, double-click it (or click it and click the Open button if one is present).

✔ To open the folder that the currently displayed folder is in, click the Up One Level button.

✔ To open other folders or other disk drives, click the down-arrow button to the right of the currently-displayed folder's name. Double-click any folder or disk drive in the list that appears.

✔ To see the kinds and sizes of files displayed, click the Show Details button that some windows and dialog boxes provide (and which is shown in Figure A-3). Or, choose View⇨Details.

✔ In Open or Save As dialog boxes, you see a Files of Type selection box (under the File Name selection box). Click that box to choose a new file type in order to import or export files from other programs.

Saving your work as a file

In order to return to a computer document that you created, you need to save your documents as a file on a disk. That disk can be either your permanent *hard disk* or a removable *diskette* (or *floppy disk*). Some programs, like Microsoft Money, save everything automatically when you exit the program, so you don't have to think much about saving files.

Most Windows programs give you three ways to save your document as a file. Choose your favorite:

✔ Choose File⇨Save from the menu bar.

✔ Press Ctrl+S.

✔ Click the diskette icon on the toolbar.

When you use these commands to save a document for the first time, your program gives you a Save As dialog box so that you can give the file a name and a location. After you save the document for the first time, these commands no longer display a dialog box at all, but simply save the document using the same name and the same location.

To make a copy of the file and give it a different name, different location, or even a different *file type,* use the File⇨Save *As* command to get to the Save As dialog box. This procedure is helpful if you need slightly different versions of the same file (for example, if you're sending the same letter to three different people).

The Save As dialog box is a close relative of the Open dialog box shown in Figure A-3. A twin, in fact. These two dialog boxes work in almost exactly the same way: You must enter the new filename, and you can also assign a folder and disk for your new file to go into, as follows:

1. **Type a name in the File Name box.**

   The suggested name is highlighted at first, so just type and your new name replaces the suggested one. Or, click the File Name box, press the Delete or Backspace key to delete the characters, and type new ones. (Omit the three-letter extension, .doc or whatever; your program supplies the extension automatically.) Use up to 256 characters, including spaces, but not the \/"*?"<> or | characters.

2. **You may browse to open a folder on a disk drive, as described in the previous section, or create a new folder as described in the next section.**

   If you do nothing else but type a name, your file simply goes into the folder the program chooses for you.

3. **Click the Save button (or, in some programs, the OK button) in the Save As dialog box.**

Managing files and folders

You're the boss when it comes to files and folders. You can move, copy, rename, or delete any file or folder on a hard disk or diskette. (Avoid moving or deleting anything in the Program Files or Windows folder, however, or you may damage programs.) Copying is especially useful: You should save a copy of any important file or folder to a diskette in case your hard disk fails.

The following instructions work whenever you have a My Computer window open on your screen.

In some programs, such as Works or Word, the following actions also work in an Open or Save (or Save As) dialog box.

✔ **Copy a file:** Right-click the file's name or icon to select the file, and choose Copy from the menu that drops down. Double-click the My Computer icon, and browse to view the contents of the disk drive or folder where you want to put the copy. Then right-click in that window and choose Paste from the drop-down menu.

✔ **Move a file:** Do exactly as described in the preceding bullet for copying a file, except, instead of choosing Copy, choose Cut.

- ✓ **Copy or move a file by dragging:** Begin with two windows open (or a window and a dialog box): one displaying the file to be moved and the other displaying the folder where you want to put the file. To move a file, click the file's icon and drag the file to its destination folder. To copy a file, hold down the Ctrl key while dragging. Release the mouse button when you're done.

- ✓ **Rename a file:** Click the file's icon or name, then click its name. The text of the name now appears highlighted within a surrounding rectangle. Type a new name, or click within the text to insert or delete text. Click anywhere outside the rectangle when you're done typing.

- ✓ **Delete or undelete a file:** Drag the file to the Recycle Bin icon on your screen to delete it. Or, click the file then press the Delete key on your keyboard; if a Confirm File Delete dialog box appears, click its Yes button. For instructions on restoring deleted files or emptying the Recycle Bin, see the discussion of the Recycle Bin icon in the section, "Viewing the Windows Desktop."

- ✓ **Manage folders:** You move, copy, rename, or delete a folder just as you do a file. When you copy, move, or delete a folder, you copy or move all of its contents with it.

- ✓ **Create a folder:** In a My Computer window, choose File➪New➪Folder. In a Save or Save As dialog box, click the New Folder button, if one is present. (Refer to Figure A-3.) The words new folder then appear, highlighted; type a name for the folder. Press the Enter key when you're done typing.

Controlling Program and Document Windows

Windows is full of windows. No surprise, right? Everywhere you look on your screen, more and more of these rectangles appear, full of cryptic controls, exhibiting odd behaviors, and obstinately refusing to show you the parts of your document you want to see. In this section, I show you how to take control of your windows.

Controlling program windows

Whenever you run a program, it does its thing entirely in a window: the *program window.* (*Sometimes* computer terms make sense!) You can run several programs at once on your PC, each one in its own window, or you can *maximize* a program's window to fill your screen.

Here's what's what in the program window:

- Every program window has a bar at the top called the *title bar*.

- Whenever you are working in a program window, that window is said to be *active*, and its title bar is colored (usually blue). Otherwise (if, say, you switch to using another program) the title bar remains a dull, sleepy gray. Any keyboard commands you use (such as Ctrl+S), apply only to the active program window.

- To select a program window (make it active and move it to the top of other windows), click its title bar.

- To move a program window, drag it by its title bar.

- To change the size of a program window, click any edge or corner (your cursor turns into a double-headed arrow) and drag.

The title bar also contains buttons (in the right-hand corner) useful for controlling the size of your program window, as shown in the Works title bar in Figure A-4:

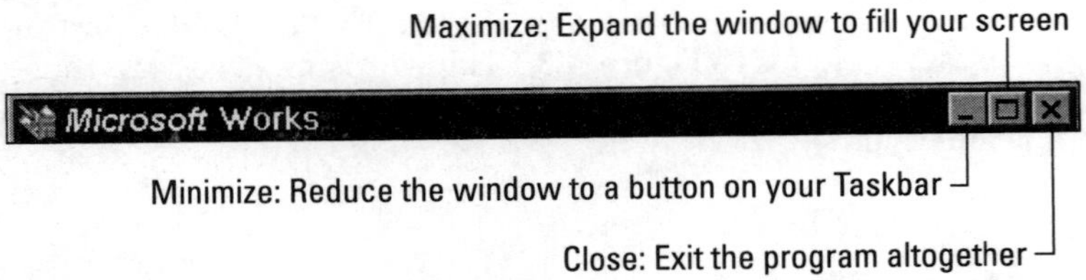

Figure A-4:
The title bar
lets you size
a program
up (or
down).

Maximize: Expand the window to fill your screen

Microsoft Works

Minimize: Reduce the window to a button on your Taskbar

Close: Exit the program altogether

Figure A-4 shows you how to minimize, maximize, and close a program Window, and defines what those terms mean. After a window has been minimized or maximized, here's how to restore it to its previous size:

- When you maximize a window, Windows replaces the maximize button with one that looks like this:

    Click this button to restore your program window to an intermediate size.

- To restore a window after it's been minimized (shrunk to a button on the Windows taskbar), click that button.

Controlling document windows

Program windows often contain even more windows. In Works and Word, for instance, whenever you create or open a document, that document gets its own Window. Document windows work very much like program windows, with a few twists as follows:

- ✔ If Window is a selection on the program's menu bar, click Window to explore the various document-window controls the program provides. Two common choices in the Window menu are Cascade (make all document windows overlap neatly) and Tile (put windows side-by-side, like tiles). Also, you can make any window active by choosing it from a numbered list at the bottom of the Window menu.

- ✔ When you minimize a document window, it shrinks to an icon or rectangle at the bottom left of the program window. Click that icon or rectangle to reinflate the document window.

- ✔ When you maximize a document window, the tiny buttons that control that document window appear just under the title bar.

Zooming

An alternative to making a window bigger is to make the document text smaller, a choice referred to as zooming out. Zooming has absolutely no effect on your document. It just changes how the document looks on your screen.

Many programs (including Works and Word) allow zooming, and provide various ways to do it. Here are two ways:

- ✔ **Choose View➪Zoom:** The Zoom dialog box zooms into view and lets you choose a magnification expressed as a percentage — the smaller the percentage, the smaller the document. You can either click the standard percentages listed, such as 75%, or type a percentage into the Custom (or similarly labeled) box.

- ✔ **Click the down-arrow to the right of the Zoom control in the toolbar:** A drop-down menu offers you the same options as the Zoom dialog box. (You can identify the Zoom control because it displays a percentage, such as 100%.)

Moving around in a document window

At the side (and perhaps at the bottom) of your document are scroll bars that let you move a document around within its document window.

- ✔ **To slide the document up or down in little increments:** Click the arrows at the top and bottom.

- ✔ **To slide the document with a lot more speed:** Click and drag the box in the middle up or down. (Or click above or below the box.) The position of this box on the scroll bar gives you a rough idea of where you are in the document. If the box is large, nearly filling the scroll bar, that means most of your document is visible in the window.

- ✔ **To slide the document horizontally (in case your window isn't wide enough to display the entire width of the document):** A horizontal scroll bar at the bottom of the window works the same way as the vertical one.

An alternative to scrolling is to use the *navigation keys* on your keyboard: the arrow keys or the Page Up, Page Down, Home, and End keys. The arrow keys move one step at a time, but the Page Up and Page Down keys move one window's worth at a time.

Ordering from the Menu Bar

When you're hungry for action, do as hungry people do everywhere: Use a menu to place your order. *Menus* are simply lists of words running horizontally (a *menu bar*) or vertically (a *drop-down menu*), from which you choose commands to give your program. Figure A-5 shows a Works menu bar. Nearly all Windows programs (and the Windows Start button, too) display menus and menu bars of some description.

Click any of the words in a menu bar, and a menu of commands drops down. Then, click one of these commands to execute it. For instance, to perform the command File➪Save, you click File on the menu bar; then click Save on the menu that drops down. Yet another menu may appear, or if a menu selection ends in an ellipsis (those ... things), a *dialog box* will spring up. (See the section "Dealing with Dialog Boxes," later in the chapter.)

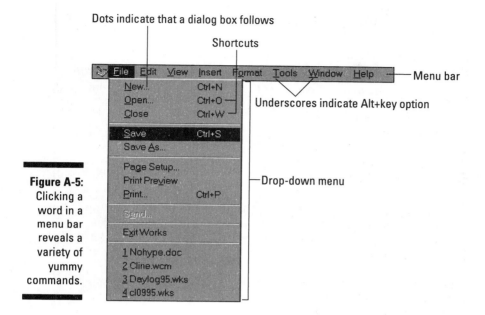

Dots indicate that a dialog box follows

Shortcuts

Menu bar

Underscores indicate Alt+key option

Drop-down menu

Figure A-5:
Clicking a
word in a
menu bar
reveals a
variety of
yummy
commands.

Shortcut keys give you another way to pick choices off menus. All those underlined letters in the menu bar of Figure A-5 are called *hot keys*. Press the Alt key *and* the hot key in any menu bar (Alt+F for File, for instance). Then, in the menu that drops down, press the hot key for your next menu choice, such as S for Save. (You may either hold the Alt key down throughout all your choices, or release it after the first choice and simply press hot keys alone.)

The offerings on menu bars are largely the same in every program. Here are some common selections on menu bars:

- ✔ **File:** Open, close, and save documents; set up the page layout; print.

- ✔ **Edit:** Copy text, numbers, and illustrations; move them, find them, replace them; also (very important) undo whatever changes you just made to your document.

- ✔ **View:** See things differently or otherwise change the way the screen looks, but without actually changing the document or other thing you're working on.

- ✔ **Insert:** Plug stuff into your document, such as illustrations from another document or file.

✔ **Format:** Change the appearance of text and numbers, and how they line up.

✔ **Tools:** Use a spelling checker, a thesaurus, or other proofreading tool. Also, change *options,* which customize the way your program operates.

✔ **Window:** Arrange the document windows or make a different window active. (See "Controlling Program and Document Windows," earlier in this appendix.)

Toiling with Toolbars

Toolbars, such as the Works toolbar shown in Figure A-6, are rows of buttons appearing just under the menu bar. Some programs, like Word, have many toolbars. Click View⊃Toolbar (or Toolbars) to enable or clear check marks that display toolbars.

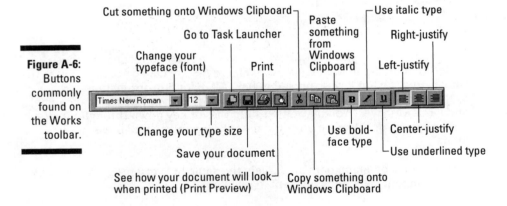

Figure A-6: Buttons commonly found on the Works toolbar.

Each button with an icon is a shortcut to some command in the menu bar. Click the button and stuff happens: Your file gets saved, for example, or you print something out. The selection of buttons available in certain toolbars may change, depending upon exactly what you are doing in a particular program.

If you forget what a button is supposed to do, just move your mouse cursor over it (don't click). In nearly all recent Windows programs, a tiny square appears with a description of the button's function.

Dealing with Dialog Boxes

Dialog boxes crop up all over the place. In a menu, a command that ends in three dots (. . .) warns you that you're about to deal with a dialog box. The dialog box's purpose in life is to let you specify important details about the command, for example, what to name the file you want to store and where to put it.

On the surface, dialog boxes look like windows, but you usually can't shrink or expand dialog boxes. (You can drag them around by their title bars, though, if they get in the way.) Internally, dialog boxes can look like darn near anything. Figure A-7 shows an example from Works.

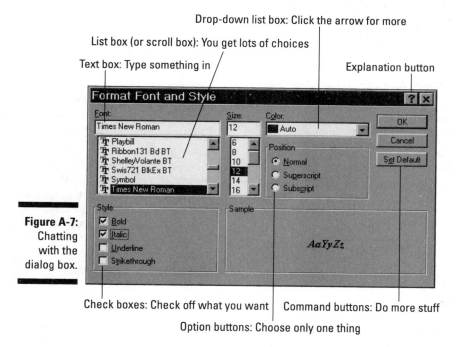

Drop-down list box: Click the arrow for more

List box (or scroll box): You get lots of choices

Text box: Type something in

Explanation button

Figure A-7:
Chatting
with the
dialog box.

Check boxes: Check off what you want | Command buttons: Do more stuff

Option buttons: Choose only one thing

The following is how this dialog box stuff works. Don't try to memorize all the names and distinctions of the thingies. I certainly don't use the names any more than I have to. Just refer back here if you get confused about a dialog box.

✔ **Explanation button (question mark):** Click this button in the title bar, and a question mark attaches itself to your cursor. Then, click a button or setting in the dialog box, and you see an explanation of that item. Click in a plain area of the dialog box to clear the explanation off the screen.

✔ **Text box:** To fill in a text box, you can type something, or sometimes you can click something in a *list box* immediately underneath the text box. When you open a text box, it usually lists some suggestion. You can delete that suggestion by pressing the Delete key, or you can change the suggestion by clicking in the box and typing in some text. Press the Backspace or Delete keys to erase single characters or text that you selected. Do *not* press the Enter key when you're done typing; click on the next item to set up in the dialog box. Click the OK button or press the Enter key when all items are as you want them.

✔ **List or scroll box:** List boxes or scroll boxes show you a list of choices. Click one of the choices, and that choice generally appears in a text box above the list. Double-click a choice, and the computer not only chooses that item, but it also tells the dialog box, "I'm done — go and do your thing!" If more text is in the list than fits in the box, a scroll bar appears alongside the list box. (Such scroll bars work like the scroll bars in your document window.)

✔ **Check boxes:** Check boxes are like tax forms, but more fun. Check off one or more things by clicking them or the box next to them. A check mark appears when an item is selected. Click the item (or the box next to it) again to deselect it.

✔ **Option (or "radio") buttons:** These buttons allow you to click only one thing in the list. The center of the button appears black when the button is selected.

✔ **Command buttons:** The most important command button is the OK button (or Close button). Click the OK button when you're ready to proceed with the task the dialog box is about (say, printing). Click Close if you have made some changes, but don't want to perform the task (printing) yet. If you want to back out of a command, click Cancel. Other command buttons may take you to yet more dialog boxes.

Finding Files

Sometimes, your files get lost in the enormous hard disk drives that most PCs have today. Windows provides a helpful feature for finding these files.

Click the Start button on the Windows taskbar, then choose Find⇨Files or Folders. The Find dialog box appears, displaying multiple cards; click a named tab to select a card. Here are the most useful things to know and their cards:

🖝 **Choose the Name & Location card if you know part of the name.**

First, press the Del key to delete any text in the Named box, then type the part of the name that you remember in that box. Substitute the * (asterisk) character for the part that you don't remember. For example, if you're looking for an invoice, and you know that the file begins with *inv,* type **inv***. To look only for Works documents, add a Works three-letter extension to the end: .wps for a word-processing file, .wks for a work-sheet file, .wdb for a database file, or .wcm for a communications file. For Word documents, end with .doc.

🖝 **Choose the Date Modified card if you know when the file or folder was created or last modified.**

First, click Find All Files Created or Modified. Then specify the date, either by clicking between and then double-clicking and typing over the dates shown or by clicking During the Previous and specifying a number of preceding months or days.

🖝 **Choose the Advanced card if you know any text that the file or folder contains.**

This selection is *really* useful because you don't have to remember anything about the document's name or location! If you wrote a letter to Mr. Smith about condominiums, just enter either Smith or condominium into the Containing Text box. Try to choose a unique word or phrase.

After you specify something on any or all of the cards, press the Enter key or click Find Now. A list of documents appears at the bottom of the Find dialog box — just double-click the document you want in order to open it!

Hollering for Help

This book covers so many topics that I can only focus on the basics. If you need help with a topic — especially a more advanced feature of a program — and this book or another *...For Dummies* book just doesn't answer it, your best alternative is to read the Help files.

When you need help *while using any program,* you can do any of the following to read the Help files:

🖝 Press the F1 key. The exact results of pressing F1 vary from program to program. In Word, for instance, pressing F1 wakes up a cartoon helper called the Office Assistant.

> ✔ Choose Help, then choose Contents to browse topics from a table of contents or choose Index to use an alphabetical index to locate topics. In some programs, such as Word, the choices are combined: Help⇨ Contents and Index.

For help on Windows itself (not one of your programs), click the Start button on the Windows Taskbar, then choose Help.

When you click Help and choose Contents and/or Index from a program's menu bar (or choose Start⇨Help from the Windows Taskbar) you get a Help Topics dialog box containing three cards with tabs sticking up like index cards. Each card gives you a different way to access the same Help documentation. Click a card's tab to use that card, as follows:

✔ **Contents:** Organizes information by topic, like a table of contents. Double-click any subject marked by a book icon to see a list of documents on that subject. Double-click any subject (or click it once, then click the Display button) to see the documentation, which is displayed in a Help dialog box. Click the Help Topics button in that dialog box to return to the Help Contents dialog box.

✔ **Index:** Organizes subjects alphabetically, like a book's index. Click the text box at the top (marked "1") and type the first few letters of a word or phrase describing what you want help on. As you type, Help looks at what you've typed so far and scrolls the list of subjects in the lower box (marked "2") to match your typing, if it can. Press the Backspace key to change your typing.

If a subject displays a folder icon, click the folder to reveal subtopics. When you see the subject you want, double-click that subject. Click the Help Topics button in that dialog box to return to the Help Contents dialog box.

✔ **Search (in Windows 98) or Find (in Windows 95):** These options search exhaustively for every occurrence of whatever text you type (say, "disk") in the box at the top of the card. Box 2 of this card displays words that begin similarly to whatever you typed (say, "disk" and "disks"); click one, then double-click any topic in box 3. (The first time you use this card, your program may ask permission to take a moment to build an index. Press the Enter key if your program does ask.)

As you are reading a Help document in a Help dialog box, you can get more information in several ways:

• Click any green, underlined text to get an explanation of that text.

• Click any Related Topics button.

• Click a button that has a tiny arrow in it (a *shortcut* indicator) to actually perform the activity described in Help.

• Click the Back button to return to previous panels.

To clear your screen of Help, click the X in the upper right-hand corner of the dialog box.

Shutting Down

To shut down your PC, click the Start button, and the Shut Down Windows dialog box appears. The choice, Shut Down the Computer, is currently chosen in that dialog box; click the Yes button. Wait until your PC screen indicates that you may now turn off the power to your computer, then turn off the power.

If a program gets stuck (doesn't respond to you), or your PC otherwise seems to have gone haywire, try the same procedure but click the Restart the Computer option before clicking the Yes button.

When you shut down your PC, any programs currently running are also shut down. If you've performed any work in those programs that has not been saved as a file, the programs prompt you to do so.

Index

YOUR ONLINE RESOURCE

WWW.DUMMIES.COM

Discover Dummies Online!

The Dummies Web Site is your fun and friendly online resource for the latest information about ...*For Dummies*® books and your favorite topics. The Web site is the place to communicate with us, exchange ideas with other ...*For Dummies* readers, chat with authors, and have fun!

Ten Fun and Useful Things You Can Do at www.dummies.com

1. Win free ...*For Dummies* books and more!
2. Register your book and be entered in a prize drawing.
3. Meet your favorite authors through the IDG Books Author Chat Series.
4. Exchange helpful information with other ...*For Dummies* readers.
5. Discover other great ...*For Dummies* books you must have!
6. Purchase Dummieswear™ exclusively from our Web site.
7. Buy ...*For Dummies* books online.
8. Talk to us. Make comments, ask questions, get answers!
9. Download free software.
10. Find additional useful resources from authors.

Link directly to these ten fun and useful things at **http://www.dummies.com/10useful**

SURF THE NET

WWW.DUMMIES.COM

For other technology titles from IDG Books Worldwide, go to **www.idgbooks.com**

Not on the Web yet? It's easy to get started with *Dummies 101*®: *The Internet For Windows*®*98* or *The Internet For Dummies*®, 5th Edition, at local retailers everywhere.

IDG BOOKS WORLDWIDE

Find other ...*For Dummies* books on these topics:

Business • Career • Databases • Food & Beverage • Games • Gardening • Graphics • Hardware
Health & Fitness • Internet and the World Wide Web • Networking • Office Suites
Operating Systems • Personal Finance • Pets • Programming • Recreation • Sports
Spreadsheets • Teacher Resources • Test Prep • Word Processing

IDG BOOKS WORLDWIDE BOOK REGISTRATION

Register
This Book
and Win!

We want to hear from you!

Visit **http://my2cents.dummies.com** to register this book and tell us how you liked it!

- Get entered in our monthly prize giveaway.

- Give us feedback about this book — tell us what you like best, what you like least, or maybe what you'd like to ask the author and us to change!

- Let us know any other *...For Dummies*® topics that interest you.

Your feedback helps us determine what books to publish, tells us what coverage to add as we revise our books, and lets us know whether we're meeting your needs as a *...For Dummies* reader. You're our most valuable resource, and what you have to say is important to us!

Not on the Web yet? It's easy to get started with *Dummies 101*®*: The Internet For Windows*® *98* or *The Internet For Dummies*®, 5th Edition, at local retailers everywhere.

Or let us know what you think by sending us a letter at the following address:

...For Dummies Book Registration
Dummies Press
7260 Shadeland Station, Suite 100
Indianapolis, IN 46256-3945
Fax 317-596-5498

™

BESTSELLING
BOOK SERIES
FROM IDG